Negotiating identities

An introduction to Asian American women's writing

HELENA GRICE

Manchester University Press
Manchester and New York

distributed exclusively in the USA by Palgrave

The right of Helena Grice to be identified as the author of this work has been
asserted by her in accordance with the Copyright, Designs and Patents Act 1988.

Published by Manchester University Press
Oxford Road, Manchester M13 9NR, UK
and Room 400, 175 Fifth Avenue, New York, NY 10010, USA
http://www.manchesteruniversitypress.co.uk

Distributed exclusively in the USA by
Palgrave, 175 Fifth Avenue, New York,
NY 10010, USA

Distributed exclusively in Canada by
UBC Press, University of British Columbia, 2029 West Mall,
Vancouver, BC, Canada V6T 1Z2

British Library Cataloguing-in-Publication Data
A catalogue record for this book is available from the British Library

Library of Congress Cataloging-in-Publication Data applied for

ISBN 0 7190 6030 3 *hardback*
ISBN 0 7190 6031 1 *paperback*

First published 2002

10 09 08 07 06 05 04 03 02   10 9 8 7 6 5 4 3 2 1

Typeset by Freelance Publishing Services, Brinscall, Lancs.
www.freelancepublishingservices.co.uk
Printed in Great Britain by Bell and Bain Ltd, Glasgow

CONTENTS

ACKNOWLEDGEMENTS

This project started out as my doctoral thesis, which was written during the period 1995–98. My greatest debt of gratitude is to my supervisor, Lyn Pykett, for finding so much time for me during her very hectic period as Head of Department. I would also like to thank Martin Padget, in his capacity as my second supervisor, for reading drafts of this work at different stages, and for providing helpful advice for further reading. Diana Chang's generosity in lending me her publicity photograph during this period is gratefully acknowledged. I would like to thank Tim Dunne, of the Department of International Politics, University of Wales, Aberystwyth, for discussions which clarified my thinking about issues of citizenship and national identity, and Tim Woods for editorial help and computer assistance, above and beyond the call of duty. In addition, I wish to acknowledge the financial support of the Department of English and the University of Wales, Aberystwyth, for postgraduate and postdoctoral research awards which enabled me to complete this project. The Department of Ethnic Studies at the University of California, Berkeley, gave me access to its splendid library during Easter 1999, and I would like to express my appreciation to them. I would also like to thank my mother for continuing financial rescue packages and unerring encouragement throughout the three years of my postgraduate study, and beyond.

Several chapters of this book incorporate material revised from the following previously published pieces and I am grateful for the permission to reprint sections of chapter 1 from 'Asian American Writing in Europe: Problems and Paradigms', *Hitting Critical Mass: A Journal of Asian American Cultural Criticism*, vol. 4:1, pp. 11–25; and from 'Asian American Feminisms: Developments, Dialogues, Departures', *Hitting Critical Mass: A Journal of Asian American Cultural Criticism*, vol. 6:2. Parts of chapter 2 first appeared in 'Asian American Women's Prose Narratives: Genre and Identity', in Esther Ghymn (ed.), *Asian American Studies: Identity, Images, and Issues Past and Present* (New York: Peter Lang, 2000), pp. 179–204; chapter 5 in 'Face-ing/De-Face-ing Racism: Physiognomy and Racism in Eur/Amerasian Texts by Women', in Yuko Matsukawa, Josephine Lee and Imogene Lim (eds), *Re/Collecting Early Asian America: Readings in Cultural History* (Philadelphia, PA: Temple University Press, 2000). Part of chapter 6 became 'Border Subjects and Territoriality: Maxine Hong Kingston's *China Men* as Frontier Literary History', *Borderlines: Studies in American Culture*, vol. 5:1 (1998), pp. 17–32.

Several colleagues and friends have been generous with their time in reading and commenting on portions of the manuscript, and I would like to thank the following: Rocío G. Davis for reading chapter 2; Anhua Gao, Hong Ying and Adeline Yen Mah for reading chapter 4; Ruth Y. Hsu and Diana Chang for reading chapter 5; Patricia Duncker for reading the introduction; Tim Woods for his very helpful (and patient!) overview of the whole manuscript, as well as the two anonymous readers who helped to shape the project in both its early and late stages. I have also benefited directly and indirectly from conversations with other friends and colleagues, so thanks to Claire Jowitt, Sarah Prescott, Yuko Matsukawa, Maria Lauret, and especially to Sau-ling Wong for her continuing patient support, gentle encouragement and inspiring example. Amy Ling did not live to see this book completed, but provided invaluable advice and feedback during the early stages. Maxine Hong Kingston, Meena Alexander and Diana Chang were kind enough to answer my questions during various stages of writing. Matthew Frost gave me the chance to embark upon this study, and I am grateful to him.

This book is dedicated to the memory of my father, John Radcliffe James Grice (1942–80); to my partner, Tim Woods, with love and appreciation; and to my baby daughter, Mary, born just as I completed the project.

TERMINOLOGY

Many of the terms used in ethnic and racial theory are applied in different ways. My usage largely follows that of Ellis Cashmore's *A Dictionary of Ethnic and Racial Theory* (London: Routledge, 1996), where more expansive definitions may be found.

Anglo is a term which in an American context means of 'European, white descent'. In this context it often denotes a culturally dominant group, and is often used, rather problematically, in opposition to 'ethnic'. It is also used interchangeably with 'Euro-American' or 'AEA' ('Anglo/Euro/American').

Asian American refers to North American writers (including Canadian) of Asian descent.

Ethnic refers to a group of people assumed to share, or who feel that they share, a common cultural descent.

Ethnicity is the sense of being 'ethnic'. This may be accentuated or de-emphasised by the individual through cultural practices.

Issei are first generation Japanese Americans.

Nikkei are Japanese Americans.

Nisei are second generation Japanese Americans.

Race was a term of classification, now largely discredited, arising out of biologist, pseudo-scientific nineteenth-century discourses. It endures as a potent signifier or trope of irreducible otherness or difference. It is often erroneously used interchangeably with 'ethnic'.

Racial differences is occasionally used here, as elsewhere, to discuss black/white dynamics of interaction.

Sansei are third generation Japanese Americans.

PREFACE

Current debates over the literary canon, the changing profile of literary and cultural studies, the increasing presence of women's and ethnic writing both within and beyond the canon: all of these factors may explain the increasing popularity of Asian American women's writing both within the USA and beyond its geographical borders. Yet the critical debate on Asian American women's writing has barely begun, especially compared with resources available for readers of African American, say, or Native American writing. Whereas a reader of Toni Morrison's *Beloved* will rarely come to the subject of slavery without any a priori knowledge of the subject, it is unlikely that a reader of Maxine Hong Kingston's *China Men* will be as familiar with the history of Chinese immigrant labourers to the USA and their crucial role in the construction of the Central Pacific Railroad. This book is a selective study of Asian American women's writing in the twentieth century, from 1911–2000, which presents an eclectic body of literature in relation to its cultural context(s), Asian American history, and in the light of both ethnic and feminist theories of women's writing. It is especially intended for British readers, who will probably be largely unfamiliar with the breadth of Asian American experience and writing. As such, I provide in the introduction a fairly lengthy discussion of the history of Asians in the United States, as well as delineating the development of their respective literatures. In so doing, the book is intended to appeal to both interested readers and students of American studies, gender studies and cultural studies, in providing an introduction to the field.

The need for contextual analysis of Asian American women's literature – in *all* of its guises – has been illustrated all too starkly recently with the publishing industry and popular readership's predilection for all things Asian. All too many readers of Arthur Golden's spectacular 1997 success, *Memoirs of a Geisha*, for example, saw cultural insights where perhaps there was only cliché, truth where there was little more than stereotype. (Perhaps even more worryingly, many readers read this fictional book by a white Anglo-Saxon Protestant writer as autobiographical.) The term 'oriental' might have been discarded along with 'red Indians', 'eskimos' and 'negroes' in favour of the more neutral and fashionable terminology of our era of political correctness, but it is not necessarily the case that racism, 'orientalism' and ethnic stereotyping have disappeared too. And despite the tremendous popularity of the works of Jung Chang, Adeline Yen Mah or Anchee Min, both in the United States and in the UK, these works are hardly ever discussed at academic level. The effect of these facts is that all too often 'Asian' writing becomes homogenised into one huge exoticised mess. To offer another example, an article in the British broadsheet newspaper *The Guardian*'s supplement 'The Editor', offered brief synopses of five 'books about China – to save you the burden of reading them'. It included texts which depicted very diverse Asian American cultures, histories and circumstances: Maxine Hong Kingston's *The Woman Warrior*, Amy Tan's *The Kitchen God's Wife*, Pang-mei Natasha Chang's *Bound Feet and Western Dress*, Adeline Yen Mah's *Falling Leaves: The True Story of an Unwanted Chinese Daughter* and Jung Chang's *Wild Swans*. Although three were set in the Cultural Revolution era in China, two in contemporary America, and three were auto/biographical, two fictional, all were reduced to an undifferentiated lowest common denominator: they were in some sense 'Asian'.

My own position as a white British woman researching the work of Asian American women writers becomes relevant here. In the process of researching this book, I have addressed the two separate but interconnected questions of ethnic and racial differences, and national and cultural differences, both of which intervene in my contact with Asian American literary and cultural forms and formations. Many explorations of American cultural forms by European critics from across the Atlantic fail to explore the problematics of their own involvement and approach, and the consequence is often a lack of cultural specificity. In 1994, Asian American critic Sau-ling Wong claimed that 'it certainly helps to be Asian American when one is interpreting Asian American literature', but conceded 'the theoretical possibility that non-Asians can manage to do excellent criticism on Asian American literature', adding, however, that 'I haven't seen a whole lot of these scholars yet'.[1] Since then, coinciding with the cultural moment that has seen a surge of interest in ethnic literatures, Asian American literature has been a focus of increasing interest for non-Asian, as well as non-American scholars, myself included. Concern has been voiced in certain ethnic quarters about the appropriation of ethnic literatures by white critics, and the perils of misreading such texts. In Asian American letters, writers such as the Chinese American Frank Chin have bewailed white (critical) interest in Asian American texts as 'racist love', and debates continue to rage in various forums over the directions in which Asian American studies ought to go.[2] As Sau-ling Wong highlights, an important difference in the positions of Asian American and Anglo/European critics respectively vis-à-vis Asian American studies is that the Asian American critic will always be in a position of noticeable advantage in the study of Asian America. He or she possesses an easy familiarity with particular linguistic and cultural nuances and idioms, and is likely to be able to draw upon a 'fund' of comparable daily experience. Indeed, and as one would expect, the literary representations and traditions of Asian America are firmly rooted in the lived experience of Asian Americans. Ethnic and racial differences operate through highlighting divisions between some individuals and by stressing connections with others. Any attempt to read and reach across these differences entails a recognition and understanding of these dynamics. Within the field of African American studies, Houston A. Baker, Jr. and Patricia Redmond have offered an especially useful discussion of the politics of white intervention and participation in the study of African American texts. They posit the necessity of 'earned participation' of white critics in what is still an 'evolving work'.[3] Such earned involvement would include the development of the disciplinary field through 'laborious research, ample scholarly production and demonstrable commitment' in such a way as to 'keep alive always both the community itself and questions of its definition at any given moment'.[4] This is a view shared by Elizabeth Abel, a white critic who explores the production of white feminist readings of black texts. Abel advocates self-reflexivity as a necessary framework for such a project:

> If we produce our readings cautiously and locate them in a self-conscious and self-critical relation to black feminist criticism, these risks, I hope, would be counterbalanced by the benefits of broadening the spectrum of interpretation, illuminating the social determinants of reading and deepening our recognition of our racial selves and the 'others' we fantasmatically construct – and thereby expanding the possibilities of dialogue across as well as about racial boundaries.[5]

Abel's model of self-reflexive reading includes the recognition of our 'racial selves' and the avoidance of implicit 'othering' produced by a white reading strategy which fails to acknowledge the importance of race in white reading. The ways in which race enters into white reading are complex, and Abel concludes that there is *no* unproblematic grounding for white readers which displaces the politics of race, so self-reflexivity is necessary as a means of recognising whiteness as both a standpoint and as a set of cultural practices. Yet, I would contend that white self-criticism may be able to offer a useful contribution to the study of black and ethnic texts by serving to endorse the racialisation of whiteness and to emphasise the role of race in the reading process.

That these debates have already been thrashed out in African American studies but have hardly begun within the field of Asian American studies is not surprising. The still nascent status of Asian American studies means that its boundaries and aims remain in constant re-negotiation, and issues such as white involvement in the field are only now being tentatively addressed. Sau-ling Wong has broached the subject at some length and notes the role of African American studies as the theoretical vanguard of this particular debate, and indeed cites white critical involvement in African American studies as one reason for a similar involvement in Asian American studies. Like Abel, Wong also advocates a reading process attentive to racial and cultural investments:

> in boundary crossing situations there is often an asymmetry of power that we don't realize. People in the dominant culture often assume that they can cross any boundary ... Readers from the dominant culture who are accustomed to believing their own reading position to be transcendent, universal, unbiased, tend to see those invested in 'minority' literatures as caught up in identity politics. In fact, they are caught up in their own identity politics too, only it's been 'naturalized', made invisible. There are certainly limits to any critical endeavor.[6]

Although focused upon the dynamics of American cultural engagement, Wong's comments pertain equally to the position of white readers beyond the geographical boundaries of America, particularly the emphasis upon denaturalised reading positions and the recognition of our own racial as well as cultural and national selves. Self-reflexive reading interrogates cultural and national as well as ethnic and racial particularities and differences. As an insistence upon racially-aware reading produces context-sensitive analyses of texts, so culturally and nationally located criticism likewise engenders an attentiveness to the social and cultural contexts that produce it. As Eva Lenox Birch notes, just as 'all writing must be seen and approached as the product of a particular historical conjuncture within a particular national context',[7] so must the critical act be sensitive to its own rootedness in social, cultural and national conditions. Such an approach avoids essentialising texts and readers, and also offers fruitful ground for contextualised and historicised analysis. So, for example, the situation of Asian American literature may usefully be compared and contrasted with the literature produced by Asian Britons, as, in places, in this study.

It is no coincidence that much of this groundbreaking work which attempts to traverse ethnic, racial, cultural and national differences, stems from a feminist epistemological basis. A feminist reading position, such as that which I adopt in this study, frequently insists upon an awareness of the problems attending the application of theoretical models to literary texts, and stresses the importance of not creating critical authority at the expense of the writing under consideration.[8] In my own reading I situate myself broadly within a feminist reading position, trying not only to read the literary text through the theoretical work, but also to go on and read the theoretical work both through and against the literary text, and thus to ensure that the theoretical basis of analysis is not privileged in any absolutist or reductionist way over the literary piece. It does, however, remain the case, as Wong warns, that 'a literature ... can't be captured by one single reading strategy' and that 'there are certainly limits to any critical endeavor'.[9] So, with this in mind, let us proceed.

Notes

1 Sau-ling Wong, 'A Conversation with Sau-ling Wong', *Tamkang Review*, 25:1 (1995), 118–33; p. 126.

2 See Elaine Kim, *Asian American Literature* (Philadelphia, PA: Temple University Press, 1982), pp. 174–89, for a discussion of Chin's views.

3 Houston A. Baker, Jr., and Patricia Redmond (eds), Introduction, *Afro-American Literary Study in the 1990s* (Chicago, IL: University of Chicago Press, 1990), p. 3.

4 *Ibid.*

5 Elizabeth Abel, 'Black Writing, White Reading: Race and the Politics of Feminist Interpretation', in Henry Louis Gates, Jr. and Kwame Anthony Appiah (eds), *Identities* (Chicago, IL: University of Chicago Press, 1995), pp. 242–70; p. 270.

6 'Conversation with Sau-ling Wong', pp. 125–6.

7 Eva Lenox Birch, *Black American Women's Writing: A Quilt of Many Colours* (Hemel Hempstead: Harvester Wheatsheaf, 1994), p. 3.

8 For a discussion of this insistence, see Beverly Skeggs (ed.), *Feminist Cultural Theory: Process and Production* (Manchester: Manchester University Press, 1995), especially Lynne Pearce's essay, 'Finding a Place from which to Write: the Methodology of Feminist Textual Practice'.

9 'Conversation with Sau-ling Wong', p. 125.

1

Introduction

In 1998, an article in the British broadsheet newspaper, *The Guardian*, noted the 'start of a great tradition ... Asian American writers who are offering a different view of life in America ... Ruth L. Ozeki, Amy Tan, Gish Jen and Mei Ng'.[1] Heralding this new literary renaissance, this article highlighted the recent rush of new publications by Asian American women, both in the United States and in the UK. Asian American writing by women first appeared in the UK with the publication in 1976 of the hugely successful memoir by Maxine Hong Kingston, *The Woman Warrior*, a text which won the National Book Critics Circle Award in that year, and which swiftly became the first classic of Asian American literature.[2] Since that time, something of a revolution has occurred in the development and visibility of both ethnic writing by women generally (the popularity of Alice Walker and Toni Morrison are such examples), and the specific expansion of published writing by Asian American women. The works of Amy Tan, Jung Chang, Anchee Min and Adeline Yen Mah, for example, have built upon and consolidated the emergence of Asian American and Asian British writing as particular corpuses, all achieving high sales figures and wide media interest. For instance, Amy Tan's well-known 1989 novel, *The Joy Luck Club*, was made into a film directed by Wayne Wang and became a box office success. The works of many Asian American writers – Kingston, Tan, Gish Jen and Bharati Mukherjee, to name but a few – are now widely taught at university level in the UK. It is clear, therefore, that there is a distinct emerging canon of Asian American women's writing, which coincides with the surge in popularity of ethnic women's writing in recent decades, as well as the recent popular predilection for all things Asian. But what exactly is Asian American women's writing, and where has it come from? This study will attempt to answer this question, as well as to survey the state of the field of Asian American women's studies, both within the United States and beyond the geographical boundaries of Asian America, in order to pay critical attention to the exciting new field of Asian women's diaspora literatures.

The evolution of Asian American literature

Although Asian American literature – defined here as literature by people of Asian descent either born in, or who have emigrated to, the United States – is undoubtedly a rapidly growing field of ethnic American literature, it should be noted that this growth has occurred mainly since the watershed period of the 1960s, which saw a massive expansion in Asian immigration to the United States, and an increased political self-awareness on the part of Asian Americans (inspired by the example of the radical social movements of the 1950s and 1960s). Yet, Asian American literature has a history which extends back to the mid-nineteenth century, and any survey of Asian American literature should pay attention to its *history*, as well as to the contemporary flourishing of Asian American literature, therefore this study begins by offering a survey of this history.

'Asian American literature' is not an ethnically or nationally bound category of writing. Instead, it is a term which is used to refer to texts written by North American writers of Asian descent, gathering together writers of diverse national origins, including Chinese, Japanese, Koreans, Filipinos, South Asians (Indians, Pakistanis, etc.) and Pacific Islanders, amongst others. This term is often also extended to include Asian Canadian writers, like Joy Kogawa, partly because Asians in the United States and Canada have had similar experiences, in terms of the conditions of social acceptance they encountered in Canada and the USA. However, despite the almost universal academic adoption of the organising rubric 'Asian American', some dissent has recently been voiced regarding the merit and academic (if not institutional) usage of such a term. Increasingly, academics working on Asian American literature choose to either discuss a particular group (Korean Americans, for example) or, more often, stress that use of the term 'Asian American', and its spatial equivalent, 'Asian America', is a limited conceptual term, an imagined geocultural space and a narrow discursive category. My use of the term in this study generally reflects the standard usage: I both accept its limitations as well as utilising its flexibility.

With this in mind, then, we must remember that the term 'Asian American' therefore not only covers an enormous variety of ethnic groups, religions, and languages, it also arguably can obscure the differences *within* these constituent groups. For example, so-called 'Chinese Americans' may trace their ancestry to mainland China, Taiwan, Hong Kong (which was of course until recently a British colony), or Singapore. Depending upon their ancestral region, they may speak Cantonese, Mandarin, or one of any number of local dialects. In addition, class differences and levels of economic security may also be obscured: there is a great deal of difference between an educated and financially secure immigrant from Hong Kong and a refugee from Vietnam. These differences become relevant in the study of Asian American literature, as particular writers often refer to, or pun upon, particular national or regional languages, religions, or other cultural practices. Maxine Hong Kingston, for example, discussed in detail in chapter 2, makes several jokes about and puns upon Cantonese words. So let us initially split the term 'Asian American' apart in order to trace the development of both these particular immigrant groups and their literary production.

Chinese American literature

Asians began emigrating to the United States in large numbers in 1849, when Chinese men began to arrive there, in order to escape the 'intense conflicts in China caused by the British Opium Wars ... the turmoil of peasant rebellions ... and the bloody strife between the *Punti* (Local People) and the *Hakkas* (Guest People) over possession of the fertile delta lands'.[3] This early immigration was mainly to California, where Chinese immigrants joined the 'Forty-Niners' in the search for gold during the period of the Californian Gold Rush. This initial surge of movement resulted in the Chinese term for the United States, 'Gold Mountain', a name that is still in use today. Early Chinese immigrants encountered harsh conditions in the United States, including what we would now call forms of institutionalised racism. The Chinese Exclusion Acts which were in force between 1882 and 1943, for example, banned the entry of certain groups of Chinese immigrants to America (notably women), and several laws were also passed restricting Chinese Americans' ability to work in California and other states. As prospecting for gold dried up in the 1850s and Chinese immigrants were made to feel increasingly unwelcome in California, many moved into railroad construction, becoming involved in the building of the transcontinental Central Pacific Railroad in the 1860s. In 1869, once the railroad was complete, this mode of employment disappeared and the Chinese immigrants either moved to Californian cities, where they took low paid service sector work as laundry workers, or entered jobs in manufacturing, or in more rural areas they became involved in agriculture and construction work. These early migrants were virtually all male; not only did Chinese tradition and culture limit the migration opportunities for women, but several laws (such as the Page Law of 1875) prohibited the emigration of Chinese women to California too. Despite this, some Chinese women travelled alone to the United States, mostly in order to become prostitutes. The fact that so many of the earliest Chinese women in America were prostitutes may explain the preponderance of images of Chinese women at this time as highly exotic and sexualised, an image which has unfortunately endured.

Owing to the difficult conditions that the Chinese immigrants (both male and female) encountered, many considered themselves *huaqiao* (overseas Chinese) who intended to return to China, and this inevitably influenced the emergence of Chinese American literature. In addition, most early immigrants were poorly educated peasants, who could neither write nor read. As a result, as Elaine Kim discusses at length in *Asian American Literature: An Introduction to the Writings and their Social Context*, early Chinese American literary production is mainly limited to a few autobiographies and oral testimonies by male writers, often in Chinese.[4] Much of this literature is heavily influenced by Chinese literary traditions, which incorporated elements reminiscent of oral culture and is often imitative of Chinese literary forms. An example of such writing is the collection *Island*, edited by Him Mark Lai, Genny Lim and Judy Yung, which is a collection of the poems (originally written in Chinese) which were carved on the walls of the immigration station on Angel Island in San Francisco Bay, through which all new immigrants to the United States had to pass, in the period up to 1940. These poems document the despair and difficulty experienced by early Chinese immigrants and are an important surviving resource. Many of the first Chinese American narratives in English were written by students. Lee Yan Phou's *When I Was a Boy in China* (1887), has recently received extensive critical attention as a proto-Asian American autobiography, and was one of the first to be written in English. *When I Was a Boy in China* describes its author's life in China before he emigrated as a student to the United States, under the aegis of the Chinese Educational Mission, and it is quite self-consciously written for an American readership. Its attempts to counteract prevailing stereotypes of Asians and Asian life are evident when Lee Yan Phou notes that 'I still continually find false ideas in America concerning Chinese customs, manners, and institutions', for example.[5] Some of the first Chinese American female writing, as Amy Ling has made clear in *Between Worlds: Women Writers of Chinese Ancestry*, was by upper-class female emigrés, including Helena Kuo, Mai-mai Sze and Lin Tai-yi, who were Chinese-born and westernised, and who often came from diplomatic backgrounds.[6] Probably the very first Chinese American woman writer was the Eurasian writer Edith Maude Eaton, who wrote stories and magazine articles under the Chinese-sounding pseudonym of Sui Sin Far, in the early twentieth century. In a time of intense Sinophobia, Eaton's stories are sensitive and elegant portrayals of the Chinese in the United States. In her best-known piece, the autobiographical essay, 'Leaves from the Mental Portfolio of an Eurasian', Eaton articulates her lifelong struggle with racism and the contradictions of ethnic identity. She published her only book of stories, *Mrs. Spring Fragrance*, in 1912; Eaton's sister Winnifred was more prolific and wrote numerous novels, under the Japanese-sounding pseudonym of Onoto Watanna. Although it may seem strange that these two sisters adopted pseudonyms in order to write, this may be explained by their sense of a need to 'mask' their true identities as Eurasians in what was undoubtedly a fiercely racist environment. At least by adopting Asian-sounding pseudonyms, the two writers were accepted on the basis of their 'exotic' Asian perspectives.

In the light of this fact, it is unsurprising that subsequent Chinese American writing continued to evince a heightened awareness of racism towards Asians. This is exemplified in Jade Snow Wong's autobiographical *Fifth Chinese Daughter* (1945), which describes Wong's experience of growing up in America as the daughter of strict and traditional Chinese parents who demanded filial piety and an adherence to Chinese expectations of women. The narrative also charts Wong's struggle to reconcile these demands with her attempts to assimilate into American society. She never successfully resolved this dilemma; on one hand she accentuates the positive aspects of her Chinese identity: she provides mouthwatering descriptions of delicious Chinese dishes (together with instructions on how to make them) and emphasises the respectability of Chinese family life. On the other hand, her autobiography illustrates her eagerness for acceptance into white society, on American terms. It is worth noting in relation to this dilemma the conditions in which Wong wrote her narrative. Although she was encouraged to write her autobiography by a white publisher, she or he extensively edited the manuscript, cutting two-thirds of the original and instructing Wong on what to include.

Owing to the gender imbalance of early Chinese American immigration, one gender-specific feature of a series of narratives written by Chinese immigrant men is their focus upon bachelor society. Louis Chu's novel *Eat a Bowl of Tea* (1961), for example, depicts the life of a group of ageing Chinese American men in Chinatown in New York, who have left their wives in China in order to search for a better existence. The men are labourers, who work in laundries and restaurants, and lead lonely, impoverished lives in cramped apartments and basements, punctuated and enlivened only by visits to prostitutes, and mah-jong games. The novel focuses upon the story of the old-timer Wah Gah and his son, Ben Loy, who is destined to live the same life as his father. Yet despite the rather depressing theme of the novel, it is a lively, often humourous and engaging account of Chinatown life. Other 'bachelor' novels include Chin Yang Lee's *Flower Drum Song* (1957) and Lin Yutang's *Chinatown Family* (1948).

Since these early publications, Chinese American writing has proliferated, with a series of well known novels and autobiographies, published in the post-war period. These include writings by several well travelled and sometimes upper-class female novelists. Diana Chang's novel *The Frontiers of Love* (1956), set in Shanghai during the Second World War; and the novels and autobiographies of Han Suyin, and Chuang Hua's experimental modernist novel *Crossings* (1968), are set in a variety of locations, including China, France and England, as well as the United States. A notable feature of more contemporary Chinese American women's writing is an emphasis upon mother–daughter relations, which can be seen in the novels and memoirs of Maxine Hong Kingston (*The Woman Warrior* (1976), *Tripmaster Monkey* (1989)), the novels of Amy Tan (*The Joy Luck Club* (1989), *The Kitchen God's Wife* (1991), *The Hundred Secret Senses* (1995), *The Bonesetter's Daughter* (2001)), and Gish Jen (*Typical American* (1992), and *Mona in the Promised Land* (1996) and these are discussed in more detail in chapter 2. These texts in particular have been phenomenally successful, perhaps because they have keyed into a popular area of attention for feminists in the late twentieth century.[7]

Japanese American literature

The pattern of development of Chinese American cultural production is largely mirrored by early Japanese, Filipino and Korean immigration and writing. Japanese people began emigrating to the United States following the economic hardships in Japan in the 1880s, at a time when the Japanese government allowed limited Japanese emigration. Unlike the gender imbalance of Chinese migration however, Japanese women emigrated too, mainly to Hawaii and California, where they became involved in agricultural work (often as sugar cane labourers). This pattern of Japanese immigration had a crucial effect on the Japanese American demographic profile in the early twentieth century, as well as upon its literary production. Since women emigrated at the same time as men (largely as a result of the 1907 'Gentleman's Agreement' between Japan and the United States, which permitted immigration for both sexes), the Japanese in the United States started families far earlier than the Chinese, so a *nisei* or second generation appeared quite swiftly. Elaine Kim argues that this led to substantial numbers of *nisei* writing from the 1920s and 1930s onwards, both male and female.[8] Possibly the first of these texts is Etsu Sugimoto's autobiographical novel *A Daughter of the Samurai*, published in 1925, which juxtaposes Sugimoto's American life with both real and fictional portraits of Japan. Like the work of the early Chinese immigrant writers, Sugimoto's narrative seems to be written with the aim of offering a favourable picture of Japanese life for the reader, and provides a similarly complimentary perspective on the United States. Elaine Kim calls her an 'ambassador of goodwill' for this reason.[9] Although Sugimoto's narrative is highly sensitive in its portrayal of Japan, it also offers veiled criticism of Japanese feudal practices, particularly concerning the treatment of women.

Another notable group of Japanese American texts is a series of autobiographies and fictions written in response to the American government's treatment of Japanese Americans during the Second World War. During this time, in response to the Japanese bombing of Pearl Harbor, the American government interned large groups of Japanese Americans in camps across the United States, labelling them 'enemy aliens'. Several Japanese Americans wrote highly critical retrospective narratives detailing their internment experiences, and these include Monica Sone's autobiographical *Nisei Daughter* (1953), John Okada's novel *No-No Boy* (1957), the short stories of Toshio Mori, in *Yokohama, California* (1949), and Hisaye Yamamoto's stories, in *Seventeen Syllables and Other Stories* (1988). Like the early Chinese American writers, these texts bear testimony to their authors' desire for acceptance in America. This is especially true of Monica Sone's interesting, and commercially successful narrative, *Nisei Daughter*, one of the most accomplished autobiographical accounts of the internment experience. An awareness of both her American readership and of growing international tensions at the time dominates *Nisei Daughter*. Sone is acutely conscious of a white readership, and seeks to project an accommodating image of Japanese Americans throughout, especially in relation to food and cultural practices. If anything, she stresses the dominance of her Americanness. For example, when she visits Japan with her family she notes that she views it through the eyes of a foreigner, and desires a return to the United States: 'This America, where I was born, surrounded by people of different extractions, was still my home' (p. 108). Sone takes care to establish a harmonious view of her life in the United States and her identity as American in a way which conforms to ideals of assimilation. Although she retains the ethnic 'piquancy' of descriptions of the odd Japanese meal or celebration, Sone emphasises that this does not interfere with her overriding identification as a 'Yankee'. Her story follows a fairly traditional autobiographical pattern, starting with early childhood, and with lots of detail about her family life. Yet she experiences racism on a regular basis, a fact which she feels continues to highlight her 'Asianness'. Her final statement, 'the Japanese and American parts of me were now blended into one', appears to assert the reconciliation of her two identities, Japanese and American. As many critics have noted however, this final resolutionary statement seems premature and unconvincing. Sone's resolutionary ending seems to signal her *desire* for a reconciliation of her problems of identity, rather than a resolution itself. Because Sone is clearly addressing a white readership, her premature claims to the resolution of her 'hyphenated identity' may signal an attempt to plead a harmonious existence of Japanese Americans in the United States during a particularly difficult period in American race relations, during the Second World War. Sone's learns that choices of identity – Japanese or American – are not always available and unlimited. Racism brings with it the shock of recognition that identity for racialised Americans may be externally imposed, for Sone as *Japanese*, however strange that identity may feel, and that an 'American' identity could remain out of reach. This learning process may be traced through a discernible loss in the narrator's confidence in herself. Early on, Sone's confidence in her ability to choose identifications shines through: 'I was a Yankee', she tells us proudly (p. 18). This contrasts sharply with her later professed need to revitalise and replenish her damaged self-image, in the wake of encounters with racism, when Sone's dampened self-confidence nearly silences her: 'I was so overcome with self-consciousness I would not bring myself to speak' (p. 131). Likewise, the style of the text, as Elaine Kim has noted, shifts from exuberance to a subdued and even stilted style in the later pages.

More recent post-war Japanese American writing includes the work of many more women: the complex, futuristic novels of Cynthia Kadohata, *The Floating World* (1989) and *In the Heart of the Valley of Love* (1992); Julie Shigekuni's novel about mothers and daughters, *A Bridge Between Us* (1995), and Gail Tsukiyama's story about Chinese girl labourers, *Women of the Silk* (1991); as well as autobiographical works by Kyoko Mori, *The Dream of Water: A Memoir* (1995), and Lydia Minatoya, *Talking to High Monks in the Snow: An Asian American Odyssey* (1993).

Korean American literature

Ronald Takaki pinpoints the beginnings of Korean immigration as 1903.[10] Like the Japanese, many of these pioneer Korean immigrants went to Hawaii, escaping Japanese aggression in Korea at the turn of the nineteenth century. As the early Korean immigration also included women, the same early appearance of a second generation occurred as it did with the Japanese. One of the most important early Korean writers was the intellectual Younghill Kang, who arrived in the United States from Korea in 1921, and who was writing at the same time as Etsu Sugimoto.[11] But unlike Sugimoto, Kang did not view himself as a guest in the United States, as Elaine Kim has observed.[12] Instead, he desperately desired both acceptance and to make America his home. Like Carlos Bulosan, Kang's perspective is simultaneously that of outsider-observer and immigrant. Kang's novels, *The Grass Roof* (1931) and *East Goes West* (1937) describe both life in Korea and the experience of Korean immigrants in America in the 1920s and 1930s, from a decidedly critical viewpoint. Like his later Chinese American counterpart, Louis Chu, Kang tended to emphasise male experiences in his work.

Surprisingly, given that Korean men and women both emigrated to America in the early twentieth century, Korean American women were slow to start publishing. Elaine Kim discusses the work that Younghill Kang produced between 1931 and 1937 at some length, but she mentions no female writers.[13] Korean American female writing really came of age in the 1980s and 1990s when Margaret K. Pai published the autobiographical *The Dreams of Two Yi-min* (1989), which recounts the life of her family in Hawaii, and Mary Paik Lee published her story of immigration to California, *Quiet Odyssey: A Pioneer Korean Woman in America* (1990). Both of these autobiographical accounts retrospectively deal with the experience of their subjects as immigrants at the beginning of the twentieth century through to the 1920s, although they were only written in the latter part of the century.

A notable exception to this lack of writing by Korean women is Kim Ronyoung's novel, *Clay Walls* (1987), published just two years before her death in 1989 at the age of sixty-three. Like *The Dreams of Two Yi-min* and *Quiet Odyssey*, *Clay Walls* tells the story of early Korean immigrants who arrived in Los Angeles in the 1920s. But unlike Pai and Lee, Kim Ronyoung's interest lies specifically in the lives that Korean immigrant women led in America. As such, the narrative stresses the story of the central female character, Haesu, and that of her daughter Faye, comparing and contrasting the experiences of first and second-generation women, including the employment opportunities available to them and their experiences of racism.

Most Korean American writers deal in different ways with the effects of the Japanese colonisation of Korea. Korean American writing is distinctive in that it has a history of political activism, both in its depiction of Korean and Korean American activists and through the political propaganda purposes of the writing itself (which is to protest colonial intervention in Korean internal affairs), elements which can be found in Mary Paik Lee's *Quiet Odyssey*, Margaret K. Pai's *The Dreams of Two Yi-Min* and Ronyoung Kim's *Clay Walls*.[14] All of these texts depict to varying degrees Korean American resistance to Japanese colonial rule, and protest against the racist treatment of Korean Americans by the American state, as well as imparting a strong nationalist spirit. But it is the writer Theresa Hak Kyung Cha who explores these political issues most extensively in a more recent text which is becoming increasingly well-known, the experimental *Dictee* (1982). Theresa Hak Kyung Cha was born in Korea in 1951 and emigrated with her family to the United States in 1962, where she lived first in Hawaii and then in San Francisco. After graduating in film and performance theory from the University of California, she embarked upon a career as a film maker and artist, and her work won several prestigious awards. Cha first published *Dictee* in 1982, the year of her premature death, and the critical acclaim accorded to the text has thus largely occurred posthumously. *Dictee* weaves together a variety of narrative modes, including poetry, journal entries, letters and excerpts from history books, to document both Korean life under Japanese colonial control and the immigrant experience in America. The text is punctuated by non-textual material, such as photographs, maps and calligraphy. Because of its complexity, *Dictee* is an intriguing text, which has been read variously as a postmodernist narrative, protest memoir and Korean American autobiography. South Korean American novelist Chang-Rae Lee's very successful first novel *Native Speaker* (1995), by contrast, raises no such questions of classification and can, unusually for an Asian American text, be characterised as genre fiction. It tells the story of a Korean American spy, Henry Park, who becomes entangled in the corrupt world of a Korean American councilman, John Kwang. It is Henry's task to uncover the secrets of Kwang's rise to power, and this endeavour is set against the backdrop of the alienating and turbulent cityscape of New York City. A gripping book, *Native Speaker* has marked something of a new departure for Asian American literature, moving as it does away from the more traditional preoccupations with ethnic identity and the processes of Americanisation.

One of those traditional images (we might even say stereotypical) of the Asian woman, is contested in Nora Okja Keller's *Comfort Woman: A Novel* (1997), which tells the story of the Korean 'comfort women'. Comfort women were young girls, usually of school age, sometimes as young as twelve, who were forcibly drafted into prostitution to service the Japanese military during its occupation of Korea between the late 1930s and 1945. Keller's protagonists in the novel are Akiko, a refugee who has fled to the United States, and her daughter by an American missionary, Beccah. Set in Hawaii, the novel charts Akiko's struggle to come to terms with her past as a comfort woman, the story of which she gradually reveals to her daughter. In relation to the concentration upon female experiences in very recent Korean American writing by women, it is possible to see how Theresa Hak Kyung Cha's work has influenced writers such as Nora Okja Keller. Critical attention is increasingly being paid to the stories of Korean military 'comfort women'. Until the late 1980s the issue had hardly been discussed. Records and documents relating to the practice have been suppressed (the Japanese government 'classified' documents relating to comfort women) and this was coupled with an intentional amnesia on the part of many of the victims.[15] It is only recently that oral testimonies, written accounts and academic research have begun to appear on the subject; apart from Keller's fictionalised account, there is now also an edited collection by several former comfort women, entitled *The True Stories of the Korean Comfort Women*.[16]

Filipino American literature

Like Korean American writing, Filipino writing has a noticeable gender imbalance. Filipinos began migrating to the United States in large numbers between 1900 and the 1920s following the United States' annexation of the Philippines. Most of these early migrants were farm and agricultural workers, although a few were students. Filipino men also often brought their wives with them, although the large majority of men who migrated were single, and unmarried women did not migrate. There are no early texts by women comparable with Carlos Bulosan's autobiographical narrative *America is in the Heart*, which was published in 1943; or Bienvenido N. Santos' *Scent of Apples: A Collection of Stories* (1979). It is only in the last years of the twentieth century that Filipino American texts by women in English have started to be widely published, the most notable example being Jessica Hagedorn's very commercially successful novel *Dogeaters* (1991), which she has subsequently followed with another novel, *The Gangster of Love* (1996). *Dogeaters* is especially interesting because it draws extensively upon vernacular modes, particularly gossip. It tells the stories of a range of Filipino characters, from the precocious and privileged young girl Pucha, to the impoverished youth Joey, who turns to prostitution as his only means of survival. Hagedorn's many characters represent the spectrum of society in the Philippines, but she favours the stories of the disenfranchised fringes of that society. As Lisa Lowe has extensively argued, Jessica Hagedorn 'radically alters the form and function of the novel and of historical narrative through explorations of alternate means for representing the history of "the popular"'.[17] She juxtaposes the discourses of history, such as Jean Mallat's 1846 history of the Philippines, with what Lowe calls popular genres, like radio melodramas, and vernacular forms like gossip, in order to cover a range of generic and discursive registers in the novel. Thus, *tsismis* (the word for gossip), becomes one of the central modes of 'knowing' in the text.

South Asian American literature

Indian American immigration, or South Asian immigration (the preferred term), has a slightly different history from those groups mentioned so far. A very short burst of immigration occurred from 1907 to 1917, after which immigration was halted by the United States Congress. This immigration was almost exclusively male: although these young men were mainly married, their wives stayed at home. In addition, the 1917 Immigration Law prohibited men from bringing their wives to America anyway. Initial South Asian immigration was largely a reaction to British colonial activities in India, but due to immigration restrictions this early wave of immigration was not sustained. Takaki notes that by 1940, the Asian Indian population in the United States numbered only 2,405, 60 per cent of whom resided in California.[18] This uneven immigration pattern helps to explain the relative absence of South Asian American writing until the 1970s and 1980s, when writers like Bharati Mukherjee (author of five novels and two collections of short stories), Meena Alexander (author of two novels, a memoir, and several poetry collections), and Chitra Banerjee Divakaruni (author of three novels) began publishing their work. Bharati Mukherjee's novels, in particular, are becoming increasingly well-known, especially her two most accomplished books, *Wife* (1975) and *Jasmine* (1989). *Wife* tells the story of Dimple Dasgupta, the daughter of middle-class Indian parents who marries Amit Basu, an engineer, and emigrates to the United

States. Dimple has high expectations of her life in America, but her experiences turn out to be very different. She encounters a world of racism and prejudice, where Amit cannot obtain the kind of work he is qualified for and Dimple herself is increasingly isolated. Dimple sees her flat as a refuge from the perilous landscape of New York beyond the front door: 'The air was never free of the sounds of sirens growing louder, or gradually fading. They were reminders of a dangerous world (even the hall was dangerous, she thought, let alone the playground and streets', and she finds herself increasingly isolated (p. 120). In fact, many of Mukherjee's novels depict the new immigrant woman trapped inside her house, and alone, for fear of what lies beyond the door. The more recent novel, *Jasmine*, by contrast, is characterised by constant movement and flight, and can almost be read as a postmodern version of *Wife*. *Jasmine's* heroine, the eponymous Jasmine Vijh, emigrates to America alone in order to escape her fate as a widow in a small Indian village. Her transformation into Jane Ripplemeyer, wife of a successful Iowa banker and mother of an adopted Vietnamese child, forms the subject of the story. But along the way, Jasmine is raped, exiled, rendered homeless and penniless, and discriminated against as an immigrant, and this reflects Mukherjee's perennial preoccupation with the fractured lives of female immigrants in America. Yet, unlike Dimple Dasgupta, Jasmine's story is resolutely one of success: she 'makes it' in the United States.

The groups whose history I have described – Chinese, Japanese, Filipinos, Koreans and South Asians – together form the earliest Asian presence in the United States. Hence it is no coincidence that these groups (and especially Chinese and Japanese Americans) have the most developed and more prolific literary traditions in America. Newer and later immigration groups include Laotians, Vietnamese and Cambodians, many of whom have emigrated since the 1965 immigration law, which abolished immigration quotas. A large proportion of these new immigrants were seeking temporary sanctuary from civil war and famine. The end of the Vietnam War in 1975, in particular, resulted in many refugees seeking asylum in the US, and continues to cast a long shadow across Asian America. Ronald Takaki observes that many Vietnamese, for example, view themselves as sojourners, and thus do not see their stay in the United States as permanent, a fact that has affected the literary production of these groups.[19] Since the 1965 law was passed, there has also been a new wave of immigration from China, the Philippines, Korea and from South Asian countries, notably from Pakistan. These bursts of immigration have invigorated the literary production of their respective ethnic groups, producing a new generation of writers. In fact, the abolition of immigrant quotas since 1965 has dramatically altered the demographic profile of Asian America. Whereas previous to this, American-born Asians outnumbered foreign-born Asians, currently the opposite is true, with 60 per cent of the population of Asian America now foreign-born. At present, Asians comprise one third of legally admitted immigrants to the United States, and Asian Americans constitute 3 per cent of the total US population (some eight million people). Of these, approximately one quarter are Chinese American, 19 per cent Filipino, and roughly 10 per cent each of Japanese, Korean, Vietnamese and South Asian Americans.

Periods of intense Asian American literary production map quite exactly on to the history of Asian reception in the United States, and on to the relationship between the United States and various Asian countries at particular moments. For example, the relatively powerful position that Japan's Meiji government enjoyed on the world stage at the end of the nineteenth century facilitated Japanese immigration and also affected the reception Japanese received in America. The Chinese, in contrast, experienced a far more hostile reception from the United States government due to China's relatively weak position at that same time. Thus, Japanese American literary production flourished quite early, but, during the Second World War when Japanese Americans were interned by the United States government, very little work was published by them in what was an anti-Japanese climate. Later, Japanese Americans retrospectively wrote about this time, in a newly conciliatory climate after the war. The close relationship between cultural acceptance and literary production is perhaps most starkly illustrated by the rapid development and proliferation of Asian American writing after the 1965 immigration law, a time which also witnessed the new social movements which sought to combat discrimination of different kinds in the United States. In particular, the education curriculum innovations that emerged out of the new social movements paved the way for more self-conscious reflections upon issues of identity and ethnicity, like those in the texts that I will discuss later in this book. In fact, the advent of Asian American studies programmes in the 1960s was a catalyst for the self-conscious advancement of Asian American interests.[20] Unlike the work of other politicised groups of the 1960s, however, Asian American studies programmes have been concerned to stress the *Americanness* of Asian America, often at the expense of the respective Asian heritage. (There is a clear difference here from other social movement writing of the period, which asserted cultural, racial or gender *difference*). This US-centric emphasis upon America and Americanisation can be detected in the proliferation of literary and autobiographical texts which have emerged since 1965, which largely focus upon the problems of assimilation and encounters with racism, and are usually set in the United States (even when, as in Maxine Hong Kingston's *The Woman Warrior*, the Asian country is 'visited' in the mind of its protagonists).

Amy Ling has recently argued that the United States is increasingly becoming more 'pro-ethnic', notably through the critical attention being paid to so-called minority literatures.[21] Ling cites the recent publication of the Heath and Norton American literature anthologies, with their extensive inclusions of non-Anglo writers, as an apposite example. She goes on to note: 'we may say with great excitement and anticipation that we are now on the brink of an Asian American literary and artistic renaissance' (p. 192). The reason for this renaissance, Ling suggests, is 'the matrix of political, social, economic, historical, and cultural forces today. The time is ripe, and the majority seems at this moment more and more ready to listen to the *other* and to its own formulations of the *other* as reflected in texts produced by these others' (p. 194). This can be seen in the recent proliferation and commercial success of much Asian American writing.

Asian American women's writing

As this study shows, Asian American literature is swiftly moving into the cultural spotlight. In this study, though, the highlighting of Asian American *women* writers perhaps requires greater justification. Women's writing has been treated as a separate locus of interest and attention increasingly in the last twenty years in literary and critical analysis. As Rita Felski writes:

> The emergence of a second wave of feminism in the late 1960s justifies the analysis of women's literature as a separate category, not because of automatic and unambiguous differences between the writings of women and men, but because of the recent cultural phenomenon of women's explicit self-identification as an oppressed group, which is in turn articulated in literary texts in the exploration of gender-specific concerns centered around the problem of female identity.[22]

The same is true of Asian American women's writing. Most of the texts discussed here identify oppression predicated upon both gender and ethnicity. Asian American women's writing and experiential realities are frequently marginalised in both canonical critical discourses and wider cultural locations. The recognition of this, and the self-identification as marginalised, throws Asian American women's textual negotiations of identity together in what Sau-ling Wong has termed 'a textual coalition'.[23] It is also the case, as Amy Ling has noted, that to focus upon the study of Asian American *women* writers is to focus upon the most significant – and prominent – texts and writers.[24] Indeed, Werner Sollors has noted that it is 'important to identify a core of women's and ethnic literatures, in order to then note how they overlap with each other and the dominant literatures, how their boundaries are blurred, and how they interact with each other'.[25]

One particular claim to be made for these texts is that they are united in the urgent negotiation and re-negotiation of the problematics of gendered, ethnicised and nationalised identity (hence the title of this book); and furthermore, that in so doing, these texts make important interventions in dominant discourses of identity and critical discussions of identity formation. Part of the uniqueness of this literature is its frequent disruption of a writer/theorist binary, as will be elaborated in chapter 3. Several writers also consciously attempt to revise traditional genres, such as the *bildungsroman*, romance narrative, or science fiction. Generic disruption in this manner constitutes a form of transformation and transgression of traditional, patriarchally-informed discursive codes, and also occurs with some frequency in this corpus of writing. Thus, it is the case that these texts become examples of what Carole Boyce Davies has termed 'uprising textualities'.[26] A further connection between the texts discussed here is the recurrence of particular thematic concerns, many of which overlap with the themes of women's writing – or sometimes ethnic writing – generally. These include a preoccupation with issues of identity, as already suggested, but also more variously include an interest in woman-to-woman identifications (especially those constructed along matrilines); an objection to limitations placed upon women by patriarchal forces; a focus upon the family; a search for viable female role models; a questioning of white male values and definitions of beauty and attractiveness (with an accompanying desire to reject the objectification of women); a sensitivity to the effects of violence against women and other trauma, such as sexual abuse; a wariness of hetero-normative approaches to sexuality; an insistence upon the importance of self-definition; an insistence upon the primacy of gossip as a valid 'genderlect'; a recognition of the phallocentricity of history and other mainstream versions of the past; a suspicion of the state as a regulatory force in women's lives; and an unease with the silencing of women's voices.

Lastly, in order to locate Asian American women's writing more thoroughly within a socio-historical context, this chapter ends by reflecting upon and surveying the specific history of Asian American women in America, especially in relation to the emergence of an Asian American feminist movement in the 1970s, 1980s and 1990s. As Sauling Wong and Jeffery Santa-Ana have recently observed, since Asian American literary and cultural criticism increasingly focuses not just upon print media, but also on theatre, film, video, photography and other visual art, popular culture, performance art, fashion, cosmetic surgery and activism, it is increasingly impossible to view literature as a separate – indeed separable – entity, and should instead be viewed in interconnection with other cultural trends.[27]

Asian American women: in and out of history

In 'A Woman-Centered Perspective on Asian American History' (1989), Sucheta Mazumbar asks:

> What did it mean to be a Chinese woman in nineteenth-century California? Or a Japanese woman on the sugar plantation in early twentieth-century Hawaii? Or a Filipina on today's electronic assembly lines in the Silicon Valley; a Korean garment worker in New York? If society has ever thought about these women, it has often been in clichés: the depraved prostitute in nineteenth-century San Francisco; the quiet, courteous, and efficient Asian female office worker today. Asian women in America have emerged not as individuals but as nameless and faceless members of an alien community. Their identity has been formed by the lore of the majority community, not by their own history, their own stories. (p. 1)

As already discussed, initial phases of Asian immigration from the mid-1800s onward did not include as many women as men, a situation which resulted in a noticeably skewed gender ratio in early Asian America. Because many of the women who did emigrate were uneducated, accounts of early Asian women's experiences of immigration to the United States are relatively scarce. Although the so-called 'Gentlemen's Agreement' of 1907–8 (which restricted Japanese immigration to wives and children of Japanese American men) resulted in an influx of Japanese women to America, it was not until the 1940s that the gender imbalance of Asian America began to radically change, largely as a result of alterations in US immigration law, and the gradual establishment of new generations of Asian Americans. The War Brides Act of 1945 enabled more extensive female immigration, as did a partial lifting of the ban on Asian immigration in the early 1940s. However, the watershed moment occurred with changes to the immigration laws in 1965, which largely saw the abolition of immigration quotas.

Asian American women's history has thus been obscured by both the conditions of female immigration and reception, and the dominance of the majority culture's versions of the past. Despite this, recent decades have witnessed the emergence of Asian American histories and oral accounts of the past. As Connie Young Yu writes, 'In Asian America there are two kinds of history. The first is what is written about us in various old volumes on immigrants and echoed in textbooks, the second is our own oral history, what we learn in the family chain of generations, (p. 33). Archival work by Asian American feminist historians like Judy Yung has excavated the particular stories of Asian American women;[28] others like Connie Young Yu have recovered the history of Chinese American women by historically 'thinking back' through their mothers, grandmothers and great-grandmothers.[29] Other historians have recorded the oral histories of Asian American women pioneers, such as historian Sucheng Chan's collaboration with Mary Paik Lee in *Quiet Odyssey: A Pioneer Korean Woman in America* (1990), or Ruth Lum McCunn's fictionalised account of the life of nineteenth-century Chinese American woman Lalu Nathoy (Anglo name Polly Bemis), in *Thousand Pieces of Gold: A Biographical Novel* (1981). Oral history projects (such as the Issei Oral History Project based in Sacramento) remain crucial means of gathering historical information about Asian American women, since statistics regarding Asian American women are difficult (sometimes impossible) to locate, as well as affording access to Asian American women's own perspectives. As Sucheng Chan notes in her preface to *Quiet Odyssey*, 'While students learn a great deal from history written in the third person (in the case of Asian immigrants, usually a faceless, nameless "they"), they become far more engaged in what they read when the information is presented through individual voices' (p. xiii). Furthermore, historically Asian American women's experiences have frequently been radically different from their male counterparts, from the first female Chinese immigrants tricked into prostitution service for a society of Chinese American bachelors, to Japanese and Korean 'picture brides', to mail-order brides' more recent experiences. Asian American women's economic and labour contributions to America have also often been obscured. Sun Bin Yim and others have discussed Korean women's crucial roles in operating family businesses, working on farms alongside their husbands, or performing domestic labour for male workers;[30] Gail Nomura has analysed Issei women's roles as active participants in the labour force, especially as sugar cane workers;[31] and much recent work has been undertaken examining the lives of Asian immigrant workers in the often highly exploitative garment and silicon production industries.[32] Recently, attention has also been paid to the connection between what Lisa Lowe has called the 'occupational ghettoization' of Asian women in the US,[33] and colonial and neocolonial activities in Asia.

As discussed in more detail in chapter 2, Maxine Hong Kingston's contribution to Asian American feminism through her life writing is particularly important, notably because of its cultural politics, derived from her gendered cross-cultural identity and its aesthetic practice, in particular the generic boundary crossings of her memoirs which are a mixture of autobiography and biography, history and myth, memory and fabulation. Such a mixture, although common in much postmodern writing, takes on a particular salience in Kingston's case since it provides her with a means to tease out the multiple threads of identity – of gender, ethnicity, class, culture and history. In this sense, Kingston's writing occupies a seminal place in the recent history of feminist thought, in particular the watershed period of the late 1970s and early 1980s when many feminist thinkers were becoming aware of the insularity of some of their traditional frames of reference, acknowledging that issues of gender cannot be separated from those of ethnicity, class and culture. In many ways, Kingston's work is symptomatic of a feminist understanding of all identities as mobile and continually open to re-negotiation. For instance, the treatment of gender identity in Kingston's writing encompasses a whole series of boundary crossings: the contradictory and conflicting definitions of womanhood that a Chinese American woman is forced to confront; the complexities of gender identity for Chinese American men, given their 'feminisation' by the dominant WASP culture; the gender crossing that Kingston attempts as the female author who places herself in the position of her male protagonists. Kingston's aesthetic practice also dramatises a feminist understanding of the links between language and identity: the acquisition of a mother tongue that is simultaneously her own and not her own, and through which the author enacts a series of transcriptions or translations backwards and forwards between Chinese and English idioms, creating in the process a hybrid discourse embodying an Asian American identity, which also gives voice to a feminist consciousness. Thus, Kingston's writing – *The Woman Warrior* in particular – may be identified as one Asian American text that influenced a paradigm shift in *all* American feminist thought.

Asian American feminism and white feminism: parallel movements?

The relationship between the burgeoning body of Asian American women's writing and the development of Asian American feminisms in the United States is a close one, particularly since both emerged in the wake of the 1950s and 1960s civil rights movements. This period saw all marginalised parties interested in the wider cultural debate galvanised by the need to end oppressions predicated upon racial, ethnic and gender 'difference'. Many Asian American women writers have been inspired by, as well as being connected to, the Asian American feminist movement. Wong and Santa Ana assert that these writers

> critiqued the oppression of Asian American women, expressed solidarity with Third World women in Asia and elsewhere, discerned connections between sexism and colonialism, challenged Orientalist stereotypes, reconstructed female ancestors' forgotten lives, claimed a matrilineal heritage on American soil, explored family dynamics, celebrated love between women, reclaimed female sexuality, and in general declared a new image: tough, powerful, resourceful, independent, and courageous.[34]

Both Asian American women's writing and Asian American feminist activism have noticeably consolidated their position on the American cultural stage in the 1990s and into the new century. Until very recently, Asian American women's role and visibility in the American women's liberation movement was relatively small. As Esther Nganling Chow points out in her perspicacious essay, 'The Feminist Movement: Where are all the Asian American Women?' (1989), the US women's movement has suffered from being predominantly white and middle class.[35] Whiteness was taken for granted as normative and as a 'given' in white feminist discourse, and patriarchal power was seen as the overriding oppression against which to organise. Asian American women's reaction against and response to the reductionism inherent in the white feminist struggles of the 1960s, 1970s and 1980s, has been self-organisation: the establishment of a separate space in which to struggle against and analyse the interconnections of racial, class and gender oppression. At the same time, this project has also involved Asian American feminists in attempting to highlight whiteness as both a standpoint and practice in feminist discourse, and to engender a greater critical self-reflexivity in the thought of white feminists.

Asian American feminist organising is also not simply the product or offshoot of the US women's liberation movement, but has other, simultaneous genealogies. For example, much work has its roots in the civil rights movements of the 1960s (such as the establishment of the

Asian American Political Alliance at UC Berkeley in 1968). And as Yen Le Espiritu makes clear in her discussion of Asian American women's movements, one reason for their genesis was Asian American women's dissatisfaction with their perceived lack of roles and marginalisation within the Asian American movement.[36] And as Ngan-ling Chow points out, many Asian American women's groups grew out of *local* community activities: women's studies courses at regional colleges, community education programmes, social service programmes (such as Asian Sisters, established in Los Angeles in 1971), and women's unions and political interest groups.[37] This move from regional organising to national, is typical especially in relation to Asian American women's political interest and activist organisations, such as Asian Immigrant Women Advocates (AIWA), Asian Women United of California, and Sakhi of New York City. Feminist and political articulations and organising by Asian American women has also often been strategic. Just as 'Asian American Studies' grew out of a conscious move to establish a political coalition, which facilitated the development of a new academic field and institutional identity, so Asian American and Asian immigrant women's organising has recognised the usefulness and counter-hegemonic possibilities of pan-ethnic alliances, despite the accompanying drawbacks.[38] In this sense, the US women of colour and Asian American feminist movements reflect the situation of the black British feminist movement, in which 'black' encompasses an entire racialised group: 'Pacific, Asian, Eastern, African, Caribbean, Latina, Native, and "mixed race"', a 'conscious coalition', 'a self-consciously constructed space where identity is not inscribed by a natural identification but a political kinship'.[39] Clearly, though, such political coalitions have their risks: the possible erasure of ethnic difference and specificity; the perceived inability to organise effectively against culturally or religiously specific oppressions; the undermining of class and caste axes, and generational connections and differences; the potential alienation of and inability to reach certain communities (for example, Yen Le Espiritu makes the point that pan-Asian organisations have primarily been the agenda of American-born and American-educated Asians, and have failed to affect Asian ethnic enclaves);[40] and the problems of inter-ethnic conflict (a recurrent criticism is the dominance of Chinese American and Japanese American influence and interests in many organisations, at the expense of other Asian American groups). Furthermore, in her essay 'Can the Subaltern Speak', Gayatri Chakravorty Spivak has cautioned that such coalitions may establish a falsely homogeneous subject position, which potentially obscures the shifting significations of 'color', 'ethnic', and 'race'.[41] Shifting demography also affects the potential for pan-Asian feminist organising: historically, in the post-war period, pan-Asian women's organisations have emerged in areas with a concentration of American-born and American-educated Asian American residents, such as San Francisco, Los Angeles and Oakland in California, and New York City. More recently, however, and especially as a result of the post-1965 influx of Asian-born immigrants, a recognition of the distinctiveness of Asian-born immigrants from their American-born, American-raised, and American-educated counterparts has led to the establishment of feminist organisations which address the particular problems such groups face. An example is the work of Asian Immigrant Women Advocates, which fights the exploitation of Asian immigrant women workers in the garment industry.[42]

Asian American feminist scholarship

Asian American feminist scholarship has been largely concerned with theorising the gender-ethnicity nexus; or the structures of Asian American women's multiple positionings: what Sandra Kumamoto Stanley calls 'multiple consciousness'; or what Amy Ling has named as 'outside the outside'; and 'between worlds'. One of the most extensive essays to date to deal with these issues is Shirley Geok-lin Lim's 1993 essay, 'Feminist and Ethnic Literary Theories in Asian American Literature'. Lim argues for an 'ethnic-cultural nuancing of conventional Euro-American feminist positions on gender/power relations and a feminist critique of ethnic-specific identity'.[43] Lim identifies the period of Asian American literary production since the publication of Maxine Hong Kingston's *The Woman Warrior* in 1976 as exemplifying a 'conscious and explicit conflict, between *women's* ideas of culture and cultural nationalism as claimed by some males'.[44] Arguing that the catalyst for this split in Asian American literary studies was the intervention of feminist critiques of literature and culture (with accompanying foci upon the mother–daughter dyad and other issues of gendered identity), Lim concludes that Asian American women writers' complex negotiations of identity provide useful paradigms of ethnic/gender identity which retain the sites of conflict between differing ideological valuations of identity, and refuse premature resolutions.

An alternative treatment of this subject may be found in Sau-ling Wong's 1992 essay 'Ethnicizing Gender: An Exploration of Sexuality as Sign in Chinese Immigrant Literature'.[45] Wong's piece marked an important moment in the evolution of Asian American feminist theory, positing as it did a new way of theorising the 'gender-ethnicity' nexus in relation to Chinese immigrant writing.[46] Wong argues that instead of the more usual theoretical move of gendering ethnicity, Asian American literature generally, and Chinese immigrant writing in particular, ethnicises gender. Wong reads three immigrant narratives: Yi Li's short story 'A Date at Age Twenty-eight', Cao Youfang's 1986 novel *American Moon*, and Bai Xianyong's story 'Excursion to Fire Island'.[47] She suggests that these three texts, amongst others, foreground sexuality as a sign amid other signs such as colour, stature, etc; and that this constitutes a challenge to the ethnic and racial stereotyping of Asian immigrants. Through her reading, she further suggests that the foregrounding of sexuality as a sign over other signs effects a revision of the ways in which the gender-ethnicity nexus is understood in Asian American criticism, from a 'double-jeopardy' model to a model in which gender and ethnicity emerge as far more fused.[48]

The gender/ethnicity problematic continues to remain a vexed issue in Asian American feminist studies, and in particular most Asian American feminist discussions of Asian American literature tend to address it to a greater or lesser extent. King-kok Cheung's 1993 analysis of the modalities of silence in Asian American women's writing, in *Articulate Silences: Hisaye Yamamoto, Maxine Hong Kingston, Joy Kogawa*, reads the work of three Asian American women writers as manifesting a particular emphasis upon the importance of silence as a strategic weapon against oppression. Cheung furthermore argues that Anglo-American criticism of women's texts has tended to valorise speech at the expense of silence, and that this Eurocentric critical perception has obscured Asian American women writers' strategic deployment of a speech–silence dichotomy as both a counter-cultural tactic and as a means of dramatising the complexities and intersections of ethnicised and gendered identity.

In her discussion of Asian immigration to the United States, and the racialised political foundations of the US nation state, Lisa Lowe has argued that the histories of citizenship and gender (in relation to the enfranchisement of white women), and the histories of citizenship and race (in relation to the enfranchisement of nonwhite males), are interconnected; in so far as the legally defined racial position of Asian Americans has always also been a gendered formation.[49] But Lowe also argues that recent attempts to organise against the exploitation of Asian immigrant female labourers (such as the work of the organisation AIWA) has to an extent disrupted this racial formation, and in so doing, highlights the intersecting axes of exploitation that Asian American women face. Lowe 'reads' the dissidence and oppositional potential of AIWA's recent campaign against garment manufacturer Jessica McClintock Inc. as comparable with the counter-cultural possibilities available through a reading of Theresa Hak Kyung Cha's text *Dictee*, or Fae Myenne Ng's novel *Bone*. In this way, too, Lowe does not seek to collapse the distinction between the 'empirical' and the 'aesthetic', but instead to situate different cultural practices within similar social and historical forms and moments of struggle. In this way, Asian American feminist cultural and aesthetic practices emerge as coterminous.

Very recent work on gender and authorship in Asian America has tended to focus less upon thematic paradigms, and more upon the strategies of assimilation that Asian American writers have adopted and adapted, in relation to a series of specific gender codes. For instance, Patricia Chu's study, *Assimilating Asians: Gendered Strategies of Authorship in Asian America* (2000), illustrates key Asian American writers' gender-based relationships to immigration, work, and forms of cultural representation. Especially innovative is Chu's reading of the early twentieth-century Chinese American writer Edith Maude Eaton (Sui Sin Far), alongside the contemporary South Asian American novelist, Bharati Mukherjee. The works of both are viewed by Chu as specifically female versions of *bildungsroman*, which connect the process of Americanisation to a female preoccupation with the domestic situation, and the position of women in society.

Finally, we turn to two particularly crucial areas of emphasis for Asian American feminists: the damage inflicted upon Asian American women by orientalist representations of Asian women, and the stereotyping of Asian women and femininity (especially what Wong and Santa Ana identify as the 'emasculation' of the Asian American male, and the 'hyperfeminization' of Asian women,[50] an issue discussed further in chapter 5). Much work has documented the reality of orientalism and yellowface in mainstream American cinema and stage. In addition to this, the widespread practice of mail order brides from Asia and the fantasies connected to twentieth-century American military engagements in the Far East that percolate to the surface in escort advertisements on television, suggest that the power of the orientalising, objectifying, and depoliticising gaze is cyclical, persistent and ubiquitous. One critic, Rocío Davis, has visited the subjects of orientalism and cultural stereotyping in her work.[51] She has analysed gay playwright David Henry Hwang's *M. Butterfly* as a subversion of the paradigms of Orientalist images of Asian women. Davis suggests that the manner in which the playwright appropriates the theme of Puccini's opera, only to reverse roles, may be considered a feminist approach to eurocentred notions of Asian femininity. Hwang weaves together fact, fiction and imagination to re-enact the drama of a desperate search for stereotypes and the tragic consequences of allowing oneself to be led by preconceived ideas about culture and gender. By invalidating many stereotypical notions of gender roles and culture, Davis asserts that Hwang offers a reading of the relations between East and West, men and women, and shows to what extent our perception is wounded by orientalist modes of thought.

Denationalisation is also a noticeable recent trend in Asian American feminist studies, as Sau-ling Wong has observed. In using this term, Wong refers to three noticeable recent phenomena in Asian American studies: the 'easing of cultural nationalist concerns',[52] academic cross-pollination between Asian American and Asian studies, and the shift towards an increasingly globalised, or diasporic, perspective. The recent collaborative feminist work of Elaine Kim and Chungmoo Choi, the work of King-Kok Cheung, and that of Lisa Lowe, are notable examples of this. Kim and Choi's jointly edited collection, *Dangerous Women: Gender and Korean Nationalism* (1998), uses feminist perspectives to analyse the position of Korean women in a global context, in relation to issues of colonialism, postcolonialism, nationalism, US interventions in Korea, the legacies of military dictatorships, and the ways in which these phenomena have affected Korean women both in Korea and in the Korean diaspora.

If Sau-ling Wong is correct in her assertion that cultural nationalist concerns have 'eased' in recent years, then this is probably due to feminist critiques of so-called Asian American cultural nationalist agendas.[53] King-kok Cheung's important 1998 essay, 'Of Men and Men: Reconstructing Chinese American Masculinity', explores issues of gender politics in Asian American literature, from a global Asian cultural perspective. Cheung argues that the representation of Asian men as 'emasculated' reflects the inextricability of gender and ethnic identity. She suggests that in response to this dominant representation, several Asian American male writers and critics have attempted to reconstruct Asian American masculinity by foregrounding and turning to Asian heroic traditions, such as martial arts, a move which has troubled Asian American feminists, leading to a conflict between Asian American feminists anxious to combat Asian American patriarchy and Asian American nationalists who have attacked what they view as Asian American feminists' reinforcement and perpetuation of negative stereotypes of Asian American men. In her attempt to reconfigure Asian American feminism, but at the same time anxious not to blunt Asian American male dissidence, in this essay Cheung explores possible avenues of reconciliation between Asian American feminist and nationalist agendas.[54]

Asian American feminist activism and publishing

Sonia Shah's recent edited collection, *Dragon Ladies: Asian American Feminists Breathe Fire* (1997), is a testimony to the current and growing vitality of the Asian American feminist movement, and the increasing politicisation of Asian American women. Surveying the whole gamut of Asian American feminist activism, including academic work, health, environmental activism, labour movements, domestic violence support organisations, sexuality, cultural representation, and the sex trade, amongst other arenas, the collection also showcases and pays homage to the contribution of individual Asian American feminist activists, including human rights activist Yuri Kochiyama, poet and performance artist Janice Mirikitani, socialist feminist Merle Woo, and writer and activist Helen Zia. In her 1989 essay, 'The Feminist Movement: Where Are All the Asian American Women?' Esther Ngan-ling Chow identified a series of barriers to Asian American feminist activism. These included psychological constraints (in the sense that the US women's movement has historically marginalised the concerns of ethnic women), cultural restrictions and dilemmas (such as language barriers for Asian immigrant women), patriarchy and other structural impediments (the juggling of responsibilities both within and beyond Asian American communities), legal-political barriers (the structural receptivity to Asian Americans; anti-Asian legislation; immigration policies), racial insensitivity and unreceptivity (both racist/capitalist patriarchy and white feminist lack of awareness), and class cleavage (particularly in the white feminist movement).[55] Chow then outlined five suggestions for an Asian American feminist course of action, which included strategies to overcome psychological barriers (such as consciousness raising, education in political awareness, networking and coalition-building); the establishment of self-awareness and cultural programmes; an analysis of the role of men in Asian American women's life struggles; white feminist education (aimed at producing an awareness in white feminist communities/organisations of ethnocentric views and practices); and pan-ethnic feminist alliances.[56] What Shah's collection, and other evidence makes clear, is that although there is still a long way to go, many of the changes and goals that Chow called for in 1989 are increasingly beginning to be achieved. A brief survey of Asian American feminist publishing in the period 1971–98 will serve to illustrate the point.

The year 1971 saw the publication of *Asian Women*, edited by Emma Gee and others, which was the first publication devoted to the subject of Asian American women. Ten years on and the seminal feminist women of colour publication, *This Bridge Called My Back: Writings by Radical Women of Color* appeared, which contained essays by Asian American feminists including Mitsuye Yamada, Merle Woo, and Nellie Wong.[57] It was not until 1989 that the next texts devoted to Asian American women appeared, with the publication of Shirley Geok-lin Lim and Mayumi Tsutakawa's collection *The Forbidden Stitch: An Asian American Women's Anthology*, and the first Asian Women United of California edition of *Making Waves: An Anthology of Writing by and about Asian American Women*. The period 1990–94 saw a series of significant publications by feminists of colour, including: *Making Face, Making Soul/Haciendo Caras: Creative and Critical Perspectives by Women of Color* edited by Gloria Anzaldúa (1990), *Skin Deep: Women Writing on Color, Culture and Identity*, edited by Elena Featherston (1994), *The Very Inside: An Anthology of Writing by Asian and Pacific Islander Lesbian and Bisexual Women*, edited by Sharon Lim-Hing (1994), and Karin Aguilar-San Juan's edited collection, *The State of Asian America: Activism and Resistance in the 1990s* (1994).

The late 1990s saw even more significant contributions to the body of writing on Asian American feminist issues. In 1997 Asian Women United of California published a sequel to their first anthology, *Making More Waves: New Writing by Asian American Women*. In the same year, Sonia Shah's edited collection, *Dragon Ladies: Asian American Feminists Breathe Fire*, was the first book-length study of Asian American feminisms. The year 1998 saw two further texts, Elaine Kim and Chungmoo Choi's edited *Dangerous Women: Gender and Korean Nationalism* and Sandra Kumamoto Stanley's edited *Other Sisterhoods: Literary Theory and U.S. Women of Color*. Most recently, 1999 saw a call for papers for a sequel to *This Bridge Called My Back*, twenty years later.[58]

This 'critical mass' of academic writing on Asian American women and feminism has also been mirrored by an explosion of significant activity by Asian American feminist organisations. Asian Women United of California (AWU) was founded in 1976 to 'promote the socioeconomic and general welfare of Asian American women'.[59] The organisation's primary work now consists of producing educational materials, including *With Silk Wings: Asian American Women at Work*, a high-school text.[60] Labour organisations, including Asian Immigrant Women Advocates (AIWA) are successfully campaigning against the exploitation of Asian American and Asian immigrant women workers, as is the pan-

Asian Committee for Asian Women (CAW), based in Hong Kong. Domestic violence organisations, particularly on the east and west coasts, have established programmes to deal with domestic violence issues faced by Asian American women, and include SAKHI and the Asian Women's Center in New York City, the Asian Women's Shelter in San Francisco, and the Asian Shelter and Advocacy Project (ASAP) in Boston. Asian American women's professional organisations include Asian Women in Business in New York City, the Asian American Journalists Association, and Catalyst. It is thus no underestimation to assert that Asian American women's creativity and activity is flourishing in the twenty first century.

Negotiating identities, mapping territories

This chapter has attempted to locate the phenomenon and success story of Asian American women's writing within a more general history of Asian America, Asian American literature and the growth of Asian American feminist studies and activism. Chapter 2 focuses specifically upon Asian American mother–daughter writing. The publication of Maxine Hong Kingston's *The Woman Warrior* in 1976 was the catalyst for the appearance of Asian American mother–daughter writing, and also marked a turning point in Asian American literature. Contemporary Asian American women's writing is notable for the recurrence of representations of both the vitality and ambivalence of the mother–daughter relationship. Women's texts across the range of Asias represented in this study address the mother–daughter bond. Chapter 2 suggests specifically that Asian American women's writing of the 1970s and 1980s challenged the 'Asian kinship nexus' by exploring the relations between Asian American mothers and daughters. This exploration also brings into question several white feminist explanations of the mother–daughter dyad in a double-edged and double-focused critique of both patriarchal, gender-blind and ethnically-blind, culturally generalist analyses of mother–daughter relations. In several texts motherhood emerges as a politically contested identity, and daughtering too is recognised as an important relational identity, one which is also deeply imbricated in questions of ethnicity and cultural identity. It is also suggested here that the emergence and persistence of Asian American mother–daughter writing has had something to do with its coincidence with white feminism's renewed attempts to theorise the mother–daughter nexus in the 1980s and 1990s, particularly in the work of Nancy Chodorow and Adrienne Rich. In discussing 'matrilineage' in

Asian American women's writing, this study mainly discusses texts written in the 1970s and 1980s, especially by Maxine Hong Kingston, Amy Tan, Joy Kogawa, as well as a 1990s text, by Julie Shigekuni.

As already discussed in relation to Maxine Hong Kingston, auto/biographical and life writing work are some of the most important ways in which Asian American women's voices from history can be recovered and heard. Auto/biographical expressions are also a means by which Asian American women are able to (re)claim a space for self articulation and representation, against a history of external representation, stereotyping and partiality, which has characterised so much writing about Asian American women. Asian American women's articulations of identity in auto/biographical modes have become an increasingly valuable academic and popular cultural commodity, from Maxine Hong Kingston's seminal life-writing in the 1970s to examples of the late 1990s, such as the popularity of texts which relate the history of China in the Cultural Revolution from women's autobiographical perspectives. In many texts by Asian American women, a self-consciousness can be detected in the relation between the structures of narrative and the construction of self. Conventional genre distinctions are often traversed so that in particular the demarcations between fiction and autobiography are challenged, and this forms the focus of chapter 3. Building upon the work of other theorists of Asian American literature, this section also suggests that many Asian American women's texts are unique in their development of new categories of prose writing, which are here alternatively named 'auto-representational fictions' and 'theoretico-narratives'. These, it is argued, can be seen as particularly Asian American forms, including writings which echo the Chinese oral form of the wooden fish song, the Japanese poetry form of *haiku*, and *Tagalog* (Filipino language) gossip. The work of Bharati Mukherjee, Ruth Lum McCunn, Hisaye Yamamoto, Jessica Hagedorn, Maxine Hong Kingston, and Aimee Liu is discussed here.

Chapter 4 departs slightly from a focus solely upon Asian *American* writing, to consider a group of texts written by both Asian American and Asian British women writers. Here, the phrase, 'writing Red China' is used, to refer to recent texts by Chinese American and Chinese British women who have written autobiographically informed narratives of their (and their families') experiences in China during and after the Cultural Revolution, including Nien Cheng's *Life and Death in Shanghai*, Jung Chang's *Wild Swans*, Anchee Min's *Red Azalea*, Adeline Yen Mah's *Falling Leaves*, Jan Wong's *Red China Blues*, Pang-Mei Natasha Chang's *Bound Feet and Western Dress*, Hong Ying's *Daughter of the River*, and

Anhua Gao's *To the Edge of the Sky*. This relatively new genre of writing has attracted large readerships and has achieved phenomenal success (both Jung Chang's *Wild Swans* and Adeline Yen Mah's *Falling Leaves* have sold over a million copies to date in the UK alone). This chapter explores the popularity of these narratives and provides a contextual history of this kind of literature.

'Writing Biraciality', chapter 5, explores the Asian American feminist re-writing of the body as signifier. If the body offers potential boundaries to the self, it becomes a battleground of both ethnic and gender identity. In our technological age, we have increasing degrees of control over our bodies and the ways in which they signify. The body is a cultural text which can be rewritten, through surgery and other interventions, to project a particular identity. Yet our bodies are constraining as well as facilitating and may signify in unwanted ways, as a racially marked subject for example. Technological intervention allows a means of altering or disguising that identity. Asian American women's texts repeatedly address the practice of reconstructing the body to project less racially marked identities, as part of a wider project of recovering a positive sense of self-identity. This emphasises the corporeality of identity as well as the connections between the internal and external body. Chapter 5 explores the intersections between body image, physiognomy, and perception, in relation to a set of twentieth century Eurasian and Amerasian texts by Diana Chang, Han Suyin, Sui Sin Far and Aimee Liu.

Chapter 6, 'Citizenship and National Identity', explores the roles of culture and the polity in defining and creating identities, in relation to two specific literary examples. Many Asian American women's constructions of identity both interrogate and interact with the United States' constructions of itself. I suggest that particular texts by Asian American women may be read as challenges to dominant constructions of national identity, constructions which sought to exclude certain Asian American groups at critical moments in American history. These include firstly: Japanese American women's narratives of internment during the Second World War, including texts by Monica Sone, Yoshiko Uchida, Joy Kogawa, Miné Okubo, and Jeanne Wakatsuki Houston; and secondly Chinese American Maxine Hong Kingston's novel/memoir/biography *China Men*, a text which retrospectively raises questions about American treatment of newly immigrant Chinese men.

Chapter 7 addresses the dynamics of space and home, a preoccupation with the idea of return as fundamental to the negotiation of an ethnicised identity. In his novel *Homebase*, Asian American Shawn Hsu

Wong writes that 'Identity is a word full of home'. The search for 'home', both as psychological construction and real location, is also a recurrent preoccupation in many Asian American women's texts. For Asian American diaspora subjects, 'home' is frequently not a space/place that can be taken for granted; it may be contested, lost, out of reach or exist simultaneously in different locations. Writing about 'home' traces a path across different communities and geopolitical spaces, and may be a difficult project for Asian American women. As this chapter shows, the ideas of home and space are particularly charged with meaning for South Asian American writers Meena Alexander, Shirley Geok-lin Lim and Sara Suleri. Furthermore, issues such as itinerancy, home-ownership, and the attachment to place, are extensively thematised in many Asian American women's texts. Domesticity is a further pre-occupation, one which often crystallises issues of gender as well.

Contemporary Asian American women's writing is marked by generic experimentation and thematic exploration. Part of its present and increasing visibility is due to the compatibility of many texts with the concerns of contemporary mainstream feminism, as well as its ability to fill an ethnic niche in the publishing marketplace. Yet the variety and range of current writing attests to a much greater impact upon the literary world still to come, and this book is partly a response to that forecast.

Notes

1   *The Guardian*, Saturday 18 July 1998.

2   According to MLA statistics, *The Woman Warrior* is the most widely taught text in American universities today.

3   Ronald Takaki, *A Different Mirror: A History of Multicultural Identity* (Boston, MA: Little, Brown, 1993), p. 192.

4   Elaine Kim, *Asian American Literature: An Introduction to the Writings and their Social Context* (Philadelphia, PA: Temple University Press, 1982), pp. 23–32.

5   Lee Yan Phou, *When I Was a Boy in China* (Boston, MA: D. Lothrop Co., 1887), p. 41.

6   Amy Ling, *Between Worlds: Women Writers of Chinese Ancestry* (New York: Pergamon, 1990), p. 14.

7   To a certain extent, then, the readership projected by the text (in this instance a feminist one) actually determines the canon.

8   Kim, *Asian American Literature*, p. 73.

9   *Ibid.*, p. 24.

10 Ronald Takaki, *Strangers from a Different Shore: A History of Asian Americans* (New York: Penguin, 1989), p. 53.

11 Younghill Kang's work is increasingly attracting academic attention. For instance, in her study, *Assimilating Asians* (2000), Patricia Chu discusses Kang's writing alongside that of Carlos Bulosan, Milton Murayama and John Okada.

12 See Kim, *Asian American Literature*, p. 32.

13 *Ibid.*, pp. 32–43.

14 For a more expansive discussion of Korean American writing and political activism, see Helena Grice, 'Placing the Korean American Subject: Theresa Hak Kyung Cha's *Dictee*' in Pauline Polkey and Alison Donnell (eds), *Representing Lives* (London: Macmillan, 2000), pp. 43–52.

15 Elaine Kim and Chungmoo Choi, *Dangerous Women: Gender and Korean Nationalism* (New York: Routledge, 1998), p. 3.

16 For more information on the comfort women, see Chunghee Sarah Soh's web page on the comfort woman project: http://userwww.sfsu/~soh/comfortwomen.html

17 Lisa Lowe, *Immigrant Acts: On Asian American Cultural Politics* (Durham, NC: Duke UP, 1996), p. 112.

18 Takaki, *Strangers from a Different Shore*, p. 314.

19 *Ibid.*, p. 455.

20 See Shirley Hune, 'Area Studies and Asian American Studies: Comparing Origins, Missions, and Frameworks', in Shirley Hune et al. (eds), *Asian Americans: Comparative and Global Perspectives* (Pullman, WA: Washington State UP, 1991), pp. 1–4.

21 Amy Ling, '"Emerging Canons" of Asian American Literature and Art', in Hune et al., *Asian Americans,* p. 191.

22 Rita Felski, *Beyond Feminist Aesthetics: Feminist Literature and Social Change* (Cambridge, MA: Harvard University Press, 1989), p. 1.

23 Sau-ling Wong, *Reading Asian American Literature: From Necessity to Extravagance* (Princeton, NJ: Princeton University Press, 1992), p. 9.

24 Amy Ling, *Between Worlds: Women Writers of Chinese Ancestry* (New York: Pergamon, 1990), p. 16.

25 Werner Sollors, 'Comments', in Winifried Siemerling and Katrin Schwenk (eds), *Cultural Difference and the Literary Text: Pluralism and the Limits of Authenticity in North American Literatures* (Iowa City, IA: University of Iowa Press, 1996), p. 3.

26 Carole Boyce Davies, *Black Women, Writing and Identity: Migrations of the Subject* (London: Routledge, 1994), p. 108.

27 Sau-ling Wong and Jeffrey Santa-Ana, 'Gender and Sexuality in Asian American Literature', *Signs: Journal of Women in Culture and Society*, 25:1 (1999), 1–91; pp. 3–4.

28 See, for example, Judy Yung, *Chinese Women of America: A Pictorial History*, and *Unbound Feet: A Social History of Chinese Women in San Francisco*. (See Bibliography.)

29 See Connie Young Yu, 'The World of Our Grandmothers', in Elaine Kim et al. (eds), *Making Waves: An Anthology of Writings by and about Asian American Women*, pp. 33–42. Other examples of this kind of work include Lisa See's family biography, *On Gold Mountain: The One-Hundred-Year Odyssey of a Chinese-American Family*, Margaret K. Pai's *The Dreams of Two Yi-min*, and Jung Chang's *Wild Swans: Three Daughters of China*. (See Bibliography.)

30 Sun Bim Yim, *Korean Women in America*; and 'Korean Immigrant Women in

Twentieth-Century America', in Kim et al. (eds), *Making Waves*, pp. 50–60.

31 Gail M. Nomura, 'Issei Working Women in Hawaii', in *ibid.*, pp. 135–48.

32 See for example, Grace Chang, 'The Global Trade in Filipina Workers', in Sonia Shah (ed.), *Dragon Ladies: Asian American Feminists Breathe Fire* (Boston: South End Press, 1997), pp. 132–51; Diane Yen-Mei Wong with Dennis Hayashi, 'Behind Unmarked Doors: Developments in the Garment Industry', in Kim et al. (eds), *Making Waves*, pp. 159–71; Rebecca Villones, 'Women in the Silicon Valley', in *ibid.*, pp. 172–6.

33 Lowe, *Immigrant Acts*, p. 270.

34 Wong and Santa-Ana, 'Gender and Sexuality', pp. 34–5.

35 Esther Ngan-ling Chow, 'The Feminist Movement: Where are all the Asian American Women?' in Kim et al. (eds), *Making Waves*, p. 362.

36 Yen Le Espiritu, *Asian American Panethnicity: Bridging Institutions and Identities* (Philadelphia: Temple University Press, 1992), pp. 47–8.

37 Chow, 'The Feminist Movement', pp. 364–5.

38 For a discussion of Asian American women and pan-ethnic alliances, see Kim et al. (eds), *Making Waves*, pp. 47–9.

39 Chow, 'The Feminist Movement', p. 3. For an analysis of the history and development of the black British feminist movement, see Heidi Safia Mirza (ed.), *Black British Feminism: A Reader*; Patricia Duncker, *Sisters and Strangers: An Introduction to Contemporary Feminist Fiction*, chapter 7, 'Writing Against Racism'; and Avtar Brah, *Cartographies of Diaspora: Contesting Identities*, chapter 1, 'Constructions of "the Asian" in post-war Britain: Culture, Politics and Identity in the pre-Thatcher Years', and chapter 3, 'Gendered Spaces: Women of South Asian Descent in 1980s Britain'. (See Bibliography.)

40 Le Espiritu, *Asian American Panethnicity*, p. 50.

41 Gayatri Chakravorty Spivak, *In Other Worlds: Essays in Cultural Politics* (New York: Routledge, 1988), p. 294.

42 Asian Immigrant Women Advocates (AIWA) organised a successful campaign against garment manufacturer Jessica McClintock Inc., in May 1992. This was to secure back pay for Asian women working for the Lucky Sewing Co., one of Jessica McClintock Inc.'s contractors.

43 Shirley Geok-lin Lim, 'Feminist and Ethnic Literary Theories in Asian American Literature', *Feminist Studies*, 19:3, Autumn (1993), p. 572.

44 *Ibid.*, p. 577.

45 Sau-ling Cynthia Wong, 'Ethnicizing Gender: An Exploration of Sexuality as Sign in Chinese Immigrant Literature', in Amy Ling and Shirley Geok-lin Lim (eds), *Reading the Literatures of Asian America* (Philadelphia, PA: Temple University Press, 1992), pp. 111–29.

46 *Ibid.*, p. 111.

47 *Ibid.*, pp. 111–29; Cao Youfang, *American Moon* (Taibei: Hongfan Shudian, 1986); Yi Li, *The Soil* (Hong Kong: Nanyue chubanshi, 1979); Bai Xianyong, *New Yorkers* (Wenxue Shuju, 1975).

48 Wong, 'Ethnicizing Gender', p. 126.

49 Lowe, *Immigrant Acts*, p. 11.

50 Here, I have mentioned quite recent work in this area. Earlier work includes Amy Ling's discussion in *Between Worlds: Women Writers of Chinese Ancestry*, pp. 10–13; Kim, *Asian American Literature*, pp. 4–22; and Renée E. Tajima, 'Lotus Blossoms Don't Bleed: Images of Asian Women', in Kim et al. (eds),

Making Waves, pp. 308–17.

51 See Rocío Davis, 'Just a Man: Subverting Stereotypes in David Henry Hwang's *M. Butterfly*', 'Asian American Literary Feminisms', ed. Helena Grice, special issue, *Hitting Critical Mass: A Journal of Asian American Cultural Criticism*, 6:2, pp. 59–74.

52 See Sau-ling Wong, 'Denationalization Reconsidered; Asian American Cultural Criticism at a Theoretical Crossroads', pp. 1–27, p. 1. (See Bibliography.)

53 For concise discussions of Asian American feminist critiques of Asian American cultural nationalism, see Jinqi Ling, *Narrating Nationalisms: Ideology and Form in Asian American Literature*, chapter 5, 'Maxine Hong Kingston's Remapping of Asian American Historical Imagination in *China Men*'; David Leiwei Li, *Imagining the Nation: Asian American Literature and Cultural Consent*, part one. Lisa Lowe's collection of occasional essays, *Immigrant Acts: On Asian American Cultural Politics* (1996), also views the cultural position of the Asian American subject in a global perspective, through a focus upon the position of Asian subjects in a global workplace, and the role of citizenship in establishing cultural identity. (See Bibliography.)

54 The examples given here are by necessity only a sample of the material available. Unfortunately, some other recent readings of Asian American women's writing have not always built upon the innovative Asian American feminist readings discussed so far. Esther Mikyung Ghymn's 1995 analysis of the thematic preoccupations of Asian American women's writing, in *Images of Asian American Women by Asian American Women Writers* (see Bibliography), misses many of the opportunities to discuss Asian American women writers' negotiation of the gender/ethnicity paradigm, despite offering some otherwise rich and lucid textual analysis of the work of Maxine Hong Kingston, Amy Tan, Yoshiko Uchida, Monica Sone, Mary Paik Lee, Kim Ronyoung, and Jade Snow Wong, amongst others. Although she mentions that 'For the Asian American woman, it has been difficult to separate issues of race and gender', and that 'issues of race and gender are both obstacles that Asian American writers have to overcome' (p. 3), the discussion is taken no further. Similarly, although Phillipa Kafka's 1997 study, *(Un)Doing the Missionary Position: Gender Asymmetry in Contemporary Asian American Women's Writing* (see Bibliography) does contain quite extensive scrutiny by women of colour criticisms of white Second Wave feminism, Kafka's primary claim for Asian American women writers is their feminist contributions *to*, not revisions and critiques *of*, white feminist theory and praxis. Her organising rubric of 'gender asymmetry' is presented as a 'global problem' (p. xviii), without, to my mind, an adequate examination of the geopolitical specificities attendant upon Asian American feminist writers' manipulation of gender/ethnic codes.

55 Chow, 'The Feminist Movement', pp. 367–70.

56 *Ibid.*, pp. 375–7.

57 Cherríe Moraga and Gloria Anzaldúa (eds), *This Bridge Called My Back: Writings by Radical Women of Color* (New York: Kitchen Table, 1981).

58 Anthologies like these are crucial in feminist practice because they provide the multi-voiced perspective which insists on recognising difference.

59 Asian Women United of California (eds), *Making Waves: An Anthology of Writing by and about Asian American Women* (Boston: Beacon Press, 1989), p. xi.

60 *With Silk Wings: Asian American Women at Work* (San Francisco, CA: Asian Women United, 1983).

2

Mother–daughter writing of the 1970s and 1980s

The publication of Kingston's *The Woman Warrior* in 1976 caused nothing less than a revolution in Asian American literary, and feminist studies. Whereas previously to this, Asian American literature was mostly read and critiqued within Asian America, *The Woman Warrior* became an almost immediate crossover hit, winning several awards in its year of publication, and virtually guaranteeing its author a celebrated place as the undisputed sovereign of Asian American writing.[1] But its impact did not end there. Since 1976, *The Woman Warrior* 'has generated a veritable industry of critical analysis';[2] and has subsequently spawned a whole new sub-genre of Asian American fiction: the fiction of matrilineage.

Perhaps because of *The Woman Warrior*'s concern with feminist issues such as emerging womanhood, identity and self, as well as mothers and daughters, the appearance of a tradition of writing about matrilineage within Asian American studies also coincided with a growth of interest in the mother–daughter dyad by mainstream feminist writers at the same time. It is important to note too that 1976, the year which saw the publication of Kingston's text, was the same year a series of seminal feminist publications appeared: Adrienne Rich's *Of Woman Born: Motherhood as Institution and as Experience*, Dorothy Dinnerstein's *The Mermaid and the Minotaur*, and Jean Baker Miller's *Toward a New Psychology of Women*. Prior to these were published Betty Friedan's *The Feminist Mystique* (1963), Kate Millet's *Sexual Politics*, Shulamith Firestone's *The Dialectic of Sex* and Anne Koedt's *The Myth of the Vaginal Orgasm* (all 1970). Within the realm of literature, feminist fiction such as Marge Piercy's *Woman on the Edge of Time* was published in 1976 too. So, *The Woman Warrior* emerged co-terminously with the emergence of feminist fiction, and at the height of feminist theorising, in America. But was this just coincidence?

As discussed at some length in the chapter 1, although the development of Asian American feminism shares a genealogy with mainstream feminism, at the same time it both lags behind, and departs from it. Contemporaneous with the consolidation of feminist agendas both within and beyond academia, women of colour were engaged in a project to both dismantle patriarchal paradigms and to question white feminism's race blindness.[3] As Nellie Wong asked in *Under Our Own Wings*, 'How can we separate our race from our sex, our sex from our race?' Maxine Hong Kingston's writing occupies an especially important place in the history of feminist thought, in particular the watershed period of the late 1970s and early 1980s when many mainstream feminist thinkers were becoming aware (or at least were being made aware) of the insularity of some of their traditional frames of reference, acknowledging that issues of gender cannot be separated from those of ethnicity, class and culture. In many ways, Kingston's work is symptomatic of a feminist understanding of all identities as mobile and continually open to re-negotiation. For instance, the treatment of gender identity in Kingston's writing encompasses a whole series of boundary crossings: the contradictory and conflicting definitions of womanhood that a Chinese American woman is forced to confront, and the complexities of gender identity for Chinese American women, given their exoticisation by WASP culture. As woman-of-colour feminist movements began to challenge mainstream feminism in this period (as discussed in chapter 1), so ethnic feminist texts like Kingston's began to gain prominence and attention from white feminist readers too, and something of a two-way exchange began to occur.

Much of this early feminist work centred upon issues of maternity, as an integral part of female identity, and as a metaphor of feminism itself. For example, the Asian American contributions to the seminal 1981 feminist anthology, *This Bridge Called My Back: Writings by Radical Women of Color*, often included a focus upon issues of motherhood, such as: Nellie Wong's essay on growing up; Genny Lim's piece on versions of womanhood; Mitsuye Yamada's pieces on the hardships of her mother's life and the connections between motherhood and stereotyping; and Merle Woo's 'Letter to Ma', in which she explicitly addressed the complexities of the mother–daughter relationship.[4] Notable fictional precursors to *The Woman Warrior* which took motherhood as their theme include Han Suyin's fictionalised autobiography, *The Crippled Tree* (1965).

The publication of *The Woman Warrior* created a new commercial market for Asian American books about maternity, and since 1976 many Asian American texts have been published which, to a greater or lesser extent, focus upon mothering and daughtering. These include: Canadian Joy Kogawa's *Obasan* (1981), Amy Tan's *The Joy Luck Club* (1989); Canadian writer Sky Lee's *Disappearing Moon Café* (1990), Gail

Tsukiyama's *Women of the Silk* (1991); Julie Shigekuni's *A Bridge Between Us* (1995), and Anita Rau Badami's *Tamarind Mem* (1996). Several other texts take mother *loss* as their theme, such as Theresa Hak Kyung Cha's *Dictee* (1982); Adeline Yen Mah's *Falling Leaves: The Story of an Unwanted Chinese Daughter* (1997); Patti Kim's *A Cab Called Reliable* (1997) and Lois-Ann Yamanaka's *Blu's Hanging* (1997).

A common feature of several Asian American mother–daughter texts is an emphasis upon adolescent perspectives. Since coming-of-age literature often illuminates and coincides with the themes of identity, parent–child relationships and a growing awareness of racial and/or gender oppression, this is not surprising. 'Daughterly' perspectives are particularly prevalent. As will be suggested later in this chapter, this daughterly perspective radically alters the emphasis upon the mother which is usually found in mother–daughter texts, and so in some ways revises the usual model of maternal–daughterly engagement (which is mother/daughter in terms of influence), to a two-way model.[5]

Increasing hybridity in the US cultural arena in the 1990s has contributed to recent challenges to traditional (Anglo) psychoanalytical discussions of maternity, and this shift can also be detected in the fictions of women of colour. Several Asian American women writers depict maternal paradigms which depart from a typical 'family romance' – or nuclear family – model, where, for instance, the grandmother or aunt may undertake a significant part of the childcare. Consequently, the biological mother cannot be said to have the kind of exclusive relationship with her child suggested in many psychoanalytically-based narratives of the mother/daughter dyad. In this chapter four Asian American women's texts will be examined as both presenting interesting maternal–daughterly paradigms, and as explicit interventions in the ongoing debate of mother–daughter relations. In order to do this, the next section provides a brief overview of the history of writing about the mother–daughter dyad, concentrating upon the period with which we are concerned, the 1970s, 1980s and early 1990s, as well as upon Anglo-American feminist scholarship which took mothering and daughtering as its subject.

Mother–daughter theory 1976–94

Whether focusing upon the oedipal or pre-oedipal, attempts to interrogate gendered subjectivity usually start with the genesis of the self. Perhaps the most powerful and certainly the most pervasive story of the self originated with Freud. Despite an absence of the maternal as a primary focus in Freud's work, he nevertheless provided us with an enduring narrative of the mother–daughter relationship.[6] Freud's contribution to theories of motherhood and daughterhood is important, despite the fact that his writings do not focus specifically on this subject because his family paradigm positions the mother as 'other' and this has tended to influence later theories. As Marianne Hirsch has made clear, Freud's 'optic' was determined by the story he took as central, the story of Oedipus.[7] Both the mother's and the daughter's relationship in the oedipal narrative are displaced by the more crucial tripartite drama of mother, father and son. Almost as an afterthought, Freud asserted that the daughter's development was different from the son's. Freud argued that the daughter's pre-oedipal relationship with the mother was 'extended, intense and ambivalent'.[8] The mother's identification with the daughter was likewise posited as stronger than that with the son and heavily imbued with narcissistic tendencies, so that, in fact, the mother would experience her daughter as an extension of herself. Unlike the boy's final rejection of his mother in favour of the Father and the Phallus, according to Freud, girls never successfully sever themselves from the relation with the mother. Despite turning to her father and becoming hostile towards her mother, as her brother does, the daughter's 'love for her father and rivalry for her mother is always tempered by love for her mother, even against her will … the internal relation and connection to the mother tend to persist in spite of her daughter's defensive manoevers' (p. 122). The female oedipal narrative is therefore a never-ending story as psychological entanglement with the mother continues as a primary identification for the girl-woman. The ongoing relationship between mother and daughter is thus fraught with the ambivalence of a desire for separation on the one hand and the need for a continuing symbiotic relation on the other.

Despite the recognition that 'the Freudian edifice is built on shaky ground' (p. 157), Freud's theory of motherhood and daughterhood is a powerful discourse still producing our own explanations of the mother–daughter dyad, into the 1990s and beyond. But in this Freudian paradigm, the mother is reduced to her function as childbearer and caretaker. In this, she is shown to be nurturing but also stifling, fulfilling but ultimately lacking. As a result of her status as an object of her child's desire within Freudian discourse, she is othered as she simply is not present or accounted for as a subject in her own right. The negative residue of the Freudian discourse of motherhood has remained long after Freudian thinking has been attacked for its 'excesses and blindnesses' (p. 157). Freudian thinking has also explicitly influenced several strains of psychoanalytic and cultural theory, the most pertinent of which can be delineated as: object relations revisions of the mother–daughter dyad; Lacan's reworking of Freudian theory in relation to language and feminist attempts to counter the oedipal story by uncovering other influential mythic versions of motherhood. Object-relations theory, in particular, has provided us with an influential reworking of Freud's theory of motherhood and daughterhood, in particular in the work of Nancy Chodorow. Freud's model of the oedipal family arrangement is both pre-text and prototext for Chodorow's seminal publication *The Reproduction of Mothering* (1978). Chodorow's revision of the Freudian paradigm is significant for the re-empowerment it could be seen to offer the mother in two ways. Firstly, her emphasis on the *mother* (as well as the daughter) shifts the 'emotional weight' and the focus of attention from the oedipal drama to the relationship between mother and daughter (p. 157). This results in a more woman-centred narrative than the peripheral status she is assigned in Freudian versions. Secondly, the continuing inter-subjectivity between mother and daughter is seen in positive terms rather than the unwelcome residual burden placed on the daughter by Freud.

Chodorow's central assertion, based on the Freudian model of the family which places man as the primary wage-earner and woman as the primary childbearer and carer, is that women are taught to mother and are subject to societal pressure to do so. As primary childrearer, the mother is the first and most important referent for the infant who therefore develops his or her sense of self in relation to her. Chodorow's work remains true to Freud in so far as she also acknowledges that the oedipal stage is different for boys and girls. Girls remain in the pre-oedipal stage much longer, in fact, they never completely leave: 'mothers tend to experience their daughters as more like, and continuous with, themselves. Correspondingly, girls tend to remain part of the dyadic primary mother–child relationship itself' (p. 168). Like Freud, Chodorow charts the daughter's struggle for independence as an ambivalent struggle for a sense of separateness and independence from her mother which is never fully successful.

However, Chodorow does go beyond Freud to suggest that as a consequence of the continuing dependence upon the mother 'girls emerge with a stronger basis for experiencing another's needs or feelings as one's own' (p. 167). Not only do girls tend to identify more strongly with others, but the girl's ego boundaries are more fluid so that in fact she even experiences herself as 'continuous with others' (p. 169). It is not just the daughter who is forced to remain in subjective interdependency with the mother, but also the mother, because as a mother she also remains intra-psychically associated with the daughter.

Chodorow also asserts that the achievement of independent selfhood becomes almost impossible for women: 'the development of a sense of autonomous self becomes difficult' (p. 212). It is at this point that the disabling connotations of this aspect of Chodorow's work start to emerge and the initial suggestion of the possibility of empowerment for the othered mother and stifled daughter of Freud's model starts to disappear. Although women's interaction is seen to be 'kin based and to cross generations' (p. 180), and the mother–daughter story has now taken centre stage, neither the mother nor the daughter ever fully appear as subjects. The mother remains trapped as (m)other, identified only with her child (and thus her biology) rather than as a subject in her own right. The daughter is unable to emerge as an autonomous subject and remains locked forever in an oedipal inter-subjective struggle with her mother. Chodorow's model is still based upon the nuclear family with the husband as the most important person in the household (despite his absence). It is a *Western* family model that is seen to reproduce mothering. Chodorow writes: 'In Western society ... households have tended to be nuclear, in that there is usually only one married couple with children in any household (and thus only one mother with young children)' (p. 57). As is discussed in more detail later in this chapter, a theory predicated upon the Western nuclear family becomes problematic in relation to the family structures of other, non-Western cultures. Asian American fiction by women often depicts a familial arrangement in which the extended family is very important. The grandmother, especially, is often the most important member of the household and also takes on a significant share of the childcare and this clearly problematises notions of a unitary identification with the mother, as well as multiplying the images of 'mother'.

Moreover, Chodorow's family model is located very firmly within a patriarchal and capitalist society. She suggests that the economic need for the father to work and the capitalist expectation that the woman will mother (and thus remain economically dependent upon the father) reinforces the reproduction of mothering in Western society. Again, if the family unit has also been subject to influence from alternative ideological environments, as is often the case for ethnic groups like Asian Americans, cultural expectations might prove quite different.

Chodorow's later book, *Femininities, Masculinities, Sexualities: Freud and Beyond* (1994), attempts to address some of the criticisms outlined above. She writes: 'I have been previously misread to be claiming a universal, idealised, usually pre-oedipally constructed mother–daughter attachment'.[9] Chodorow argues that she has been misinterpreted and that she is concerned not with making prescriptive generalisations but with identifying patterns. Theoretically, this is a shift in focus from the theory as prototext to the theory explicating empirical examples. Chodorow also recognises that theories of motherhood and daughterhood are multiply situated discourses and it is this eclecticism that she uses to counter charges of cultural essentialism:

> I have yet to come across any woman patient, or any narrative (fictional, autobiographical, biographical, poetic) written from the daughter's point of view … from whatever cultural group – for whom in the broadest sense we could say that 'love' for a daughter's mother was not central.[10]

It is significant that one of the texts that Chodorow cites as an example is Asian American writer Amy Tan's *The Joy Luck Club*, a text which, this study argues, is itself intervening in the mother–daughter discussion.

It is perhaps here that Chodorow comes closest to recognising the problem with Anglo-American psychoanalytic theories of the mother–daughter relationship. Psychoanalytic theories, by definition and by practice, deal with the psychic, the psychological, inner realm, a space which can be perceived as ahistorical, acultural and non-specific. As a gendered discourse, however, psychoanalytic theory has been a focus of attention for feminists anxious to revise Freudian and Freudian-derived theories of the gender-specific acquisition of subjectivity which in different ways have continued to position woman – as mother or as daughter – as other.[11] This search for a way to revise Freudian theory has been a return again and again to the origins of psychoanalytic theory. When Chodorow defends her psychoanalytic approach, she is attempting to historicise and acculturate her analysand by turning to more historically and culturally specific discourses such as autobiography and fiction for examples/evidence. (It is also the case that here the text also *becomes* the analysand so that Chodorow can be seen to be entering the very different theoretical arena of psychoanalytically-influenced *literary* theory. This shift in discursive arenas arguably allows Chodorow more freedom because there is less pressure in this discourse for an empirical base to a thesis.) Implicit in this defensive move by Chodorow is the recognition that we need to turn to more externally located discourses for specificity and cultural difference in our analysis of the mother–daughter relationship.

The influence of Adrienne Rich's work upon feminist theory generally and theories of maternality in particular is also important. Rich's

1977 book *Of Woman Born: Motherhood as Experience and as Institution* still to some extent acknowledges a debt to psychoanalysis, but links this far more explicitly to the social arena. Rich differentiates between motherhood on the one hand as experience, in terms of the psychological and social interaction between mother and child, and motherhood as institution, which outlines the mother's capacity as an instrument of patriarchy used to educate her child in patriarchal expectations: 'patriarchy depends upon the mother to act as a conservative influence, imprinting future adults with patriarchal values'.[12] This seems quite close to Chodorow's theory of the reproduction of mothering as essential for the perpetuation of patriarchy by tying the mother's role in society to her biology. The two writers here do to some extent meet, which is not surprising as the works of both are products of the same historical environment. Rich's analysis does, however, differ from Chodorow's in three fundamental ways. Like Chodorow, Rich is concerned with a Western nuclear family model. But perhaps due to Rich's own experience of cultural marginalisation as a Jewish American woman, she recognises that cultural difference renders problematic those reductionist theories of motherhood based on a Western nuclear family model. Ethnicity is explicitly recognised as a variable, producing different and diverse forms of mothering. Rich is also far more interested than Chodorow in textual representations of the mother–daughter cathexis and she uses examples drawn from ethnically diverse writing like Navaho literary theory and Asian American poetry.

Perhaps the most significant way in which Rich departs from Chodorow is her explanation of the ambivalence in the mother–daughter dyad. Whereas Chodorow sees this ambivalence wholly in psychoanalytic terms as a contradictory urge for separation on one hand and a desire for intra-psychic dependency on the other, on the part of both mother and daughter, Rich explains the ambivalence far more from the daughter's viewpoint. Although acknowledging that both 'mothers and daughters alike hunger for, pull away from, make possible and impossible for each other' (p. 218), Rich focuses predominantly on the daughter's pain and ambivalence towards her mother. She names this 'matrophobia' which is not the fear of one's mother, but the fear of becoming one's mother. Significantly then, the daughter's negative feelings are predicated upon her recognition of the connectedness with the mother: that she is like her and may become more like her. Rich portrays this ambivalence far more in social terms (although matrophobia is also seen as a psychoanalytic phenomenon): it is also the social position of the mother that is feared, as a woman in a patriarchal society:

> Many daughters live in rage at their mothers for having accepted, too readily and passively, whatever comes … a mother's victimisation does not merely humiliate her, it mutilates the daughter who watches her for clues as to what it means to be a woman, like the traditional foot-bound Chinese woman, she passes on her own affliction. (p. 243)

Significantly, Rich's 1995 revised edition of *Of Woman Born* contains a new chapter entitled 'Motherhood and Daughterhood'. Her earlier text has attained cultural authority and a prototypic status in mother–daughter theory. Rich's revised edition, by taking account of the daughter's perspective as it does, locates itself very firmly within the new era of texts intervening in the ongoing debate about mother and daughter relations. To some extent, Rich is responding to texts like those of the Asian American women writers discussed later in this chapter. As Amy Tan and Maxine Hong Kingston, for example, are themselves intervening in mother–daughter debates, so Rich is entering into dialogic engagement with new theories and paradigms as suggested in texts like Tan's *The Joy Luck Club* and *The Kitchen God's Wife*. In her revised chapter on mothers and daughters, Rich refers to Amy Tan's work in particular, as an example of the new daughterly textual representations. Fiction and theory thus to some extent converge and merge. Like Tan, Rich describes daughtering in active terms, which serves to take some of the pressure off the mother: both actively contribute to the dyadic relation and play a role in constituting each other's subjectivity. Rich's description of the mother–daughter drama thus closely mirrors those representations found in Asian American women's writing.

Asian American mother–daughter writing

This section explores five particular specificities of Asian American mother–daughter writing. These are: the varied definitions of mothering to be found in Asian American women's writing; the predominance of 'daughterly' perspectives; the manner in which mother loss is also figured as the loss of a 'mother' culture; the use of a framework of matrilineality for storytelling; and an emphasis upon the ambivalence of maternal influence.

In Asian American women's writing, the maternal voice or presence is often defined more loosely than is seen in Chodorow's theory of the nuclear family. The grandmother, aunt, or even a mother-surrogate or mythic mother may constitute the maternal presence in the text. By expanding the narrow definition of motherhood to be found in Western discourses such as psychoanalysis, women writers of colour are able to bypass the pitfalls of essentialising notions of mothering in their work. For example, in both Joy Kogawa's *Obasan* and Cynthia Kadohata's *The Floating World* it is an elderly female relative who serves as the maternal figure in relation to whom the female protagonist is by turns drawn towards and distanced from. In Amy Tan's *The Joy Luck Club*, Gail Tsukiyama's *Women Of The Silk* and Fiona Cheong's *The Scent of the Gods* the mother-surrogate becomes a replacement nurturer, teacher and custodian of cultural values. Tsukiyama's 1991 novel *Women of the Silk* tells the story of a group of women who worked in China's silk industry in 1926. The female characters of the novel forge a sisterhood in the harsh conditions in which they work, which eventually leads to a strike against their atrocious working conditions. In *Women of the Silk* the idea of a mother surrogacy is crucial. The central female character, Pei, was separated from her mother at the age of seven when she was sold by her impoverished family into silk work. The maternal figure Auntie Yee acts as a surrogate mother to all the girls living in the boarding house in the silk village, both by guiding the girls and disciplining them. Another example, Tan's *The Joy Luck Club*, is the story of a series of mothers and their daughters, and the surrogate mothers in this text are protagonist Jing-Mei's actual aunts, Lindo, An-Mei and Ying-Ying who stand in for Suyuan Woo, Jing-Mei's birth mother, who has died. These aunts assume responsibility for Jing-Mei and for the passing on of the matrilineage. A final text, Fiona Cheong's 1991 novel *The Scent of the Gods* is the story of a young girl, Su Yen, growing up in Singapore in the 1960s. She lives with her family, but in *The Scent of the Gods* it is the grandmother who stands in for the absent mother, who again has died. As these examples show, maternality takes on a broader meaning in many Asian American novels because of extended patterns of filiality and varieties of mothering.

So the diversity of maternal presences in Asian American women's writing is striking. There is no unitary form of motherhood in these texts and all adopt 'daughterly' viewpoints, towards the actual or imagined filial connection with other women. Marina Heung has discussed *The Joy Luck Club* as a daughter-text addressing the mother(s).[13] The act of addressing the mother of course in part constitutes her as a listening, if not speaking, subject. Many of these narratives by Asian American women, including *The Joy Luck Club*, *The Woman Warrior*, *Women of the Silk* and Sky Lee's novel *Disappearing Moon Café* are all dedicated to the author's mother. Maxine Hong Kingston also dedicates her text to her father but has made clear in a recent article that *The Woman Warrior* tells 'the women's stories'.[14] Julie Shigekuni's *A Bridge Between Us* is dedicated to her grandmothers. The mother is also mentioned as an important influence or the text is partly inscribed to her in *The Scent of the Gods*, *Obasan*, Lydia Minatoya's autobiography *Talking to High Monks in the Snow* and Andrea Louie's novel *Moon Cakes*, amongst others. The mother is therefore frequently acknowledged textually to be both an important influence upon the daughter-author but is also a source of inspiration. In this way, then, a matrilineage is constructed textually: the daughters are acknowledging a debt to the mothers as source of their stories. With the exception of *Disappearing Moon Café* all these fictions are narrated by a daughter, with the mother as the central focus of attention, and in narrating her story the daughter constitutes her mother's subjectivity textually. Not only is the maternal both foregrounded and seen as an important influence, though, but Joy Kogawa's *Obasan*, Amy Tan's *The Joy Luck Club*, Julie Shigekuni's *A Bridge Between Us* and Maxine Hong Kingston's *The Woman Warrior* are all texts which are very actively engaged in a search for, and often a struggle with, the mother. In this sense, the mother is, for different reasons, lost or separated from the daughter.

The loss of the mother is also partly a loss of the mother-culture, so that mothering and daughtering also become textual tropes for the diaspora situation. The daughter's situation as a 'hyphenated' ethnic subject often alienates her from her mother, more rooted as the mother often is in the ancestral/'mother' culture. The daughter's differing social and cultural embeddedness thus often results in a barrier between mother and daughter which needs to be traversed in order to recover mother-figure and mother-culture. Asian American women's writing can perhaps be seen therefore to offer a more culturally-specific discourse of mothering and daughtering than the work of Chodorow, Rich and others suggests, offering as it does an account of the social, historical and trans-cultural forces intervening in and complicating the mother's and daughter's mutual engagement. The search for the mother is often a symbolic search for cultural roots but also is an attempt to reconstitute the mother through memory, and the recovery of the mother in the text is frequently enacted through the reconstitution of a matrilineage. Matrilines are posited in these narratives as a counter tactic to the loss of the maternal. Although the matrilineage it is always there, due to cultural and/or familial separation it is hidden or lost and needs to be recovered. In her essay on matrilineage, Nan Bauer Maglin identifies five interconnecting themes in the literature of matrilineage:

the recognition by the daughter that her voice is not entirely her own; the importance of trying to really see one's mother in spite of or beyond the blindnesses and skewed vision that growing up together causes; the amazement and humility about the strength of our mothers; the need to recite one's matrilineage, to find a ritual both to get back there and preserve it and still, the anger and despair about the pain and silence borne and handed on from mother to daughter.[15]

Bauer Maglin's themes are immediately recognisable in the work of many Asian American women writers. Matrilineal storytelling becomes a conceptual framework for the intra-psychic mother–daughter relationship. It addresses the inter-subjectivity between mother and daughter in listening to the voices and stories of both and acknowledging that both are intertwined. The ambiguity present in the mother–daughter relationship is recognised and struggled with as part of the daughter's search for the mother in the attempt to recover her textually. The reconstruction of the matrilineal connection by the daughter is therefore a political, feminist-inspired move. Subjectivity is subsequently constructed through links between women, and this inter-subjectivity is acknowledged to be a source of power. Most mother–daughter theory rooted in a psychoanalytic tradition sees separation rather than continuing psychological interdependency as the ultimate goal, but several matrilineal texts by Asian American women writers refute this and instead identify interconnectedness between women as a mutually affirming objective in itself. This pattern can be seen in the four texts chosen here: (two Chinese American, two Japanese American) *The Joy Luck Club*, *The Woman Warrior*, *Obasan* and *A Bridge Between Us* and where, in each case, the maternal is lost and needs to be rediscovered. These stories subsequently function as both elegy and eulogy to the mother. The daughter's lament and longing for the mother leads to a search and finally a rediscovery of the maternal through matrilineal storytelling. The mother's story is also frequently indistinguishable from the wider history of the mother's ethnic group, and thus the manner in which mother-figure relates to mother-culture is accentuated. The Japanese American mother-figure Aunt Emily, for example, tells Naomi in *Obasan*: 'You are your history. If you cut any of it off you're an amputee'.[16] In *Obasan*, the mother's tale is that of the destruction caused at Nagasaki by the atomic bomb, and Naomi's mother's experience is set against the backdrop of this past. Chinese American Jing-Mei Woo's mother Suyuan Woo in Tan's *The Joy Luck Club* was a victim of the Japanese invasion of China in the Second World War, and so her story is representative of a whole period of history too. The narrator's mother in *The Woman Warrior* tells a less war-torn but equally embattled story of female persecution and struggle in Canton.

The mother's ensuing separation from her daughter is sometimes physical (when she is dead, for instance), but it is always psychological. The mothers in these stories are frequently seen to think and behave in what is perceived to be an alien way by their daughters. Amy Tan and Maxine Hong Kingston both attribute this psychological alienation to cultural differences between mother and daughter. In all cases, the mother bears an un-hyphenated identity as Chinese or Japanese, say, and the daughter bears a hyphenated identity as Chinese-American or Japanese-American.

Cultural difference and matrilineality also map on to a language dynamic in these texts. Jing-Mei Woo notes that 'My mother and I never really understood each other's meanings and I seemed to hear less than what was said, while my mother heard more'.[17] The mothers and daughters do not communicate successfully in Tan's and Kingston's works, mainly due to cultural differences and inter-cultural misunderstanding, and until this gap can be bridged, matrilineal healing through storytelling cannot take place. These cultural differences are seen operating linguistically: the mothers speak what Tan calls 'their special language' – a pidgin dialect which the daughters mostly understand, but do not speak (p. 34).[18] This further precludes maternal-daughterly communication. As Marina Heung notes: 'Language is an instrument of intersubjectivity … as a medium of transmission from mothers to daughters'.[19] The mother tongue consequently becomes a sign of difference between mother and daughter. Maternal silence can be literal, as it is in the case of Suyuan Woo and Naomi's mother (both of whom are dead), but it is also figurative. Often the mother *is* speaking, but the daughter is not present as a recipient or addressee of the mother's speech either because she is not listening or cannot yet understand.

When the daughters do start to listen to their mothers, maternal silence is broken, and the subjective cultural histories of the mothers are transformed into inter-subjective dialogue with the daughters. Speech thus proves therapeutic, a talking cure for personal tragedy and struggle. In *Obasan*, speech also functions as a partial panacea for the previously literally unspeakable tragedy of the atomic holocaust in Japan. Cultural histories like those of Nagasaki are repeatedly represented as burdensome. In *Obasan*, Naomi notes: 'All our ordinary stories are changed in time, altered as much by the present as the present is shaped by the past. Potent and pervasive as a prairie dust storm, memories and dreams seep and mingle through cracks, settling on furniture and into upholstery' (p. 30). The act of telling one's story is also an act of unburdening the self. Grandma Kato writes in her letters about Nagasaki: 'If these matters are sent away in this letter, perhaps they will depart a little from our souls ... for the burden of these words, forgive me' (p. 283). The mother's monologue thus becomes dialogue as the gap between mother and daughter closes.

Accompanying the longing for the mother is the desire for recognition or praise from the mother by the daughter. The Asian American daughters in these narratives are repeatedly seen to be striving for success in order to please their mothers. This is seen most extensively in Tan's *The Joy Luck Club* where each of the mothers exerts pressure upon her daughter to succeed, producing the desire to please the mother in the daughter. In one instance, in *The Woman Warrior*, Maxine's comment: 'I got straight A's, Mama', is met with indifference. Maxine wryly comments in the voice of her mother: 'My American life has been such a disappointment'.[20]

In *Ethnic Passages: Literary Immigrants in Twentieth Century America*, Thomas Ferraro suggests that the ethnic mother's ambition for her daughter acts as another form of oppression.[21] One of the contradictory messages that the Asian American daughters receive from their mothers is that on one hand, they are taught to become the good wives and mothers that patriarchy requires in the way that Rich and Chodorow have outlined. However, they are also offered liberatory possibilities in the form of cultural fictions and myths of female selfhood which constitute part of the matrilineal inheritance. Examples include the stories of Ts'ai Yen and Fa Mu Lan in *The Woman Warrior*, or The Queen of the Western Skies in *The Joy Luck Club*.[22] Beyond this, the mother herself often constitutes a female – even feminist – model. Brave Orchid, Maxine's mother in *The Woman Warrior*, is one such figure. Her very name symbolises her identity as a warrior woman.[23] Brave Orchid's story charts her various struggles against institutions and individuals: her struggle to become a doctor, her fight for the professionalisation of other women and her battle of wills with the literal as well as figurative ghosts that she encounters. Brave Orchid therefore represents female heroism and strength and yet simultaneously suppresses her own daughter's voice, freedom and individuality. Unsurprisingly, the young Maxine finds herself confused by her role model. Brave Orchid's linguistic messages are similarly ambivalent. Her daughter describes her frequently uttering powerfully repressive Chinese idioms such as 'girls are maggots in the rice' (p. 45). Yet her mother also teaches her the song of the warrior woman: 'she said I would grow up a wife and slave', Maxine writes, 'but she taught me the song of the warrior woman' (p. 22). Brave Orchid thus offers two versions of female identity to her daughter. As symbolised by her name, Brave Orchid embodies both the warrior woman and the wife/slave – 'brave' with male, warrior associations and 'orchid' signifying femininity. Maxine chooses heroism over female subserviance and docility: 'I am not going to be a slave or a wife', she tells her mother (p. 22). Maxine thus accepts the inheritance of her mother's fighting spirit, and uses it to fight patriarchy: 'If I took the sword', she says in response to a sexist and racist employer, 'I would put colour and wrinkles into his shirt' (p. 50).

Other female, we might even call feminist, models include Naomi's mother in *Obasan*, who, after the holocaust, stays in Nagasaki rather than bring the burden of her tragedy home to her family. Naomi describes her as 'Martyr mother' (p. 290). Similarly, in *The Joy Luck Club*, Jing-Mei Woo is told of her mother Suyuan's sacrifices saving her two children in the Japanese invasion of Kweilin. Her aunt tells her: 'Your mother was a very strong woman, a good mother' (p. 39). Jing-Mei is offered her mother's story as a tale of female strength to aspire to (her aunts recite her story to persuade Jing-Mei to go to China), but her mother also carries the ambition for her daughter that Ferraro suggests is repressive. Jing-Mei says: 'My mother believed that you could be anything you wanted to be in America' (p. 132). Suyuan Woo, as well as the other Joy Luck mothers/aunties, and Kingston's mother Brave Orchid all put pressure on the daughters in the way outlined by Ferraro. The mothers have subscribed to the American dream and now live their ambitions through their daughters. Perhaps it is this pressure to become 'warrior women', to borrow Kingston's phrase, in the footsteps of their mothers that may explain the matrophobia that can be detected on the part of many of these Asian American daughters. Matrophobia (not the fear of the mother but the fear of *becoming* one's mother in Adrienne Rich's definition) is displayed in most extreme form in *The Joy Luck Club*, when Lindo Jong notes her daughter's horror when someone comments on her similarity to her mother in looks.

The daughter's path from separation or sometimes rejection from the mother towards matrilineality is often initiated by another maternal figure, that of the *obasan* or aunt. As I suggested earlier, in common with other forms of ethnic writing, Asian American women's writing is important in the way it depicts alternative maternal economies influencing the daughter in formative ways. Extended family becomes much more important and the aunt or *obasan* is one such example. '*Obasan*' is a Japanese term for an elder female relative, a grandmother or an aunt; it stands for an aunt in the novel of the same name. Aunts and *obasans* are often seen to be as important as mothers, equally strong and with the potential to be woman warriors too. In *Obasan*, for instance, Naomi's Aunt Emily is described as a 'word warrior', and constitutes a very dominant influence upon her niece's life (p. 39). However, as discussed later in this chapter, Asian American daughters recognise that maternal power is often ambivalent: it can easily be transformed into a weapon against them. In a telling moment in *The Woman Warrior* Maxine says of her no-name aunt:

> My aunt haunts me – her ghost drawn to me because now, after fifty years of neglect, I alone devote pages of paper to her ... I do not think she always means me well. I am telling on her, and she was a spite suicide, drowning herself in the drinking water. The Chinese are always very frightened of the drowned one, whose weeping ghost, wet hair hanging and skin bloated, waits silently by the water to pull down a substitute. (p. 22)

In this quotation, Maxine links the power of the aunt to the power of the ghost, so the no-name aunt becomes doubly potent. By reading her aunt's suicide as a form of revenge, Maxine gives her aunt power which she wields over her family and the village.The aunt-as-woman-warrior often uses her strength for revenge, which, like the mother women warriors, locates her as a feminist heroine within the daughter's text. Several aunt-figures, like Fa Mu Lan in 'White Tigers', become female avengers. The woman warrior is, often, a *word* warrior. Maxine Hong Kingston writes: 'The idioms for revenge are "report a crime" and "report to five families". The reporting is the vengeance – not the beheading, not the gutting, but the words' (p. 53). Mothers and aunts alike become word warriors. In *Obasan*, Aunt Emily fights relentlessly for Japanese American governmental redress for internment during the Second World War. Her battle is fought with words – the literal reporting of a crime – because she will not stop talking and asking for redress. It is also through words that Aunt Emily persuades her niece to take up arms and become a female avenger too, by becoming involved in the redress movement. She urges Naomi: 'Write the vision and make it plain'(p. 38). In *Itsuka*, the sequel to *Obasan*, Aunt Emily paradigmatically tells Naomi: 'I've had to be a fighter ... there's been a lot to fight about'.[24] In *Itsuka*, it is the loss of one aunt (Obasan) that spurs another aunt (Aunt Emily) to force Naomi to face her past. When Obasan dies, Aunt Emily sweeps Naomi off to visit her mother's grave in Japan where Naomi experiences the sense of a return to both the maternal and maternal culture when she dreams of her mother: 'I see

Mother's face, her eyes gently oblique ... the dream was my final sign-post in my steadfast journey toward Mother'.[25] Having reconciled her-self with her mother and her mother's fate, Naomi is now able to face her wider cultural history which is so closely linked to her own mother's story. Aunt Emily turns Naomi into a word warrior herself, fighting for governmental redress, and it is through both Aunt Emily and Obasan that Naomi comes to the recognition that 'to be without history is to be unlived crystal'.[26] Aunt Emily is thus also a feminist model for her niece. Likewise, in *The Woman Warrior*, it is the various mothers and aunties as woman warriors who urge Maxine to become a word warrior. She writes: 'I could make myself a warrior like the swordswoman who drives me' (p. 49). Here it is Fa Mu Lan who exerts pressure on Maxine to take up arms. Later, it is her mother, Brave Orchid:

> When we Chinese girls listened to the adults talking-story, we learned that we failed if we grew up to be but wives or slaves. We could be heroines, swordswomen ... my mother told [stories] that followed swordswomen through woods and palaces for years ... [my mother] taught me the song of the warrior woman, Fa Mu Lan. I would have to grow up a warrior woman. (p. 26)

Maxine's mother goes further in urging her daughter to become a word warrior by actually incising her fraenum, 'so that you would not be tongue-tied' (p. 148). All the maternal figures – aunts and mothers – in *The Woman Warrior* join to urge Maxine to become a woman warrior herself. Fa Mu Lan, the no-name aunt, Brave Orchid, and even her weak-est aunt, Moon Orchid, unite to urge Maxine into battle. Moon Orchid offers symbolic strength when she gives Maxine a series of paper effi-gies of warriors, including, significantly, a warrior poet and an effigy of Fa Mu Lan herself. Moon Orchid tells her niece: 'this is Fa Mu Lan ... she was a woman warrior, and really existed' (p. 111).

Maxine Hong Kingston, *The Woman Warrior* (1976)

The Woman Warrior recounts the childhood experiences of a young girl, who is caught between her inherited Chinese (Cantonese) culture, and the American culture of her upbringing in Stockton, California. Kingston juxtaposes and interweaves her adolescent confusion and perspective with an ironic adult commentary upon her experiences. The text is split into five sections, each episode tracking Kingston's theme of the development of the young girl into the inspirational figure of the woman warrior. Each section relates the story of a particular woman who is formative in the narrator's life, and these maternal figures are

both actual and mythical, ghostly and real presences in the young girl's life.

The narrative opens with an injunction to silence: 'You must not tell anyone', Kingston's mother warns her, before going on to recount the true story of Kingston's aunt's illegitimate pregnancy, shame, and eventual suicide (p. 11). This 'no name aunt' hovers as an absent presence throughout Kingston's story, serving to reinforce the sense of an almost overwhelming burden of Chinese patriarchal culture on the women in the text. This initial section explores the debilitating effects of Chinese patriarchal culture upon females. The 'no name aunt' is a victim of the Chinese village community which ostracises her after she becomes pregnant. Finally, she drowns herself in the drinking-water well. Her story is told to the young narrator by her mother as a cautionary tale: it is both a warning not to 'humiliate' her parents, by becoming pregnant herself, but also, and more crucially, it serves as an injunction against passing on this story of familial shame (p. 13). The narrator, though, makes her own use of this tale: as a 'story to grow up on', she uses her aunt's biography as an inspirational emancipatory narrative, preferring to view her aunt as less of a failure, and more as a heroine who successfully wrought vengeance upon those who spurned and controlled her, by throwing her body into the family drinking well (p. 13). Rather than obeying her mother, she is 'telling' on her aunt, and her family, to the reader, although at the same time she recognises the perils attendant upon that telling, as she notes that her aunt 'does not always mean me well' (p. 22).

This opening section demonstrates the young girl's ability to sift through the cultural fragments that she inherits via her mother and to make use of them for her own purposes. She recognises, though, the confusions and contradictions she faces in separating out her two worlds: 'Chinese-Americans', she asks, 'when you try to understand what things in you are Chinese, how do you separate what is peculiar to childhood, to poverty, insanities, one family, your mother who marked your growing with stories, from what is Chinese? What is Chinese tradition and what is the movies?' (p. 13).

The second section, 'White Tigers', introduces the no name woman's counterpart in the text, the mythical and legendary character of Fa Mu Lan, or the woman warrior. The narrator's mother, Brave Orchid, also tells this story. Brave Orchid's ambivalence in guiding and instructing her daughter is that on one hand, she offers her daughter emancipatory narratives of female avengers, such as the woman warrior, but on the other, she stresses the perils and pitfalls of womanhood through the narrative of the no name woman. Kingston notes: 'When we Chinese girls listened to the adults talking-story, we learned that we failed if we grew up to be but wives or slaves. We could be heroines, swordswomen' (p. 25). The young girl's dilemma is that she must decide whether to become a woman warrior, or a no-name woman, and also to reconcile the two visions of her ancestral culture that she receives via these narratives. The narrator says of her mother: 'She said I would grow up a wife and a slave, but she taught me the song of the warrior woman' (p. 26).

The young girl resolutely chooses to become a woman warrior. Fa Mu Lan's escapades are given central significance in the narrative, and are related in a quasi-mythical manner, with Fa Mu Lan herself handling the story in the first person. This strategy accentuates the young girl's heightened identification with her heroine. The character of Fa Mu Lan is loosely based upon the Chinese 'Ballad of Mulan', as Sau-ling Wong has noted.[27] However, as Wong goes on to point out, Fa Mu Lan has 'gained the status of a topos' in Chinese literature, and there are many versions of the story in circulation (p. 28). Kingston's own version should be read as a fantasy, as the whole 'White Tigers' section of the text is meant to operate on a mythic and non-naturalistic level. As Kingston herself has noted: 'Fa Mu Lan is a fantasy that inspires the girls' psyches and their politics. The myths transform lives and are themselves changed'.[28] Although Kingston has moulded the myth to suit her purposes, the version of the Fa Mu Lan story that we find in *The Woman Warrior* is faithful to some of the basic plot elements of the story, whilst changing others. Traditional versions, as Sau-ling Wong explains it, tend to emphasise the character's battles and hardships as a woman warrior, rather than her transformation into a warrior-figure (p. 30). Kingston's story, unlike traditional versions, opens with the childhood heroine's encounter with an old couple who train her in martial arts, skills essential for her transformation into a woman warrior. Part of this training is the girl's endurance test in the land of the white tigers, which gives this section of the text its name. She must survive without food, shelter or warmth in an inhospitable climate alongside the white tigers as a rite of passage in her transformation into the figure of the woman warrior. She then leaves her mentors and teachers in the mountains and returns to her village, ready to avenge the wrongs done to her family and fellow villagers. Kingston has also added the next section of the narrative, when Fa Mu Lan's parents carve a list of grievances onto her back, which it is her mission to avenge. Thus equipped, Fa Mu Lan gathers an army of village men, and, disguised as a man herself, leads her army to victory after victory, pausing only long enough to give birth to her child. Kingston's version ends, in line with traditional versions, with the woman warrior returning to live a life of filial piety with her parents-in-law.

Many of the elements of the Fa Mu Lan story added by Kingston correspond to fragments of other and equally well-known parables. In particular, the back-carving incident corresponds to the popular story of Ngak Fei, a male heroic figure who has characters carved on his back by his mother, also demanding his service in honour of his kinspeople. Similarly, many elements of Kingston's Fa Mu Lan story reflect classical Chinese narratives of warrior revenge and peasant revolution.

The Fa Mu Lan story is immediately juxtaposed by Kingston with this comment on the narrator's own life: 'My American life has been such a disappointment' (p. 47). Through connecting the young girl's life to that of Fa Mu Lan at this moment, Kingston shifts the narrative perspective from a mythical mode focusing upon the woman warrior to that of her mother, Brave Orchid. It is at this point in the text that we see the Chinese American daughter struggling to reconcile the para-doxical versions of femininity and identity with which she is confronted via her mother's stories and teachings. On the one hand, she is inured to hearing Chinese sayings such as 'Feeding girls is feeding cowbirds', whilst on the other hand, she listens to her mother 'talking-story' about Fa Mu Lan (p. 48). On the one hand, she busies herself turning 'Ameri-can-feminine, or no dates', whilst on the other, she 'went away to col-lege – Berkeley in the sixties – and I studied, and I marched to save the world' (p. 49). On the one hand, she tells us that there 'is a Chinese word for the female *I* – which is 'slave'. Break the women with their own tongues!' (p. 49), while on the other, she imagines her own re-venge upon racism and sexism:

> To avenge my family, I'd have to storm across China to take back our farm from the Communists; I'd have to rage across the United States to take back the laundry in New York and the one in California. ... A descendent of eighty pole fighters, I ought to be able to set out confidently, march straight down our street, get going right now. (p. 50)

Kingston's solution, from the vantage point of adulthood, is her writ-ing. At the end of this section, she notes:

> The swordswoman and I are not so dissimilar. May my people understand the resemblance soon so that I can return to them. What we have in com-mon are the words at our backs. The idioms for *revenge* are 'report a crime' and 'report to five families'. The reporting is the vengeance – not the be-heading, not the gutting, but the words. (p. 53)

Textual vengeance is precisely the vengeance that Kingston chooses to take.

'Shaman', the third section of the novel, deals with Brave Orchid's life. As a pioneering doctor and scholar in China, war medic, vanquisher of ghosts, emancipator of Chinese girl slaves, expert and adventurous cook, competent mother and tireless labourer in her laundry in America, Brave Orchid herself functions as a model of female strength and accomplishment, and as an admirable survivor in her daughter's imagination. As Kingston sharply contrasts the mythical woman warrior's victories with her own 'voice unreliable' attempts to shout down the 'stupid racists', so she distinguishes between her mother's valiant deeds and her 'slum grubby' existence as an immigrant in America (p. 50; p. 52). Crucially, Brave Orchid's life is related textually. The narrator herself has to piece together her mother's history by sifting through the textual fragments she discovers: Brave Orchid's medical diploma, graduation photographs and photographs of her father. Although this material is partly supplemented by Brave Orchid's stories about her life, the narrator is left to imaginatively reconstruct the missing sections of her mother's life. In fact, all of the narrator's experiences of China, including mythical narratives, are mediated textually; even her knowledge of her relatives and ancestors in China is gleaned from letters to her parents.

The fourth section, 'At the Western Palace', continues the narrator's exploration of her mother's life, but shifts the focus to America. We are introduced to the narrator's aunt, Moon Orchid, who comes to stay with her sister. The opposite of her sister in spirit, Moon Orchid is a frail and anxious woman, with little personality of her own. Once ensconced in her sister's house, she takes to trailing after her nephews and nieces, the narrator included, and verbally echoing their actions and movements. Moon Orchid's flimsy appearance is reflected in the present that she gives to Maxine: a paper cutout of Fa Mu Lan. Whereas her sister gives the young girl tangible role models to which to aspire, Moon Orchid is able only to offer fragile, paper effigies. This inefficacy continues when Moon Orchid fails to live up to her sister's expectations of her existence in America, and goes mad. As many commentators have observed, Moon Orchid thus reflects the 'lunacy' of her name.

Names are in fact crucial in the text. Not only does namelessness erase identity – hence the no-name woman – but the naming system in the text reflects the characters' functions in the narrator's life. As David Leiwei Li has explored in intriguing detail, all of the woman share the same family name, that of 'Orchid'.[29] Fa Mu Lan roughly translates as 'wood orchid'; Kingston's mother is 'Brave Orchid', her aunt 'Moon

Orchid', and the final woman we encounter in the fifth section, Ts'ai Yen, is 'Sylvan Orchid'. This naming serves to connect all the women in the text through a linguistic link which stresses the symbolic as well as actual kinship ties which exist amongst them, as well as their shared role as mother-figures for the young narrator. For Chinese-speaking readers, however, there is a further symbolic significance in this naming structure. Although 'Orchid' is a traditional female surname, and 'Moon Orchid' is a possible name, 'Brave Orchid' is not. This is because although 'orchid' carries female connotations in Chinese, 'Brave' carries male, warrior connotations, and this male/female, yin/yang clash would not be conceivable. Thus, the name Brave Orchid denies the confines of femininity, as too does the bearer of the name. The same is true of Fa Mu Lan. In contrast, 'Moon Orchid' is a traditional name, carrying significations of both femininity and lunacy, as does the narrator's aunt.

The final section, 'A Song for a Barbarian Reed Pipe', unites the previous sections, weaving together the narratives of mother and daughter. In so doing, this section extensively interrogates the problems and paradoxes of the mother–daughter nexus. This is particularly apparent in relation to a speech–silence dichotomy. Kingston has already charted the narrator's sometime hostility towards the mother tongue, as well as her attempts to try to escape it. Frequently the site of a repressive representation of women, her move to escape Chinese as the language of repression and turn to English as the language of individualism runs parallel to her attempt to free herself from what she regards as a stifling maternal influence. Partly this desire for dissociation from the mother tongue is due to the embarrassment she feels at her parents' lack of accomplishment in English. For the narrator, her mother's poor English amplifies her humiliation at school: her own taciturnity causes her teachers to seek parental involvement, only to discover that 'my parents did not understand English' (p. 149). The daughter's hostility also results from the mother's attempts to press her language knowledge into service for the mother. Repeatedly, the daughter's humiliation is accentuated by her mother's insistence that she act as translator. As Kingston notes: 'You can't entrust your voice to the Chinese, either; they want to capture your voice for their own use. They want to fix up your tongue to speak for them. "How much less can you sell it for?" we have to say' (p. 152). But for the young girl, this maternal pressure paradoxically results in silencing or mangling her speech. Brave Orchid's instructions 'You just translate', preclude the narrator from doing so effectively, so her speech becomes warped: '"My motherseztagimmesomecandy," I said to the druggist' (p. 153; p. 154).

But gradually, the daughter moves away from regarding her mother and her language as negative. This move is engendered by a recognition on the daughter's part that the mother's language is actually more similar to her own than she had realised. The mother tongue is not actually Chinese; rather it is a mixture of Chinese and American, and this becomes the language of mother–daughter communication. A recognition of this shared lexicon, and the decision to speak – and write – it, completes the move towards resolution between mother and daughter, so that ending her text, Kingston is able to say, 'it translated well' (p. 186).

The young girl's inability to converse confidently in English is also linked to a crisis of selfhood. She tell us: 'I could not understand "I". The Chinese "I" has seven strokes, intricacies. How could the American "I", assuredly wearing a hat like the Chinese, have only three strokes, the middle so straight?' (p. 150). The narrator's taciturnity is thus linked to her struggle to reconcile conflicting Chinese and American cultural inheritances. Her resolution is not to collapse these dualities and contradictions, but instead to accommodate them. The final story that the narrator relates is one told by her mother, that of the singing poetess, Ts'ai Yen. A real historical figure, Ts'ai Yen lived in AD 175, the daughter of a scholar. She was captured and made to live in 'barbarian' lands for twelve years. She composed the long poem, 'Eighteen Stanzas for a Barbarian Reed Pipe', based upon her time in captivity, from which the final section of Kingston's work takes its title. As with her other uses of Chinese myths, Kingston has edited and changed this one to fit her purpose. Most notably, the Ts'ai Yen story emphasises that those estranged from an ancestral country will retain a psychological link with that culture, but also, more crucially, that this separation can be harnessed for creative purposes, as Ts'ai Yen did, and as Kingston does too. The Ts'ai Yen story is narrated by both mother and daughter, Kingston tells us: 'The beginning is hers, the ending, mine' (p. 184). At this point, both stories and individuals merge together, so that the daughter contributes to the mother's text and vice-versa.

In *The Woman Warrior*, as in *The Joy Luck Club*, discussed later in this chapter, the mother-figure is seen from the daughter's perspective as the point of origin. As already shown, Brave Orchid's subjectivity dominates the text, as she also dominates her daughter's subjectivity. Kingston is actually presenting us with an *inter*-subjective arrangement: the daughter's identity partly depends upon that of her mother, but also the other women she perceives as foremothers, such as Fa Mu Lan and the 'no name woman'. So the formative foremothers are both family members: Brave Orchid, Moon Orchid and Kingston's no name aunt and also mythical characters: Fa Mu Lan and Ts'ai Yen, and through this Kingston constructs a whole spectrum of maternity and maternal influence.

The matrilineal connection between the young Kingston and her blood relative foremothers also hinges upon the act of storytelling. Kingston's autobiographical text (subtitled 'memoirs') is also the bio-graphical story of her mother and her aunts. This both emphasises the matrilineage and also reinforces the inter-subjectivity; the boundaries of the self as written are fluid, so that, through the stories told, Kingston and her foremothers' subjectivities are not clearly separable.

The presentation of each of the women in the text, including Kingston, as participating in an inter-subjective engagement with each other is a feminist move to affirm the subjectivity of women for whom identity has, for one reason or another, been obliterated. Kingston's aunt, Moon Orchid, in particular, has little subjectivity of her own and is seen in the text living her life echoing the actions of others. By de-picting an inter-subjective arrangement with her aunt as she does, Kingston thus gives her subjectivity. The same is true of her no name aunt: Kingston names her by telling her story, an act which also consti-tutes her subjectivity. Kingston's 'talking story', as in Tan's *The Joy Luck Club*, also becomes a feminist act because she locates the maternal presences in the text within an alternative subjective economy: one that is female-centred. The recognition that women's lives are shaped and affected in formative ways by other women is important: in *The Woman Warrior*, as in *Obasan* and *The Joy Luck Club*, the mother–daugh-ter drama is not displaced by the more important/enduring oedipal spectacle, but is instead central.

Ironically, the very features of *The Woman Warrior* which made it a hit with feminist readers also served to precipitate its rejection by the Asian American cultural nationalists. Where feminist readers celebrated the text's emphasis upon the complexities of gender identity, some Asian American critics lamented what they viewed as the book's tendency to exoticise Asian American experiences. As Ben Tong observed, the text was 'a fashionable feminist work written with white acceptance in mind'.[30] At stake in this reception was the central debate over Kingston's 'Asiancy': the extent to which she remained faithful to her Asian as well as American cultural roots. For many early feminist reviewers, this ques-tion was simply immaterial. David Leiwei Li cites Sara Blackburn's 1977 review in *Ms* magazine, in which she labelled the book 'a psychic tran-script of every woman I know – class, age, race or ethnicity be damned'.[31]

The tendency to value *The Woman Warrior* for the manner in which it adheres to white feminist preoccupations is widespread in Anglo criticism of the text. For example, Sidonie Smith has explored the text from the perspective of filiality and women's autobiographical storytelling; Leigh Gilmore has built upon this work in analysing Kingston's focus upon the body in her quest for self-representation.

Maxine Hong Kingston's critical status as the proto-feminist of Asian American letters undoubtedly requires *The Woman Warrior*, the text upon which this reputation rests, to assume a rather inordinate burden. This is especially the case when we consider Kingston's own comment on her book: 'It would not just be a family book or an American book or a woman's book but a world book, and at the same moment, my book'.[32] Yet it is not just in the realm of mother–daughter relations that *The Woman Warrior* qualifies as feminist. Its many themes also include several other feminist ones: female connectedness; compassion towards female characters; childbirth; dating; and the demystification of sex. Its extra-textual history is also a feminist one. As Katie King analyses in *Theory in its Feminist Travels: Conversations in U.S. Women's Movements*, feminism resides in many diverse sites, including arenas not always considered 'theoretical'. The ruckus surrounding the reception of *The Woman Warrior* somewhat paradoxically itself served to promote the text's feminist politics, and in so doing, recruited both readers and critics to its cause. To this day it remains the case that Asian American feminist critics seem to feel obliged to defend the book's feminist stance, as culturally legitimate within an ethnic feminist agenda, as well as in relation to white feminism.[33]

Joy Kogawa, *Obasan* (1981)

Joy Kogawa is actually a Japanese Canadian writer, who was born in Vancouver, British Columbia, in 1935 to *issei* (first-generation Japanese immigrants). *Obasan* and its sequel, *Itsuka* (1992) are Joy Kogawa's partly autobiographical novels about the Japanese Canadian relocation experience during the Second World War and its aftermath. Kogawa's novels are partly based upon the author's personal experience during the war, as well as documents and papers from the period (many of the quotations are from the Public Archives of Canada and the letters of activist Muriel Kitigawa). Both novels have received extensive critical attention and acclaim in North America: *Obasan* won the Books in Canada First Novel Award in 1981, the Canadian Authors Association Book of the Year Award in 1982 and the Before Columbus

Foundation American Book Award in 1982. Of the two novels, *Obasan* is undoubtedly the better-known. Whereas *Itsuka* picks up the story of the redress movement in Canada, *Obasan* deals with the relocation experience itself and its devastating effects upon the individuals who were involved.

During the Second World War, after the bombing of Pearl Harbor in December 1941, Canada declared the Pacific Coast a strategic military zone and forced between twenty-one to twenty-three thousand Japanese Canadians to leave their homes in British Columbia and move to various ghost towns in the interior, leaving behind their possessions and often splitting up families. Those who refused to comply faced incarceration in a camp in Angler, Ontario. Vacated properties belonging to the relocated Japanese Canadians were confiscated by the state and auctioned. Later, in 1944, Japanese Canadians were given the harsh choice of relocation to even more remote areas, or deportation to Japan. Kogawa (who herself experienced relocation along with her family), relates this history and its debilitating effects upon Japanese Canadians in *Obasan*, from the first-person perspective of her female narrator, Naomi Nakane.

The novel is a lyrical and moving narrative about the relocation and its aftermath. *Obasan*'s narrative structure is cyclical, oscillating between the narrative present in 1972, through a series of flashbacks to the period between 1941 and 1951. Although the time of the narrative present is the post-relocation life of Naomi, the continuing dominance of the past upon Naomi's present is signalled through the repeated returns to her history through her consciousness. The novel opens in 1972, when Naomi and her uncle Isamu are contemplating the night sky together in a field near the family house in Granton, where they had been moved to in 1951. Then the narrative switches to September of the same year, to the school where Naomi teaches in Cecil, Alberta, and where she is interrupted by a telephone call informing her of her uncle's death. Naomi then returns to the family home in Granton, to comfort her aunt, the eponymous Obasan, the wife of Uncle Isamu. Obasan is a taciturn woman, who communicates with her niece through half-phrases, gestures and her many silences. Yet we at once realise that Naomi and her aunt share a special bond, which does not operate through verbal forms of communication. For example, at this point, Naomi observes of Obasan: 'The language of her grief is silence. She has learned it well, its idioms, its nuances. Over the years, silence within her small body has grown large and powerful' (p. 17). The next section sees Naomi remembering her uncle when she was a child. This sets the novel's narrative pattern of shifting between past and present via Naomi's memories. It becomes clear that Naomi's memories of both her childhood and the relocation are blurred and unclear, and that many gaps in the story remain. The task which confronts Naomi throughout the novel is to piece together her fragments of memory, with the information that she is able to glean from others, in order to learn the full story of her history. This history has seen her family scattered across Canada and Japan, the mysterious disappearance of her mother in Japan, the loss of the family home, and the death of several of her close relatives. The quest is partly frustrated by the elder relatives' reluctance to discuss the past with either the child or adult Naomi. Obasan is especially unforthcoming: 'Her answers are always oblique and the full story never emerges in a direct line' (p. 22). The comment Naomi most frequently hears is 'Kodomo no tame' or 'for the sake of the children', as the reason why her elder relatives withhold the truth of her past from her. Despite the family's reluctance to recall the past openly, it continues to affect their present lives, Naomi's included. She notes:

> We're trapped, Obasan and I, by our memories of the dead – all our dead – those who refuse to bury themselves. Like threads of old spiderwebs, still sticky and hovering, the past waits for us to submit, or depart. When I least expect it, a memory comes skittering out of the dark, spinning and netting the air, ready to snap me up and ensnare me in old and complex puzzles. Just a glimpse of a worn-out patchwork quilt and the old question comes thudding out of the night again like a giant moth. Why did my mother not return? After all these years, I find myself wondering, but with the dullness of expecting no response. (pp. 30–1)

At the beginning of chapter 13, Naomi describes her mother's inexplicable disappearance from the family home. The narrative then becomes the journal of Aunt Emily, written in the form of letters to Naomi's missing mother in Japan, and which extends to two chapters. Although this fills in some of the gaps for Naomi, the central puzzle of her mother's disappearance remains. From this point on, the narrative becomes more thoroughly concerned with the family's ordeal during the series of relocations that they are forced to make. Chapters 14 to 33 chart the moves from the British Columbian coast into the interior, each time to a more remote and less comfortable environment. As with the earlier sections of the novel, these events are interspersed with Naomi's more pensive and intensely personal reflections upon the family history, and the narrative continues to shift between different temporal anchors.

There are multiple maternal presences in *Obasan*: Aunt Emily, Obasan and Naomi's mother, of whom only Aunt Emily can be seen as a fully speaking subject. Obasan's *issei* status (as a first generation immigrant) in part explains her taciturnity and almost precarious presence in the text. The silence is also the curse of her family history of persecution and extermination. Naomi's biological mother is both presence and absence, she is often described in the text as 'a fragile presence' (p. 23). Each mother-figure has an individual story within the wider cultural narrative of the Japanese genocide in the Second World War and the Japanese Canadian relocation policy at the same time. Naomi's mother was killed at Nagasaki and Obasan was interned in Canada so the stories of these two mothers are also the histories of Naomi's ethnic group. Naomi's daughterly search for subjectivity and journey towards the affirmation of matrilineal connection with Obasan, Aunt Emily and her real mother is linked to her gradual education in and understanding of her cultural and ethnic history. She is aided in this by one of the maternal presences, Aunt Emily, who is the cultural custodian in the text. It is Aunt Emily who enables Naomi to hear the language of both her *nisei* mother and *issei obasan*. Aunt Emily is founder of the movement for governmental redress for Japanese Canadians and it is her insistence on Naomi's engagement with her history that forces a confrontation with the cultural narratives of persecution. Naomi's education in Japanese Canadian history is also a journey towards self-discovery in which she learns that it is her history and her mother's that makes her the person that she is now.

The constitution of the matrilineage and thus of maternal subjectivity is charted in the text through a maternal movement from silence to speech. The silence has been engendered by the mother's mutilation at Nagasaki. Her subsequent plea 'Do not tell' to the other mother-figures produces a silence only broken by Naomi's awakening desire to learn of her and her mother's past. The inability to speak of Nagasaki can only be broken by Naomi's recognition of the weight – and thus value – of inherited cultural chronicles.

We learn that at one time, crucially pre-Nagasaki, the matrilineage was strong: 'each night, from the very beginning before I could talk, there were the same stories, the voices of my mother or my father or Obasan or Grandma Kato, soft through the filter of my sleepiness, carrying me away to a shadowy ancestry' (p. 66). The matrilineage is broken by Nagasaki and Naomi's later pleas for maternal stories are refused: '"Please tell me about Mother," I would say as a child to Obasan. I was consumed by the question. Devoured alive. But Obasan gave me no answers. I did not have, I never have had, the key to the vault of her thoughts' (p. 31).

It is only after her uncle's death that Emily gives Naomi that key: a package of letters and papers about Japanese Canadian history, crucially including her mother's diary. This diary stresses matrilineal connection: '"Dearest Nesan" her entries begin. The sight of the word "Nesan" cuts into me with a peculiar sensation of pain and tenderness. It means "older sister" and was what Aunt Emily always called Mother. Grandma Kato also called Mother "Nesan" from time to time, especially if she was talking to Aunt Emily' (p. 56). This interconnectedness between her female ancestors awakens Naomi to the existence and importance of the matrilineage: 'the book feels heavy with voices from the past – a connection to Mother and Grandma Kato I did not know existed' (p. 56). Naomi feels a need to take her place in the matrilineage, which will be enacted textually through reading her aunt's papers: 'I feel a strong urge to put everything aside and read the journal' (p. 56).

Naomi needs to actively reconstruct the matrilineage as she inherits a fragmented family history. The family has been fragmented physically by the atomic holocaust and the Canadian government's policy of dispersal, which has left the Katos geographically dispersed and diminished by death. Symbolically, the matrilineage needs to be reconstructed by Naomi piecing together the stories that she inherits: 'only fragments relate me to them now, to this young woman, my mother, and me, her infant daughter. Fragments of fragments. Parts of a house. Segments of stories' (p. 64).

In keeping with Bauer Maglin's recognition of the celebratory aspect of matrilineage, Naomi's awakening sense of matrilineal connection fosters a new belief in the power of her mothers. Symbolically, Emily gives Naomi a Book of Knowledge in which she finds stories of strong, conquering women warriors: 'Could I, I wonder, ever do the things that they do? Could I hide in a wagon of hay and not cry out if I were stabbed by a bayonet?' (p. 87).

Finally, at the end of chapter 36, when the family have congregated (in the narrative present) for Uncle Isamu's funeral, it is agreed that Naomi and her brother Stephen should be told the truth of their mother's disappearance in Japan many years earlier. In the presence of the community elder, Nakayama-Sensei, and in a quasi-religious and highly charged atmosphere, the letters from Japan which unlock the secrets of the past are read. Nakayama-Sensei says to Naomi and her brother: 'your mother is speaking. Listen carefully to her voice' (p. 279). Through the letters of Naomi's Grandma Kato, Naomi and her brother learn that their mother died as a result of the atomic holocaust in

Nagasaki. The description of the bombing and its effect upon Naomi's mother and others is detailed and horrific:

> The woman was utterly disfigured. Her nose and one cheek were almost gone. Great wounds and pustules covered her entire face and body. She was completely bald. She sat in a cloud of flies, and maggots wriggled among her wounds. As Grandma watched her, the woman gave her a vacant gaze, then let out a cry. It was my mother. (p. 286)

The letters state that Naomi's mother died some time later. The two final brief chapters following this episode depict Naomi's meditation upon her mother's fate and her search for a way to pay homage to her mother and her suffering:

> Silent mother, you do not speak or write. You do not reach through the night to enter morning, but remain in the voicelessness. From the extremity of much dying, the only sound that reaches me now is the sigh of your remembered breath, a wordless word. How shall I attend that speech, Mother, how shall I trace that wave? (p. 289)

In common with the rest of the novel, Naomi's attentiveness to her mother's memory and story at this point is figured through a speech/silence dichotomy, as the above quotation shows. Now that Naomi has heard (rather than simply imagined) her mother's story, she is able to find a kind of peace, and it is with this image that the novel closes.

Rich and Chodorow have both discussed the mother's role in educating her daughter to be a good daughter within patriarchal society. In *Obasan*, the mother acts in an entirely different way by offering the daughter liberatory narratives of female strength and emancipation. It is only when Naomi accepts the legacy of her cultural heritage as taught by Aunt Emily that the silence of Obasan and her mother is broken. When the mother speaks, it is through the matrilineage: her story comes to Naomi through the letters sent from Grandma Kato to her daughter, Aunt Emily. We learn that the silence imposed by Naomi's mother was a defence strategy against the horrors of Nagasaki: 'the horror would surely die sooner, they felt, if they refused to speak' (p. 282). After Naomi's mother has spoken through her letters, her daughter speaks too so that both mother's and daughter's stories are told together and intertwine. Naomi significantly reproaches her mother for her silence: 'Silent Mother, you do not speak or write. You do not reach through the night to enter morning, but remain in the voicelessness' (p. 289). By concluding her story both with her and for her, Naomi recovers her mother from this voicelessness and thus reconstitutes her subjectivity. This is no easy project though: at this point Naomi betrays a daughterly anxiety that she will not hear her mother's story or do justice to it. She asks: 'How shall I attend that speech, Mother, how shall I trace that wave?' (p. 289), demonstrating her yearning towards, but also fear of, her mother, almost a matrophobic anxiety. Naomi's daughterly status means that she is forced to confront her mother's separation: 'First you could not, then you chose not to come' (p. 290). Naomi goes on to voice the intersubjectivity between her and her mother, through a statement of empathy for her mother: 'Beneath the hiding I am there with you ... Young Mother at Nagasaki, am I not also there?' (p. 290). Naomi imagines this interconnectedness in terms of a tree and thus literalises the metaphor of the family tree: 'Your leg is a tree trunk and I am branch, vine, butterfly. I am joined to your limbs by right of birth, child of your flesh, leaf of your bough' (p. 291). She envisages her closeness with her mother through an imagined return to infancy. Ultimately, then, the matrilineage affirms maternal and daughterly subjectivity in the text because it is a form of speech that breaks the silence: 'Gentle Mother, we were lost together in our silences. Our wordlessness was our mutual destruction' (p. 291). When Naomi recovers her mother's voice and thus her subjectivity she releases the spell of silence also preventing Obasan from speaking and remembering. The text closes with Obasan sifting through her collection of long untouched photographs. The matrilineal connection has been recovered.

Amy Tan, *The Joy Luck Club* (1989)

Published more than ten years after *The Woman Warrior*, Amy Tan's first novel *The Joy Luck Club* tells the story of four women (Suyuan, An-mei, Lindo and Ying-Ying) who were born in China, and who later emigrated to the United States. All four women have American-born daughters (Jing-mei, Rose, Waverly and Lena), and it is the intergenerational relationships between these eight women which preoccupies Tan's novel. Like Kingston's narrative, it has been phenomenally successful. Starting with advance dustjacket praise from Alice Walker and Louise Erdrich, amongst others, it stayed for nine months on the *New York Times* bestseller list, was reprinted in hardback twenty-seven times, selling more than a quarter of a million copies in hardback alone. Echoing the success of Kingston's novel, it was also a finalist for the National Book Critics Circle Award, as well as the National Book Award. As Penny Perrick wryly observed in 1991, 'Whether by a quirk of literary fate or because it is their psychological destiny, Chinese American women seem to have won the world rights to the mother–daughter relationship'.[34] Clearly, Maxine Hong Kingston to some extent paved the way for Tan's success, in so far as her own work popularised the themes of female friendship and filiality, and in this sense at least, both texts appear to be fashioned from the same cloth. Yet, as Sau-ling Wong points out in a perspicacious essay on Tan, entitled 'Sugar Sisterhood: Situating the Amy Tan Phenomenon', Tan's text has been marketed quite differently from Kingston's:

> Like Maxine Hong Kingston's *The Woman Warrior* (1976), *The Joy Luck Club* is a crossover hit by a female ethnic writer; it also straddles the worlds of 'mass' literature and 'respectable' literature, stocking the shelves of airport newsstands as well as university bookstores, generating coffee table discussions as well as conference papers.[35]

Wong suggests that the key to Tan's success lies in the convergence of a specific Asian American matrilineal tradition (which she delineates in some detail), and a white feminist ideological need for matrilineal literature, a need which is also bound up in orientalist discourse. Wong suggests that Tan herself colludes in the purveyance of an exotic China to a white readership, and this is very reminiscent of early reactions to Kingston's writing. We should remember that Kingston, too, was fiercely attacked for her perceived exoticisation of Chinese American culture twenty years earlier. Aside from these similarities, one very noticeable difference between the two texts is an element Wong gestures towards in the quotation above: Tan's novel is something of a lowbrow cultural version of Kingston's. Whereas Kingston's preoccupation with the mother–daughter dyad is but part of an extensive meditation upon intercultural and intra-cultural understanding, Tan's concern with mothers and daughters is the predominant focus. Similarly, despite its tight structure, Tan's novel lacks the formal complexity and elegance of *The Woman Warrior*, with its palimpsestic narration, polyvocality, and shifting cultural registers.

Of the four texts discussed in this section, a matrilineage is constructed most explicitly in *The Joy Luck Club*. Mother–daughter relations are both emphasised and foregrounded. Each section of the text itself begins with a mythical Chinese parable about the relations between mothers and daughters. Structurally, the organising framework of the text, the separate narratives of four mothers and four daughters, is explicitly concerned with the construction of a matrilineage, and all of the sections are either narratives of separation from, or connection to, the mother. Daughter Jing-Mei Woo's story opens the text and it immediately sets the theme of matrilineage: her mother Suyuan Woo has died, and Jing-Mei has been asked by the other mothers to take her place at the weekly mah-jong game. Mah-jong is a Chinese game played with dice and tiles, in which four corners, or winds, compete. The mah-jong game structurally acts as a trope in the novel for the matrilineage – it is both a connection between the mothers, but also the daughters. In this opening section, the matrilineal connection is seen to be both symbolically and actually threatened, through the collapse of the mah-jong game. The other mah-jong players want Jing-Mei to go to China to learn about and reconnect with her maternal history by meeting her mother's first children. Jing-Mei's unease at this proposition represents her ambivalence towards matrilineality and this in turn threatens the psychological link between her and her mother. Because Jing-Mei's story is the framing narrative in the text the pattern is thus set of both a yearning towards, and a resistance to the matrilineage. Like *The Woman Warrior*, the matrilineage in *The Joy Luck Club* works through 'talking story', with the mothers reciting tales of their lives to their daughters.

Following Jing-Mei's section are the three narratives of the mothers, Lindo, An-Mei and Ying-Ying. These sections are preoccupied with the threatened disruption of the matrilineal connection, initiated by Jing-Mei's paradigmatic rejection of her maternal history. All the mothers go on to tell stories of the separation from and/or loss of their own mothers: An-Mei's of her own mother's banishment from the family home; Lindo of how she was given to another family in marriage and Ying-Ying of the separation from her mother at the festival of the Moon Lady. Lindo expresses their collective anxiety when she says of her daughter: 'I worry that … she will forget'.[36] The mothers' mournings of the loss of their own mothers strengthens the growing sense of the disappearance of the matrilineage. Ying-Ying says of her own daughter: 'we are lost, she and I, unseen and not seeing, unheard and not hearing, unknown by others' (p. 67). Even though the loss is actually of the connection between mothers and daughters, the mother's inability to break free from her daughter here is expressed in her continuing identification with her: although her daughter has elected to move away from the mother, the mother sees this as a tragedy for *both*.

The mothers' narratives of feared or actual loss or separation within the mother–daughter dyad are balanced by the following narratives of their daughters. It is significant within the symbolic construction of the text that Tan has the daughters follow the mothers, which could be seen as a hint of resolution. These daughterly stories articulate four concerns specifically related to the matrilineage. All of the daughters pay homage to the power of their mothers, an aspect of the literature of matrilineage outlined by Nan Bauer earlier. Both Rose and Lena also

believe that their mothers have magical powers. The mothers are celebrated as all-knowing, as Lena says, 'to this day, I believe my mother
has the mysterious ability to see things before they happen' (p. 149).
Often, this power is passed on to the daughter: 'my mother taught me
the art of invisible strength' (p. 89). However, in the world of mother–
daughter relations this recognition of strength cannot be read as a simple
celebratory gesture, as some critics do.[37] The daughters recognise that
whilst maternal power can be passed on to the daughters, it can as
easily be used against them. For instance, daughter Waverly Jong's reluctance to tell her mother about her husband-to-be stems from the
knowledge of her mother's power, as she notes: 'my mother knows
how to hit a nerve' (p. 170). Similarly, the nightmares that another
daughter, Rose Hsu Jordan, suffers from as a child stem from her
mother's power over her. She says of her mother 'The power of her
words was … strong' (p. 185). Through instances like these, we can
see that Tan's attitude towards mothering in the novel is complex, perhaps even contradictory. She seems to veer between a celebratory impulse, which does nothing to demystify mothering as an activity, and a
far more negative version in which the all-powerful and all-knowing
mothers become suffocating and damaging influences upon their daughters. The mothers know the daughters better than anyone else and are
repeatedly shown as looking beyond their daughters' representations
of their behaviour. Lena's mother tells her husband that she does not
like ice cream, for example, and Jing-Mei's mother knew that her daughter would pick the inferior crab at a feast, because she would have
done that herself.

Despite the recognition of closeness and similarities, the Joy Luck
daughters struggle against their mothers and the imposition of a matrilineage. Jing-Mei actively tries to reject the mother–daughter bond: 'I
wish I wasn't your daughter' she tells Suyuan (p. 142), as Waverly does
too when her own mother demands: 'embarrass you be my daughter?'
(p. 99). The struggle is enacted in an attempt to escape the stifling and
repressing imposition that the mother's influence is perceived to be.
Partly this is a result of the mother's situation as mediator of the Chinese
mother-culture, a cultural inheritance the daughters are not sure that
they want. Because matrilineality cuts across cultural lines in the novel,
the acceptance of the connection to the mother is also an acceptance of
this cultural inheritance, further problematising an already complex
relationship.

Towards the end of the novel, the daughters ultimately initiate
attempts to reinstate the matrilineal connection, and this provides the

forward thrust of the plot. It is Lena's dream of a daughter saving her
mother that symbolically enacts this move. Then, after her mother's
death, Jing-Mei starts to play the piano, an act that would have pleased
her mother. Rose takes the advice from her mother that she has previously rejected and Waverly visits her mother and tells of their shared
genealogy. These initial actions all begin to signal the affirmation and
acceptance of the matrilineage on the part of the daughters. This acceptance is both a recognition of the inter-subjective connection between mother and daughter, and an acceptance of the mother culture.
This move is then extended by the following three mothers' narratives,
which affirm the reinstated matrilineage through a series of stories the
mothers tell about the cultural history and genealogy they share with
their offspring. An-Mei relates the tale of the reconciliation and re-
union she experienced with her own mother years earlier. Ying-Ying
talks about both the physical closeness she shares with her daughter:
'she and I shared the same body', as well as the inter-subjective engagement between them: 'there is a part of her mind that is a part of
mine', before seeking to strengthen the connection between them by
storytelling about her past: 'and now I must tell her everything about
my own past. It is the only way to penetrate her skin and pull her to
where she can be saved' (pp. 242–52). So, matrilineal healing of the
rift between mother and daughter, as in *The Woman Warrior* and *Obasan*
takes place through storytelling. Thomas Ferraro describes this impuls
to 'talk-story' as the Chinese mothers and daughters call it, as a 'possible antidote' to the wounds both mothers and daughters have sustained in these texts, and it certainly seems to become an increasingly
urgent and important project in the mothers' eyes.[38] The fourth mother
Lindo, also tries to heal the rift between her and her daughter in a
episode at the hairdressers called 'Double Face'. As her own and her
daughter's similar faces are reflected in the same hairdresser's mirror
('these two faces, I think, so much the same!'), she remembers a similar occasion with her own mother and notes: 'I am seeing myself an
my mother' again enforcing the matrilineal connection (p. 256). Th
move towards matrilineage and the recognition of inter-subjective d
pendency is reflected structurally in the final sections of the novel. F
the most part, the novel uses a first-person narrative mode, but in the
last sections the narrative voice shifts from first-person address to
more deliberate second-person address: the daughter figure is the sp
cifically intended listener. The section titles: 'Double Face', 'Half an
Half' and 'Two Kinds' also reflect the coupling in the mother–daughter
dyad. Finally, Jing-Mei's return to China completes the return to

maternality. The matrilineage is thus confirmed both in east and west: Jing-Mei's visit to China and her meeting with her Chinese sisters also symbolises the acceptance of culture-as-motherhood too.

In these three texts, matrilineage works in the ways outlined by Nan Bauer: through the mediation of cultural expectations (here, through shared culture, Chinese or Japanese), through the celebration of the mother, through reciting the matrilineage, through the recognition that the mother's and daughter's voices are linked, and also through the acknowledgement of the ambiguities present in the relationship. Kingston's text also betrays a preoccupation with the psychological and genealogical connections between herself and her mother. She tells us: 'I am really a Dragon, as she is a Dragon, both of us born in Dragon years. I am practically a first daughter of a first daughter' (p. 101). Tan depicts a similar episode when Ying-Ying tells us she and her daughter are both Tigers. In both cases, the links between mother and daughter are reiterated through the metaphor of Chinese birth sign mythology. The daughters in all three texts are thus seen to be orientated (literally) towards the mother, who is seen as the point of origin and the source of subjectivity.

Julie Shigekuni, *A Bridge Between Us* (1995)

In some ways, Julie Shigekuni's more recent novel, *A Bridge Between Us*, departs from the texts that I have discussed so far, because it focuses almost exclusively on the negative aspects of the mother–daughter relationship. Set in the contemporary period, it is a story of four generations of Japanese American women who all live in the same house in San Francisco, bound together not just by physical proximity, but also by matrilineal obligation and the weight of familial tradition. In alternating chapters, the four women relate their own life stories and experiences, as well as revealing the secrets and tensions that exist between them and the other women. The narrative is similarly structured to *The Joy Luck Club*, with five sections, each subdivided into the individual sections by each woman. Head of the family is the ancient malevolent matriarch Reiko, who terrorises her daughter, Rio, and her daughter-in-law, Tomoe, on a daily basis. Her daughter Rio says of her:

> Granny was causing trouble even before she was Granny. Long before she became the great-grand-pain-in-the-ass that she's been to Tomoe's children she was Goro's out-of-control grandmother who locked him in the closet to teach him about life. She taught me about life, that's for sure. She is the mother to whom I owe everything, including the $537 balance

remaining on the money I borrowed to have my hysterectomy ten years ago, in addition to another kind of balance I seem never to have possessed at all. She was my mother before she was Goro's grandmother, and now she's Granny to the children. But she was never just plain Reiko. Reiko was always the *princess*, the spoiled daughter of a rich man who never had to lift a finger. Look where that's gotten her … Look where it's gotten me.[39]

Rio's attitude towards her mother betrays all of the ambivalence of the mother–daughter dyad, expressing both inextricable ties and a sense of suffocation. Crucially, Reiko's relationship as a mother to Rio works in entirely opposite ways to the manner outlined by Nancy Chodorow. Rather than teaching her to mother, Reiko pays for Rio's hysterectomy.

It is the female members who are removed from each other by at least one generation who forge a bond, rather than mother and daughter. Whereas Reiko and Rio fail to connect on any level with each other – although Rio is bound to her mother by fear, and although they live in the same house, they have not spoken for years – Reiko's only positive tie is with her granddaughter Nomi, who is both drawn towards and away from the grandmother who wields such power in the house. Both Rio's daughter-in-law Tomoe and Nomi provide the connective tissue that ties the household together, the symbolic 'bridge' of the novel's title. As the youngest daughter of the house, Nomi especially feels the weight of matriarchal presence and influence, as well as assuming the burden of holding the female members of the family together. When Rio tries to commit suicide, Nomi notes that 'I am to blame' (p. 49). Shigekuni's novel demonstrates the inextricable yet stifling ties of intimacy and obligation that can bind women to their mothers. One way in which this is achieved is by employing architectural metaphors in order to illustrate the hierarchy of the women within the household: Reiko lives at the top of the house, Rio at the bottom, separated by Tomoe. Like Tan's *The Joy Luck Club*, *A Bridge Between Us* uses a series of disconnected first-person narratives to relate the stories of the women. As in Tan's novel, this narrative technique structurally represents the simultaneous isolation and interconnections with the other female family members that these women experience. The matrilineal connection between the women also symbolically ruptures at certain points: not only does Reiko pay for Rio's hysterectomy, thus preventing her from having further children, but when Nomi gives birth to a child herself, it is surrendered for adoption. The novel draws to a climax when the paralysing matrilineal connections between the women are broken permanently by the death of Rio. The novel ends symbolically with Tomoe and Nomi released from the burden of matrilineal and matriarchal control in the house.

As in both *The Woman Warrior* and *The Joy Luck Club*, male perspectives are marginalised in the novel. Although the novel is actually about the intersecting lives of two entire families – men included – and we are given the family trees of both the Hito and Kanemori families, only one male character, Rio's husband Tadashi, is accorded any real narrative attention. In this manner, Shigekuni not only underscores her primary concern with female connectedness, but also emphasises the overriding strength of the matriline.

All these texts seem to conform, to varying degrees, to a Chodorowian explanation of the mother–daughter relationship. Similarly, Rich's discussion of the mother's role in socialising her daughter and conditioning her in patriarchal values is suggested especially in Brave Orchid's treatment of her daughter. Yet all four writers seem to conform to these theories of motherly and daughterly inter-subjectivity only in order to then question them. As a mediator of the ancestral culture (Chinese or Japanese) the mother-figure often represents mother-land. This complicates the daughter's dealings with her mother so that the contradictory acts that she engages in chart her desire on one hand to reconcile herself with her mother as the psychological but also the cultural point of origin, and her fear of what cultural impositions accompany this reconciliation. Similarly, the daughter's ambivalence is echoed in the mother's suspicion of the 'new' culture as she sees it manifested in her daughter. In *The Joy Luck Club* for instance, the mother is suspicious of the daughter's American gadgets, telephones and Sony Walkmans. Significantly, these four Asian American women writers move beyond the terms of both Chodorow's and Rich's explanations of the mother–daughter relationship by positing a resolution to the eternal ambivalence inherent within it. Tan, Kingston and Kogawa, in particular, all rescue the mother by suggesting ways in which the daughter and mother may reconcile their difference. This reconciliation is in part an acknowledgement of the strength of seeing difference as diversity. As Asian American women, these writers are themselves both inside and outside Western culture. Psychoanalytic discourses in particular regard this simultaneous insider/outsider positioning as problematic, because the urge for assimilation on one hand and separation on the other, as seen in the mother–daughter dyad, is regarded as unsatisfactory. Difference in psychoanalytic discourses is the root of all subsequent problems: the girl endlessly desires both a separation from her mother and a penis and the boy rivals the father for mastery of the mother. However, excepting Julie Shigekuni, the Asian American women writers discussed here all regard difference in positive terms: by being both inside and outside of Western culture, or equally inside and outside of the respective Asian culture, one may choose which versions of womanhood to privilege. Clearly the different ways in which the maternal can be seen to be present in these texts also challenges unitary theories of mothering which reduce women to their biology: in several cases the maternal figure as formative influence is not a biological mother. It therefore seems that in several ways Asian American women writers can be regarded as finding new ways of writing the maternal in their work. Mothering is becoming not just a more diverse activity, but in these texts it is also seen to be altogether more positive.

Notes

1 David Leiwei Li cites statistics in which *Time* magazine rated *The Woman Warrior* as one of the top ten nonfiction works of the 1970s; and notes that Kingston was the most prominent ethnic woman writer of the 1970s and 1980s, her popularity predating that of both Alice Walker and Toni Morrison. See his *Imagining the Nation: Asian American Literature and Cultural Consent* (Stanford, CA: Stanford University Press, 1998), p. 57.

2 Sau-ling Wong and Jeffrey Santa-Ana, 'Gender and Sexuality in Asian American Literature', *Signs: Journal of Women in Culture and Society*, 25:1 (1999), 1–91, p. 35.

3 For example, Mitsuye Yamada's 1979 essay, 'Invisibility is an Unnatural Disaster: Reflections of an Asian American Woman', pp. 35–40, and her 1981 essay, 'Asian Pacific American Women and Feminism', pp. 71–5, both in Cherríe Moraga and Gloria Anzaldúa (eds), *This Bridge Called My Back: Writings by Radical Women of Color* (New York: Kitchen Table: Women of Color Press, 1981), critiqued the non-inclusion of Asian American women in feminist activist organisations.

4 See Nellie Wong, 'When I Was Growing Up'; Genny Lim 'Wonder Woman'; and Mitsuye Yamada, 'Asian Pacific American Women and Feminism', in Cherríe Moraga and Gloria Anzaldúa (eds), *This Bridge Called My Back: Writings by Radical Women of Color* (New York: Kitchen Table: Women of Color Press, 1981).

5 Mainstream mother–daughter writing of the period viewed the mother as particularly influential, in such works as Nancy Friday's *My Mother/My Self: The Daughter's Search for Identity* (New York: Delacorte, 1977), and Kim Chernin's *In My Mother's House* (New York: Harper Row, 1983).

6 For a more expansive discussion of the absence of the maternal in Freud's work see Nancy Chodorow, *Femininities, Masculinities, Sexualities: Freud and Beyond* (Lexington, KY: University of Kentucky Press, 1994).

7 Marianne Hirsch, *The Mother/Daughter Plot: Narrative, Psychoanalysis, Feminism* (Bloomington and Indianapolis, IN: Indiana University Press, 1989), p. 2.

8 Nancy Chodorow, *The Reproduction of Mothering: Psychoanalysis and the Sociology of Gender* (Berkeley, CA: University of California Press, 1978), p. 109. All further page references are to this edition and are cited in parentheses.

9   Chodorow, *Femininities, Masculinities, Sexualities*, p. 112.

10   *Ibid.*, p. 82.

11   I am thinking here of the work of feminist theorists like Juliet Mitchell, Jessica Benjamin, Jane Flax and Jean Baker Miller.

12   Adrienne Rich, *Of Woman Born: Motherhood as Experience and as Institution* (London: Virago, 1977), p. 34. All further page references are to this edition and are cited in parentheses.

13   Marina Heung, 'Mother Text/Daughter Text: Matrilineage in Amy Tan's *The Joy Luck Club*', *Feminist Studies*, 19:3, Autumn (1993), pp. 597–616.

14   Maxine Hong Kingston, 'Personal Statement', in Shirley Geok-lin Lim (ed.), *Approaches to Teaching Maxine Hong Kingston's 'The Woman Warrior'* (New York: MLA, 1991), pp. 23–5.

15   Nan Bauer Maglin, '"Don't forget the bridge that you crossed over on": The Literature of Matrilineage', in Cathy N. Davidson and E. M. Broner (eds), *The Lost Tradition: Mothers and Daughters in Literature* (New York: Frederick Ungar, 1980), p. 258.

16   Joy Kogawa, *Obasan* (New York: Anchor/Doubleday, 1994), p. 60. All further page references are to this edition and are cited in parentheses.

17   Amy Tan, *The Joy Luck Club* (London: Minerva, 1990), p.37. All references are to this edition and hereafter are given parenthetically in the text.

18   'Pidgin English' was a term originally coined to describe the language used between Chinese and Europeans.

19   Heung, 'Mother Text/Daughter Text', p. 604.

20   Maxine Hong Kingston, *The Woman Warrior* (London: Picador, 1981), p. 47. All further page references are to this edition and are cited in parentheses.

21   Thomas J. Ferraro, *Ethnic Passages: Literary Immigrants in Twentieth Century America* (Chicago, IL and London: University of Chicago Press, 1993).

22   The Queen of the Western Skies is a parable about a grandmother and a granddaughter. The granddaughter is the Queen of the Western Skies and she teaches both mother and grandmother how to lose hope, but not innocence and how to laugh forever. In short, she teaches female resilience and strength. Both Ts'ai Yen and Fa Mu Lan, the woman warrior, likewise displayed great female strength. Fa Mu Lan defeated many enemies in battle, pausing only to give birth, and Ts'ai Yen also fought and gave birth soon after, but her main strength was to emerge singing in the face of her barbarian captors.

23   As David Leiwei Li makes clear in his illuminating essay on naming in *The Woman Warrior*, although 'Orchid' signifies femininity, and is a traditional Chinese name for a woman, 'Brave Orchid' would not be an acceptable name in Chinese. 'Brave' carries male, warrior significations, the opposite of 'Orchid', so that the name means 'woman, man'. Thus, Brave Orchid is a warrior woman. See David Leiwei Li, 'The Naming of a Chinese-American "I": Cross-Cultural Sign/ifications in *The Woman Warrior*', *Criticism*, 30:4, Autumn (1988), pp. 497–515; p. 502.

24   Joy Kogawa, *Itsuka* (New York: Anchor/Doubleday, 1994), p. 63.

25   *Ibid.*, p. 104.

26   *Ibid.*, p. 321.

27   Sau-ling Wong, 'Kingston's Handling of Traditional Chinese Sources', in *Approaches to Teaching Maxine Hong Kingston's "The Woman Warrior"*, pp. 26–36; p. 28. All references to this article are hereafter given in parentheses in the text.

28 Maxine Hong Kingston, 'Personal Statement', in *Approaches to Teaching Maxine Hong Kingston's The Woman Warrior*, p. 24.

29 Leiwei Li, 'The Naming of a Chinese American "I"'.

30 Ben Tong, 'Critics of Admirer Sees Dumb Racist', *San Francisco Journal*, 11 May 1977, p. 20.

31 David Leiwei Li, *Imagining the Nation: Asian American Literature and Cultural Consent* (CA: Stanford University Press, 1998), p. 49.

32 Maxine Hong Kingston, 'Cultural Mis-readings by American Reviewers', in Guy Amirthagayam (ed.), *Asian and Western Writers in Dialogue*, (London: Macmillan, 1982), pp. 55–65; pp. 64–5.

33 Feminist defenders of *The Woman Warrior* include Elaine Kim, Sau-ling Wong and King-kok Cheung.

34 Penny Perrick, 'Daughters of America', *Sunday Times Book Review*, 14 July 1991, p. 6.

35 Sau-ling Cynthia Wong, 'Sugar Sisterhood: Situating the Amy Tan Phenomenon', in David Palumbo-Liu (ed.), *The Ethnic Canon: Histories, Institutions, and Interventions* (Minneapolis: University of Minnesota Press, 1995), pp. 174–210; p. 175.

36 Amy Tan, *The Joy Luck Club* (London: Minerva, 1990), p. 49. All further page references are to this edition and are cited in parentheses.

37 See Suzanna Danuta Walters, *Lives Together/Worlds Apart: Mothers and Daughters in Popular Culture*, pp. 180–4; and Heung, 'Mother Text/Daughter Text'.

38 Ferraro, *Ethnic Passages*, p. 159.

39 Julie Shigekuni, *A Bridge Between Us* (New York: Anchor, 1995), pp. 53–4. All further page references are to this edition and are cited in parentheses.

3

Genre and identity

> It is up to the writer to transcend trendy categories
> (Maxine Hong Kingston, 'Cultural Mis-readings by American Reviewers')
>
> No matter that critics question what my genre is – fiction? nonfiction? –
> there is a reader in every audience who will ask: 'How's your mother doing?'
> (Maxine Hong Kingston, 'Personal Statement')
>
> A woman's fiction of identity shapes the identity of her fiction
> (Joan Lidoff, 'Autobiography in a Different Voice: *The Woman Warrior*
> and the Question of Genre')

Shirley Goek-lin Lim has recently claimed:

> As a distinctive corpus, Asian American women's writing goes back only to
> the early twentieth century with the life stories of elite Asian women liv-
> ing in the United States. But writers such as Maxine Hong Kingston, Joy
> Kogawa, Bharati Mukherjee, Hualing Nieh … and others collectively are
> creating a body of literature that inscribes as central the experience of
> Asian American women in which the Asian American is still the model,
> because invisible, minority.[1]

It is no coincidence that Shirley Goek-lin Lim refers only to prose writers, or that this study of the work of Asian American women writers
also focuses predominantly upon prose narratives. As Asian American
feminist critics Sau-ling Wong and Amy Ling have both pointed out,
'prose narratives – novels, novellas, autobiographies, short stories' largely
constitute the corpus of writing by Asian American women.[2] Such a
concentration, is also, in Amy Ling's words, is 'to focus … on the most
significant texts and writers'.[3] Whilst recognising that increasingly, Asian
American women are also publishing volumes of poetry and drama, to
which this study occasionally refers,[4] here the discussion is mainly concentrated upon other forms of literary production by Asian American
women.

Theories of genre

Any study claiming the discussion of 'prose narratives' as its subject necessarily finds itself implicated in questions of genre. An imprecise term, 'prose narrative' gathers together such diverse kinds of writing as novels, autobiography, biography, journals, short stories and novellas – forms with very different histories, expectations and rules. These categories further split into more kinds of writing: adventure stories, allegories, fables, fairy tales, elegies, epics, fantasies, romances, science fiction, pastoral, ghost stories or novels of manners. When discussing these specific kinds of prose narrative, we use the term 'genre'. 'Genre' has been variously described as a 'horizon of expectation' (Tzvetan Todorov),[5] a 'social contract' (Fredric Jameson),[6] or 'a set of expectations, a set of instructions' (Jonathan Culler).[7] Each of these definitions asserts the *law* of genre, that is, genre is thought of as a set of regulations to which the author is expected to adhere and the reader expects to find.[8] Yet, as Jacques Derrida has argued, a closer analysis of the law of genre reveals it as something of a red herring. Derrida's argument in his essay, 'The Law of Genre', is paraphrased by Derek Attridge:

> The question of *genre* – literary genre but also gender, genus, and taxonomy more generally – brings with it the question of law, since it implies an institutionalized classification, an enforceable principle of non-contamination and non-contradiction. But genre always potentially exceeds the boundaries that bring it into being, for a member of a genre always signals its membership by an explicit or implicit mark; its relation to the generic field is, in the terminology of speech act theory, a matter of *mention* as well as *use*.[9]

In his essay, as Attridge explains here, Derrida emphasises the slipperiness of the law of genre. Although in our critical definitions and discussions genre is often posited as a highly regulated form of literary discourse (Helen Carr suggests that genres are 'best understood as particular forms of discourse'),[10] when transferred to the literary material, such definitions prove less than watertight, and it is this state of affairs which accounts for the continuation of the question of genre as a vexed issue in contemporary literary studies.

A survey of the history of genre theory also reveals its gender blindness. Traditional studies of genre ignore questions of gender. Even such recent works as Todorov's *Genres in Discourse*, which analyses genre from a structuralist viewpoint, or Marjorie Perloff's edited collection *Postmodern Genres*, fail to address adequately the relationship between gender and genre, notably as a result of the scarcity of examples by women.[11] Critical attempts to gender genre have taken place predominantly within the feminist sphere. Increasingly, women's fiction is being scrutinised for the ways in which it uses, misuses and abuses certain genres. For example, such works as Anne Cranny-Francis's *Feminist Fiction* or Rita Felski's *Beyond Feminist Aesthetics: Feminist Literature and Social Change* track women writers' use and abuse of genres like the romance or the confession.[12] Sally Munt's *Murder by the Book: Feminism and the Crime Novel* interrogates women writers' adoption of the detective novel, while Lucie Armitt's analysis of female science fiction in *Theorising the Fantastic* would be yet another example.[13] Nancy A. Walker's *Feminist Alternatives: Irony and Fantasy in the Contemporary Novel by Women* addresses the ways in which women writers have imported aspects of genres such as fantasy into other kinds of writing.[14] In addition, Rachel Blau DuPlessis' *Writing Beyond the Ending: Narrative Strategies of Twentieth-Century Women Writers* takes as its focus the manner in which both codes of gender and genre are reassessed by women writers in their work.[15] A final example, a wider-ranging study, Helen Carr's 1989 edited collection, *From My Guy to Sci-Fi: Genre and Women's Writing in the Postmodern World*, provides a useful overview of women writers' revision of a range of genres, including the romance, the detective novel, science fiction, poetry and auto/biography.[16] Carr's collection is also particularly useful in its inclusion of the manipulation of genres by women of colour, including Asian British writers and Caribbean women writers.

A slightly different, but parallel line of feminist inquiry has taken autobiography as its focus in gendering a specific genre. Early work revisited the territory of male autobiography criticism, such as the work of James Olney (*Metaphors of Self: The Meaning of Autobiography* and *Autobiography: Essays Theoretical and Critical*) or Phillipe Lejeune (*Le Pacte Autobiographique*) in order to highlight the absence of women's texts from the critically-created corpus of auto/biography.[17] Examples include Estelle C. Jelinek's edited collection *Women's Autobiography: Essays in Criticism*, Domna Stanton's edited *The Female Autograph* and Elizabeth W. Bruss's *Autobiographical Acts: The Changing Situation of a Literary Genre.*[18] Two collections, Bella Brodzki and Celeste Schenck's *Life/Lines: Theorizing Women's Autobiography* and Shari Benstock's *The Private Self*, of the same year (1988), built upon this early work by theorising works of autobiography by women previously excluded from the canon of autobiography.[19] Most recently, the work of Sidonie Smith (*A Poetics of Women's Autobiography* and *Subjectivity, Identity and the Body*),[20] Françoise Lionnet (*Autobiographical Voices: Race, Gender, Self-Portraiture* and *Postcolonial Representations: Women, Literature,*

Identity),[21] Leigh Gilmore (*Autobiographics: A Feminist Theory of Self-Representation*)[22] and Linda Anderson (*Women and Autobiography in the Twentieth Century: Remembered Futures*)[23] has furthered the critical discussion of women's auto/biography by developing highly sophisticated analytical approaches specific to women's auto/biographical writing as a genre. Smith's focus is on the fictions and fictiveness of subjectivity, which she later links to the body, Anderson's nostalgia, memory and the search for 'home', Gilmore focuses on 'autobiographics' as a multiply-situated discursive practice and Lionnet explores the '*métissage*' or cultural braiding of Francophone women writers' cultural productions. Yet, excepting Lionnet's work, none of these studies offer a sufficient account of the intersection of ethnicity and gender in relation to autobiography. Anderson only briefly discusses Audre Lorde's *Zami: A New Spelling of My Name*. Both Gilmore and Smith discuss Kingston's *The Woman Warrior* at length, but in each case, Kingston's text emerges as an ethnic variation of women's reworking of autobiography. Sidonie Smith views Kingston's position as one residing on the margins of culture, a location resulting in a textual self-consciousness about her position as an ethnic woman writing in an androcentric and ethnocentric culture. Smith partly falls into the trap of 'adding on' ethnicity as a variable to the liminality of the woman writer as a result of her gender, a mathematical move whereby the ethnic woman's autobiography becomes 'doubly or triply the subject of other people's representations'.[24] Gilmore's *Autobiographics* likewise discusses *The Woman Warrior* as its main ethnic text, viewing it as a creation story through the representation of the female body. Gilmore offers a persuasive reading, but once more one which privileges gender representational politics over those of ethnicity.[25]

In contrast to these works, Françoise Lionnet's *Autobiographical Voices: Race, Gender, Self-Portraiture*, as its title suggests, seeks to subvert the move whereby white feminism has privileged the politics of gender over ethnicity in its theories of autobiographical identity. Lionnet's analysis of the work of Maya Angelou, Zora Neale Hurston, Marysé Condé and Marie-Therese Humbert as '*métis*' (culturally mixed) writers demonstrates the ways in which gender and ethnicity may be 'braided together' theoretically in a manner which does not subordinate one aspect of identity over another, in order to 'encourage lateral relations'.[26]

Lionnet's theory of '*métissage*' (cultural 'braiding') is specific to her focus upon certain postcolonial women writers. As with Lionnet, it is contended in this study that writing by Asian American women must be read from (and as) a theoretically formulated position, like *métissage*, which arises out of its own terms of production, histories, languages and cultural constructs. This is not to advocate a form of theoretical essentialism, but instead to avoid the kind of theoretical appropriation I have already outlined in which difference is dissolved or elided in favour of the furthering of a Euro-American political–theoretical agenda. Asian American feminist criticism has already begun to do this. All of the main studies of Asian American writing by women address, to lesser or greater extents, the specificities of that writing, and articles devoted to the particularities of Asian American women's writing are appearing increasingly regularly. Yet, at the time of writing, there are only three works devoted solely to the specificities and commonalities of writing by Asian American women: Amy Ling's *Between Worlds* is specific to Chinese American women writers and King-kok Cheung's *Articulate Silences* to three female Asian American writers, two Japanese American and one Chinese American. Esther Ghymn's *Images of Asian American Women by Asian American Women Writers* covers a wide range of writers, but with quite a narrow thematic focus. Questions of genre are addressed at some point in all of the main studies of Asian American literature, usually focusing upon prose narratives, especially autobiography. Building upon this work, this chapter explores Asian American women's particular adoption and adaptation of genres and seeks a reading strategy and theoretical paradigm attentive to the nuances of Asian American women's literary production.

Asian American women's texts – a generic history

The publishing marketplace has had, and continues to have, an extensive influence upon the generic profile of Asian American women's writing, as it does in other areas too. As Amy Ling has shown, early Chinese American women writers were under pressure to provide texts for an orientalist market, texts which fed the dominant culture's appetite for exotic tales of depraved Chinatowns and their inhabitants.[27] More recently, King-kok Cheung has attributed the predominance of autobiography within the body of Asian American women's writing to 'trade publishers' predilection for Asian American personal narratives'.[28] She suggests that the popularity of autobiographical texts may reside in the extent to which they conform to what David Palumbo-Liu has called 'model-minority discourse' – a narrative in which 'problems' of ethnicity and gender are resolved in a *bildungsroman*-esque narrative.[29] Or it may be the case that stories tracking the writing/written subject's assimilation into the dominant culture fulfil a cultural need for a literature which resolves problems of ethnicity and difference (examples would include the novels of Amy Tan and Gish Jen, as well as autobiographical works like Monica Sone's *Nisei Daughter*).[30] Cheung also suggests that the predominance of autobiographical narratives may be due to the tastes of a reading public which judges American minority writers by the ethnic content of their work, ignoring works which don't dwell upon problems of ethnic identity.[31] This clearly also raises questions about the hierarchy of genre. That autobiography is an extremely popular form is well documented.[32] Likewise, the extensive and extending market for ethnic autobiography has been noted by observers.[33] Yet these conditions of reception also tell us something about the relative values of literary genres. Valuing Asian American works predominantly as autobiography (particularly when the generic identity of the text is not clear-cut) is one way in which these texts are routinely devalued as literature: autobiography has traditionally been regarded as an inferior form to fiction and other literary genres.[34] Readers often search for the autobiographical content of a text by an ethnic woman writer, as if this is most interesting, or appropriate. For example, Ann Rayson notes that for ethnic writers 'autobiography becomes the proper form for the transmission of cultural reality and myth'.[35] Texts which negotiate the problematics of identity, particularly those by culturally marginalised subjects, are all too often read autobiographically, whatever the generic identity of the text, as if a discussion of identity can only ever go hand-in-hand with a project of self-representation. But, as Julia Watson and Sidonie Smith have observed, autobiographical writing is only one of a range of forms of life writing.[36] Aware of this, Asian American feminist critic Shirley Goek-lin Lim, in discussing Asian American women's writing, prefers to speak of 'life stories', rather than of 'autobiography', as her term allows for a range of styles and differing degrees of referentiality. This enables her, for example, to place Joy Kogawa's fictional account of the Japanese American internment experience in *Obasan* alongside Monica Sone's *Nisei Daughter*, a text presented as an autobiography of the same experience, in order to show how Kogawa's work is 'a fiction which impersonates the discourse of autobiography while at the same time ... mask[ing] the genre of autobiography'.[37]

Autobiography, along with other kinds of life writing, has often been used by those in culturally marginal positions (such as the Asian American women we are concerned with here) to assert the validity of their experience.[38] Autobiography carries its own kind of textual authority, one that rests upon a claim of its veracity and thus irrefutability as a culturally authoritative narrative. At particular moments, certain Asian American women writers, in common with members of other culturally marginalised groups, have had recourse to the autobiographical as a counter-cultural medium in which to express their own versions of identity and experience in opposition to 'dominant' versions and paradigms. Most notably this occurred when several Japanese American women wrote autobiographical texts protesting, refuting and revising 'dominant' American versions of the Japanese American internment experience in the Second World War, which are discussed in chapter 6. Another way in which the truth-claim of autobiography has been taken up and used by Asian American women writers is as a currency of cultural exchange, in which 'ambassadors of goodwill' sought to sell Asia, Asians and Asian Americans to white America, especially during tense periods in the history of Asian Americans.[39] A notable example of this is Jade Snow Wong's 1945 autobiography, *Fifth Chinese Daughter*.[40] Sau-ling Wong has alternatively named this kind of writing 'autobiography as guided Chinatown tour',[41] referring to its authors' well-meaning if misguided attempts to offer a culturally compatible portrayal of Asian American life in America for white readers.

Whatever the reason, autobiography, autobiographical fiction and other permutations of life writing are undeniably prominent forms within the corpus of Asian American women's writing. Yet these exist alongside and within other forms too, not just recognisably American/Western forms like the novel, or short stories, but other specifically Asian American forms, a point elaborated later. This introduces another crucial point: that the specificities of cultural location extensively affect – even dictate – the forms or genres chosen. One example of this is the ongoing debate in Asian American letters over the 'Asian Americanness' or not of autobiographical forms of writing. Several critics have queried Asian American writers' use and access to a form of writing which is heavily imbricated in a Judeo-Christian Western tradition of thought about the self, as well as a form possibly incompatible with certain Chinese and Japanese behavioural codes and traditions.[42] This view has also been vehemently contested. This debate, coined the Asian American 'pen wars', has most recently centered upon the writer Maxine Hong Kingston, whose work *The Woman Warrior* has been lambasted in certain quarters for its purported pandering to a white readership. Critics such as Benjamin Tong and Jeffery Chan asserted that the text was obviously fictional, and that its publishing identity as an autobiography or as a memoir reeked of racist marketing ploys.[43] Asian American critic Frank Chin further attacked what he saw as the book's suspect generic status on the grounds that the autobiography is not a Chinese form, so Chinese Americans should not – indeed cannot – use it without 'selling out'.[44] But to raise such an objection is to assume that Asian literary forms constitute the main literary inheritance for a group of writers often at least equally influenced by American/Western forms of writing, and ignores the fact that diverse cultural influences may lead to the creation of hybrid textual forms. Chin, Tong and others seem to be subscribing to a highly problematic notion of generic purity as linked to cultural purity, the validity of which would probably not withstand recent theories of cultural exchange and hybridity.

The much-debated troubling generic identity of *The Woman Warrior* and the 'pen wars' surrounding its reception also raise the question – or more accurately the problem – of readership for many ethnic writers. Much of the criticism levelled at *The Woman Warrior* by Asian American critics like Frank Chin, Ben Tong and Jeffery Chan ensued from their belief in the responsibilities, as they saw them, of the ethnic writer to his or her ethnic community. This view was set out in the manifesto for Asian American writers, authored by Frank Chin together with Jeffery Chan, Lawson Inada and Shawn Wong, in the introduction to *Aiiieeee!*.[45] In this piece, these authors' ideas about cultural and generic purity versus the 'contamination' found in texts like Kingston's (their terms are 'real and 'fake') were linked to the idea of the 'ideal' Asian American writers as super-masculine, who would combat racist stereotyping of Asian Americans as emasculated Charlie Chan figures. (This combatorial view of writing obviously has ironic resonances in Kingston's own work). These and other critics have condemned Kingston for her failure to render Chinese language, myths and traditions accurately, and for failing to represent faithfully the sociohistorical reality of the experience of Chinese Americans (as they see it) in her work. Katheryn Fong has summed up these objections, in addressing Kingston, suggesting that the 'problem is that non-Chinese are reading your fiction as true accounts of Chinese and Chinese American history'.[46] Furthermore, several male Chinese American critics, notably including the *Aiiieeee!* group, have accused Kingston of writing a fashionable feminist work aiming for white acceptance. All these charges rest upon an understanding of the ethnic writer's role in her community as an ambassador to white society, with a duty to her 'own' ethnic group. They also proceed from a hyper-awareness of Anglo society. Kingston's wholehearted rejection of such responsibilities attests to her self-made role as an ethnic 'trickster', manipulating literary tools like the form of her work as a means of avoiding precisely the kind of ethnic pigeonholing about which the *Aiiieeee!* critics and others have been so anxious. *The Woman Warrior* masquerades as a series of different kinds of writing, without ever faithfully fulfilling the readerly expectations of any one mode. In so doing, it addresses different readerships by turns. Kingston has discussed how her use of cultural reference points like the Fa Mu Lan myth allows her to hail, or exclude, certain groups of readers at different points in her narrative. Genre acts as one such reference point in the text, teasingly suggesting itself as autobiography, myth, or fiction in turn. In this sense, Kingston manipulates her own readership. Yet, as suggested later in this chapter, she partly lost that control once the text moved into the publishing marketplace, as the continuing tendency to read her work as a faithful rendering of her own reality and experience shows.

Asian American forms, as Lisa Lowe has argued, are forms in flux, because as a body Asian American literature continues to be developed and extended as new groups add their particular textual permutations to the corpus (a recent example is Thai American writing).[47] Assigning texts to a particular genre therefore fails to take account of the dynamic ways in which Asian American women writers adopt, adapt and abandon certain generic categories. If, as Michael M. J. Fischer has argued, being Asian American 'exists only as an exploratory project, a matter of finding a voice and style', then part of that project is the active creation of forms of writing apposite to the task of negotiating different identities.[48] Talking of 'genre' is, in fact, a less than helpful way in which to approach the multitudinousness of Asian American women's writing.[49] Whilst some texts clearly are recognisable as novels, or biographies, many more blend other discursive modes in dynamic ways. It is unfortunate that the mixing of genres and discourses is so often perceived by readers and critics as a problem. If genre is a contract between author and reader, then the failure to obey the law on the part of the author necessitates a less censorious reading on the part of the reader than is evident in the responses to Kingston's work by Chin et. al. Genre is never as stable as its promise, as Derrida has illustrated. In fact, as Helen Carr notes, 'Genres represent a set of conventions whose parameters are redrawn with each new book and each new reading'.[50] Many women writers, in common with other culturally underprivileged groups, as Leslie Dick notes, engage in 'ripping the genre off', by 'making use of the elements of the genre, while discarding the implicit values of the genre as institution', as a subversive strategy in which genres are destabilised and new textual identities are created.[51] This study attempts to avoid the 'fixing' of the generic categories of these works, and to remain attentive to the diverse kinds of writing. With this end in mind, this study deliberately avoids assigning texts to a particular genre and instead uses that critical evasion, 'text'. This also emphasises the role that readers and critics, as well as publishers and writers, play in assigning the generic status of a text. Kingston's frustration at always being read autobiographically, cited in my opening epigraph, is only the most well-known example.[52] This study, therefore, rarely reads a text as being straightforwardly, or self-evidently autobiographical, biographical, fictional or historical, but instead usually refers to the most noticeable emphasis or emphases that are evident in that text. This way of reading, hopefully, recognises the fluidity and sophistication of the discursive modes in these works. Within the different ethnic groups and diverse texts gathered together in the name of writing by Asian American women, there are, of course, very different histories of the use of discursive modes, which are particular to the immigrant patterns and reception of that group in the United States. It is thus necessary at this point to delineate the development of particular Asian American women's literatures, forms and genres by separating Asian American women's writing into its composite ethnic groupings.

Chinese American women's writing, as Sau-ling Wong and Amy Ling have demonstrated, has the longest history of any of the groupings of Asian American women's writing.[53] This is despite the relatively late immigration of Chinese women to America in comparison to men, and the economically and educatively disadvantaged profile of those who did emigrate early in Chinese America's history.[54] As I noted in the introduction, early Chinese American women immigrants were either indentured prostitutes or 'paper brides' who did not or could not write. The first Chinese American women's writings were often life stories. In fact, Sau-ling Wong notes that from the turn of the century, autobiographical narratives were a very popular form.[55] Another, slightly later, form of writing that emerged was novels focusing upon communist China from the critical perspective of America.[56] Increasingly, these different kinds of writing were blurred and Chinese American women's writing became more mixed-genre. Notably, this included the diasporic writings of upper-class emigrés, like Chuang Hua (*Crossings*), Mai-mai Sze (*Echo of a Cry*) and Han Suyin (*The Crippled Tree*), texts which reside rather precariously in and between traditional generic categories.[57]

Chinese American female literary production has always developed unevenly, reflecting an immigrant history which in turn saw Chinese women banned from, then encouraged to emigrate to the United States. There are several identifiable phases of Chinese American female literary production, three of which have been discussed in chapter 1.[58]

Another, recently prevalent, phase has seen writers focusing upon matrilineality, which as discussed in chapter 2, is a phenomenon often read by white feminist critics as productive of, or at least coinciding with, the cultural moment which has seen a surge of interest in mother/daughter writing and theory.[59] Most of these texts were written in the 1970s and the 1980s and may been seen as drawing upon and reacting to popular discourses of the same time.

Japanese American female literary production is mainly that of second and third generation writers (*nisei* and *sansei* respectively). First generation, or *issei*, mainly wrote in Japanese, using traditional Japanese forms like *haiku*, *tanka* or *senryu*.[60] Women *nisei* mainly became active in literary production from the 1940s onwards, producing amongst other kinds of writing, short prose pieces for the many Japanese American vernacular newspapers that appeared on the West coast.[61] In particular, the experience of the Second World War, during which many Japanese Americans were incarcerated by the American government and Japanese Canadians interned by the Canadian government, prompted several Japanese American women to write in the form of life stories, poems and fictions, and these authors included Hisaye Yamamoto, Jeanne Wakatsuki Houston, Miné Okubo, Joy Kogawa, Yoshiko Uchida, Monica Sone and Mitsuye Yamada, whose work is discussed in chapter 6. *Sansei*, or third generation, Japanese American women, have become even more formally experimental, reacting to and dabbling in postmodern narrative modes, from Janice Mirikitani's activist writing, or Sylvia Watanabe's fiction/history *Talking to the Dead*, to Cynthia Kadohata's formally experimental, haunting works *The Floating World* and *In the Heart of the Valley of Love*.

As observed in the introduction, early Korean American writers were mainly male, but a group of women writers produced works in the 1980s and 1990s, notably including autobiographies: Mary Paik Lee's *Quiet Odyssey*, Margaret K. Pai's *The Dreams of Two Yi-Min*, Theresa Hak Kyung Cha's *Dictee*; as well as novels: Ronyoung Kim's *Clay Walls*, for example. As a result of the politically turbulent history of their ancestral country, Korean American female writers have often produced texts politically activist in both tone and form, which, especially in the case of *Dictee*, defy traditional generic classification.

South Asian American women's writing, like Chinese American and Korean American women's writing, really came of age in the 1970s and 1980s. Most of these writers are middle or upper-class, high caste, well educated women; three are academics.[62] This fact is reflected in the development of a South Asian American memoir/fiction-as-theory, seen in the work of Meena Alexander (*Fault Lines*), Sara Suleri (*Meatless Days*) and Shirley Geok-lin Lim (*Among the White Moon Faces*), which are discussed more extensively. Other 'critical fictionalists' include the highly prolific Bharati Mukherjee, and, more recently, Chitra Banerjee Divakaruni.[63] In contrast to the prolific, varied and generically adventurous literary production of those ethnic groups discussed so far, Filipina American writing and Vietnamese American women's writing has been markedly absent. The exceptions include Filipina American writer Jessica Hagedorn's *Dogeaters*, and the work of Vietnamese American Wendy Larsen.

Each of these ethnic groupings draws upon and mixes their respective Asian literary traditions in their work, as well as drawing upon American (Western) traditions, in a way that engenders particularly Asian American forms.[64] For example, Maxine Hong Kingston and Amy Tan utilise the Chinese tradition of 'talking-story' as a structuring device within their prose narratives. 'Talking story', as its name suggests, is the female Chinese practice of telling stories, often from one generation to the next.[65] In Kingston's *The Woman Warrior* and Tan's *The Joy Luck Club*, *The Kitchen God's Wife* and *The Hundred Secret Senses*, the maternal habit of talking story serves to organise the narrative. Kingkok Cheung has explored the ways in which Kingston's use of talk-story allows her to cross and problematise genre categories: 'Her recourse to talk-story – which blurs the distinction between straight facts and pure fiction – accomplishes two key objectives: to reclaim a past and, more decisively, to envision a different future'.[66] Cheung suggests that Kingston 'uses fantasy the way other women writers ... use science fiction, historical romance, or utopian novels'.[67] That is to say, in common with other women writers, Kingston, and Amy Tan too, deliberately misuse and problematise certain generic conventions, not only to underscore the elusiveness of generic fixity, but also as a means of imagining both different kinds of writing and the experiences that writing communicates. As Asian American writers, both women are able to bring to the feminist project of problematising genre diverse forms of narrative, both oral and textual, culled from Asian as well as American cultures.

A similar case may be found in the way that Chinese American writer Ruth Lum McCunn has taken up and reworked the Chinese form of the 'wooden fish song' as a narrative device in her 1995 historical novel, *Wooden Fish Songs*. The novel is set in the nineteenth century, and tells the true story of nineteenth century pioneer, Lue Gim Gong. Lue travels to the United States, where he becomes a renowned horticulturalist. His story is told by the three women with whom he becomes involved. The wooden fish is a Chinese percussion instrument, and wooden fish songs were the laments sung by Chinese women left behind by husbands seeking to make their fortunes in America. In McCunn's historical novel, the wooden fish songs form the structure of the narrative as a series of laments by the three women attached to the male character, Lue Gim Gong. Two women, one Chinese, one American, Sum Jui and Fanny Burlingame, each relate part of Lue Gim Gong's story, one bound up with their own. Later in the narration a third voice is added, that of an observer, Sheba, the daughter of a slave. By utilising the form of the wooden fish song within the historical narrative, McCunn is able to portray the story of Lue through the simultaneous and cross-cultural lenses of two narrative traditions, those of the wooden fish song and the historical novel. In so doing, McCunn gestures to both the history of Chinese immigration to the United States as a backdrop to Lue's, Sum Jui's and Fanny's stories, and also to the isolation and dislo-cation caused by that history to the individuals involved. This isolation and displacement is further emphasised by the introduction of Sheba's narrative, one preoccupied with issues of imprisonment and hardship. As with Tan's and Kingston's work, the text is generically hybrid, a mix-ture of the wooden fish song and the historical novel, reflective of the cultural hybridity of the experiences that it relates. It also betrays McCunn's feminist concern to foreground female experience too. Although the story is principally Lue's, the narration is handled entirely by the three women, stressing that the story of male immigration to the United States is also the tale of its effects upon the women with whom those men were involved, a story often eclipsed in narratives of this experience. As with the tradition of talking-story, too, the form of the wooden fish song is also specifically female, and McCunn's use of this form acknowledges the existence of a strong Chinese female tradition of oral narrative which is one element of her literary inheritance.

In another example, Japanese American Hisaye Yamamoto's 1988 short story, 'Seventeen Syllables' skilfully blends Japanese and Ameri-can/Western forms of writing. The seventeen syllables of the story's title refer to the highly formal structure of the Japanese poetry form of *haiku*. Yamamoto's story relates the experience of young *nisei* girl Rosie, who, impatient with the stultifying life of her family, finds excitement in the form of an illicit meeting with the family's Chicano helper, Jesus Carrasco. Rosie's preoccupation with her own life overshadows that of her mother, an *issei* woman forced to marry beneath her social class due to a pregnancy in Japan. Rosie's mother seeks solace from her unhappy marriage through the composition of *haiku*, a form traditionally associated with the refined classes in Japan. When she wins a *haiku* competition, she is awarded with a beautiful Japanese 'floating world' painting.[68] In an act of anger, her husband sets fire to the painting, thus symbolically also consigning Rosie's mother's life as an artist to the flames too. Rosie's mother's story and unhappiness only emerge at this point, towards the end of the story, when, as she watches the painting burn, she asks her daughter never to marry. It is Rosie's mother's *haiku* that structures the narrative. The story opens with one *haiku* example, as Rosie's mother patiently explains the symbolism and sparse images of her latest effort to an uncomprehending daughter.[69] Later, we witness Rosie chuckling over a less serious and poorly crafted *haiku* that she comes across. Rosie's uneducated response to her mother's talented efforts thematises the generational chasm between mother and daughter. But the *haiku* has significance in the story beyond the thematic. Yamamoto also uses the *haiku* as a submerged structuring device in her story. The story may be split into three sections, reflective of the three lines which make up the *haiku* form: Rosie's innocence, Rosie's induction into sexual experience with Jesus and Rosie's subsequent realisation of her mother's unhappiness. These stages are punctuated by two pivotal actions: Rosie and Jesus's meeting, and the burning of the painting. Also reflective of the *haiku* form is the space given to each section. The story is narrated from Rosie's perspective, and the event that she feels to be most important, her meeting with Jesus, forms the central, and most extended section of the story, as in a *haiku*, the central line of seven syllables is the longest. Yet, as the *haiku* must be taken in its entirety in order to appreciate its full meaning, so in reading Yamamoto's story must we view all of the events as contributing to Rosie's awakening. In addition, although at first reading, the story appears rather minimal in detail, the significance resides below the surface, accessible only by careful interpretation, which is also the case with *haiku*.

A final example is the use Jessica Hagedorn makes of gossip in her very compelling pop novel about The Phillipines, *Dogeaters*. Gossip becomes the central linguistic currency of the text, and is used as the primary form of discourse by a range of characters, including the young, rich girl, Pucha, and the young and poor youth, Joey, who is forced into prostitution in order to make ends meet. Although Hagedorn also makes use of a range of other discourses, such as history, or the language of radio melodrama, gossip is used to destabilise and subvert both the generic and discursive registers of the text. Thus, *tsismis* (Tagalog for gossip), in its very leakiness as a narrative not contained – it is described in *Dogeaters* as a form which 'ebbs and flows' – and a narrative which is often exaggerated, typifies the generic and discursive lawlessness of much Asian American women's writing.[70]

Mixed genre writing/theoretico-narratives/auto-representational fictions

Sau-ling Wong has suggested that we need to view Asian American literature as 'an emergent and evolving textual coalition', an approach which seeks to stress the collective, politically activist mode of discourse produced by many Asian American writers, while at the same time marking the heterogeneity of the field (a 'coalition' is a *temporary* alliance of *distinct* groups).[71] Building upon this, Asian American women's writing may be thought of as a textual coalition in its own right, in its various attempts to write/right the wrongs of racism, sexism and colonialism. This is not to imply that somehow Asian American women writers speak as one group, but rather to emphasise a mode of intertextual, symbiotic influence which functions through a sense of a textual community. Community, as Bonnie TuSmith has shown us, is fundamental in the creation of political coalitions; nowhere is this more the case than with ethnic groupings.[72] Ethnic group identification works through a sense of community/commonality: a member identifies with and is identified as part of that ethnic group.[73] As TuSmith has argued, ethnic literary history must be understood not in terms of individualism, as is often the case with white, male literary history, but in terms of a collectivist, communal interaction.[74] Critics such as Elaine Kim and Mary Dearborn have explored the communal/community orientation of ethnic literature: Kim of Asian American writing, and Dearborn of ethnic women's writing generally.[75] Drawing the work of Kim, Dearborn and TuSmith together, it is possible to view the specific ways in which Asian American women writers have recourse to, and proceed from, notions of collectivity and community in their work.

Many Asian American women writers incorporate a very strong sense of community within their work. Maxine Hong Kingston, Theresa Hak Kyung Cha and Amy Tan, to name but three writers, have produced polyvocal texts, in which many voices, perspectives and stories are heard. In this sense, these writers utilise the oral traditions of their inherited Asian cultures, in the case of Chinese Americans Tan and Kingston, of 'talking-story', or in the case of Chinese American Ruth Lum McCunn of the wooden fish song. Storytelling, in this sense of polyvocality, is a communal act. TuSmith views this act as a vernacular act, in the sense that the vernacular – folklore, myth, talk-story – works as the literary material.[76] The use of vernacular codes and forms by Asian American women writers creates a community, one united by common speech acts. The use, for example, of a Chinese American vernacular links writers like Amy Tan, Gish Jen and Maxine Hong Kingston together, amongst others. Likewise, the vernacular Japanese American folktale Momotaro (the story of a boy who was born of a peach) links Joy Kogawa's novel *Obasan* and Lydia Minatoya's *Talking to High Monks in the Snow*, since both make use of this in their narratives. Vernacular texts like those written by these Asian American women writers provide the opportunity to blend different discourses or narrative/literary modes within the same text. Thus, Maxine Hong Kingston and Theresa Hak Kyung Cha, for example, recite history alongside the inherited oral narratives of their ancestors. This may at once destabilise the literary authority of certain genres, whilst according others a greater authority. (This is discussed in more detail in an analysis of Maxine Hong Kingston's *China Men* in chapter 6.)

Community is also created in these texts through their relationship with other texts. Most of the works discussed here are by second generation Asian American women. This creates a sense of generational community, and it is possible to approach many works as 'daughter' texts in contrast to earlier 'mother' works, as discussed in chapter 2 on mother–daughter writing. Sau-ling Wong, too, has defined generational differences as crucial to a theoretical approach to Asian American autobiographical writing.[77] Chinese American writers like Maxine Hong Kingston, Amy Tan, Andrea Louie, Gish Jen, Aimee Liu, Jade Snow Wong, Chuang Hua, Julie Shigekuni, Arlene Chai and Evelyn Lau may all be thought of as 'daughter' writers. Likewise, Japanese American writers Joy Kogawa, Monica Sone, Yoshiko Uchida, Miné Okubo, Lydia Minatoya and Hisaye Yamamoto are also all 'daughter' writers (they are all *nisei*, or second generation) sharing a commonality of cultural experiences.[78]

This model of Asian American women's literary history is by definition genealogical, but it also serves to emphasise the communal aspects of Asian American cultural production, and thus offers a fruitful alternative to both androcentric and ethnocentric models of literary history. TuSmith's work shows us that a paradigm which stresses community, offers us an ethnic-sensitive version of ethnic literary history contrary to traditional accounts which stress the individuality of the artist.[79] Likewise, evolutionary paradigms of literary history, whilst useful, must take care not to stress modes of *vertical* influence (in the sense of a genealogy of writers) at the expense of forms of *horizontal* influence (in the sense of a contemporary peer-group), which are important as well. It is therefore useful to think of Asian American women's writing as a textual coalition bound simultaneously by the threads of communal experiences, goals, orientations or texts, across certain barriers of space, culture and time. I am thus primarily interested in the intertextual relations both between works by second generation Asian American women and in their relationship with earlier writers and forms of narrative, viewed here as a form of inter-generational community.

These writers are also linked through a sense of the need to intervene in dominant discussions of identity formation. As Donald Geollnicht has recently pointed out, we need to read Asian American women's texts as both theoretically informed and informing.[80] Reading creative texts as theory usually occurs in relation to Euro-American texts, often by men. As Goellnicht notes: 'texts by writers like Maxine Hong Kingston and Joy Kogawa are classified as autobiography or fiction, or autobiographical fiction, but rarely as theoretical fictions or fictionalized theory'.[81] But many Asian American women's texts are not just reflective of contemporary debates about mothers and daughters, identity, or language, but actively seek to intervene and interject into these arguments. One example would be Kingston's *The Woman Warrior*, which has mainly been read as autobiography. Knopf's decision to publish it as autobiography, with the Library of Congress classification as 'biography', largely influenced this reception. The text won the National Book Critics Circle Award for best nonfiction in 1976. Yet the subtitle is 'memoirs', a third different classification. The text itself is a disjunctive series of five separate but interlinked personal and cultural memories. Therefore, both intra-textually and extra-textually the text offers itself as a series of conflicting generic categories, as memoir, auto/biography or as another category, one attested or suggested by the texture of the text itself. *The Woman Warrior*'s hazy generic status has not just troubled autobiography theorists, but has actively revised theories of women's autobiographies.[82] It is an important theoretical text in its own right, a theoretical text lurking beneath a slippery textual guise.

Another example would be *The Joy Luck Club*, which has not just keyed into, but has actively revised theories of mother–daughter relations. As discussed in chapter 2, Nancy Chodorow, one of the most influential theorists of the mother–daughter dyad, has used Tan's novel to revise her theories of mothering and daughtering.[83] Yet another example would be the way that Miné Okubo's *Citizen 13660* successfully contested dominant versions of national identity in her own autobiographical narrative of the Japanese American internment story, a challenge so successful that the text was actually used as evidence at the United States internment reparation hearings in the 1980s.[84]

Thus it is the very form of these texts, to use Goellnicht's term, as 'theoretico-narratives' which serves to destabilise genre theories.[85] The existence of these texts within and between different discourses serves to challenge those discourses. This is a strategy whereby minority women writers offer a potent feminist and ethnic assault upon phallocentric laws of genre as well as upon androcentric and ethnocentric discourses of identity.[86] The question to ask, then, as Linda Anderson poses it, is not how far a work is autobiographical, or even how entitled we are to read it in that way, but rather how that text speaks to and revises problems of identity.[87]

Memory is one place where identity is formed.[88] Various kinds of prose writing inscribe memory in differing ways. The texts considered in this study mostly refuse the assignation of particular generic identities and instead insist upon new textual identities of their own, ones which speak to the slippery and elusive nature of recollection. Scholarship in the 1990s taking ethnic texts as its subject has asserted the importance of memory for ethnic writers in the negotiation of identity.[89] The personal recollections of ethnic subjects, in common with other culturally marginal subjects, may contradict other 'official' or culturally authoritative versions of the past. Many culturally marginal writers foreground the workings of memory in their work, and this is also the case in much writing by Asian American women. Such an emphasis is useful for the way that it allows us to read what the text does not say, as much as what it does. The insistence upon the workings of memory as incomplete, flawed, often ahistorical, subjective, may, for example, open the way to acknowledge certain textual excesses,[90] such as silence, or forgetting, not accounted for within conventional theories of the representation of the past. Recent work on the role of memory in ethnic writing has recognised ways in which it has destabilised traditional generic categories:

> Memory ... shapes narrative forms and strategies toward reclaiming a suppressed past and helps the process of re-visioning that is essential to gaining control over one's life and future. The ethnic narrative thus becomes, in Stuart Hall's phrase, 'an act of cultural recovery', and the emergent ethnicity embedded therein develops a new relationship to the past, which is to be recovered through both memory and narrative. These strategies of the ethnic writer often deny the validity of the linear progression of the traditional narrative.[91]

Many ethnic American writers remember the racism that culture has asked them to forget; ethnic American women writers also remember oppressions that are the result of the combined effects of racism and sexism. The emphasis upon and use of memory in ethnic American women's texts is partly responsible for the ways in which these writers upset the apple cart of genre. The workings of memory in a text cut across and through generic categories, touching upon and mixing the processes of officially-authorised memory (history) with personal histories (autobiography, memoir, journals) as a counter-cultural tactic. At the same time an emphasis upon the processes of remembering acknowledges the partiality and fictiveness of that process. The workings of collective memory may also be foregrounded, as they are inscribed culturally through songs and stories. Thus a text like Joy Kogawa's *Obasan* has a textual identity part-fictional, part-historical, part-autobiographical, in the manner in which it recalls the treatment of Japanese Canadians during the Second World War. In this sense it is what Goellnicht calls an 'auto-representational fiction'.[92] But it is also a 'theoretico-narrative', to continue with Goellnicht's terminology, because it also intervenes in and forces a revision of the ways in which we have explained not just the past, but the strategies by which we represent that past.

Asian American female memory often privileges the vernacular. Myths, folklore, bedtime stories and other vernacular forms are used as valid versions of the past alongside, often over and above, other forms like laws and written histories. For instance, Kingston's *China Men* or Theresa Hak Kyung Cha's *Dictee* foreground the stories of their ancestors, inherited via journals and conversations, over maps, histories or 'The Laws', to quote Kingston.[93] Excavating the workings of memory in many of these narratives allows us to progress from considering questions of genre and to avoid categorising these works in reductionist ways. *The Woman Warrior* is precisely *not* an autobiography, but neither is it a fiction, a history, or a memoir. It is self-consciously a 'rememory', to borrow Toni Morrison's well-known phrase, which listens to and speaks the multifariousness of the past as we receive it, through both legacies of orality and textual modes of inscription.[94]

The main focus of this study is often the mixed-discourse, theoretically self-conscious writing already discussed. However, not all of the texts that I address can be subsumed under the paradigm of 'theoretico-narratives'. There are other traditions and genres of writing by Asian American women, for example biographical work or literary history, which have quite separate trajectories of development. In common with much feminist work in the 1970s, this kind of writing seeks to uncover and recount the stories of 'ordinary' or forgotten Asian American women.[95] Examples of this kind of work include Ruth Lum McCunn's *Thousand Pieces of Gold*, which tells the story of Chinese American woman pioneer, Lalu Nathoy (Anglo name Polly Bemis), Lisa See's family biography, *On Gold Mountain: The One-Hundred-Year Odyssey of a Chinese-American Family* and Annette White-Parks's literary biography, *Sui Sin Far/Edith Maude Eaton: A Literary Biography*.[96] This kind of writing has done important cultural and political work in raising and developing Asian American political consciousness. Such writing is clearly not totally separable from more theoretically self-conscious writing, indeed, in its formulation of discourses of identity, and the political motives of writing, there is much overlap.

Another important kind of Asian American women's writing which deserves separate mention is the anthology, which has functioned as the textual sword in the rise of Asian American women's political solidarity (Cynthia G. Franklin has called it 'activist anthologizing'). Two seminal anthologies, published in the same year, *The Forbidden Stitch: An Asian American Women's Anthology* and Asian Women United of California's *Making Waves: An Anthology of Writings By And About Asian American Women* illustrate this.[97] The very title of *Making Waves* speaks of its interventionist stance. And as Cynthia G. Franklin observes, 'these anthologies demonstrate the possibility of creating identity-based communities not based upon exclusions'.[98] The anthology is an example of a kind of Asian American women's textual coalition working in practice. In fact, many of the Asian American women involved in the writing and production of these anthologies are also writers and academics in their own right, as well as community activists beyond the academy. The anthology also illustrates the ways in which an Asian American textual coalition not only intervenes ideologically in dominant discourses defining identity, but also how it works pragmatically and institutionally to bypass the restrictions of the publishing marketplace and academic institution. Most of these anthologies have been published by relatively small, politically motivated presses, such as Calyx Books in Oregon. This tradition is still continuing, with recent examples including Sharon Lim-Hing's edited collection, *The Very Inside: An Anthology of Writing by Asian and Pacific Islander Lesbian and Bisexual Women* (1994); Sylvia Watanabe and Carol Bruchac's edited *Home to Stay: Asian American Women's Fiction* (New York: Greenfield Review Press, 1990), Garrett Hongo's edited *Under Western Eyes: Personal Essays from Asian America* (1995) and Sonia Shah's *Dragon Ladies: Asian American*

Feminists Breathe Fire (1997).[99] Hongo's collection further illustrates the
extent to which Asian American writing cuts across and through generic
categories. Its subtitle, 'personal essays' announces a kind of writing
which is rooted in the personal, yet is not recognisable as autobiography, and is distinct from the short story, academic essay or any other
form. The continuing growth of this kind of mixed genre prose is not
just specific to Asian American women's writing, it is also an increasingly popular form in other areas of ethnic, feminist and women's writing.[100] Clearly, this may be attributed to the political and ideological
motive and force of this sort of collectivist textual coalition. Anthologies further destabilise genre categories. Do we take the material text,
its contents or its declared generic status (if there is one) as a guide to
that text's genre? The anthologies referred to above are all multi-genre,
mixing recognisable and new kinds of writing together.[101]

All the texts discussed so far define themselves, or are defined by
their marketing, as 'Asian American'. Some are more obviously marketed
as 'ethnic' texts than others, such as Maria Hong's edited collection, *Growing Up Asian American*, or the novels of Amy Tan and Gish Jen, who are
both writers who have been marketed as addressing – and resolving –
problems of ethnic identity.[102] However, many texts by Asian American
women writers do not address questions of ethnic identity, but instead
deal with other issues. Some, like Evelyn Lau's novel *Other Women*, are
not discernibly Asian American in content at all.[103] Such works have often been ignored by a readership which seems to prefer texts which deal
with questions of ethnic identity. Other texts may be categorised as genre
fiction: Cynthia Kadohata's *In the Heart of the Valley of Love* as science
fiction, Han Suyin's *Winter Love* as lesbian romance. Since ethnic and
gender identity is central to the work of the majority of Asian American
women writers, this is what this study focuses upon, remaining aware,
however, that this concentration on identity-centred texts at the expense
of other themes and preoccupations risks reproducing the tendency
whereby white readers search for the ethnic content of a work, to the
detriment of other issues. The increasing appearance of writers who do
not address such questions, but are instead publishing other kinds of
writing, may be suggestive of the increasing diversity and maturity of
Asian American women's writing, no longer contained by and within an
ethnic niche of the publishing marketplace. It may also be argued that
this is also a sign of increasing acceptance within the United States of the
'fact' of ethnic and cultural diversity.

Notes

1 Shirley Geok-lin Lim, 'Japanese American Women's Life Stories: Maternality in Monica Sone's *Nisei Daughter* and Joy Kogawa's *Obasan*', *Feminist Studies*, 16:2 (Summer, 1990), 289–312; p. 309.

2 Sau-ling Wong, *Reading Asian American Literature: From Necessity to Extravagance* (Princeton, NJ: Princeton University Press), p. 12.

3 Amy Ling, *Between Worlds: Women Writers of Chinese Ancestry* (New York and London: Pergamon, 1990), p. 16.

4 Most notably, prominent Asian American women poets include Mitsuye Yamada, Janice Mirikitani, Cathy Song, Genny Lim, Geraldine Kudaka and Kimiko Hahn. Asian American female dramatists are less numerous, and their work less available, another reason for their absence in this study. However, for a discussion of their work, see Josephine Lee, *Performing Asian America: Race and Ethnicity on the Contemporary Stage* (Philadelphia, PA: Temple University Press, 1997).

5 Tzvetan Todorov, *Genres in Discourse* (New York: Cambridge University Press, 1990), p. 18.

6 Fredric Jameson, 'Postmodern Consumer Society', in Hal Foster (ed.), *Postmodern Culture* (London: Pluto, 1985), pp. 111–25.

7 Jonathan Culler, 'Towards a Theory of Non-Genre Literature', in Raymond Federman (ed.), *Surfiction* (Chicago: Swallow Press, 1981), pp. 255–62.

8 See Jacques Derrida, 'The Law of Genre', *Glyph 7* (Baltimore, MD: Johns Hopkins University Press, 1980).

9 Jacques Derrida, *Acts of Literature*, ed. Derek Attridge (London: Routledge, 1992), p. 221.

10 Helen Carr, 'Genre and Women's Writing in the Postmodern World', in Helen Carr (ed.), *From My Guy to Sci-Fi: Genre and Women's Writing in the Postmodern World* (London: Pandora, 1989), pp. 3–14; p. 8.

11 Marjorie Perloff (ed.), *Postmodern Genres* (Norman, OK, and London: University of Oklahoma Press, 1989).

12 Anne Cranny-Francis, *Feminist Fiction* (Cambridge: Polity Press, 1990); Rita Felski, *Beyond Feminist Aesthetics: Feminist Literature and Social Change* (Cambridge, MA: Harvard University Press, 1989).

13 Sally R. Munt, *Murder by the Book? Feminism and the Crime Novel* (London: Routledge, 1994), Lucie Armitt, *Theorising the Fantastic* (London: Edward Arnold, 1996).

14 Nancy A. Walker, *Feminist Alternatives: Irony and Fantasy in the Contemporary Novel by Women* (Jackson, MS, and London: University Press of Mississippi, 1990).

15 Rachel Blau DuPlessis, *Writing Beyond the Ending: Narrative Strategies of Twentieth-Century Women Writers* (Bloomington, IN: Indiana University Press, 1985).

16 Helen Carr (ed.), *From My Guy to Sci Fi: Genre and Women's Writing in the Postmodern World* (London: Pandora, 1989).

17 James Olney (ed.), *Metaphors of Self: The Meaning of Autobiography* (Princeton, NJ: Princeton University Press, 1972); and *Autobiography: Essays Theoretical and Critical* (Princeton, NJ: Princeton University Press, 1980); Philippe Lejeune, *Le Pacte Autobiographique* (Paris: Seuil, 1975).

18 Estelle C. Jelinek (ed.), *Women's Autobiography: Essays in Criticism* (Bloomington, IN: Indiana University Press, 1980); Domna Stanton (ed.), *The*

Female Autograph (Chicago, IL: University of Chicago Press, 1987); Elizabeth W. Bruss, *Autobiographical Acts: The Changing Situation of a Literary Genre* (Baltimore, MD: Johns Hopkins University Press, 1976).

19 Bella Brodzki and Celeste Schenck (eds), *Life/Lines: Theorizing Women's Autobiography* (Ithaca, NY: Cornell University Press, 1988); Shari Benstock (ed.), *The Private Self* (Chapel Hill, NC: University of North Carolina Press, 1988).

20 Sidonie Smith, *A Poetics of Women's Autobiography: Marginality and the Fictions of Self-Representation* (Bloomington, IN: Indiana University Press, 1987) and *Subjectivity, Identity and the Body: Women's Autobiographical Practices in the Twentieth Century* (Bloomington, IN: Indiana University Press, 1993).

21 Françoise Lionnet, *Autobiographical Voices: Race, Gender, Self-Portraiture* (Ithaca, NY: Cornell University Press, 1989) and *Postcolonial Representations: Women, Literature, Identity* (Ithaca, NY: Cornell University Press, 1995).

22 Leigh Gilmore, *Autobiographics: A Feminist Theory of Self-Representation* (Ithaca, NY: Cornell University Press, 1994).

23 Linda Anderson, *Women and Autobiography in the Twentieth Century: Remembered Futures* (Hemel Hempstead: Harvester Wheatsheaf, 1997).

24 Smith, *A Poetics of Women's Autobiography*, p. 51.

25 *The Woman Warrior* is discussed as a bodily representation alongside Cherríe Moraga's *Loving in the War Years*. I do not want to charge Gilmore with either essentialising or reducing Kingston's work: her analysis of bodily identity is astute and persuasive. Yet, although the work of women of colour is quite well represented here (Kingston, Moraga, Lorde and Sandra Cisneros), Gilmore does not focus upon these writers' negotiation of their gendered and ethnicised identities at length. The same may be said, to a lesser extent, of Sidonie Smith's discussion of bodily identity in *The Woman Warrior*.

26 Lionnet, *Autobiographical Voices*, p. 7.

27 Ling, *Between Worlds*, p. 10.

28 King-kok Cheung, 'Re-viewing Asian American Literary Studies', in King-kok Cheung (ed.), *An Interethnic Companion to Asian American Literature*, (New York: Cambridge University Press, 1997), pp. 17–20.

29 *Ibid.* See also David Palumbo-Liu, 'Model Minority Discourse and the Course of Healing', in Abdul JanMohamed (ed.), *Minority Discourse: Ideological Containment and Utopian/Heterotopian Potentials* (New York: Oxford University Press, forthcoming).

30 See Cheung, as 'Re-viewing Asian American Literary Studies'. This is a point also made by Sau-ling Wong. See Sau-ling Wong, 'Sugar Sisterhood: Situating the Amy Tan Phenomenon', in David Palumbo Liu (ed.), *The Ethnic Canon: Histories, Institutions, and Interventions* (Minneapolis, MN: University of Minnesota Press, 1995), pp. 174–210.

31 *Ibid.*

32 See Benstock (ed.), *The Private Self* and Brodski and Schenck (eds), *Life/Lines* for commentary on the increasing popularity of autobiography.

33 A point attested to by Paul Eakin's edited collection, *American Autobiography: Retrospect and Prospect* (Madison, WI: University of Wisconsin Press, 1991), and James R. Payne's edited collection, *Multicultural Autobiography: American Lives* (Knoxville, TN: University of Tennessee Press, 1992).

34 Amy Tan, in particular, has suffered from being read autobiographically in this way. LeiLani Nishime reminds us that the problems of generic distinctions are endemic to Asian American literature, because, as Trinh T. Minh Ha has put it, 'the *minor*-ity's voice is always *personal*'. LeiLani Nishime, 'Engendering Genre: Gender and Nationalism in *China Men* and *The Woman Warrior*', *Melus*, 28:1, Spring (1995), 67–82; p. 69.

35 Ann Rayson, 'Beneath the Mask: Autobiographies of Japanese-American Women', *Melus*, 14:1, Spring (1987), 43–57; p. 44.

36 Julia Watson and Sidonie Smith, 'De/Colonization and the Politics of Discourse in Women's Autobiographical Practices', in Julia Watson and Sidonie Smith (eds), *De/Colonizing the Subject: The Politics of Gender in Women's Autobiography*, (Minneapolis, MN: University of Minnesota Press, 1992), pp. xiii–xxxi; p. xvi.

37 Lim, 'Japanese American Women's Life Stories', p. 301.

38 This is especially the case for Japanese American women, who wrote autobiographies of their time in internment camps in the Second World War, in order to contest 'national' versions of their story.

39 The phrase 'ambassadors of goodwill' is Elaine Kim's. See Elaine Kim, Asian *American Literature: An Introduction to the Writings and their Social Context* (Philadelphia, PA: Temple University Press, 1982), pp. 24–32.

40 Wong's text is discussed in chapter 1.

41 For a lucid discussion of this phenomenon, see Sau-ling Wong, 'Autobiography as Guided Chinatown Tour? Maxine Hong Kingston's *The Woman Warrior* and the Chinese American Autobiographical Controversy', in Payne (ed.), *Multicultural Autobiography*, pp. 248–79.

42 This debate has been played out over the last few years, most notably relating to the cultural authenticity – or not – of Kingston's *The Woman Warrior*. Frank Chin, one of Kingston's harshest critics, has been most vocal in denouncing her work as culturally inauthentic and pandering to a white readership, arguing that the autobiography is not an Asian American form. Many Asian American feminist critics have come to Kingston's defence. For a concise summary of this debate, see King-kok Cheung, *Articulate Silences: Hisaye Yamamoto, Maxine Hong Kingston, Joy Kogawa* (Ithaca, NY: Cornell University Press, 1993), p. 78.

43 Benjamin Tong, 'Critics of Admirer Sees Dumb Racist', *Journal* (San Francisco), 11 May 1977, p. 20; Jeffery Chan, 'Letters: The Mysterious West', *New York Review of Books*, 28 April 1977, p. 41.

44 Frank Chin, 'This Is Not an Autobiography', *Genre*, 18:2 (1985), 109–30.

45 Frank Chin et. al., (eds), *Aiiieeee! An Anthology of Asian-American Writers* (Washington, DC: Howard University Press, 1983).

46 Katheryn Fong, 'Woman's Review of "Woman Warrior"', *Journal* (San Francisco), 25 January 1978, p. 6.

47 See Lisa Lowe, *Immigrant Acts: On Asian American Cultural Politics* (Durham, NC: Duke University Press, 1996), especially chapter 3, 'Heterogeneity, Hybridity, Multiplicity: Marking Asian American Differences'.

48 See Michael M. J. Fischer, 'Ethnicity and the Post-Modern Arts of Memory', in James Clifford and George E. Marcus (eds), *Writing Culture: The Poetics and Politics of Ethnography* (Berkeley, CA: University of California Press, 1986), p. 210.

49 Furthermore, talking of 'genre' seems problematic in that it is a term which in usage has referred mainly to literary modes. The increasing cross-pollination over discursive boundaries, such as between history and literature, requires that we use 'discourse' rather than 'genre', as history cannot properly be considered a genre. More appropriately, we should speak of 'historical discourse'.

50 Carr (ed.), *From My Guy to Sci-Fi*, p. 7.
51 Leslie Dick, 'Feminism, Writing, Postmodernism', in Carr (ed.), *From My Guy to Sci-Fi*, pp. 204–14; p. 209.
52 See Cheung, *Articulate Silences* for a discussion of this.
53 See Ling, *Between Worlds*, pp. 9–17; also Sau-ling Wong, 'Chinese American Literature', in Cheung (ed.), *An Interethnic Companion*, p. 41.
54 See Ling's discussion of Chinese women's history, in Ling, *Between Worlds*, pp. 9–17.
55 See Wong, 'Chinese American Literature', pp. 46–7.
56 For a more detailed rendering of this history, see Amy Ling's discussion in Ling, *Between Worlds*, especially her section, 'Focus on China: Stances'. Other texts in this tradition would include the phenomenally successful Jung Chang, *Wild Swans* (London: Flamingo, 1993), Anchee Min, *Red Azalea* (London: Victor Gollancz, 1993) and Jan Wong, *Red China Blues* (London: Bantam, 1997).
57 Amy Ling and Sau-ling Wong both discuss these works as a separate form in themselves, one dictated by cultural multi-situatedness. See Ling, *Between Worlds*, pp. 106–12; and Wong, 'Chinese American Literature', p. 49.
58 A similar delineation may be found in Wong, 'Chinese American Literature'.
59 Perhaps I should talk about phases as well as strains here because, as Sau-ling Wong has argued, although matrilineal writing is currently prospering, texts focusing upon matrilineality may be traced back through the century. This further attests to the need for a model of literary history of Asian American women's writing which can account for diachronic as well as synchronic modes of influence.
60 See Stan Yogi, 'Japanese American Literature', in Cheung (ed.), *An Interethnic Companion*, p. 126.
61 Hisaye Yamamoto, in particular, published – and continues to publish – in such papers as *Rafu Shimpo*.
62 A point made by Ketu H. Katrak. See 'South Asian American Literature', in Cheung (ed.), *An Interethnic Companion*, p. 194.
63 I use the term 'critical fiction' here to designate a work in which politics speak critically and importantly through a text identified mainly as fiction. This definition is taken from Philomena Mariani (ed.), *Critical Fictions: The Politics of Imaginative Writing* (Seattle, WA: Bay Press, 1991), and I view this as a form of theoretically informed and informing writing, characteristic of much Asian American women's writing.
64 My use of the term 'Asian American forms' needs qualifying at this point. I do not mean that there are forms of writing characteristic of Asian Americans as a group, but instead that there are Chinese American, Japanese American or Filipino American forms, specific to that ethnic group. The way that these works are collectively Asian American in form may be that they share a textual/generic hybridity reflective of the 'between worlds' status of their authors. In this sense, we may also talk about ethnic, immigrant, or even postcolonial forms.
65 King-kok Cheung notes that talking-story is a female practice. See Cheung, *Articulate Silences*, p. 102.

66 *Ibid.*, p. 121.

67 *Ibid.*, p. 123.

68 The 'floating world' painting is another organisational device. It is used most extensively by Cynthia Kadohata in *The Floating World*, where a Japanese form (the 'floating world' painting) is transposed as both a metaphor and a structure for a novel about ethnic dislocation in America.

69 Stories by Asian American women often use artistic creativity as a language in its own right. As Rosie's mother 'speaks' through her poetry compositon here, so the mother figure in R. A. Sasaki's story 'The Loom' speaks through her knitting.

70 See Lowe, *Immigrant Acts*, p. 112.

71 See Wong, *Reading Asian American Literature*, pp. 9–17.

72 See Bonnie TuSmith, *All My Relatives: Community in Contemporary Ethnic American Literatures* (Ann Arbor, MI: University of Michigan Press, 1993), p. 13.

73 This is a point also made in relation to Japanese Americans in Stephen S. Fugita and David O'Brien, *Japanese American Ethnicity: The Persistence of Community* (Seattle, WA: University of Washington Press, 1991).

74 TuSmith, *All My Relatives*, pp. 16–24.

75 See Kim, *Asian American Literature*; and Mary Dearborn, *Pocahontas's Daughters: Gender and Ethnicity in American Culture* (New York: Oxford University Press, 1986), both cited in TuSmith, *All My Relatives*, p. 21. More recent work on the question of redefining ethnic literary history may be found in A. LaVonne Brown Ruoff and Jerry W. Ward, Jr., (eds), *Redefining American Literary History* (New York: MLA, 1990).

76 See TuSmith, *All My Relatives*, pp. 25–6.

77 See Sau-ling Wong, 'Immigrant Autobiography: Some Questions of Definition and Approach', in Eakin (ed.), *American Autobiography*, pp. 147–51.

78 All of these women lived through the experience of being interned by the American government during the Second World War.

79 TuSmith, *All My Relatives*, pp. 19–32.

80 Donald C. Goellnicht, 'Blurring Boundaries: Asian American Literature as Theory', in Cheung, *An Interethnic Companion*, p. 340. I am indebted to Goellnicht's work in this piece in shaping my own approach.

81 *Ibid.*, p. 341.

82 This revision has taken place through the work of autobiography theorists Sidonie Smith and Leigh Gilmore, amongst others.

83 See Nancy Chodorow, *Femininities, Masculinities, Sexualities: Freud and Beyond* (Lexington, KY: University of Kentucky Press, 1994).

84 A point which I elaborate further in chapter 6.

85 Goellnicht, 'Blurring Boundaries', p. 351; p. 356.

86 It is necessary to clarify my use of the terms 'discourse' and 'genre' at this particular point. I use 'discourse' to refer to the language of a particular subject, with corresponding power structures and ideologies. A genre is a highly formally regulated form of literary discourse.

87 Anderson, *Women and Autobiography in the Twentieth Century*, p. 115.

88 *Ibid.*, p. 10.

89 See, for example, the two collections by Amritjit Singh, Joseph T. Skerrett, Jr. and Robert E. Hogan (eds), *Memory, Narrative, and Identity: New Essays in Ethnic American Literatures* (Boston, MA: Northeastern University Press, 1994) and *Memory and Cultural Politics: New Approaches to Ethnic American Literatures* (Boston, MA: Northeastern University Press, 1996). Also see Fischer, 'Ethnicity and the Post-Modern Arts of Memory'.

90   A textual excess such as silence becomes evident when one searches for what has been left out of the narrative. Work in this area includes King-kok Cheung's *Articulate Silences*.

91   Singh, Skerrett and Hogan (eds), *Memory, Narrative, and Identity*, p. 19.

92   Goellnicht, 'Blurring Boundaries', p. 152.

93   Kingston, for example, juxtaposes her relatives' memories alongside the official inscription of the past via 'the laws' in her text, *China Men*.

94   Toni Morrison, 'Rootedness: The Ancestor as Foundation', in Mari Evans (ed.), *Black Women Writers: A Critical Evaluation* (New York: Anchor/Doubleday, 1984), pp. 339–45.

95   This kind of writing is closely in line with the early feminist endeavour of recovering women's lives and stories.

96   See Bibliography.

97   I only mention a brief selection here. For details of these, and other, anthologies, see Bibliography.

98   Cynthia G. Franklin, *Writing Women's Communities: The Politics and Poetics of Contemporary Multi-Genre Anthologies* (Madison, WI: The University of Wisconsin Press, 1997).

99   Although Hongo's text is not limited to Asian American women, it contains many important contributions. For bibliographic details, see the Bibliography.

100 I am thinking here in particular of two collections: Cherríe Moraga and Gloria Anzaldúa's edited collection, *This Bridge Called My Back: Writings by Radical Women of Color* (New York: Kitchen Table: Women of Color Press, 1983) and Elena Featherston's edited anthology, *Skin Deep: Women Writing on Color, Culture and Identity* (Freedom, CA: The Crossing Press, 1994).

101 See Cynthia G. Franklin's discussion of multi-ethnic, multi-genre anthologies in *Writing Women's Communities: The Politics and Poetics of Contemporary Multi-Genre Anthologies* (Madison, WI: University of Wisconsin Press, 1997). Franklin discusses Asian American examples as well.

102 This is a point made succinctly by King-kok Cheung, who has also noted the success of texts dealing with ethnic issues in soft focus, whereas those writers who 'rage' over racism are largely ignored. See Cheung, 'Re-viewing Asian American Literary Studies', especially pp. 17–20.

103 In a conference paper, Sneja Gunew has commented upon the manner in which Lau actively disassociates herself from ethnic identifications. Sneja Gunew, 'Operatic Karaoke: the pitfalls of seeking diasporic legitimations' (unpublished paper), 'Transformations: Thinking through Feminism' conference, Institute of Women's Studies, Lancaster University, 17–19 July, 1997.

4

Writing Red China: recent Chinese American/British narratives

Chinese lives during this century are stranger than fiction, they are so dramatic and so strange to an outside eye that you don't need to embellish them.

(Jung Chang)[1]

In recent years, the reading public has clearly developed a taste for accounts of suffering and hardship under Communist rule in China. Publishers have responded eagerly with memoirs chronicling family misfortune, emotional and cultural deprivation, and political victimization by a totalitarian regime. Though these accounts vary, they often reproduce a view of China's history which reinforces stereotypes and assumes ignorance on the part of their readers. Indeed, many memoirs of life in China suggest a kind of contemporary orientalism in which China appears as a radically other, despotic and brutal world.

(Harriet Evans)[2]

When Jung Chang published *Wild Swans: Three Daughters of China* in 1991, it received widespread critical acclaim, as well as commercial success, including winning the 1992 NCR Book Award. Much of this critical attention focused upon the text's *novelty*, as a personal memoir and history of China during the period after the Communist Party gained control, and of the Cultural Revolution. This chapter will contextualise Chang's work within a wider history of writing about Communist China, and in so doing, will advance three separate arguments. Firstly, it will be suggested that Chang's work is not in fact a new form of writing, but instead can be located within a long – and continuing – tradition of both Chinese American and British writing. Chang's book did however usher in a renewed literary interest in Communist China, as can be seen in the plethora of texts which 'write Red China', which have appeared since 1991. These include writing by women from mainland Red China, who were born into early generation Communist families: Anchee Min's *Red Azalea* (1993), Hong Ying's (1998) memoir, *Daughter of the River*, Meihong Xu's *Daughter of China* (also 1998), Anhua Gao's

To the Edge of the Sky (2000), Aiping Mu's *Vermilion Gate* (2000), Ting-xing Ye's *A Leaf in the Bitter Wind* (2000), and Liu Hong's fictionalised *Startling Moon* (2001), as well as texts by women born outside of the mainland such as Jan Wong's *Red China Blues* (1996; Wong was born in Canada), Pang-Mei Natasha Chang's *Bound Feet and Western Dress* (1996; Chang is Chinese American), and Adeline Yen Mah's *Falling Leaves: The True Story of an Unwanted Chinese Daughter* (1997 – Mah was born and brought up in Hong Kong).[3] Many of these narratives provide a unique range of inside perspectives – especially of women's experiences – on a country which has not only undergone radical political changes through-out the twentieth century, but which has also largely been closed to the West, and in this sense, this study will argue that an important new sub-genre of women's writing is emerging. For one reason or another, it has fallen to a group of expatriate women to be spokespersons for their country's history. Narratives by this group of women writers, this study will show, also further elide the distinctions between 'Asian American', 'Asian British' and 'Asian Asian' writing, which is becoming increasingly commonplace, as commentators like Sau-ling Wong have observed.[4] Finally, this chapter will suggest that the critical reception of these recent books about Communist China may be symptomatic of a cultural resurgence of orientalism.

Critical histories

The critical reception of and reaction to Jung Chang's *Wild Swans* be-trays a certain confusion about how to characterise her work. This is partly engendered by the title itself, in particular the subtitle, 'Three Daughters of China', which suggests that the text is at once a personal history/biography/memoir, and an example of Chinese American women's writing about matrilineality, which has been so popular in recent years with the success of Maxine Hong Kingston's and Amy Tan's work. In fact, the critical confusion over the generic status of Chang's work is very reminiscent of a similar uncertainty surrounding Maxine Hong Kingston's *The Woman Warrior* nearly twenty years earlier, which is discussed in chapter 2. This textual dual identity has also been cre-ated by Chang herself, who has said in an interview that whilst the text is primarily a personal history of the Cultural Revolution, 'on a smaller scale … it is the process of understanding my mother'.[5] Of the many reviews of the book when it first appeared, several located it within very different generic traditions. Lucy Hughes-Hallet, writing in the *Independent*, read it as 'popular history at its most compelling', illustrating the 'pleasures of good historical fiction'.[6] Richard Heller also read it as 'living history', whilst Martin Amis located it as both 'family memoir' and as 'social history'. Several other reviews found similarities between *Wild Swans* and more popular fiction: Caroline Moorehead declared it 'a loving family saga', whilst Edward Behr went even further, labelling it 'real-life saga', and compared it with the soap opera *Dynasty*! An even more bizarre interpretation, by Carolyn See, announced it as several different things at once: 'a mad adventure story, a fairy tale of courage – calm and measured history'. Minette Marrin summed up these various confusions in her interpretation of the text as 'an unusual masterpiece – not only a popular bestseller … it has also received serious critical attention'.

The point of relating these reviews is that *Wild Swans* has been received in very different ways by a reading public who cannot seem to get enough of writing about Communist China in contemporary times. However, as discussed in chapter 3, the assumptions which accompany the generic label attached to a text differ widely, and these differences are in fact crucial in explaining the cultural reception of *Wild Swans* and other similar texts. This study suggests that the critical reception of *Wild Swans* and other texts which 'write Red China', has not differentiated adequately between different genres of writing about Communist China, resulting in the confusion already outlined over just exactly how to characterise these texts. This is partly due to the marketing of these books by publishers eager to cash in on a cultural moment which has seen Communist China become a fad for Western readers, so that as this chapter shows, each subsequently published text is declared to be in the same vein as the last, a claim which in fact often masks very real differences in style, tone, location, social circumstances, intended audience and focus.[7] There are crucial differences too, in the distance between each author and her story: Jung Chang took many years to articulate her experiences; while Anhua Gao's narrative appeared barely six years after her arrival in Britain.

Reviewing *Wild Swans* in the *New York Review of Books*, Jonathan Mirsky read the text alongside Feng Jicai's *Voices from the Whirlwind: An Oral History of the Chinese Cultural Revolution*, published in the same year. In an attempt to link Chang's very extensive and detailed memoir of her family's experiences during the Cultural Revolution with the necessarily shorter and more episodic reminiscences to be found in *Voices from the Whirlwind*, Mirsky proposes a common unifying category: 'literature of the wounded'.[8] In yet another attempt to generically 'fix' Chang's text, Mirsky argues that what these texts have in common is that they are 'intimate studies in persecution'. While Mirsky's claim may have some basis in the many dreadful incidents that Chang relates, it seems a rather facile gesture to link this writing to a currently fashionable (but in some ways highly problematic) critical discourse on the 'literatures of trauma', in a move which effectively obscures the cultural and historical specificities of the period 1909–78 in China. Extending Mirsky's description to other texts illustrates the problems with this category. Certainly, all the texts discussed here take as their central focus and organising rubric the central character/author's suffering and pain at the mercy of a totalitarian regime. Yet although all of these texts deal to varying degrees with the negative aspects of the Cultural Revolution, including torture, persecution, execution and famine, several also address other forms of trauma as well. This is often a specific form of gender trauma. Adeline Yen Mah's *Falling Leaves*, for example, also extensively describes the mistreatment and neglect she suffered at the hands of her family as an unwanted daughter, and in fact this preoccupation at times obscures the narrative of the Cultural Revolution with which it is juxtaposed. Anhua Gao's *To the Edge of the Sky* is partly her story of abuse at the hands of a vicious husband. Similarly, Hong Ying's *Daughter of the River* tracks its narrator's attempts to uncover the mysterious familial secrets which seem to cause her family to resent her (and which, it turns out, relate to her identity as an illegitimate daughter), which are related alongside the events of the Cultural Revolution. It is difficult to see how Mirsky's label, 'literature of the wounded', can adequately describe the content of all of these narratives without either reducing the different kinds and levels of suffering to one, or ignoring the gender aspects of many of these accounts. Despite this, Mirsky's label does have useful analogies to the ways in which testimonial literature of the Holocaust and other traumatic experiences have been characterised, by critics like Kalí Tal, Cathy Caruth, and others. Tal has argued that any literature which 'bears witness' on one level is aggressively political, emotionally charged and culturally sensitive, and furthermore that it is the politically sensitive aspects of a narrative that come to dominate the text, to be privileged over other thematic concerns or dimensions, and in this sense at least, Mirsky's label perhaps has some validity.[9]

Red Azalea by Anchee Min, was published in 1993, just two years after *Wild Swans*, and betrays its publisher's eagerness to capitalise on the success of Chang's text, as well as upon Amy Tan's *The Kitchen God's Wife*, which had appeared the year before, and which is also a personal story set against a background of China in the twentieth century (notably the 1930s). Min's story is particularly sensational, as she became a film star in Mao's China, and led something of a high-flying life. *Red Azalea* was reviewed by Amy Tan for the dustjacket, in which, in big bold type, she finds Min's memoir 'riveting ... this is not just another book on the cultural revolution'. Like *Wild Swans*, a wider survey of the reviews of Min's memoir also reveals a wide spectrum of generic interpretations of the text.

Later narratives, such as *Bound Feet and Western Dress*, by Pang-Mei Natasha Chang and *Red China Blues* by Jan Wong (published in the same year, 1996, by the same press, Bantam) actually share little in common, although the *New York Times* described both as part of the 'family memoir genre'. *Bound Feet and Western Dress* is actually written by a first generation Chinese American woman, who relates the story of her great-aunt after spending many hours of taped interviewing. Yu-i, Chang's aunt, lived through the Cultural Revolution, and *Bound Feet* describes these years, alongside Yu-i's own story of female resistance and bravery: the title refers to her childhood refusal to have her feet bound.[10] It covers the period from 1900, when Yu-i was born, to her death in 1989. Like *Wild Swans*, it includes a chronology of events which juxtaposes Yu-i's story with the events of the Cultural Revolution. In contrast, Jan Wong's *Red China Blues* is a personal memoir about the author's experience of travelling from her home in Canada to China in order to become involved in the Cultural Revolution in the 1980s. Wong's narrative thus only covers a short period and has a quite different, externalised – and certainly more limited – perspective on Communist China. Yet Bantam quite obviously marketed the two books together: *Red China Blues* is advertised within the pages of *Bound Feet*.

Adeline Yen Mah's *Falling Leaves: The True Story of an Unwanted Chinese Daughter*, is arguably one of the most commercially successful of these books (it spent more than thirty weeks on *The Times* bestseller list, and to date has sold almost half a million copies in Britain alone). Possibly owing to its subtitle, which again suggested a connection with Chinese American writing about mothers and daughters, it was reviewed by Amy Tan for the dustjacket, who described it, this time in large red type, as 'riveting ... I am still haunted by Mah's memoir. A marvel of memory'. Apart from the fact that Amy Tan only seems to have one thing to say about these texts, that they are 'riveting', it is significant that she is repeatedly asked to review them, not just as a well-known Chinese American writer, but also because of the publishers' attempts to connect these texts about Communist China with the commercially successful subject of Chinese experience and Chinese American mothers

and daughters. This can also be seen in one of the most recent of these
texts, by the Chinese expatriate and poet, Hong Ying. Her partly
fictionalised memoir *Daughter of the River* was published in 1997.
Despite its title, this book is not substantially about matrilineality:
'daughter of the river' refers to the Yangtze river, on the bank of which
Hong Ying grew up, in a slum. Yet the review which is printed on the
back cover, originally published in *The Times*, connects Hong Ying's
narrative with both *Wild Swans* and Tan's *The Joy Luck Club*: 'Dealing
as it does with the nightmare of Mao's China, comparisons with Jung
Chang's *Wild Swans* will be inevitable, but Ying's book more closely
resembles Amy Tan's *The Joy Luck Club*'.

All of this critical confusion can be summed up in the one of the
latest texts to be published, *Daughter of China: The True Story of Forbidden Love in Modern China*, by Meihong Xu. Reviewed for the dustjacket
by Anchee Min, author of *Red Azalea*, the blurb announces it 'as dramatic as *Wild Swans*, as moving as *Falling Leaves* and as revealing as
Memoirs of a Geisha, *Daughter of China* tells how a nation's troubled
history shaped the destiny of one remarkable young woman'.

Precursors: early writing against Red China

These contemporary texts share commercial as well as critical success,
although they have not yet received substantial critical analysis. However, although they have been accepted to a certain extent as a *new*
body of writing, they do in fact have important precursors in Chinese
American literature. In her book *Between Worlds: Women Writers of
Chinese Ancestry*, Amy Ling discusses a range of texts by Chinese American women which focused upon China after the Communist Party gained
control, and which according to Ling, took a 'critical and negative stance'
towards this period in China's history. In a section entitled 'Life in the
People's Republic of China: The Critical Stance', Ling discusses a series
of key auto/biographical texts about Communist China, including the
autobiography by Maria Yen published in 1954, *The Umbrella Garden*,
which relates Yen's experiences as a student of the National Beijing
University in the late 1940s; Sansan's memoir *Eighth Moon*, published
in 1964, the story of a child who grew up separated from her parents in
the People's Republic; Yuan-tsung Chen's autobiographical novel *The
Dragon's Village*, published in 1980, charting Chen's experiences as a
land reformer in the 1950s and 1960s; and a more recent precursor to
the texts discussed here, Nien Cheng's *Life and Death in Shanghai*, the
story of an upper-class wife of an ambassador, who became a political

prisoner, which was published in 1987. As with the more contemporary writers under discussion here, these women 'found publishers and a ready audience for expressions of discontent'.[11] As Ling makes clear, because the United States regarded China as a dangerous enemy in the 1950s (this was after all the period when the House UnAmerican Activities Committee was active under Senator Joseph McCarthy), the political climate was even riper for books about Communist China than it is today. In this section of her study, Ling also discusses the novels of Eileen Chang, published in the 1950s and 1960s. Chang's novels are particularly interesting, both as fictionalised documents of the Cultural Revolution era, and in the light of the critical acclaim that they have received.[12]

Eileen Chang (Zhang Ai-ling), *The Rice Sprout Song* (1955)

Eileen Chang was a Chinese woman writer of upper-class and educated background who emigrated to the United States as a young adult. She was born and raised in China's old society, although her perspective on the Communist Party has much in common with later writers. She is the author of several novels, including *The Rice Sprout Song* (1955), *The Naked Earth* (1956) and *Rouge of the North* (1967). She is also the author of the acclaimed novella, *The Golden Cangue* (1943), which draws heavily upon her experience of her father's opium habit and the familial destruction this caused. This piece was later to be expanded into her novel, *The Rouge of the North*.[13]

Chang's critical reputation largely rests upon her 1955 novel, *The Rice Sprout Song*, which, like *The Naked Earth*, was originally written in Chinese, but was later translated into English by the writer herself. Like *The Naked Earth*, *The Rice Sprout Song* deals with the period of Chinese history Chang experienced: Communist China, and the failure of the government during this time. Significantly, both novels were commissioned by the United States Information Agency, for barely-concealed propaganda purposes. The initial inspiration for *The Rice Sprout Song* was an article written by a Communist Party cadre who had been involved in quelling a peasant attack upon a granary store during a period of particular hardship. The party member asked in his article how the ideals of the Communist Party could have gone so wrong, so much so that the party was against the people it sought to help. He subsequently published a retraction of these earlier views, and it is these two viewpoints expressed by the party member that Chang explores in her novel. *The Rice Sprout Song* is more successful than *The Naked Earth* in transcending the narrow contractual brief within which Chang was forced to work, as she herself has admitted. The novel offers a subtle but sophisticated critique of the values spawned by Communist China through the dual lenses of both the peasant hardship created by the Revolution and subsequent government, and the party itself. So the novel opens with a peasant village wedding and then proceeds through the lives of party members such as Ku, the party intellectual prone to petty deceptions. The contact between Ku and peasant hardship poignantly illustrates the distance between the ideals and the realities of Communist China. Juxtaposed with these two, is the situation of the higher-ranking party member, Comrade Wong, whose demands upon the peasants culminates in a riot which he is forced to viciously quell. These individuals provide the means for Chang to demonstrate the impossible demands and conditions of survival in Communist China, as well as the fracture of both party ideas and ideals, as Wong finally notes: 'We have failed'. The rice sprout song, or *yanko*, itself, is the dance of the revolution that ultimately provides a powerful and ironic symbol in Chang's novel.

Chang's critical reputation predominantly rests upon *The Golden Cangue* and *The Rice Sprout Song*. Although one critic has described Chang as 'the only novelist of real competence who has deserted Red China and written of life in that country from this side of the Bamboo curtain', her work may be compared with Nien Cheng's autobiographical *Life and Death in Shanghai* (1986), another account of the period of the Cultural Revolution and its aftermath, grounded in the personal experience of the author.[14] Chang's work has also been compared by Amy Ling with other Chinese women writers who have made the United States their home, including Han Suyin, Helena Kuo, Hazel Lin and Yuan-tsung Chen. As the renowned Chinese literary expert C. T. Hsia has noted, *The Rice Sprout Song*'s position at the forefront of Chinese writing in English extends beyond its linguistic boundaries, so that it may be considered to be 'among the classics of Chinese fiction'.[15] Partly the novel's importance may be attributed to the critical and ruthlessly unsentimental account that it offers of life in Communist China, in which respect it may be placed alongside Maria Yen's *The Umbrella Garden: A Picture of Student Life in Red China* (1954) and Yuan-tsung Chen's *The Dragon's Village* (1980). However, *The Rice Sprout Song*'s reputation is equally explained by Chang's literary skill. As Amy Ling has noted, Chang's sparse but effective descriptions and striking images also contribute much to the success of this novel.

New orientalisms?

One of the concerns in this study about the conditions of marketing and reception of the more recent of these texts about Communist China is that we may in fact be witnessing the birth of a new orientalism, as Harriet Evans also observed in the quotation opening this chapter. In Edward Said's definition, 'orientalism' is a perspective on world relations in which the West produces a particular version of the 'Orient', which then serves to justify its subjugation as culturally, morally and politically inferior to the West.[16] Many of these narratives about the atrocities which occurred in Communist China have been key in retrospectively confirming China for the West as a politically and socially draconian state. In some cases this has been very blatant, as in Eileen Chang's case where the United States actually sponsored her anti-Communist narratives.[17] This may be a strategy of containment: with the collapse of Communist Russia, China has become the new cultural, political and economic target, especially in the light of the events which took place in Tiananmen Square on 4 June 1989, and the current global spotlight upon China's poor record of human rights.[18] Asia has long since emerged as a double front of threat and encroachment in the West (the so-called 'Yellow Peril', which in the Cold War era took the form of a fear of the spread of Communism); today, Asian states have become prominent rivals in the global economy, and yet Asian immigrants to the United States and elsewhere are still a necessary internally racialised labour force as well. Orientalist discourses continue to define Asians as culturally and racially 'other', at a time when the United States is economically at war with Asia, and this is partly manifested in a neo-orientalist fascination with all things Asian.[19] For example, it can be suggested that the publishing industry's current predilection for texts about the 'orient' may also account for the success of Arthur Golden's 1997 novel about geisha life in Japan from the 1920s to the 1960s, *Memoirs of a Geisha*. As anyone who has read it will know, this book serves up a mixture of tantalising eroticism and exoticism, culminating in the blow-by-blow account of the geisha Sayuri's *mizuage*, or deflowering, by one of her patrons. Although it is a novel, it is presented as a memoir, complete with a false 'translator's' note regarding the sincerity of Sayuri's story. This narrative ruse has been so successful that several reviewers have reported reading it without becoming aware of its fictional status; a mistake I too made when reading it.[20] It has been phenomenally successful – selling over a million copies in Britain – and has the dubious honour of becoming another Spielberg movie.[21] The perils of homogenising texts which to varying degrees 'write the east', can

perhaps best be illustrated by a recent article in the British broadsheet
newspaper *The Guardian*'s supplement 'The Editor', which presented
'five novels about women in China, to save you the burden of reading
them'.[22] These 'Five of a Kind' included Kingston's *The Woman Warrior*,
Tan's *The Kitchen God's Wife*, Chang's *Bound Feet*, Mah's *Falling Leaves*
and Chang's *Wild Swans*. The item reduces Chinese American writing
to its lowest common denominator: the final section of each brief review gives the 'best Chinese proverb cited'! In another case, an article
by Vanessa Thorpe in *The Observer* commented upon the manner in
which 'the East is Read: How the Orient captivated the West'. She noted:

> First came *Wild Swans*, then *Falling Leaves*. Now an equally authentic story
> about rural China … is expected to surpass both those bestsellers. … The
> book business is still prepared to bank on the British reader's obsession
> with all things oriental. With Arthur Golden's semi-factual study of Japan,
> *Memoirs of a Geisha*, still selling well, hunger for detailed chronicles of
> lives lived out in far flung places grows unabated.[23]

The Observer article cites a fiction editor at a prominent publishing house,
who observes that 'there is still an interest in story-telling that is exotic
and yet fairly familiar. *Memoirs of a Geisha*, for instance, was an extraordinary story, with no Westerners in it, yet somehow readers here
are able to relate to it'.[24] It seems that, as these comments indicate,
publishers are currently engaged in selling a reading public an
orientalism that continues to be extremely profitable, one which continues to fetishise Asia and Asians: it is precisely the *absence* of 'Westerners', along with the *presence* of the 'exotic' East, that is attractive.
Ultimately, that publishers seem to have happened upon a highly successful, if unspoken, narrative formula may have more to do with the
content of these texts than with artistic merit or political integrity, although these are undoubtedly also present.

Central to the conditions of reception of these texts, are issues of
representation and reading. Clearly, for these writers, although representation is to some extent under their authorial control, reading is
not. Yet, as John McLeod warns, and as the critical reception of many
of these texts demonstrate, 'the act of reading in postcolonial contexts
is by no means a neutral activity. *How* we read is just as important as
what we read'.[25] It is clear that several of these narratives were intended
by their authors to be exposés of China's hypocrisy and the severity of
elements of the Communist regime during the twentieth century, often
from a gendered perspective. However, if we recognise that these texts
(like all texts) are sites of 'multiaccentuality' or sites of pluralistic meaning, one can account for their potential 'derailment'. By this, I mean

that there is the possibility that these texts may be construed or consumed as appealing to the stereotypical assumptions about China's cultural difference (or cultural *inferiority*). In this respect, the texts may inadvertently fall prey to the neo-orientalist impetus in the West. So whilst their authors *produce* them as critiques of Maoist China, they are *consumed* by a readership which is fixated upon a neo-orientalist exoticism and voyeurism. This is especially the case if we consider the gender politics at stake within this literature. As this chapter demonstrates, the uniqueness of several narratives – notably *Wild Swans*, *Bound Feet and Western Dress*, and *Falling Leaves* – stems from the portrait of *women's* lives that each provides. However, precisely because many stereotypical images of Asian women have emerged from the very same experiences that these texts describe, such as foot-binding and prostitution, these narratives may (albeit inadvertently) ultimately invite a voyeuristic fascination.

The critical responses outlined here, are, of course, characteristic of texts which slide across generic divides. It is apparent that much of the criticism in this study is levelled at reviews of these texts, as no substantial critical work has yet been written, in the vein of Amy Ling's extensive analysis of early writing about Communist China. This may perhaps be unfair criticism, although it could be argued that reviews of books, especially when so many illustrate the same approach, do function as de facto indexes of the prevailing cultural 'zeitgeist'. Perhaps the title and organising rubric 'writing Red China' in this chapter, does little to disentangle the specificities of these texts. We should not ignore the complexity of these texts, which after all, appeal to a variety of different readerships, from popular consumers of literary exotica, interested observers of China to students of Asian American literature. But what we need is sustained, specific and generically-sensitive analysis of these texts and the ways in which they write Red China from differing social and cultural perspectives. In short, we need to sensitise our readings to both neo-colonial dynamics and class and gender axes. The rest of this chapter, therefore, offers readings of several of these narratives.

Jung Chang, *Wild Swans* (1991)

Jung Chang's style in *Wild Swans* is informal yet compelling, and so it is not surprising that this auto/biographical text has been hailed by critics as a masterpiece of popular historical writing. Chang's skill is evident in her masterful blending of personal testimony and popular history in the vein of historian Howard Zinn.[26] Accompanied by many pictures, the narrative, written in the first person, traces Chang's family life against the backdrop of China's changing fortunes. Included in the autobiography is a chronology which charts the rise and fall of the Kuomintang, and the rise of the Communist Party, alongside corresponding events in the lives of the Chang family. Chang's family were not only extensively affected by the Japanese occupation, the fall of the Kuomintang and the Cultural Revolution, but were also actively involved in these changes. For instance, her grandmother became the concubine of the chief warlord General Xue, her father was governor of Yibin, her mother a head of public affairs in Yibin, and Jung Chang herself a member of the Red Guard. The pictures which accompany the text are particularly important in documenting the tandem histories of the Changs alongside a more general history of twentieth-century China. Many of the photographs show the Changs in their official capacities: Jung's grandfather, General Xue Zhi-heng, in his official uniform; Jung's parents in Communist Party uniforms; Jung as a Red Guard; and Jung's father's funeral in 1975, which depicts an official reading the Communist Party's valedictory. The many photographs are, in fact, one of the most remarkable features of the text, marking its distinction from several other 'Red China' life writings. They offer an intensely personal perspective upon this turbulent period of Chinese history.

Something of a contemporary publishing phenomenon the world over, *Wild Swans* is still banned in China, Chang's native country and the subject of the narrative.[27] Chang has said in response to this: 'I feel very angry and frustrated. I would love mainland Chinese to read my book. There is a Chinese translation which I worked on myself, published in Hong Kong and Taiwan.'[28] The fact that *Wild Swans* is banned in China is not entirely surprising though. The subject of the book is the social and political upheaval of twentieth-century China, which is told through the lives and perspectives of three generations of women: Jung Chang, her mother and her grandmother. Chang's grandmother, Yu-fang, was born into the feudal society of China in 1909, just two years before the Manchu Empire was overthrown, precipitating one of the bloodiest periods in China's history, when regional warlords reigned. Yu-fang's life was typical of Chinese women's lives in the early twentieth century: she endured foot-binding and had a very restricted existence as a result. In 1924, three years before Chiang-Kai-shek and the Kuomintang took control of China, Yu-fang became the concubine of General Xue Zhi-heng, a powerful chief of police in Peking. She bore him a daughter, Chang's mother, Bao Qin (or De-hong/'wild swan') in

1931. After General Xue's death two years later, Yu-Fang escaped from Peking with her infant daughter, and subsequently met and married a respectable middle-class doctor, Dr Xia, who was almost forty years her senior. This period coincided with the growth and consolidation of the Communist Party, against the backdrop of Japanese aggression in Manchuria, and eventually across China, culminating in the proclamation of the People's Republic in 1949. It was also during this period after the overthrow of the Kuomintang, that Chang's mother, now a young adult, joined the Communist Party, first becoming a student leader, then a member of the Communist Youth League. She also met and married Chang's father, Wang Yu, who became a Maoist guerilla soldier. As a civil servant herself, and as the wife of a party official, Bao Qin gained certain privileges, and Jung and her four siblings enjoyed a relatively secure upbringing until the first years of the 1960s. Jung Chang herself became a Red Guard briefly in 1966. Eventually, however, the ritual party purgings and human rights atrocities occurring at the time invaded the young girl's world when the tide turned against her parents in the early 1960s. Both parents became scapegoats and were punished as enemies of the people, and Jung was banished to the countryside to be re-educated as a peasant in Deyang. As part of her punishment and humiliation, Jung's mother was forced to kneel on broken glass. Jung herself was forced to become a 'barefoot doctor', serving the Communist Party as a medic, despite her lack of training. Jung's father died in 1975, barely three years after his release from a detainment camp. In 1978, the same year as Deng Xiaoping returned to power, Jung, now an educated twenty-six year old, won a scholarship to Britain, which then became her home. It was not until after her mother's visit in 1988, though, that Jung made the decision to commit her story to paper:

> in 1988 my mother came to England to visit me. For the first time, she told me the story of her life and that of my grandmother. When she returned to Chengdu, I sat down and let my memory surge out and the unshed tears flood my mind. I decided to write *Wild Swans*. The past was no longer too painful to recall because I had found love and fulfillment and therefore tranquillity. (p. 673)

Censorship of Chang's story was thus not just official and public, it also existed on a private level. Chang seems to have suffered from an almost intentional amnesia about her past. Yet, as with many traumatic histories, Chang found writing *Wild Swans* simultaneously both difficult and yet cathartic. She has said:

> The process of writing was perhaps more painful, but afterwards it became cathartic because I no longer have the terrible nightmares that I

used to have when I first came to Britain. I came over in 1978, Mao had just died in 1976, and China began to open up. For the first time scholarships to go the West to study were awarded on academic merit. If my mother had spoken out against the Communists to me when I was a child, I would not have been allowed to come.[29]

In fact, it was Chang's mother who instigated the writing process. As Chang observes:

> Inevitably when you write a book you have to be selective editorially, but there was nothing I left out because it was too painful. In fact before my mother told me the story in 1988, I tried to write something about my past, but I couldn't dig deep into my memory. Then my mother told me her story and she struck me as being so honest, she really let herself go, and felt I was drawing strength from her so I was really able to open myself up to face the most painful parts.[30]

As an invaluable personalised testament to the horrors of the Cultural Revolution era, and as a useful historical perspective on Mao's impact upon China in the last century, *Wild Swans* is still unparalleled. Although it offers insights into the brutality and deep corruption that existed within Mao's China, it is most interesting in its depiction of Chinese women's lives through the century. Chang's grandmother's experience, with her 'three inch golden lilies', or bound feet, was exceptionally burdensome to her, and limited, in comparison with her daughter's life as a revolutionary. Yet this was disempowering in its own way, as was Jung's life before leaving China in 1978. The text also functions as a tribute to Chang's female forebears, especially by foregrounding their personal stories against the epic sweep of China's history. *Wild Swans* thus successfully combines family history and personal testimony with other documentary forms (Chang includes a family tree, a chronology, and an extensive list of illustrations).

Hong Ying, *Daughter of the River* (1997)

In some ways, *Daughter of the River* is the most remarkable of these books which deal with twentieth-century Chinese history. Unlike all of the other texts discussed here, Hong Ying's memoir tells the story of a particularly disenfranchised young woman, and therefore adds a unique class dimension to this corpus of writing.[31] This is less a book written from the inside, than a book written from below. Whereas Jung Chang, Adeline Yen Mah, Anhua Gao, Anchee Min, Nien Cheng and Meihong Xu occupied fairly comfortable positions in China's social hierarchy (in the case of Anchee Min as a Chinese film star, Adeline Yen Mah as the daughter of an affluent Shanghai family, and for Nien Cheng as the upper-class wife of an ambassador), Hong Ying was the daughter of peasants, and grew up in a slum on the Yangtze river, in Chongqing, in Sichuan Province. Her perspective is thus of the underside of Chinese society, of a raw existence without food, income, and in unhygienic conditions. Thus the very fact that Hong Ying has been able to write her memoir is in itself remarkable.

Unlike *Wild Swans* or *To the Edge of the Sky*, *Daughter of the River* does not have the epic sweep of a century's history; but only deals with the period of the 1980s. This is partly because of Ying's youthful age (she was born in 1962, at the height of the Cultural Revolution, and only embarks upon her story as she turns eighteen) and partly due to Ying's emphasis upon her own personal story, and that of her immediate family, rather than with China's history in general. Her perspective is likewise limited by her social circumstances. As a member of an uneducated peasant family, Hong Ying simply did not have an intellectualised, or even broad perspective on Mao's machinations and China's political and economic changes, except where they directly infringed upon the circumstances of her immediate community. When she does refer to an incident or moment in China's history, or an action taken by Mao, it is invariably filtered through her community, and is often reported as unsubstantiated hearsay. Her narrative thus deals with the experience of ordinary, poor, Chinese people and the manner in which they were affected by the turbulent years of the Cultural Revolution and its aftermath.

Like most of the other narratives, this is a first-person account, but it is also one which is characterised by an intensity of feeling, and a sparse narrative style. Hong Ying is also a poet, and this is very apparent in her striking prose style, which lends an almost surreal quality to the text. This sparseness is also underscored by the extreme, almost unbelievable poverty that Ying describes:

> The hills in South Bank teem with simple wooden thatched sheds made of asphalt felt and asbestos board. Rickety and darkened by weather, they have something sinister about them. When you enter the dark, misshapen courtyards off twisting little lanes, it is all but impossible to find your way back out; these are home to millions of people engaged in coolie labour. Along the meandering lines of South Bank there are hardly any sewers or garbage-collecting facilities, so the accumulated filth spills out into roadside ditches and runs down the hills. (pp. 3–4)

In Hong Ying's words, the river and the lives it supports take on a quasimagical, if horrific, quality:

> The other side of the river is as different as night from day. The centre of
> the city might as well be in another world, with red flags everywhere you
> look and rousing political songs filling the air … South Bank … is the city's
> garbage dump, an unsalvageable slum; a curtain of mist above the river
> hides this dark corner, this rotting urban appendix, from sight. (p. 5)

Hong Ying lived with her family of five siblings and her parents in an
unheated two-room slum by the river, where they shared a communal
kitchen and yard with several other families. Washing took place in the
river, and sewage was poured into the street. Both of her parents worked
as coolie labourers, on wages of just two *yuan* a day. It was this employment that prevented the family from starving during the great famine
which swept across China in the late 1950s. Ying's mother's life was
especially hard. She became the sole wage earner after Ying's father
was forced to retire on disability benefit, due to failing sight. She was
fired from her job when she offended the head of her residents' committee and lost her work permit. With her job went her ability to contribute to the family income, and the Hong's life deteriorated as a result.
She also suffered from poor health. Ying writes:

> Decades of coolie labour had left Mother with heart problems, anaemia
> that eventually developed into high blood pressure, rheumatism, a dam-
> aged hip, and aches and pains all over. It wasn't until I entered middle
> school that she managed to find different work: stoking a boiler in the
> shipyard. (p. 11)

Ying's own life was equally impoverished. She was born in the midst of
the famine, and grew up rarely having enough to eat: 'Hunger was my
embryonic education. Mother and daughter survived the ordeal, but
only after the spectre of hunger was indelibly stamped in my mind' (p.
41). Peasant hardship became a condition of her childhood existence.
As she grew up, she spent long hours helping out with domestic chores,
in addition to her schoolwork. During this period, Ying had a very problematic relationship with her mother, who often seemed angered by
the young girl. This puzzled Ying, as it hinted at some forgotten crime,
and part of the thrust of the narrative is Ying's attempt to discover what
exactly causes the inexplicable guilt by which she feels constantly bur-
dened. Eventually, Ying persuades her elder sister to tell her the story
of their parents' life, and it is this which forms the central section of the
narrative. At the same time, Ying struggled to continue with her studies, and to prepare for the local college entrance examination, although
this was against her mother's wishes (as well as beyond her parents'
pocket). She is increasingly forced into subterfuge to maintain her learning, including surreptitiously borrowing books from her neighbour,

Auntie Zhang, and eventually embarking upon a sexual relationship with her history tutor. This proved disastrous: Ying became pregnant and was forced to have an abortion, without anaesthetic, and she subsequently failed the college examination. It is this particular predicament which highlights Ying's trying and limited circumstances as a young, poor Chinese woman. Lacking either political connections or financial security, Ying is in an especially precarious position when she discovers her pregnancy, as she observes: '"Pre-marital pregnancy!" I'd learned in school, even as a little girl, that this was the most shameless sin of all, scarier than death itself ... My life would be ruined, and all because of this child' (pp. 252–3).

Finally, towards the end of the narrative, Ying's mother reveals the reason why Ying has always felt unwelcome in the family: she was the illegitimate offspring of an affair Ying's mother had with a young visiting bookkeeper. Ying's mother wanted to have an abortion, but was prevented from doing so by Ying's father, who compassionately insisted that the sins of the parents should not affect the child, and thus, Ying was born, but grew up in the shadow of her mother's guilt and animosity, as well as the resentment of her siblings. She was not only vilified as the 'daughter of a slut' (p. 208), but was also held responsible for the food shortage that the family endured during the famine. Disillusioned, Ying left home, and became an impoverished underground poet. Eventually, she was able to study at the Lu Xun Literature Academy for Writers in Beijing, and this marked Ying's moment of escape from the poverty and uncertainty of her childhood.

Hong Ying's story is thus primarily that of her own adolescence, and her accompanying dawning sexual and emotional awareness, set against the backdrop of China in the 1980s. As such, it provides a uniquely personalised, as well as sensitive and lyrical, account of life in China at the end of the twentieth century. In this sense it is a useful contemporary counterpart to the story of Adeline Yen Mah, which is equally individual, but focuses upon the period up to the 1980s (as well as from a very different class perspective). Ying's story is also closely juxtaposed with that of her mother. The fate of both women was determined by their gender: in each case, a pregnancy outside of wedlock is shown to irrevocably alter the lives of both, in an intolerant China.

Adeline Yen Mah, *Falling Leaves: The True Story of an Unwanted Chinese Daughter* (1997)

Falling Leaves has followed closely in the footsteps of *Wild Swans*. Like Chang's book, Mah's book has sold well: the current figures are three hundred and fifty thousand copies in the UK alone. Adeline Yen Mah was encouraged to write *Falling Leaves* by her friend Jung Chang, the historian Jon Halliday (who also aided Jung Chang), and also by her agent Toby Eady (also Chang's agent, and agent to Hong Ying).[32] Like many of the other writers discussed here, this was no easy feat, as Mah asserts in her author's note:

> This is a true story. Much of it was painful and difficult to write but I felt compelled to do so. I continue to have deep feelings towards many members of my family and harbour no wish to hurt anyone unnecessarily. I have therefore disguised the Christian names of all my living siblings, their spouses and their children. However, my parents' names are real, so are all the events described.

Born 'Jun-ling' in the 1930s in Shanghai, Adeline Yen Mah did not write her memoir until the 1980s, when she was in her fifties. Her narrative is cyclical, starting with a family gathering in Hong Kong in 1988, on the occasion of Mah's father's death, before travelling back in time to the late nineteenth century. Like Jung Chang's story, Mah's is distinctive in its emphasis upon female experience, here predominately that of Adeline herself, but also of her 'grand-aunt', grandmother, aunt, mother and stepmother. Like *Wild Swans* (and perhaps even more so), it therefore offers a detailed account of the shifting social and political circumstances of Chinese women's lives throughout the twentieth century.[33] In fact, the narrative is defined by the presence of a series of strong female influences in Adeline's life, not all of them positive. Adeline's stepmother, Jeanne (called 'Niang' by Adeline), in particular, is a vitriolic and pernicious influence upon Adeline, and in many ways, Jeanne's persecution of her step-daughter defines Adeline's story.

The narrative starts with the issue of foot-binding, a defining (because ultimately debilitating) experience for Chinese women at the start of the twentieth century. Adeline's grand-aunt refused to have her feet bound, and this started her life as a relatively emancipated woman of her time. She learned to horse-ride, was educated, never married, and generally cut an imposing, striking and somewhat unusual figure. Adeline recalls:

> I remember Grand Aunt as a tall, imposing figure, treated with great esteem by every member of our family. Even Ye Ye and Father deferred to her

every wish, which was remarkable in a society where women were dis-
dained. Out of respect, we children were instructed to call her ... 'Gong
Gong', which meant Great Uncle. It was common practice for high-achiev-
ing women within the clan to assume the male equivalent of their female
titles. ... Erect, dignified, her feet unbound, she had a striking presence, in
contrast to the obsequious demeanour befitting women of her time. (p. 8)

In 1924 Adeline's aunt founded her own bank in Shanghai, the Shanghai Women's Bank, which became a highly successful venture. Adeline's
aunt was thus a powerful and influential female role model in the young
girl's life, as something of a pioneer, as Adeline notes: 'It is impossible
to overestimate the scale of her achievement. In a feudal society where
the very idea of a woman being capable of simple everyday decisions,
let alone important business negotiations, was scoffed at, Grand Aunt's
courage was extraordinary' (p. 9). These events occurred long before
Mah's birth, and the narrative goes on to describe Mah's grandmother's
marriage, her birthing of seven children, the life of Mah's aunt Baba,
the marriage of Adeline's parents, and her mother's death during childbirth. Of these events, Mah's grandmother's and mother's lives stand in
stark contrast to the liberated existence enjoyed by Mah's Grand Aunt.
Mah's grandmother, although not much younger than Grand Aunt, had
bound feet, and this affected her ability to lead a normal life. Mah is
careful to emphasise this for the reader:

> At the age of three, Grandmother's feet had been wrapped tightly with a
> long, narrow cloth bandage, forcing the four lateral toes under the soles so
> that only the big toe protruded. The bandage was tightened daily for a
> number of years, squeezing the toes painfully inwards and permanently
> arresting the foot's growth in order to achieve the tiny feet so prized by
> Chinese men. Women were in effect crippled and their inability to walk
> with ease was a symbol both of their subservience and of their family's
> wealth. Grandmother's feet caused her pain throughout her life. Later, she
> braved social ridicule rather than inflict this suffering on her own daugh-
> ter. (p. 11)

Adeline's mother, Miss Ren, also had a troubled life. Although Adeline's
parents were happy, and had four children, Adeline's mother experienced tremendous difficulties in childbirth, and finally died after giving birth to Adeline. In its own way, this event was catastrophic for
Adeline, as Adeline was subsequently thought to carry bad luck by
her family, and was virtually ostracised as a result. Like Hong Ying,
she became an 'unwanted Chinese daughter'. After her father remar-
ried, Adeline's life became a misery. Adeline's stepmother Jeanne had
expensive tastes and a vindictive, spiteful nature. She re-named all of
her step-children (Jun-ling became Adeline) and banished them below-

stairs, blatantly favouring her own children; she belittled her husband's surviving relatives, and established a quasi-dictatorship in her husband's house. But it was Adeline who was singled out for the harshest treatment. Eventually, in 1948, barely a teenager, Adeline was placed as a boarder in a convent named St. Joseph's, in Tianjin, many miles north of her home, where she was forbidden to communicate with the rest of her family. Finally rescued by her aunt, as all residents of Tianjin were fleeing from the Communists, Adeline was taken to Hong Kong to be briefly reunited with her family, before being re-enrolled in a convent in Hong Kong, and then in England. At this point, Adeline ponders her possible fate with trepidation:

> Girls were a cheap commodity in China. Unwanted daughters were peddled as virtual slaves, sometimes by brokers, to unknown families. Once sold, a child's destiny was at the whim of her buyer. She had no papers and no rights. A few lucky ones became legally adopted by their owners. Many more were subjected to beatings and other abuses. Prostitution or even death were the fate of some child slaves. ... I did not know what Niang's intentions were but my future was in her hands. (p. 100)

Adeline eventually transcends her family's treatment, and becomes a successful doctor, married to a Chinese American, with a son, and based in New York City. Her siblings likewise find a semblance of happiness away from Niang and her machinations. Yet Niang continued to influence and harass her step-children, culminating in her manouevres to disinherit them following Adeline's father's death in 1988.

Throughout the narrative, Mah intersperses her story with the events shaping China at the time. In a curious manner, the personal incidents affecting Adeline at particular moments seem to be reflected in the wider political and social changes occurring in China at the same time. When Adeline is sent away to school, the family rupture this engenders is mirrored in the political turmoil of the Communist victory over the Kuomintang, and the end of Japanese occupation. Similarly, at the moment in 1976 when Mao Zedong dies, and Deng Xiaoping begins to reform China, China becomes accessible to Adeline again, not just as a tourist, but members of her family welcome her home as well. Finally, too, it is suggested that Niang's death in 1990 was hastened by the impending return of Hong Kong to Chinese control, symbolising Adeline's release from a lifetime of repressive familial as well as political influence upon her.

Anhua Gao, *To the Edge of the Sky* (2000)

Like Jung Chang, Anhua Gao felt the need to bear testimony to the horrors she both witnessed and endured during her life in China. She has said: 'I wanted the world to know the truth about China. People living outside didn't really understand what happened'. Like Chang, too, Gao also wanted to pay homage to her parents, who were unable to tell their own story: 'Because my parents died a long time ago I could not do my duty and look after them, I was too young. So I have written a book for them' (dustjacket). Although Gao's narrative starts slightly later than Chang's (in 1926), it covers roughly the same period of Chinese history, ending with Gao's escape to the West in 1994. As with *Wild Swans* she also makes use of many illustrations, as well as a map of China.

Gao's perspective on the story of the Cultural Revolution is, like Jung Chang's, that of insider–observer. Gao's parents, both People's Liberation Army officials, were hailed as revolutionary martyrs by Mao, and this label served to protect Anhua and her siblings from the harsh reality of advancing Communism in China for many years. However, both died prematurely (of a combination of poor nutrition and inadequate medical care), leaving Anhua, her brother, and two sisters, orphans at the mercy of disinterested and uncaring relatives, who separated the vulnerable children, thus initiating their induction into life in the new China. From this point onwards, Gao's life proved increasingly difficult. She was zealous both in her academic studies, and her desire to serve Mao. She became a Young Pioneer, then a Red Guard, and studied Mao's teachings so hard that she collapsed with exhaustion. She relates this period of her life in a curiously detached manner, and although she stresses her revolutionary fervour at this point, her narrative misses no opportunity to highlight the hypocrisy and hardship permeating the lives of Chinese people at this time. A notable instance of this is the chapter dealing with the so-called 'Great Leap Forward' in 1958. This was Mao's attempt to accelerate the development of China into a modern industrialised economy to rival the most advanced Western countries. It was also an effort to reverse the stirrings of discontent that had begun in the wake of Mao's last campaign, the so-called 'Anti-Rightist Campaign'. This was a virtual witch hunt, in which 5 per cent of every work unit in China was 'outed' by their peers as rightists, and persecuted. Gao writes:

> After the Anti-rightist campaign, the Chinese people had been silenced. Their enthusiasm for socialist reconstruction waned to almost nothing,

causing consternation in Beijing. In the spring of 1958 Mao decided to launch yet another campaign in an attempt to save his face and to revive interest in Communism. He called it the Great Leap Forward. He wanted to prove to the world how clever he was by building the Chinese economy many times faster than any capitalist country in the West. (p. 64)

The Great Leap Forward consisted of two strategies. The first was to 'eliminate the four pests, flies, bedbugs, mice and sparrows' (p. 65). In a section typical of Gao's narrative style, she dispassionately describes the Chinese people's attempts to implement this policy, despite its ludicrousness. Typically, too, though, she does not miss the chance to offer her own view of this incident, and not without an element of wry irony:

> Of course, you will think, How stupid! What about all the insects that the birds eat? But when Chairman Mao said we should kill the birds, we did it without question. He was always right. We, the people, followed him blindly, as we followed the emperor's instructions in the old days. Mao was our inspiration and our leader. We worshipped him as a god. The Chinese people were not allowed to belong to any religious group, so Mao became the focus of our spiritual needs. He wished it to be so, and it was. (p. 65)

The second strategy of the Great Leap Forward was to expediently increase iron and steel production across China. This involved the mass surrender of implements fashioned from these materials, including vast numbers of cooking items and farming equipment. As a result, the Great Leap Forward precipitated one of the worst famines in China's history. As Gao bitterly observes, 'The "Great Leap Forward" catapulted China back at least twenty years' (p. 67).

Like millions of other Chinese, Anhua Gao was intimidated into silence and acquiescence against her better judgement during the Cultural Revolution, as she watched countless friends, relatives and teachers denounced as counter-revolutionaries, and tortured. Although she relates her growing misgivings and disillusionment with Mao's China, she does not dare to speak critically in the open until much later. At one point, she notes:

> By this time I had lost all interest in taking part in the Cultural Revolution. All the people I loved and respected most were dead or in disgrace – my teachers, uncles, aunties, and friends. None, as far as I knew, had done anything against China, or the Communist Party, or Chairman Mao. (p. 166)

Meanwhile, Gao's troubles continued. She joined the army in an effort to escape deployment to the countryside, only to find herself denounced by her own sister as a bourgeois decadent and expelled. She was then banished to work as an assembly worker in the Nanjing Radio Factory, where she was diagnosed as suffering from Meniere's Disease, a debilitating condition which plagued her for many years.

Like Adeline Yen Mah and Hong Ying, Gao's story is noticeably marked by gender oppression. Her marriage to a young family friend, Zhao Lin, proved disastrous, as he turned out to be a wife-batterer, and she suffers quite extreme emotional and physical abuse at his hands. Shortly after they had a child, Little Yan, Lin died in a freak accident, leaving Anhua a vulnerable penniless widow, and single mother. Then came her harshest test. In 1985 Anhua was arrested and accused of being an 'enemy agent and a foreign-paid spy' (p. 311), dragged away from her home by force and thrown into the *Wawaqiao*, a Communist prison, torture and interrogation centre. Gao was imprisoned for two months, with little idea of what crime she was accused of committing, before being released when the State Security Bureau failed to prove any charges against her. Despite this, Gao left prison to find her life in tatters; she had no job, no income, and a tarnished political record which meant that everyone, from former friends to family, shunned her. It was at this point that Gao decided to rebel, by speaking out against the injustices she had endured in Mao's new China. Gao finally succeeded in exonerating herself, and finding work. The narrative concludes in a manner very reminiscent of Meihong Xu's *Daughter of China*. Anhua resolves to find a way to leave China, and she does this by corresponding, and finally falling in love with, a British man. She married him, and eventually, in 1994, moved to England to begin a new life. The value that she places upon this is that she is able to leave the persecution so endemic in China behind:

> At two p. m. on 15 December 1994, I climbed the steps to board the Air China Boeing 747 bound for the United Kingdom, soon to be my second Motherland. I was flying to a land where there was no State Security Bureau, no 'unseen eyes' ever ready to betray the unwary, a land where I would no longer be frightened of political victimization or of what I might say, or even of what I might think. (p. 398)

If nation states are underwritten by history, then they can also be under*mined* by it. In writing Red China, the women discussed in this chapter, from Eileen Chang to Anhua Gao, are inserting a range of female voices into the cultural discourse revisiting China's twentieth century history. At the same time, although it may be strategically and politically productive to foreground female history, and thus to gain access to previously obscured or suppressed perspectives, it is important that readers recognise the differences between these representations of Chinese women. It remains to be seen whether the mounting popular interest in Asia contributes to the efforts of Asian Americanists and other parties, who are interested in furthering a multicultural agenda, and increasing inter-ethnic and inter-cultural awareness and understanding.

Notes

1   See HarperCollins web site: www.fireandwater.com/Jung Chang

2   Harriet Evans, 'Dangers of Arrogance', *TLS*, 4 July 1997 (no. 4918), p. 29.

3   Other fictional texts also address China's turbulent history, of course, and these include Amy Tan's *The Kitchen God's Wife* (1991), Han Suyin's *Destination Chungking* (1942) and Aimee Liu's *Cloud Mountain* (1997).

4   All of these writers are foreign-born, and thus American or British nativity is not a prerequisite for their qualification as Asian British or Asian American. It has only been possible for many of these writers to tell their stories after they have left the oppressive political climate of China and the accompanying censorship of China's history. Thus, the transmutation of their stories from Chinese to Chinese American or Chinese British becomes a necessary pre-requisite of their existence.

5   'Sour Sweet', *Bookcase*, Summer 1993, p. 7.

6   These, and the following quotations from reviews of *Wild Swans*, are taken from the book jacket.

7   Harriet Evans further suggests that the genre of popular history/memoir writing is not fit for its purpose here, and that we should be wary of turning to memoir writing as a means of explaining the past. See Evans, 'Dangers of Arrogance', p. 29.

8   Jonathan Mirsky, 'Literature of the Wounded', *The New York Review of Books*, 5 March 1992, pp. 6–10.

9   Kalí Tal, *Worlds of Hurt: Reading the Literature of Trauma* (New York: Cambridge University Press, 1996).

10   Literature which deals with the subject of foot-binding in China, a common practice from the Tang dynasty until 1949, is becoming increasingly popular, as the success of Pang-Mei Natasha Chang's novel, *Bound Feet and Western Dress* illustrates. A recent example is Kathryn Harrison's novel, *The Binding Chair*, published in 2000.

11   Amy Ling, *Between Worlds: Women Writers of Chinese Ancestry* (New York: Pergamon, 1991), p. 85.

12   Despite the critical attention accorded to Chang's work, it should be noted, as C. T. Hsia does, that her writing never achieved the success of her contemporaries, the Chinese American writers Han Suyin or Pearl Buck, probably due to the serious subject of Chang's work. See C. T. Hsia, *A History of Modern Chinese Fiction* (Bloomington, IN: Indiana University Press, 1999), p. 389. Chang is, however, enjoying something of a renaissance in popularity, especially since the republication of *The Rice Sprout Song* and *The Rouge of the North* by California University Press in 1998.

13   Jung Chang reviewed *The Rouge of the North* for the dustjacket, upon its republication. She said that 'Eileen Chang beautifully and movingly evokes 20th-century China and the hearts and minds of Chinese women'.

14 Preston Schoyer, 'The Smell of a Hidden World', *Saturday Review*, 21 May 1955.

15 Hsia, *A History of Modern Chinese Fiction*, p. 389.

16 The 'Orient' in this sense is used as a collective noun encompassing Asia, Africa and the Middle East.

17 Eileen Chang was not the only writer to be sponsored by the United States information agency for propaganda purposes during this period. Following the success of her autobiography, *Fifth Chinese Daughter*, in 1953 Jade Snow Wong was sponsored by the US State Department to undertake a tour promoting her experiences of America.

18 However, as Han Suyin has noted, such memoirs are also appearing in China as well. She mentions Dou Houying's memoir, *Stones in the Wall*, and writes: '1978 also sees the advent of a new literature, called "literature of the wounded". The recital of the sufferings and humiliations endured by so many Party and non-Party intellectuals during the Cultural Revolution. Harrowing stories, which, after a while, stale because of a certain sameness' (Han Suyin, *Wind in my Sleeve: China, Autobiography, History* (London: Cape, 1992) p. 32).

19 Paradoxically, just as orientalism survives in various Western media perspectives, so its inverse, occidentalism, was – and continues to be – used by China as a strategy of containment as well.

20 This example clearly underscores the extent to which genre is implicated in orientalism.

21 Texts about geishas have proliferated in the last couple of years, and include Liza Dalby, *Geisha* (London: Vintage, 2000); Lesley Downer, *Geisha* (London: Headline, 2000); and Kyoko Aihara, *Geisha* (London: Carlton Books, 2000).

22 'Five of a Kind', *The Editor*, 5 December 1998, p. 16.

23 Vanessa Thorpe, 'The East is Read: How the Orient Captivated the West', *The Observer*, 16 April 2000, p. 16.

24 *Ibid.*

25 John McLeod, *Beginning Postcolonialism* (Manchester: Manchester University Press, 2000), p. 33.

26 Chang's next project is a book about Mao.

27 Although they will not release the exact figures, Chang's publishers HarperCollins describe *Wild Swans* as 'the biggest-selling non-fiction paperback in recent publishing history'. It is estimated that the UK sales alone amount to two million.

28 HarperCollinsUK web site, www.fireandwater.com

29 *Ibid.*

30 *Ibid.*

31 Hong Ying's reputation as a writer has been very uneven, especially in China. Her fictional stories have been attacked for their salacious content, and some critics have noted that Hong Ying's work panders to Western attitudes, and is tarnished by her descriptions of sexual activities. My thanks to Anhua Gao for pointing this out to me.

32 Adeline Yen Mah was also encouraged by Nien Cheng, whom she acknowledges in *Falling Leaves*.

33 It should be noted, however, that Adeline Yen Mah was born and raised in a rich family in Hong Kong, and this has inevitably influenced her perspective on the history of mainland red China. My thanks to Adeline for reminding me of this.

5

Writing biraciality: five Eurasian/Amerasian women's texts

A recurrent preoccupation in Asian American women's writing through-out the twentieth century, and specifically in texts both by and about Eurasian or Amerasian women, is the question of *visible* racial iden-tity.[1] It is possible to identify a concern with the way that the ethnic subject is marked by her physiognomy in texts about Eurasians from Sui Sin Far's 1911 autobiography to Aimee Liu's 1994 novel, *Face*. These discussions identify a correlation between the body and psychology; between the politics of corporeality and the dynamics of selfhood. This is represented in differing ways, but all of the books discussed here assert the primacy of the body-as-text, and the body as a dominant signifier of racial identity. As character Maibelle Chung paradigmatically tells her brother in Aimee Liu's novel *Face*: 'Aren't you ignoring one fundamental factor? ... Looks! Skin color. Hair. Eyes. Body type. Far as most whites are concerned, Chinese are Chinese – for that matter, any Oriental is Chinese – and blacks are black. No difference where they were born or what language they speak.'[2] The discussion of visible ra-cial identity in these texts is contextually specific in that it is a dynamic of cross-cultural engagement. The move on the part of Eurasian women writers to interrogate the relationship between exterior and interior subjectivity relates to their position as liminal ethnic subjects in the United States. Occasionally this exploration may pertain to their posi-tion in Asian countries as well. For example, in the case of the central character Sylvia Chen in Diana Chang's 1956 novel *The Frontiers of Love*, her position as a woman of mixed ancestry in an Asian country (China) places her as much an outsider there as other Asian Americans have felt themselves to be in the United States.

Read together, the corpus of texts discussed in this chapter func-tion as a record of differing psychological responses to shifting racist environments. As such, they also chart the history of interaction be-tween Eurasians and Anglo Americans throughout the twentieth cen-tury. Thus, for example, for the Eurasian sisters Edith and Winnifred Eaton (Sui Sin Far and Onoto Watanna), their experience as new ethnic subjects in America at the start of the twentieth century was characterised by feelings of exclusion and inferiority in the face of extreme racism, a racism which was supported by pseudo-scientific discourses of racial hierarchies. Racism is highly durable, however, so a delineation of Eurasian women's writing up to the present day sadly continues to demonstrate both the potency of racist phenomena and the psychological effects of racism upon ethnic subjects.

In constructing links between texts written as much as eighty years apart, the intention here is not to homogenise them. As textual responses to appearance-instigated racism they illustrate historical, geographical and cultural divergencies which should not be erased. It is important, for example, to recognise that the particular situation of early twentieth-century Eurasian women, whose experience was often characterised by an acute sense of ambivalence, was partly produced by late nineteenth and early twentieth-century anti-miscegenation discourses, the credibility of which had eroded by the time Eurasian writer Aimee Liu published *Face* in 1994.[3] The commonality between these texts is not based on an assumed transhistoric racial/ethnic similarity or sensibility, but is instead predicated upon a shared encounter with racism and its concomitant psychoactive effects. Furthermore, these textual rejoinders to racism actually serve to highlight an historical shift in the way that 'race' is understood. An historical survey of these texts shows the ways that they are linked to the historical evolution of discourses of race in America from a biological, pseudo-scientific understanding to a far less stable interpretation. This shift may alternatively be tracked through a change in the way 'race' is understood as a classificatory term, to its more prevalent later usage as a non-specific signifier of difference. In particular, this chapter links my discussion of early Eurasian women's textual responses to racism, to an understanding of race in relation to physiognomy, and contends that discourses of the 'science' of physiognomy surface in many of these earlier works, although they continue to have a residual influence in late twentieth-century works too, and suggests why this might be the case.

A brief history of physiognomy

Physiognomy: the form of one's features, expression and body, is also understood as the art of judging character from facial characteristics. Therefore, although physiognomy may refer simply to corporeal form, it is also used (as frequently in this study) specifically in relation to the face. As Thomas F. Gossett has made clear in *Race: The History of an*

Idea in America, there has long existed a science of physiognomy which attempted to link physiognomic characteristics with racial difference. As early as 1610, Giovan Della Ponta published *On the Physiognomy of Man*, an analysis focusing in depth on facial characteristics, which read 'facial features as a kind of graphism or writing which in turn is in need of the systematic decoding that physiognomy claimed to provide'.[4] In 1684, a study was made by one Francois Bernier, on the relationship between the face, the body and racial classifications. Bernier is held to have coined the term 'race', so that from its genesis, 'race' has been identified as a form of categorisation associated with physiognomic features.[5] Indeed, racial classification was, and despite being discredited, to some limited extent, continues to be understood in terms of shared prototypic features.[6] As Gossett goes on to show, theories of physiognomy and scientific racism contributed significantly to the construction of the idea of race, especially in the United States. As ideological scaffolding supporting the building of institutionalised racism like slavery, the science of physiognomy was crucial. For example, the comparative study of crania of African Americans and Caucasian Americans supposedly revealed significant intelligence differences, which in turn functioned to support notions of white racial superiority.[7] Because the idea of race, as Joseph Rothschild notes, 'had no inherent cultural meaning ... predating its use as a device for imposing and enforcing stratification and segmentation', race as a concept has always been *racist*, because of its role in the production of prejudice based on the belief of the superiority of races.[8] This kind of essentialist racism produced a tendency to read cultural differences between groups as absolute and inextricably tied to biology.

Clearly, then, the assumption that the face and other physiognomic features may be read as clues to internal characteristics endorses biologist theories of race, and of racial superiority. The 'supposition ... that conduct can be deduced from physical form' is capable of producing a very invidious racism.[9] As Juliana Schiesari notes, 'a working definition of racism can be found precisely in the attempts by the "science" of physiognomy to attribute common behavioural characteristics to shared physical features'.[10] Because of their recognition that any theory of physiognomic difference works as an ideological apparatus preserving both racial hierarchies and stereotypes, and that racism continues to work in a physiognomic currency, many Eurasian women writers have often investigated and explored the imagined correlation between physiognomy and behaviour in their work. This is partly because there is a history of using such connections in order to derogate Asians in popular cultural media, as Elaine Kim makes clear in her discussion of images of Asians in Anglo fiction and film.[11]

Asian Americans have been subject to essentialist racism since the mid-nineteenth century. Gompers' and Gustadt's 1908 piece, *Meat vs. Rice: American Manhood against Asiatic Coolieism: Which Shall Survive* is an example of one such text. One of the assertions of this article was that the Chinese were 'without nerves and without digestion'.[12] Another early twentieth-century 'explanation' of Chinese 'inferiority' by Henry George stated that the 'Chinaman was capable of learning up to a certain point of adolescence … but unlike the Caucasian he had a limited point of development beyond which it was impossible for him to go'.[13] A later example quoted by Elaine Kim from Wallace Irwin's *The Seed of the Sun* in 1921 notes that Asians are 'ridiculously clad, superstition-ridden, dishonest, crafty, cruel … marginal members of the human race who lack the courage, intelligence, skill, and the will to do anything about the oppressive conditions that surround them'.[14] Unfortunately, as Kim shows, these representations are not specific to the earlier part of the twentieth century: Kim cites examples as recent as 1969, as well as an example from a 1980 Charlie Chan film, where he is described as 'wise, smiling, pudgy … symbol of the sagacity, kindliness, and charm of the Chinese people'.[15] Such racist conclusions about groups of people based on their biology have evolved and produced enduring images and stereotypes of cultural groups. As Schiesani writes: 'at its worst physiognomy … proceeded to a highly suspect classification of humanity based upon the assumed behaviour imputed to derive from bodily types. Anatomical difference thus became the pretext for prejudicial moral judgements.'[16] As Elaine Kim shows, these early representations of Asian Americans which make assumptions about behaviour based on physiognomic characteristics have continued up to the present day. Thus, Asian American women writers have inherited a tradition of representing Asian Americans encumbered by such images. In her important article, 'Ethnic Subject, Ethnic Sign, and the Difficulty of Rehabilitative Representation: Chinatown in Some Works of Chinese American Fiction', Sau-ling Cynthia Wong poses the vexed question: 'when subject and sign have both been altered by the gaze of white society, how is a Chinese American writer to represent his/her own experiences?'[17] Although Sau-ling Wong's discussion relates to representing Chinatown, several aspects of her argument may be usefully transposed onto a discussion of the rehabilitative representation of the female Eurasian subject. Wong's analysis in this piece draws upon semiology to explore the process of representing (and misrepresenting)

Chinatown. She uses William Boelhower's work on ethnic semiosis to suggest that the 'cultural product' of Chinatown (that is, the dominant cultural image of Chinatown) is created by a process of joint semiosis, in which the gaze of the dominator and the dominated (the white and the ethnic subject respectively) engage in a 'process of mutual constitution' to represent Chinatown.[18] Wong notes (and this is where she differs from Boelhower) that this mutual semiosis/gaze 'hardly implies equal partnership', because the gaze of the ethnic subject is economically and discursively less powerful than that of the white subject.[19] Wong's analysis of this process is useful because it firstly acknowledges that for the ethnic subject *self*-representation is not always possible, precisely because the 'gaze of white society dominates', and as she notes 'the "Chinaman" no longer fully owns his experiences'.[20] The question then, is again how exactly to divorce ethnic self-representation from the debilitating images with which it has been saddled? Secondly, because of the potency of the white gaze, Wong states that the ethnic subject is 'now *marked* ... singled out, blemished'.[21] And thirdly, the ramification of the all-powerful and controlling white gaze is that ethnic self-representation becomes highly problematic and fraught with near-insurmountable difficulty: 'the Orientalizing sign may become so pervasive and invasive as to monopolise all expression. When that happens, the subjectivity of the ethnic subject is in danger of being drained from any effort at self representation.'[22] This discussion opened with the suggestion that there is a concern with the relationship between corporeality and selfhood. It is the politics of representation which mediate this relationship. As Wong shows, in the process of joint semiosis, the gaze of the dominated ethnic subject is less potent than that of the dominator. The ethnic subject therefore lacks agency to control self-representation; and as the controlling white gaze marks the ethnic subject as ethnic, 'other', the body becomes the dominant signifier. Thus, being caught in the racialising gaze of another constitutes a crisis of self and self-representation.

Spec(tac)ular acts

Sau-ling Wong goes on to suggest that in the gaze of the white voyeur, 'Chinatown means *spectacle*'.[23] I would suggest that the Eurasian subject himself or herself, too, becomes a spectacle in the way that Wong posits, because she or he too becomes an object attracting the sight of the white cultural voyeur. Likewise, representation itself is a 'spectacular act', which can, as Wong warns, all too easily reinforce the ethnic subject as a spectacle. Indeed, the process of mutual gazing/semiosis proposed by Boelhower and elaborated by Wong may also be called a spectacular act or exchange, as it also functions as an unequal form of representation in which the ethnicising/racialising (Anglo) gaze produces the ethnic subject as a spectacle of 'otherness'.

In the racialising gaze, which fails to acknowledge individual response/nuance, the subjectivity of the individual disappears. The face, the eyes and other physiognomic features visibly signify difference from a culturally normalised ethnic or racial majority; and through the gaze as spectacular act the 'minority' ethnic subject is objectified. Eurasian writers like Sui Sin Far (Edith Maude Eaton), Onoto Watanna (Winnifred Eaton), Han Suyin, Diana Chang, and Aimee Liu depict different ways in which they (in the case of auto/biographical works) or their characters (in fictional examples) could begin to escape this objectification, and thus begin to pave the way for a possible rehabilitative representation of the Eurasian subject.[24]

R. D. Laing has written: 'Self identity ("I" looking at "me") is constituted not only by our looking at ourselves, but also by our looking at others looking at us and our reconstitution of and alteration of these views of others about us'.[25] It is this consciousness of the spectacular act that surfaces repeatedly as an anxiety in Eurasian texts by women, from early autobiographical works up to recent fiction. The spectacular act here becomes a *specular interaction*, as the ethnic subject finds her self-identity produced by, and reflected back to her, by another. For instance, the Eurasian character Sylvia Chen in *The Frontiers of Love* constantly attracts unwanted attention: 'people never ceased to be curious about her'.[26] Sylvia Chen tries to avoid this marking by averting her face from the racialising gaze: 'she averted her face' is a recurrent phrase in the novel. This awareness of the gaze is what W. E. B. Du Bois called 'double consciousness', which is the sense of watching one's self-image being produced by another.[27]

Anti-miscegenation discourses and the Eurasian subject

Although an awareness of the gaze surfaces as a preoccupation in many Asian American texts by women, it is for Eurasian women that the crisis of selfhood is most entangled with corporeal identity.[28] The Eurasian, a mix of Caucasian and Asian, presents a visibly literalised hybridity, as her identity appears to be embodied in her appearance. The body/face again functions as text. This divided external identity produces an even more conflicting sense of selfhood, as Amy Ling writes: 'Coexisting and unresolvable opposites are daily experiences for bicultural people and particularly for Eurasians … By which race shall one be known?'[29] In her study of race, Ruth Frankenberg notes that '"Chineseness", "Blackness", and "Whiteness"' are states of being in theories of racial superiority, so that 'the "half" or "mixed" person … does not belong anywhere'.[30] Like the better-known figure of the 'tragic mulatta', the Eurasian was often depicted in popular (Anglo) cultural fictions as out of place, stranded between two states of being. Elaine Kim notes that 'the dilemma of the Eurasian in Anglo-American literature is unresolvable. He [sic] must either accept life as it is, with its injustices and inequalities, or he must die'.[31] The Eurasian, like the mulatto/a, thus constitutes a threat to essentialist theories of racial superiority precisely because, as Nancy Bentley writes in relation to mulattos in Antebellum fiction: 'the person of mixed black and white parentage stood precisely at the place where nature and culture could come unbound'.[32] And as Frankenberg asserts, any theory of race predicated upon the assumption that racial differences are absolute and tied to biological belonging will be troubled[33] by the miscegenated subject. Nancy Bentley's work on the mulatto identifies a cultural preoccupation with how to classify the American subject who is neither black nor white and the underlying cultural anxiety this causes, which, she argues, is evident in the production of terms to classify the miscegenated subject like 'octoroon' and 'quadroon'.[34] Frankenberg argues that this cultural anxiety is manifested in a discourse against interracial relationships which claims that mixed race children don't – and can't – fit in.[35] It is such cultural anxieties and anti-miscegenation discourses that resulted in the Californian miscegenation laws, pertaining to Negroes, Mulattos and Mongolians, which were active from 1880 until they were finally declared unconstitutional in 1967 by the United States Supreme Court. Anti-miscegenation arguments circulating at the time of the first of these laws bear testimony to a cultural abhorrence and fear of miscegenation. In a letter to Kentaro Keneko in 1892, anthropologist Herbert Spencer claimed: 'if you mix the constitutions of two widely divergent varieties which have severally become adapted to widely divergent modes of life, you get a constitution which is adapted to the mode of life of neither – a constitution which will not work properly, because it is not fitted for any set of conditions whatever'.[36] This quite startling example of social Darwinism, which equates 'race' with 'species', produces an argument which implicitly suggests that miscegenation is also mutation.

Like the case of the mulatto/a, there are many early twentieth-century Anglo cultural fictions written about – against – the Eurasian (comparable in many ways with mid/late nineteenth-century texts like

Mayne Reid's *The Quadroon* or H. L. Hosmer's *Adela the Octoroon*).[37]
These texts also demonstrate the abhorrence of miscegenation seen in
fiction about the mulatto/a, as well as an emphasis on their position as
doubly liminal subjects. Early twentieth-century examples include
Wallace Irwin's *The Seed of the Sun*, where the Eurasian character feels
that 'the dragon's tail of the Orient is fastened to the goat's head of
Europe';[38] Achmed Abdullah's 'A Simple Act of Piety', in whose Eurasian
protagonist's body, we are told, 'the Chinese blood in her veins, shrewd,
patient, scotched the violence of her passion, her American impulse to
clamour loudly for right and justice and fairness';[39] and Rex Beach's
Son of the Gods[40] amongst others. In fiction and autobiography both by
and about Eurasians, there is a corresponding preoccupation with the
identity of the miscegenated subject, which is linked, in different ways,
to corporeality (although it does not result in death). In particular, both
the fiction and the autobiographies of the Eurasian sisters Edith Maude
Eaton (Sui Sin Far) and Winnifred Eaton (Onoto Watanna) betray such
a concern. Both sisters were writing between 1899 and 1925, at the
same time as Anglo writers like Wallace Irwin and Rex Beach, and their
work produces the same preoccupation with miscegenation and its effects that can be seen in their contemporary, Herbert Spencer's 1892
letter. As Amy Ling makes clear in her discussion of the Eaton sisters in
Between Worlds, the autobiographies of both – Winnifred's partly
fictionalised *Me: A Book of Remembrance* (1915) and Edith's essay 'Leaves
from the Mental Portfolio of an Eurasian' (1912) – engage with the
bigotry they both experienced as Eurasians.

Early Eurasian writing: the Eaton sisters

Edith Maude Eaton (1865–1914) and her sister Winnifred (1875–1954)
are widely held to be the first Asian American writers. Their parents (a
Chinese mother and an English father) emigrated to the United States,
and then Canada, in 1874. The family, with a total of sixteen children,
was extremely poor. Despite this, the arts flourished in the household,
and all of the children were encouraged to write. As teenagers, both
sisters began publishing poems and articles in the local newspapers.
Although neither woman looked particularly Asian, both chose to assert Asian identities when embarking upon their literary careers.

By the time that *Me: A Book of Remembrance* was published in 1915,
its author, Winnifred Eaton, had been using the Japanese-sounding pen
name 'Onoto Watanna' for several years.[41] Although she was, like her
sister, actually a Eurasian of Chinese ancestry, Winnifred chose a

Japanese name in order to mask an undesirable identity. *Me* charts Eaton's dissimulations as a Eurasian woman at a particularly difficult moment in Chinese American history, when Sinophobia had reached an all-time high. Winnifred decided to publish under a Japanese pseudonym, a more ethnically-compatible identity in the early twentieth century, partly because her physical appearance prevented her from passing as white. Yet, a publishing identity obscures physical appearance, so Winnifred's disguise must have served other purposes. In fact, she was partly forced to continue an authorial ruse that she had started much earlier, when she had invented a Japanese ancestry for herself for her entry in *Who's Who*. But in contrast to many of her fictional works, *Me* was published anonymously, a textual disguise as effective as her physical passing as Japanese. However, Winnifred filled the text with clues as to her ethnic identity. For example, she explores in detail the desire to 'pass' in *Me*. She describes Nora, her corresponding character, as 'a native of a far distant land'. [42] Yet the lack of ethnic specificity here is a form of identity evasion. Through Nora, Winnifred extensively explores the psychological anguish of being Eurasian, but in a very indirect way. Nora attempts to deflect the racialising gaze of those 'interested' in her or those 'puzzled' by her nationality: 'People stared at me ... but in a different sort of way, as if I interested them or they were puzzled to know my nationality' (p. 166). *Me* also shows an awareness of the spectacular act, as Winnifred notes: 'I would have given anything to look less foreign. My darkness marked and crushed me' (p. 166). It is interesting to note, as Ling does, that *Me* reveals a consciousness of the gendering, as well as the racialising gaze, so that it is clear that Winnifred was conscious of both pressures upon her appearance.

Me's reviewers caught the scent of Winnifred's evasive publishing tactics. As Linda Trinh Moser has pointed out, both the *Chicago Tribune* (21 August 1915) and *The New York Times Book Review* (22 August 1915) guessed that the author was Eurasian. [43] Shortly after, on 10 October, *The New York Times Book Review* declared that Onoto Watanna was *Me*'s author. None of the reviewers detected Winnifred's real identity as Chinese Eurasian, and so we must conclude that her technologies of writerly evasion were at least partly successful.

Edith Maude Eaton was much more open than her sister about her biracial identity. She first used her pseudonym, Sui Sin Far, in 1896. Her pseudonym worked quite the opposite way to Winnifred's: by adopting the name Sui Sin Far, Edith actually declared her ethnic identity far more than her given Anglo name was able to do. [44] Edith used her ethnic identity in order to actively combat and confront racial prejudices. [45]

Edith's autobiography, 'Leaves from the Mental Portfolio of an Eurasian', like *Me*, discusses the connection between physiognomy and racism in detail, but she is especially concerned with Eurasian identity. She uses personal anecdote to describe her growing awareness of Eurasian identity:

> I meet a half Chinese, half white girl. Her face is plastered with a thick white coat of paint and her eyelids and eyebrows are blackened so that the shape of her eyes and the whole expression of her face is changed. She was born in the East, and at the age of eighteen came West … It is not difficult, in a land like California, for a half Chinese, half white girl to pass as one of Spanish or Mexican origin. This the poor child does, though she lives in nervous dread of being discovered.[46]

Edith clearly disapproves of this girl's passing tactics, and rejects technologies of racial disguise as a means of coping with biracial identity in a hostile environment, whereby she would, rather like her sister, 'carry a fan in my hand, wear a pair of scarlet beaded slippers, live in New York, and come of high birth' (p. 189); despite this, she empathises with the psychological feelings that are their motivation. Edith's encounter with her racial double, when she sees another Chinese person for the first time, leads her to 'recoil with a sense of shock' (p. 189). Amy Ling's discussion of 'Leaves' emphasises Edith's double consciousness, whereby racial taunts along physiognomic lines, such as 'yellowface, pig-tail', produce a negative self-image and a tendency to blame miscegenation for all her bodily ills, and as Amy Ling notes 'she attributes her life-long physical frailty to the social burden of being a Eurasian'.[47]

For both sisters, the social environment into which they were born as Eurasians in America presented them with a dilemma to which they reacted in different ways. Whereas Edith chose to stand up to anti-miscegenation feeling and racism, Winnifred chose to avoid it. Winnifred's autobiography, *Me*, is a fully developed narrative of Nora Ascouth's coming-of-age in both north America and Jamaica; 'Leaves' in contrast focuses almost exclusively upon ethnicity, chronicling the suffering Edith endured from the age of four simply for being Eurasian. For both Edith and Winnifred, though, being Eurasian exacted a tremendous psychological and physical cost.

Edith, in particular, was also aware of gendered racism. At one point in her narrative, she describes having to endure degrading assumptions by Anglo men. She is approached by a sailor on leave, who assumes that since she is Chinese, she must be a comfort girl, or prostitute. Yet her accounts of such instances of racial prejudice are not simply a criticism of Anglos: she also points out that racial prejudice works the other way too. Overall, both accounts describe the ferment of racial complexity that emerges in the birth of a multi-ethnic society at the beginning of the twentieth century.

Diana Chang, *The Frontiers of Love* (1956)

Later fiction and autobiography by Eurasians continues to demonstrate debates over the conflicting identity produced by miscegenation, which again is often instigated by the racialising and gendering gaze. In Diana Chang's 1956 novel *The Frontiers of Love*, we are told that the female Eurasian protagonist, Sylvia Chen, 'was both as American as her own mother, and as Chinese as her father. She could not deny her own ambivalence' (p. 19). Like Edith Maude Eaton, Diana Chang is quite open about her own Eurasian identity, as her dustjacket for the University of Washington Press edition of *The Frontiers of Love* shows: her photograph clearly advertises the fact, and the accompanying biography includes details of her mixed ancestry, as well as of her childhood spent in Shanghai and Beijing.[48] Eurasian identity, and the crisis of self that may result, is actually the subject of very little of Chang's work, but is a prevalent theme in her first and most successful novel, *The Frontiers of Love*.[49] It was published in 1956 to critical acclaim, with many contemporary reviews approving of Chang's description of the 'tragic' Eurasian figure of Sylvia Chen. Samantha Ramu Rau, for example, in *The New York Review of Books*, described Chen as 'a tragically ineffectual figure', and observed that Chang offers 'a convincing and interior view of the Eurasian world, so to speak, from the inside looking out and embracing both the political and emotional dilemmas of that twilit no-man's land'.[50] Yet Chang does not simply subscribe to and reproduce the stereotype of the miscegenated subject, but extensively explores the social and historical contingencies of Eurasian identity. Written in 1956, but set in 1945, the context of *The Frontiers of Love* is the Second World War, a time of particular intensity and instability for racialised subjects in Euro-American cultural milieu. The novel also asserts its geopolitical specificity as a reason for the confusion of identity experienced by its Eurasian characters: 'People were true to nothing in Shanghai; they belonged only to the surface values of both East and West and leaned heavily toward the exoticism of the West. If one did not hold carefully to one's sense of self, one might wake up one morning looking for one's face, so easily lost' (p. 87). Chang's novel both extensively thematises and literalises the problematics of biracial identity. Its setting is biracial, as Shanghai is described explicitly as a Eurasian city (Shanghai was, and still is, a particularly Westernised city enclave in China). In fact, Chang has elsewhere insisted upon this geographical specificity in the novel, asserting that 'while it is about identity, it is not about ethnicity here', referring to the United States. In *The Frontiers of Love* Diana Chang interrogates anti-miscegenation ideas as they are articulated by the novel's several Eurasian characters, in the context of Western idea(l)s of beauty. Each of the Eurasian characters privately struggle with their own confusing racial identity, as this example shows:

> Poor Paul, Sylvia thought, and that was more accurate. My brother, she thought, seeing him as he had been at six, angelic and so beautiful (part porcelain and part flame) he had been painful to look at. At their best, half-breeds who had Chinese blood in them had fine features, thin skins and eyes that caught the light in a blaze. So much tragedy seemed to lie beneath Paul's physical perfection, his puzzling Chinese-Western looks, which seemed like an optical illusion. (p. 144)

Here, we see one of the central female characters pondering the burden of biracial appearance. Sylvia's subscription to a stereotypical image of the 'tragic' Eurasian in this passage is subtly undermined by Chang. The viewpoint is that of an observer, Sylvia, and it is the sense of the gaze in this section that highlights Sylvia's internalisation of acute double consciousness. The pain here is not Paul's, but crucially it is Sylvia's, as she identifies her brother's looks with her own sense of inferiority. Sylvia's ambivalence about her identity is often reflected, and thus accentuated, by others' reaction to her when in public, as the following passage shows:

> she averted her face as she passed them ... (people never ceased to be curious about her), a slight girl of twenty, tanned to an even brown by the Shanghai sun. Her eyes were startlingly large, dilated, as her father said ... but her hair was not all black; she walked with all the freedom and impatience of a foreigner, yet in her there was something inescapably oriental. (p. 5)

Sylvia's sense of contradictory identity is mirrored by her observer's *assumed* reaction to her physiognomy. Once more the viewpoint in this passage is Sylvia's own, and therefore we identify the reactions of the passer-by to be projected by Sylvia herself.

As Shirley Geok-lin Lim has made clear, Chang's preoccupation with the question of biracial identity is not the only concern of *The Frontiers of Love*, as the novel's title itself suggests. She observes: 'In Chang's novels, the question of stereotypes, ethnicity, duality, and the forging of a new identity fall under a larger existentialist theme'.[51] As much as it is about these issues, it is also a love story, as well as an elegant and extensive meditation upon the exilic and diasporic existence of its many characters.

Han Suyin, *The Crippled Tree* (1965)

Han Suyin is one of the most prolific of Asian American women writers. During a literary career which has spanned some four decades, she has written over seven novels, a multi-volume autobiography, and several nonfiction works, including biographies of Chiang Kai-shek and Mao Tse-tung. Born 'Rosalie Chou' in 1917, a Eurasian of Belgian and Chinese ancestry, Han Suyin has had a varied career, as the wife of a Kuomintang army officer, doctor and finally as a writer. She has lived in China, Hong Kong, England and the United States. Like the Eaton sisters, she adopted a pseudonym in order to write. This was not in order to mask her biraciality, though, but instead was used by Han to distance her writing persona from her identity as the wife of a diplomat, as she explains in the foreword to her first novel:

> But the authorship of the book could not, at the time, be publicly acknowledged, and for an odd reason. I had become, if only temporarily, through my husband, a member of my country's diplomatic corps. Ladies of the diplomatic corps do not write books. The set in which I lived considered writing an unwomanly occupation, destructive of one's moral character, like acting.[52]

Having published her first novel, *Destination Chungking*, under the pseudonym of Han Suyin in 1942, she has continued to use this pen name ever since. However, in her autobiographical works she reverts to referring to herself by her natal name, Rosalie Chou.

The Crippled Tree is the first volume of Han's autobiography, although it does not adhere to the traditional conventions of autobiographical writing, but mixes generic modes. The subtitle of the text is 'China, Biography, History, Autobiography'. Rosalie's story is told against the backdrop of China's early twentieth-century history, and Han intersperses the narrative with poems, excerpts from her father's and uncle's autobiographies, and letters as well. In this sense, *The Crippled Tree* is typical of Han's writing, which tends to adopt a wide purview. Han blends the various narrative perspectives in the text with acuity, and relates her own in the third person. Her story is that of the experience of growing up as a Eurasian, and Han Suyin/Rosalie Chou unusually finds this both positive and negative, as Amy Ling observes: 'Han Suyin turns handicaps into advantages; the legacy of her bicultural, biracial

heritage, she proudly asserts, has prepared her for the world's incoher-
ence and inconsistencies'.[53] An instance of this is her use of the metaphor of the crippled tree to describe her Eurasian identity. Han refuses
to let this overcome her and asserts that 'I would not be a crippled tree,
marring the landscape with its own malady'.[54] She also returns to this
metaphor near the end of the text, stating that 'although the tree was
crippled, it has gone on living, and who knows but that its fruit shall be
sweeter and better than that of any other?' (p. 317). Despite these
positive assertions, though, Han Suyin does document several encounters with racial prejudice, significantly including her parents. Early in
her life, she recalls hearing herself described as 'A mixed blood,
Marguerite's offspring', and wryly observes that 'the way they said it, I
must have sounded like excreta' (p. 203). In *The Crippled Tree*, it is her
Caucasian mother, rather than an anonymous passer-by, who forces
Rosalie to confront the racialising gaze: 'Look at yourself! You a Chinese. You will never be Chinese, and let me tell you why: the Chinese
will not have you! Never, never! They won't accept you. They will call
you "yang kweitse" devil from over the ocean, as they call me. They
will call you half-caste and mixed-blood, for that is what you are' (p.416).
Like *The Frontiers of Love*, the racialising gaze in this instance is linked
to context, as Rosalie and her mother are both outsiders in China, due
to their Caucasian blood. Rosalie's mother suggests that in this Chinese
context, it is Rosalie's *non*-Chineseness, rather than her Chineseness,
that is significant. Repeatedly in Eurasian writing, the failure to signify
as either wholly Caucasian or Asian is presented in negative terms, as
the Eurasian defines herself as a non-member of either racial group,
rather than a member of both.[55] Sylvia Chen notes that she looks 'not
even Aryan, but just non-Chinese'.[56] Physiognomy is repeatedly held
responsible for a fractured sense of identity. Blood is to blame, as Edith
Eaton writes: 'the white blood in our veins fights valiantly for the Chinese
half of us'.[57]

Another way in which anti-miscegenation discourses surface in
many of these early and mid twentieth-century texts is through images
of mutation, homelessness and tragedy. Like the mulatto/a, the Eurasian is depicted as a tragic figure who belongs nowhere, as in this
example from Winnifred Eaton/Onoto Watanna's novel *His Royal Nibs*:
'Tragic faces of half-breeds, pawns of an undesired fate. Something of
wildness, something of sadness, something of intense longing and wist-
fulness looked from the strange eyes of the breeds'.[58] In this quotation,
the face and eyes again signal otherness, a tragic and sad otherness. It
is the language of mutation that surfaces in *The Frontiers of Love* as we

are told that Sylvia Chen's father 'could hardly bear to pronounce the word "Eurasian"; it was as though his seed had produced mavericks, a mutation'.[59] In Han Suyin's *The Crippled Tree*, too, Rosalie's father, like Sylvia's father, regrets producing Eurasian children: 'My children would belong nowhere. Always there would be this double load for them, no place they could call their own land, their true home. No house for them in the world. Eurasians, despised by everyone.'[60] Thus, as in Anglo portrayals, in these Asian American women's texts, from the early autobiographies of the Eatons to Chang's 1956 novel, we see that the Eurasian is represented as visibly embodying the racial split that reproduces a fractured sense of identity, and this works through the racialising gaze. This bodily split, and its relationship with the gaze, is symbolised much later in Aimee Liu's *Face*, by character Maibelle Chung's self portrait, which is called 'Oriental I', a 'wall-sized mosaic of one hundred forty-four separate photographs of disconnected body parts'.[61] This self portrait expresses the bodily fragmentation all these women experience in the face of the racialising and gendering gaze. As Patricia Waugh observes: 'As a consequence of their social alienation, women experience their body as parts, "objects", rather than integrated wholes'.[62] This is even more the case for the Eurasian subject, who feels herself to be alienated both due to her gender and racial identity.

There is a difference between Anglo and Asian American portrayals of the Eurasian's situation, however. Anglo portrayals, as Kim notes, offer no possibility for coming to terms with one's mixed racial ancestry: 'most of the stories about Eurasians end with the death of the protagonist. The only real victory possible ... is mistaken identity'.[63] This is in marked contrast to Asian American depictions, where even if the option of choosing to pass for one racial identity solely is available, it is rejected: both of the Eaton sisters chose to swap between identities as Asian and Caucasian, thus manipulating their position for their own gain. So for the Eatons, self-representation *was* possible, although it remained linked to feelings of inferiority. In Han Suyin's *The Crippled Tree*, Rosalie finds a way to come to terms with her identity by accepting the inevitability of self division:

> In Rosalie a fragmentation of the total self occurred ... Others born like her of two worlds, who chose not to accept this splitting, fragmentation of monolithic identity into several selves, found themselves later unable to face the contradictions latent in their own beings ... In Rosalie the necessity of knowing mutually contradictory truths without assuming any one of them to be the whole truth, became in childhood the only way to live on, to live and to remain substantial. (p. 369)

It seems, therefore, that one form of rehabilitative representation of the Eurasian subject's predicament is to posit a way of coping with the contradictions of biracial identity: which for both the Eatons and Rosalie Chou/Han Suyin is an acceptance of those contradictions. It is not surprising that it is not Anglo representations of Eurasians, where there is a vested interest in preserving racial hierarchies and classifications, where we find such rehabilitative writing, nor that it should be the project of Eurasian women themselves, to rescue Eurasian subjectivity from association with anti-miscegenation arguments.

In texts like *The Crippled Tree* and *The Frontiers of Love*, the Eurasian's awareness of the inevitability of self-division replaces her desire for racial wholeness and her yearning for an unfragmented selfhood, which is denied to her with each engagement with the racialising/gendering gaze. Rosalind Coward notes that: 'looking has become a crucial aspect of sexual relations, not because of any natural impulse, but because it is one of the ways in which domination and subordination are expressed'.[64] Looking is an aspect of racial, as well as sexual, relations. Frequently, Eurasian women are seen in these texts trying to evade the gaze, precisely because it signals subordination within a racial and gender hierarchy, by turning away as Sylvia Chen does: 'she averted her face'. Yet it is not just the gaze of the voyeur that must be avoided, it is also the reflection of one's body image in a mirror, the act of specularisation. The inability to control self-image is often presented through the use of the mirror-as-trope in these texts. As Lydia Minatoya describes it 'sometimes I catch sight of my reflection in a store window … and I am shocked to see that I am oriental'.[65] This woman's encounter with her self-image here constitutes as much of a shock to her as it did to Edith Eaton when she saw another Chinese person for the first time. Negative external identity is reimposed each time, as *Face* character Maibelle Chung notes, 'I see myself'.[66]

Gendered responses and the technologies of race

For Eurasian women in these texts, the double consciousness of the racialising gaze is rendered further threatening by the double bind of the awareness of gender as well as racial differences. For these women are not only caught in the racialising gaze, they are also caught in the gendering gaze. As Teresa de Lauretis writes: 'concurrent representation of the female body as the *locus* of sexuality, site of visual pleasure, or lure of the gaze is so pervasive in our culture … it necessarily constitutes a starting point for any understanding of … the construction of social subjects, its presence in all forms of subjectivity.'[67] The recognition of the hegemony of the gaze in our culture owes much to Laura Mulvey's now seminal essay, 'Visual Pleasure and Narrative Cinema'. Sau-ling Wong's piece, 'Ethnic Subject, Ethnic Sign', alluded to at length earlier in this chapter, draws mainly upon William Boelhower's thesis on ethnic semiosis for its theoretical substructure. But it is in the area of film criticism, pioneered by Mulvey in 'Visual Pleasure', where we find the confluence of feminist theories of the fetishisation of female sexuality and the semiotics of representation. It is useful to reiterate two assertions of Mulvey's essay here. Like Wong, she stresses the power of the gaze, but also the compulsiveness: 'curiosity and the wish to look intermingle with a fascination with likeness and recognition: the human face, the human body, the relationship between the human form and its surroundings'.[68] The compulsion to look reinforces the hegemony of the gaze. But it is women who are objects of this gaze: 'women are simultaneously looked at and displayed, with their appearance coded, for strong visual and erotic impact so that they can be said to connote *to-be-looked-at-ness*'.[69] Thus, the ethnic subject finds herself prey to objectification as both an ethnic and female spectacle, drawing the gaze of the white/male spectator. This process of objectification can be seen to produce the pressure to conform to dominant definitions of beauty. Many early Eurasian women's texts repeatedly articulate both a yearning for and a recognition of the failure to achieve those standards. Elsewhere, for other women, it is their eyes in particular which are the orientalising sign. Sylvia Chen in *The Frontiers of Love* is recognised as part-Chinese precisely because 'her eyes were startlingly large, dilated' (p. 5).

In the earlier texts discussed in this chapter, tactics of disguise are often employed as a means of escaping the racialising gaze, notably through 'passing' by dressing in particular ways. Winnifred Eaton/Onoto Watanna and Edith Eaton/Sui Sin Far also used textual strategies to mask their identities, by adopting pseudonyms. In notable contrast, texts written in the late twentieth century depict women who find themselves marked as outsiders by their physiognomy resorting to a sliding scale of cosmetic technologies in order to align their appearance with the contextual norm.[70] This move illustrates a shift in the way that race is understood, as well as charting the development of cosmetic technologies. Earlier in this chapter it was argued that race as a term has changed in meaning and this is demonstrated through a reading of these Eurasian women's texts, where 'race' is seen to be an idea, like 'gender', in flux. In her study, *Consumer Culture*, Celia Lury describes this shift: '*from* a racism tied to a biological understanding of race in which identity is fixed or naturalised *to* a racism in which race is a cultural category in which racial identity is represented as a matter of style, and is the subject of choice.'[71] The claim that racial difference may be seen as a question of aesthetics, rather than a political reality is a contentious one; but it may constitute one attempt at rehabilitative representation. If racial identity can be seen as something to choose to 'wear' – or not – then this would signal a move from objectified subject devoid of agency to a position whereby self-representation was possible.[72] Lury cites Susan Willis's argument that this move *is* possible, and furthermore can be seen in the well documented case of Michael Jackson's self-representation through physical transformation.[73] This constitutes a technology of race. In *Technologies of Gender: Essays on Theory, Film, and Fiction*, Teresa de Lauretis notes that 'gender ... both as representation and as self-representation is the product of various technologies ... institutional discourses, epistemologies, and critical practices'.[74] The move from regarding gender, like race as a biological category to regarding it as a culturally constructed entity, subject to change, is echoed by de Lauretis. Certainly, this possibility is explored in one of the texts of interest here. In *Face*, the central character Maibelle Chung bumps into one of the 'Yellow Butterflies', a woman whose Asian features she had admired as a child, and finds that she has tried to erase her orientalising features: 'Much later, between years of college, I ran into one of the Yellow Butterflies selling panty hose at Bloomingdale's. She'd had her eyes done, had the lids lifted, folded, and cut until the almond shape was gone and with it her exotic, imperious beauty. Now she looked innocent. Cute. She could pass for American.'[75] This woman's attempts to erase the orientalising sign of her physiognomy is the result of the double consciousness of the spectacular act defining her from the outside. For this woman, self-image seems to reside close to the surface; the pressure to attain standards of occidental attractiveness engenders an acute awareness of the *look* as well as her *looks*. Late twentieth-century technologies enable her to change her appearance in ways not open to women in the earlier texts discussed here, where women's ultimate defence was evasion. Yet, it remains that cosmetic technologies may be only provisionally welcomed as a means of escaping the racialising gaze, because the gendering gaze is still there, and the culture of othering through looking also remains undisturbed, just deflected. In fact, diminishing encounters with the racialising gaze only reinforces the hegemony of the gendering gaze; as is seen in the example quoted above, this woman exchanges her racialising appearance for one which conforms to American stereotypes of Anglo 'girl-next-door' attractiveness. Ultimately, Liu's representation of the spectacular act in *Face* is just as debilitating for the women who encounter it, as for the Eaton sisters almost ninety years earlier.

Aimee Liu, *Face* (1994)

A contemporary text, which has been very successful, Aimee Liu's 1994 novel *Face* tracks its female subject's struggle to come to terms with an incident of abuse, which is linked to her physical identity as Eurasian. *Face* tells the story of character Maibelle Chung's search for her identity in New York's Chinatown, where she grew up, and where she finally recollects that she was raped as a child. Maibelle is the daughter of a Chinese photojournalist and his wife. She was raised in New York's Chinatown, but left with her family during her teenage years. As an adult, Maibelle is haunted by an inexplicable compulsion to return to Chinatown, where she is sure that she can uncover the reasons for her ongoing nightmares that hint at a suppressed traumatic past. Maibelle Chung's quest for identity is mapped by her struggle to remember and confront the incident of rape that she has erased from her memory.

It is in *Face* that the violence and violation of the racialising, as well as gendering, gaze is explored in most detail. Maibelle Chung's quest for identity is mapped through her relationship with the racialising gaze and the spectacular act. As a Eurasian, she is both inside and outside of Chinatown physiognomically, and her geographical exist- ence mirrors this; she moves out of Chinatown, but returns repeatedly as a tourist, which renders her an outsider.

The novel opens with a discussion of Maibelle's experience grow- ing up in Chinatown psychologically as an insider, whilst marked as a foreigner by her appearance. Although Chinatown was familiar to her, shown by her olfactory recognition, she knew the smell 'as well as my name' (p. 1), her physiognomy places her as an non-member: 'I see myself in these memories as a tall, pale, redheaded girl ... too-wide eyes the color of jade and only a vague oriental cast. Against the rest of the Mott Street crowd I stand out like a vivid flaw in a bolt of jet-black silk' (p. 1). Maibelle's relationship with the Chinatown that used to be her home continues to be characterised by ambivalence when she leaves Chinatown as a child, but she nevertheless retains a psychological con- nection with it, partly due to her father, who is Chinese, but also be- cause something repeatedly draws her back. She initially returns to undertake a photographic assignment for a friend, and it is these visits that reawaken her contradictory feelings towards the place where she grew up. She returns in the role of an outsider as a tourist, when she photographs her surroundings: 'It's all different, I tell myself. That souvenir sign "Tourist Welcome", means you now' (p. 133). She engages in a spectacular act herself through the lens of her camera when she starts photographing her surroundings, but finds herself accidentally embroiled in a demonstration against the kind of racial and cultural voyeurism in which she is involved. Maibelle significantly feels *herself* being watched: 'I can't shake the feeling that I'm being watched' and 'I sense the concealed faces watching' (p. 133), as if she is identifying with the angry sentiments of the Chinese she herself has returned to photograph. She simultaneously feels herself to be both a spectacle and a spectator in Chinatown. Paradoxically, she raises her camera – the instrument of spectatorship – as a defence against appearing as a spectacle herself, by masking her face: 'I hold my circle of glass to my face as if it could protect me' (p. 138). Maibelle's voyeurism of the Chinatown spectacle means that she herself adopts a racialising gaze when watching other Chinese: 'Suddenly one of the protesters, a man with a ponytail, spins around barking like a seal. The roundness of his face, like a plate, registers. I release the shutter' (p. 139). It is the man's physiognomy, the *roundness of his face*, that triggers Maibelle's spectatorship at this moment. The man reacts to Maibelle as a foreigner/spectator, not recognising her as part-Chinese and asks her 'Come to the Chinatown zoo, lady?' (p. 139). Moments later, Maibelle finds herself taunted by a group of young boys who again fail to see her as part-Chinese, calling her 'Lou fan', which means 'barbarian/outsider' (p. 139). Maibelle again defends herself against the gaping boys by using her camera as a weapon (symbolised by the double meaning of the word shoot), so that she turns from spectacle to spectator: 'I turn quickly, raising the Leica, shoot them once, twice, three times dead on, and start running' (p. 140). It is incidents like this, where Maibelle finds herself treated as a foreigner, that cause her to note: 'Living in Chinatown, things happened that made me feel like an outcast' (p. 140).

Despite her paradoxical attempts to sever links with Chinatown by photographing it, in order to move from spectacle to spectator, Maibelle's preoccupation with Chinatown continues. As the narrative progresses, she starts to remember the childhood she suppressed and it emerges that her confusion over her identity and inability to relinquish Chinatown as a psychological influence upon her result from her suppression of a rape in Chinatown one night when she returned as a fourteen year old to take photographs. The rape is a pivotal moment in Maibelle's relationship with the racialising gaze and her oscillation between the position of spectator and spectacle. Maibelle, aged fourteen, is distanced from Chinatown both geographically and culturally now she has moved upstate, and has returned as a tourist to 'shoot the storefronts. The ginseng and strangled ducks. The dancing chicken' (p. 303), all the spectacles to which tourists are attracted when visiting Chinatown. Psychologically, she begins to feel a part of her surroundings once more: 'Chinatown wrapped around me as if I'd never left' (p. 303). Maibelle's sense of belonging is so strong at this point that she even begins to assimilate her appearance into her environment: 'Even my own reflection – taller, paler, and more out of place than ever – seemed part of the package luring me back, no longer cause to run away' (p. 303). Maibelle's activities as a tourist are separated from her feeling of belonging, and, armed with this new sense of security, she begins to photograph a group of boys, who obligingly pose for her. Their response is then to turn her act of violation back on her by taking her to a deserted building nearby and gang-raping her. One act of colonisation is reciprocated by another (although not equal); it is an act of gender, as well as racial violence. The whole ordeal is described in a highly racially- and colour-charged way, which repeatedly plays along 'colorist' lines.[76] For example, Maibelle's recognition of the danger her attackers represent is described using colorist coding: 'So much black. Hair, eyes, clothing, sunglasses' (p. 306). Here, for Maibelle, the black hair and eyes that she lacks, and which mark her attackers as Chinese in the dim light, function textually as a trope for threat and evil intent. Later, during their rape, her assailants taunt her in colorist terms, calling her '"Bai xiangku". White witch' (p. 307). It is significant that during the rape itself, Maibelle doesn't look at her aggressors, she 'felt rather than saw them closing in' (p. 306). She thus refuses to face her attackers and to engage in the exchange of recognition that is part of the spectacular act. After the rape, though, Maibelle's defiance is to gaze at her attackers, literally facing them down, without looking away: 'I stared into the flame the fat one kept waving at me. I didn't blink. Again and again, until the muscles around my eyes burned with the effort of keeping them wide' (p. 308). Maibelle's defiance partly works by staring with the wide-eyed look that she knows occidentalises her in the eyes of her all-Chinese rapists. The recognition that her eyes are an occidentalising sign for her attackers allows her to use their racialising gaze as a defence, as she later says: 'I retreated back into my crazy eyes' (p. 308). Maibelle's punishment and rejection as non-Chinese, a 'white witch', by the Chinatown boys here is linked with gender violence too. The episode works through both racial and gender tensions, and both colorist cod-ing and the racialising gaze mark the distance between Maibelle and her attackers. The incident is only later linked to Maibelle through her appearance as only part-Chinese, because 'the girl had red hair, was a teenager. Rumor was, she came from outside' (p. 329).

Maibelle's attempts to recover her suppressed memories of this rape years later involve her in utilising another means of remembering the past, taking photographs. During her repeated returns to Chinatown in search of her past, Maibelle photographs her surroundings in an attempt to recapture her past experiences. Her photography repeat-edly functions in the novel as the means by which she is able to control her surroundings and experiences, but, crucially, when she returns to Chinatown, she loses this control.

The narrative of *Face* opens at a point when the central female character is undergoing the psychological anguish of a traumatic past which she has yet to exorcise. Maibelle's memories slowly return, as she herself returns to the scene of the traumatic event. Her journey into her memory tracks her concurrent research into her father's own story, as a photojournalist in China. Crucially, the two stories are linked through the use of photography as a means of recording the past; as Maibelle's father tells her, 'the best photographs tell stories better than words' (p. 286). Maibelle's father's own story is also submerged, and only emerges simultaneously with Maibelle's discovery of the truth of her own trauma. It eventually transpires that Maibelle's father witnessed a bombing in Shanghai in 1935, in which his own father was killed, an event he photographed for *Life* magazine. He tells her this story in the hope that it will help her to come to terms with her own past: 'Only when the question of identity is settled can we do justice to other concerns', he tells her (p. 292). Like her father, Maibelle had also recorded her own trauma the night of her rape, photographing her attackers before they raped her. But, like her father's photographs, those pictures were never developed and so photography as a source of memory is shown to fail in the text. Maibelle must let her body remember what the photographs did not record.

Maibelle's memories of abuse are linked to her parents' own sto-ries of suffering. She struggles against a shroud of familial silence about the past in order to recover her own story. The abuse she experienced is linked to her identity as Eurasian, and the cathartic process of re-membering, tracks her reconciliation with her biracial ethnic identity. The narrative works retrospectively, with the protagonist travelling back through her past in order to forge a new future. Structurally, the narrative patterns the fragmented return of submerged memories. The novel is also episodic in structure, oscillating between past and present, and thus memory also determines the form of the text.

Rehabilitative representations?

But is it possible to escape the gaze? Avenues of release are only tentatively journeyed in these texts. Maibelle Chung, for one, finds relief from her crisis of identity by turning her gaze outward. She returns to the scene of her rape and photographs it. Once more, the camera provides defence for her and allows her to become the spectator rather than the spectacle: 'the camera offers a removed chamber where I can rest and wait for the glare to subside. The frame controls what I see, lens and shutter give me something to do with my hands' (p. 338). Maibelle's photography of the scene of her rape allows her to (re)colonise the episode and it is this process that provides a release. Symbolically, when Maibelle catches the fire escape in the lens of her camera, she sees her escape route, the escape route that she failed to notice on the night of her rape, and this signals her escape from the racialising/ gendering gaze. *Face* closes with Maibelle's encounter with her racial double:

> The child's eyes are elongated, beautifully carved with the same perfectly smooth, flat lids that I used to admire in the Yellow Butterflies. But that's where the resemblance ends. As I lean close I see this child's eyes are not black or even dark brown. They are flecked with color, radiating like a wheel – slivers of grey, amber, green, but deep in the center as unearthly and hypnotic as a summer pool, they are pure blue. (p. 341)

Because Maibelle's gaze has finally turned outward, she is able to photograph the child: 'I begin to record what I see' (p. 341).

Notes

1 'Eurasian' refers to people of mixed European and Asian ancestry; 'Amerasian' usually designates people of mixed *American* and Asian ancestry. The term 'Amerasian' has also been used to refer to biracial children born of American servicemen during the Vietnam war.

2 Aimee Liu, *Face* (London: Headline Review Press, 1994), p. 55. All further page references are to this edition and are given in parentheses.

3 However, although certainly for white Americans, the credibility of anti-miscegenation thinking of old has eroded, there are still vocal groups who adamantly oppose inter-racial unions. It is also the case, that for some Asian Americans, the 'marrying out' of Asian women is seen as a betrayal of Asians, a move that will gradually thin out the Asian American population. My thanks

to Ruth Hsu for pointing this out to me.

4   Juliana Schiesari, 'The Face of Domestication: Physiognomy, Gender Politics, and Humanism's Others', in Margo Hendricks and Patricia Parker (eds), *Women, 'Race', and Writing in the Early Modern Period* (London: Routledge, 1994), p. 57.

5   Maggie Humm, *The Dictionary of Feminist Theory* (Hemel Hempstead: Harvester Wheatsheaf, 1989), p. 182.

6   Joseph Rothschild, *Ethnopolitics: A Conceptual Framework* (New York: Columbia University Press, 1981), p. 87.

7   See Gossett's discussion of nineteenth-century anthropology in *Race: The History of an Idea in America* (Dallas, TX: Southern Methodist University Press, 1975), especially pp. 73–4.

8   Rothschild, *Ethnopolitics*, p. 87.

9   Schiesari, 'The Face of Domestication', p. 60.

10 *Ibid.*, p. 57.

11 See Elaine Kim, *Asian American Literature: An Introduction to the Writings and their Social Context* (Philadelphia, PA: Temple University Press, 1982), especially chapter 1.

12 Gossett, *Race*, p. 291. These examples are taken from Kim's work.

13 *Ibid.*, p. 290.

14 Kim, *Asian American Literature*, p. 6.

15 *Ibid.*, p. 18.

16 Schiesari, 'The Face of Domestication', p. 57.

17 Sau-ling Wong, 'Ethnic Subject, Ethnic Sign, and the Difficulty of Rehabilitative Representation: Chinatown in Some Works of Chinese American Fiction', *The Yearbook of English Studies*, 24 (1994) pp. 251–62; p. 251.

18 *Ibid.*

19 *Ibid.*, p. 252.

20 *Ibid.*

21 *Ibid.*

22 *Ibid.*

23 *Ibid.*, p. 253.

24 Four of the five texts discussed in this chapter have autobiographical emphases, which in itself may attest to the psychological pressures of biraciality felt by each author.

25 H. Phillipson Laing and A. R. Lee, *Interpersonal Perception* (London: Tavistock, 1966), pp. 5–6; quoted in Amy Ling, *Between Worlds: Women Writers of Chinese Ancestry* (New York: Pergamon, 1990), p. 34.

26 Diana Chang, *The Frontiers of Love* (Seattle, WA: University of Washington Press, 1994), p. 5. All further page references are to this edition and are cited in parentheses.

27 See Amy Ling's interesting discussion of the relation between double consciousness and the writings of the Eaton sisters in Ling, *Between Worlds*, pp. 21–55.

28 An awareness of the racialising gaze is very prevalent in the poetry of Marilyn Chin and Janice Mirikitani, autobiographical writing by Fiona Cheong, Lydia Minatoya and Nellie Wong, and fiction by Ronyoung Kim and Amy Tan. Stereotypes, too, often work through a physiognomic currency. Maxine Hong Kingston has extensively interrogated the subject of racial stereotyping in her novel, *Tripmaster Monkey: His Fake Book* (London: Picador, 1989).

29 Ling, *Between Worlds*, p. 112.

30 Ruth Frankenberg, *White Women, Race Matters: The Social Construction of Whiteness* (Minneapolis, MN: University of Minnesota Press, 1993), p. 95.

31 Kim, *Asian American Literature*, p. 9.

32 Nancy Bentley, 'White Slaves: The Mulatto Hero in Antebellum Fiction', in Michael Moon and Cathy N. Davidson (eds), *Subjects and Citizens: Nation, Race, and Gender From Oroonoko to Anita Hill* (Durham, NC: Duke University Press, 1995), p. 198. It should also be noted, though, that the predominance of the black/white miscegenation discourse has elided the existence of other blood-mixing/inter-racial histories in the United States, such as the Black Seminoles, the intermarriage of Native Americans, Spanish and gringos, or the intermarriage of Sikhs and Mexicans. One of the problems that yellow Asians face in the United States is the predominance of the black–white paradigm. To some extent, this predominance erases the white–yellow–other racial hierarchy. I am grateful to Ruth Hsu for reminding me of this point.

33 I mean to evoke Judith Butler's use of 'trouble' here. See Judith Butler, *Gender Trouble: Feminism and the Subversion of Identity* (New York: Routledge, 1990).

34 Bentley, 'White Slaves', p. 198.

35 Frankenberg, *White Women, Race Matters*, p. 95.

36 Quoted in Gossett, *Race: The History of an Idea in America*, p. 151.

37 These examples are discussed by Nancy Bentley in 'White Slaves'.

38 Wallace Irwin, *The Seed of the Sun* (New York: Arno Press, 1978), p. 51. This, and the following examples, are taken from Elaine Kim's discussion in *Asian American Literature*, pp. 3–22.

39 Achmed Abdullah, 'A Simple Act of Piety', in *The Honourable Gentleman and Other Stories* (New York: Knickerbocker Press, 1919), p. 219.

40 Rex Beach, *Son of the Gods* (New York: Harper and Brothers, 1929).

41 Winnifred even invented a Japanese history for herself, claiming that she was born in Nagasaki, and that she had a Japanese noblewoman for a mother.

42 'Passing' is the surreptitious crossing of the colour line. See Onoto Watanna, *Me, a Book of Remembrance* (1915; Jackson: University of Mississippi Press, 1997), p. 3.

43 Linda Trinh Moser, 'Afterword', in Watanna, *Me*, p. 365.

44 This may explain why Edith's writing is much better-known than her sister's. This is beginning to change however. In his 1997 book, Harold Bloom includes discussions of both sisters' work. See Harold Bloom (ed.), *Asian American Women Writers* (Philadelphia, PA: Chelsea House, 1997).

45 Edith took personally all insults to the Chinese and assumed the role of a warrior defending an unjustly maligned ethnic group. She frequently uses the word 'battle' in her essay, both literally and figuratively.

46 Edith Maude Eaton, 'Leaves From the Mental Portfolio of An Eurasian', the *Independent*, 21 January 1909, p. 187. All further page references are to this article and are given in parentheses.

47 Ling, *Between Worlds*, p. 35.

48 My thanks to Diana Chang for lending her publicity photograph to me, and for reading and responding to an earlier draft of this chapter.

49 Diana Chang has said, however, that she often subsumes aspects of her Eurasian background 'in the interests of other truths and recognitions'. See Bloom (ed.), *Asian American Women Writers*, p. 1.

50   Samantha Ramu Rau, 'The Need to Belong', *The New York Times Book Review*, 23 September 1956, p. 4.

51   Shirley Geok-lin Lim, 'Twelve Asian American Writers: In Search of Self-Definition', in A. LaVonne Brown Ruoff and Jerry W. Ward Jr. (eds), *Redefining American Literary History* (New York: MLA, 1990), p. 249.

52   Han Suyin, *Destination Chungking* (1942; Harmondsworth: Penguin, 1960), p. 8.

53   Amy Ling, *Between Worlds*, p. 115.

54   Han Suyin, *The Crippled Tree: China, Biography, History, Autobiography* (London: Lowe and Brydore, 1965), p. 18. All references are to this edition and hereafter are given parenthetically in the text.

55   A recent Eurasian text which deals with the negative aspects of biraciality is Elizabeth Kim's 2000 memoir, *Ten Thousand Sorrows* (London: Transworld, 2000). Another interesting contemporary text takes biraciality in Hawaii as its subject. See Marie Hara and Nora Okja Keller (eds), *Intersecting Circles: The Voices of Hapa Women in Poetry and Prose* (Honolulu, HI: Bamboo Ridge, 1999). 'Hapa' means mixed-blood.

56   Chang, *The Frontiers of Love*, p. 86.

57   Sui Sin Far (pseud. Edith Maude Eaton), 'Leaves from the Mental Portfolio of an Eurasian', in Edith Blicksilver (ed.), *The Ethnic American Woman: Problems, Protests, Lifestyles* (Dubuque, IA: Kendall/Hunt, 1978), p. 216.

58   Onoto Watanna, *His Royal Nibs* (New York: W. J.Watt, 1925), pp. 245–6.

59   Diana Chang, *The Frontiers of Love* (1956; Seattle, WA: University of Washington Press, 1994), p. 162.

60   Han Suyin, *The Crippled Tree* (New York: Putnam, 1965), p. 290.

61   Liu, *Face*, p. 172.

62   Patricia Waugh, *Feminine Fictions: Revisiting the Postmodern* (London: Routledge, 1989), p. 178.

63   Kim, *Asian American Literature*, p. 9.

64   Rosalind Coward, *Female Desire: Women's Sexuality Today* (London: Paladin, 1984), p. 76.

65   Lydia Minatoya, *Talking to High Monks in the Snow* (New York: HarperCollins, 1992), p. 58.

66   Liu, *Face*, p. 1.

67   Teresa de Lauretis, *Alice Doesn't: Feminism, Semiotics Cinema* (London: Macmillan, 1984), p. 38.

68   Laura Mulvey, 'Visual Pleasure and Narrative Cinema', *Screen*, 16:3, Autumn (1975), 6–18; p. 9.

69   *Ibid.*, p. 11.

70   Maxine Hong Kingston, in particular, has commented at length on the use of cosmetic surgery by Asian American women to anglicise their looks in *Tripmaster Monkey*, in which the character Wittman Ah Sing engages in a lengthy indictment of such practices.

71   Celia Lury, *Consumer Culture* (Cambridge: Polity, 1996), p. 165.

72   Clearly, though, the use of such technology is a highly suspect strategy. It is also predicated upon access to wealth, and ultimately only serves to legitimate hegemonic discourses of white standards of beauty.

73   Michael Jackson's whitening has been severely criticised by African Americans.

In response, Jackson now claims that he suffers from a rare skin disease.

74 Teresa de Lauretis, *Technologies of Gender: Essays on Theory, Film, and Fiction* (London: Macmillan, 1987), p. ix.

75 Liu, *Face*, p. 2.

76 'Colorism' is often used by writers to signify thematically, and a whole signifying system can be identified based upon the culturally constructed correlation between physiognomic features and personal characteristics. Blue eyes, for instance, may suggest innocence or beauty. In Asian American women's fiction, the eyes and skin in particular are often seen to represent the most extreme difference from white standards of beauty, and, as such, often function as a trope of otherness. Examples of this include Ronyoung Kim's novel *Clay Walls*, Nellie Wong's poem 'When I Was Growing Up', Fiona Cheong's short piece, 'Natives', and Janice Mirikitani's poem 'Recipe for Round Eyes'. See selections in Juliana Chang (ed.), *Quiet Fire: A Historical Anthology of Asian American Poetry 1982–1970* (New York: Asian American Writers' Workshop, 1996); Janice Mirikitani, *We, the Dangerous*; Elaine Kim et al. (eds), *Making Waves*; and Shirley Geok-lin Lim and Mayumi Tsutakawa (eds), *The Forbidden Stitch* (see Bibliography).

6

Citizenship and national identity: cultural forms and formations

This chapter turns to questions of national identity as explored by a group of Japanese American women writers and by Chinese American writer Maxine Hong Kingston. It focuses upon these examples as they illustrate two very different means by which Asian American women writers have sought to interrogate, negotiate, or renegotiate an externally imposed national identity, in Kingston's case for her ancestors, and thus, by implication, for herself too; in the case of the Japanese American women considered here, for themselves as second-generation Japanese Americans.

National identity and citizenship

'National' identity may be defined in different ways and by utilising different discourses. These may be fictional, historical, auto/biographical or cartographical; but legal discourse is dominant in the definition of national identity, and the legal discourse of national identity is that of citizenship. However a particular group seeks to claim a particular national identity through cultural productions and practices, until that claimed national identity is legitimated and recognised through citizenship, as the formal means by which the nation recognises its members, that claimed national identity remains provisional.[1]

'Citizens inhabit the political space of the nation, a space that is, at once, juridically legislated, territorially situated, and culturally embodied'.[2] This chapter reviews the negotiation of Asian American identity in relation to the institution and condition of citizenship. This analysis proceeds from the assumption that the 'state matters … as a source of identity for its citizens', and that by 'establishing boundaries, the state plays a large role in determining identity. American citizenship is established within the boundaries set by the American state'.[3] Citizenship, as Hill and Hughes have argued, is the medium through which the individual identifies with and is identified by the nation state: 'Since the Renaissance, the modern nation state has been the unit of political identification ... where the individual's relationship to that nation is based upon a model of citizenship'.[4] It is thus a formalised means through which the state confers a national identity upon the individual and through which the individual participates in the national state. The liberal ideal of citizenship stresses the equality the state seeks to confer upon its citizens: 'All citizens have the same political rights: to vote, to run for office, to speak freely, to assemble, and so forth'.[5] As such, citizenship is predicated upon a model of inclusion rather than exclusion and is 'traditionally conceived of in terms of participation'.[6] The institution of citizenship also demands a reciprocal relationship both between state and subject and between subjects. Thus the state both confers upon and protects the rights of the individual who in turn abides by the rules of citizenship, so it may also be noted that 'citizenship is about how citizens see and treat others – and how they are viewed and treated by others'.[7]

However, as Lisa Lowe and Will Kymlicka have shown, the state of citizenship is often a site of contradiction for racialised Americans, such as the Asian American women we are concerned with here.[8] Kymlicka has argued that citizenship assumes the existence of a homogeneous polis, and therefore demands that its ethnic members shed their ethnicity in favour of assimilation in order that this may be realised. As Kymlicka notes, 'citizenship cannot perform if it is group-differentiated'.[9] The assimilationist pressure that the institution of citizenship exerts upon its individuals creates problems for racialised Americans' ethnic identities. In particular, the erasure of the particularities of ethnic identity and identification often result in a sense of self-negation, as Iris Marion Young has observed: 'Self-annihilation is an unreasonable and unjust requirement of citizenship. The fiction, poetry and songs of American cultural minorities brim over with the pain and loss such demands inflict, documenting how thoroughly assimilationist values violate basic respect for persons.'[10]

Lisa Lowe's work on citizenship and Asian American identity throws this issue into particular relief. Her seminal piece on citizenship and national identity, 'Immigration, Citizenship, Racialization', offers a 'materialist critique of the institution of citizenship' in order 'to name the genealogy of the legal exclusion, disenfranchisement, and restricted enfranchisement of Asian immigrants *as* a genealogy of the American institution of citizenship'.[11] Lowe's materialist analysis of the links between citizenship and Asian American identity views this relationship through the lens of the 'importance of Asia in the development of Western capitalism globally and the use of Asian labor in the development of capitalist America'.[12] She suggests that Asian American culture emerges within this formation as an alternative site and the place where the 'contradictions of immigrant history are read, performed, and critiqued'.[13] In Lowe's analysis minority culture and minority cultural forms emerge as the places where the minority subject speaks, contests, revises and reinvents national versions of history and identity:

> Culture is the medium of the *present* – the imagined equivalences and identification through which the individual invents lived relationship with the national collective – but it is simultaneously the site that mediates the *past*, through which history is grasped as difference, as fragments, shocks, and flashes of disjunction. It is through culture that the subject becomes, acts, and speaks itself as 'American.' It is likewise in culture that individuals and collectivities struggle and remember, and, in that difficult remembering, imagine and practice both subject and community differently.[14]

Asian American cultural forms are thus posited by Lowe as the site of the emergence of the subject and through which the individual speaks her identity as 'American'. Asian American culture becomes the location of alternative versions of history and identity to national forms precisely because of Asian America's continuing cultural distance from the national spaces and narratives from which it is excluded. As Lowe notes, 'the Asian American, even as citizen, continues to be located outside the cultural and racial boundaries of the nation'.[15] The Asian American *citizen*, then, continues to be culturally and politically located at the margins of the polity but this position leads to 'cultural products emerging out of the contradictions of immigrant marginality which displace the fiction of reconciliation, disrupt the myth of national identity by revealing its gaps and fissures, and intervene in the narrative of national development'.[16] The particular experience of the Asian American citizenry thus reveals the contradictions and provisions of the state of citizenhood for racialised subjects and displays the fiction of political homogeneity by revealing that citizenship is in fact a partial institution which treats individuals on a differential and group-specific basis.

The state also imposes identity upon some ethnic individuals through debarment from citizenship, through legislation. Enforced *dis*identification from the nation state in this manner has been the result of a series of legislative moves to label particular groups of Asian immigrants at particular moments in history as 'aliens ineligible for citizenship'. The 'alien ineligible for citizenship' has even less agency for self-definition within the boundaries of the national polity than the racialised citizen. Yet, paradoxically, 'alien' status has, at times in United States history, worked to expose the partiality of citizenship. During the Second World War Japanese Americans were interned as 'enemy aliens' on the basis of their ethnicity, *regardless* of their citizenship status, which highlighted the failure of the insurances that the conferment of citizenship claimed to provide.[17] 'Citizenship' is an oppositional category, in that it works in opposition to the notion of the state 'alien', yet the move to intern Japanese Americans reneged upon the privileges proceeding from this difference. In addition, as Ronald Takaki has shown, even the conferment of citizenship did not always dissolve Asian American difference into the national polity.[18]

The history of American treatment of Asian immigrants and of Asian American citizens therefore mirrors the patterns and histories of American national, cultural and legal acceptance and incorporation of Asian Americans into the polity.[19] This chapter is concerned with the particular history of two groups of Asian Americans: Japanese Americans and Chinese Americans who, at different junctures in American immigration history, suffered especially critical changes in their status as Americans. In each case, at a particular moment, national identity comes to dominate the identity of the individuals in question.

Asian American writers and national identity

The Japanese American narratives chosen here are a group of texts dealing with the experience of incarceration and relocation to which most Japanese Americans were subjected following the bombing of Pearl Harbor in 1941. These acts of incarceration and relocation demonstrate how the state imposed a national identity upon a particular group of people, against which they had little power of objection. The texts under consideration may be collectively named 'Japanese American internment narratives', as their subject is the experience of internment and relocation and the effects of this upon Japanese American identity. These texts are all written after the war, at varying degrees of distance from the experience, and they attempt to heal the damage done by internment. All are autobiographical, and they are read here as deliberate textual reformulations of Japanese American identity, as a means of coping with the deformation of identity caused by internment.[20] The autobiographical form functions as a kind of 'talking cure', as autobiographical discourse offers a way of bearing testimony as well as extending its authority as a discourse of 'truth' to these women's stories.[21] Two claims can be made for these texts. Firstly, they can be read psychoanalytically as examples of a textual talking cure, which, as is shown in individual discussions of each text, has varying degrees of success as a panacea for the damage wreaked by the internment experience. Secondly, these texts are offered as examples of the kind of alternative cultural site through which the subject imagines herself as 'American' in the way outlined by Lisa Lowe, and through which the subject seeks to connect to a national identity through writing, despite the limitations imposed upon that project by an externally imposed national identity as a result of internment. Kalí Tal has mapped these two aims as the desire that the text will function as both personally and politically reconstitutive.[22] These two aims are sometimes in contradiction, however. In attempting to achieve personal regeneration through writing, these writers often reveal the self-negation the experience of internment and dislocation caused. It is difficult to see how the same texts so marked by self-negation and erasure would be able, with any degree of success, to assert a viable alternative national identity to those versions of national identity imposed upon these Japanese American women through internment.

The autobiographical internment narratives are not the only retrospective narratives revisiting internment as a defining moment in the formation of Japanese American female identity. This chapter includes a discussion of Joy Kogawa's novelistic retelling of the internment story in *Obasan* as a way into a discussion of the use of form, genre and discourse as means of claiming national identity. Kogawa's use of fiction affords her a greater freedom in which to revisit, contest and revise the internment and relocation story; in contrast, the autobiographical form adopted by the other writers, despite its status as a 'truth-telling' discourse, actually delimits both the narrative and authorising possibilities for those writers.

Maxine Hong Kingston's *China Men* tries to claim a national identity in a very different way. She textually revisits the history of Chinese Americans – her history too – in an attempt to claim America for her Chinese American ancestors, in a way which will construct a heritage in America for herself too. This involves Kingston in an exploration of the differing ways in which national identity is formulated and engages her with various different discourses, through which identity may be inscribed: history, fiction, biography, cartography and the legal discourse of citizenship are all explored as discourses producing national identity. Kingston recognises that these discourses offer different degrees of legitimated national identity, but seeks to break down the hierarchy in which citizenship is seen to extend the only state-sanctioned and wholly inclusive identity, and in which fictional discourse is only able to confer a limited national identity. Certain discourses carry more epistemological authority than others, but in Kingston's retelling, the discursive bound-aries policing this are blurred in a way which works to begin to ques-tion that authority.

Japanese American internment narratives

Japanese Americans have shared with Chinese Americans the experi-ence of white hostility, legislation such as exclusion acts and anti-naturalisation laws, but it is the period of the Second World War especially which proved to be the most cataclysmic moment in Japanese American history and which had the most damaging effects upon the development of a sense of national identity. As was the case for Chinese Americans, there were also generational differences in the legal and political status and inclusion of Japanese Americans. The *issei*, or first generation, were born in Japan, and as a result of anti-naturalisation laws were debarred from citizenship until after the Second World War. This meant the first generation Japanese Americans, like first genera-tion Chinese Americans, remained 'aliens ineligible for citizenship', on the rim of the national polity. However, for both second generation Chinese Americans and second generation Japanese Americans, or *nisei*, as American-born subjects they were automatically entitled to hold citi-zenship. This generational divergence in national status was, for Japanese Americans, thrown into horrible relief during the Second World War, because first and second generations were treated differently ac-cording to their citizenship status. As a result of the gradual unease with Japanese presence in America after the bombing of Pearl Harbor, and in response to increasingly insistent calls for Japanese American containment, President Roosevelt passed Executive Order 9066, effec-tively interning the majority of the Japanese American population of the United States for the duration of the war. Two thirds of the intern-ees were American citizens, a fact which did not affect their treatment immediately. Thus, citizens and aliens alike were treated as 'enemy aliens'. It was only near the close of the war that the state decided to offer *nisei* men with citizenship the 'privilege' of leaving the camps in order to fight for the United States, thus differentiating between citizen and non-citizen. This whole experience had a catastrophic effect upon Japanese American identity long after the camps were closed down, and this subject is related in several autobiographies by Japanese Ameri-can women.

The Japanese American experience of internment during the pe-riod 1941–46 uniquely illustrates the failure of the institution of citizenship to extend equal rights and protection to all of its members regardless of individual group memberships.[23] The incarceration of Japanese Americans regardless of their citizenship status starkly demonstrates that the state treated them on the basis of race and ethnic ancestry rather than on the legal basis of political membership. As well as leading to a questioning of the existence of democracy in America, as Elaine Kim has noted, this experience forced many Japanese Americans to consider what racial identity really meant.[24] As Amy Iwasaki Mass notes, 'President Roosevelt's decision to incarcerate all Japanese Americans on the West Coast during World War II created an identity crisis'.[25] The texts that were written shortly after the war betray the anxieties attendant upon the reformulation of selfhood in the wake of internment and its debilitating consequences, as well as protesting and documenting the internment experience in the context of legal membership and equality in the United States. Miné Okubo's *Citizen 13660* (1946), Monica Sone's *Nisei Daughter* (1953), Yoshiko Uchida's *Desert Exile: The Uprooting of a Japanese–American Family* (1966) and Jeanne Wakatsuki Houston's *Farewell to Manzanar* (1973), may be read together as cultural texts portraying internment, in different ways, and to different extents, as a pivotal moment in the formation of Japanese American female identity. All four women were child or teenage internees at camps across the west coast of the United States. Okubo and Uchida were incarcerated at Tanforan Assembly centre, then Topaz Camp; Sone at Pullayup Camp and then Camp Minidoka, and Houston at Manzanar Camp. All the texts are first-person narrative accounts, although Houston's *Farewell to Manzanar* was actually written by her husband, James Houston, after hours of taped conversations with his wife, a fact that as suggested later in this chapter, has important ramifications for how we read her story. Uchida's text includes supplementary photographs and *Citizen 13660* is half comprised of Okubo's own illustrations of camp life. All the texts bear traces of the anxiety accompanying the textual telling or testimony of internment to a possibly hostile readership. These stories, in Priscilla Wald's words, reveal 'their authors' uneasy awareness of a larger story controlling their stories'.[26] That story changes from the period immediately post-internment when Sone published *Nisei Daughter*, to the 1973 publication of *Farewell to Manzanar* in a significantly more conciliatory climate. Each author, aware that she was writing against a competing national version of her tale, which accentuated the *necessity* of internment, invokes the authority of her own experience as a counter-tactic. Each also stresses the *individuality* of her story, as Uchida, for example, notes: 'My story is a very personal one, and I speak only for myself'.[27] Yet all the women locate their stories within the national and political context of internment and its contravention of citizenship rights. One means by which these writers revise the larger national story of the necessity of internment is by emphasising the *Americanness* of these stories. Some of these texts, Uchida's most notably, reach beyond the boundaries of their own ethnic group story in an attempt to connect their individual experiences with defining, but always somehow just out of reach, narratives of national identity.

None of the texts deliver undivided, assimilated subjects.[28] Rather, these texts yield versions of self-identity at odds with the nation's conception of 'alien subjects' and contrary to citizenship's requirement for assimilated subjects. However, these women are not divided by loyalty to both the United States and Japan, as the justificatory official discourse defending internment would have us believe, but are instead divided by the demands upon them to choose between loyalties. The binary demand of the experience of internment was that the Japanese American subject must choose between Japanese and American affiliations. This identification choice was coercively enforced through incarceration on the grounds of 'enemy alien' identity, in so far as Japanese Americans were assumed to have a primary loyalty to Japan which overrode any subsequent loyalty to the United States. However, midwar the goalposts shifted. Under pressure for new recruits, the government distributed a loyalty questionnaire to all *issei* and *nisei*, forcing them to admit loyalty to one country only. The pressure was to express loyalty to the United States, and thereby relinquish political affiliation (via citizenship) to the other country, Japan. The ultimate goal of this move on the part of the state was to create an all-*nisei* combat unit composed of loyal Japanese American citizens. The dilemma thus facing *nisei* and *issei* presented with this questionnaire was whether to claim loyalty to the United States, something they had been doing since the bombing of Pearl Harbor anyway, and thereby risk losing their citizenship of Japan, a move that under the current internment conditions would have effectively rendered them stateless persons. Whether individuals chose American or Japanese identification determined their subsequent externally imposed official identity within the polity. Enemy aliens, those who declined to swear allegiance to the United States, were branded as 'disloyal', and were transferred to disloyalty camps. 'Loyal' *nisei* possessing citizenship were eventually allowed to leave the camps and to return to civilian life, and in the short term, were given the opportunity to further 'prove' their loyalty by fighting for the United States. The crisis of identity that the initial shock of internment brought is followed in each text by the inner turmoil and agony engendered by the loyalty questionnaires later.

Joy Kogawa's semi-autobiographical novels *Obasan* and *Itsuka* may be placed alongside the earlier internment narratives both as a means of connection and as a point of departure. *Obasan* also renders the internment experience through a first-person narrative, but it differs from earlier responses to internment in several important ways. Published in 1981, and thus the most recent internment narrative, *Obasan* recounts the Japanese Canadian experience of the Second World War through the story of protagonist Naomi Nakane. Canadian treatment of Japanese North Americans differed from treatment in the United States. Japanese Canadians were not interned, but they were still subjected to enforced relocations to the geographical as well as cultural margins of the polity. Thus *Obasan* shares with the earlier texts by Japanese Americans the trauma and delimiting effects of displacement and dispossession if not of outright incarceration. However, *Obasan* comprises a less continuous narrative than the autobiographical accounts of internment. Its novelistic form is characterised by textual ellipsis, rupture and chronological disjunction in sharp contrast to the often deceptively 'seamless' accounts of the earlier writers. *Itsuka*, the sequel to *Obasan*, bears mention here, as it picks up the redress story, and was published in 1992 at a point when it had become clear that redress proceedings would take place. It thus serves the same function as the prefaces to the autobiographical Japanese American narratives.

Each story demonstrates in its painful rendering of the damaging period of the Second World War the struggle with a well-nigh unmanageable history. Indeed, several writers draw comparisons between their own stories and the contemporary concentration camp incarcerations of the Holocaust. These narratives both show and speak of the self-negation which was the result of internment. For Jeanne Wakatsuki Houston, for example, the self-erasure that internment produced was so total that she was unable to write her own story. It is also evident in the almost complete *issei* silence about internment: an *issei* has yet to write an internment narrative.[29] This kind of silence may be a form of cultural coping, as Kalí Tal suggests in her study, *Worlds of Hurt*; the 'disappearance strategy' as she names it, whereby 'a refusal to admit to the existence of a particular kind of trauma', coupled with the difficulties of speaking in spite of official silencing of the internment story, may result in taciturnity on the subject.[30] Indeed, the *issei*'s desire to forget about internment after the war is well documented, an erasure of the past explored extensively in Kogawa's novels. In particular,

Obasan's cyclical structure indicates Naomi's unsuccessful struggle to forget the past, while *Itsuka* charts this struggle on a wider scale, depicting the *issei* determination to bury a history of which they were ashamed.[31]

Obasan admits the struggle with history through its formal cyclical structure. Earlier autobiographical accounts also indicate this struggle formally, although in different ways. Another coping strategy is the construction of continuous narratives which attempt to dissolve, undermine and deny the particular consequences of internment for self-identification and to absorb the internment experience within a *bildungsroman* developmental autobiographical narrative.[32] For Benedict Anderson, a recognition of the discontinuity between past and present provokes a desire for continuity, evident in the production of narratives of identity.[33] These Japanese American internment autobiographies demonstrate the desire to de-emphasise the rupture internment caused in the process of self-formation through the location of the internment experience within a larger developmental story. However, in the case of Okubo's *Citizen 13660*, Uchida's *Desert Exile* and Kogawa's *Obasan*, the rupture caused by internment is marked textually, through omission in *Citizen 13660*, discontinuous narrative in *Obasan*, and through the choice of pictures in *Desert Exile*. This rupture is also figured through a spatial discontinuity. Sau-ling Wong has discussed the theme of mobility as a defining trope of American literature, bespeaking freedom of possibility and the vast openness of the American landscape.[34] Against this background, she explores the particular form of immobility caused by internment and the enforced mobility engendered by relocation that preoccupies Japanese American stories of relocation. She suggests that different degrees of enforced/impaired mobility result in narratives about 'undoing', contrary to their apparent conformation to a *bildungsroman*-esque developmental narrative of the self in formation. The 'undoing' is both spatial, legal and personal. It is spatial in terms of dispossession, legal in terms of the violation of citizenship rights and this results in the deformation of national identity as well as a damaging self-negation.

The urge expressed in these texts has been described by Kalí Tal, speaking of Holocaust literature, as 'the urge to bear witness, to carry the tale of horror back to the halls of "normalcy"'.[35] She continues: 'Each of these authors articulates the belief that he or she is a storyteller with a mission; their response as survivors is to bear the tale. Each one also affirms the process of storytelling as a personally reconstitutive act, and expresses the hope that it will also be a socially reconstitutive act'.[36] This situation equally pertains to the Japanese American autobiographical narratives of internment. Okubo and Uchida, for example, stress the socially reconstitutive function of their writing especially strongly. In contrast, Sone and Houston refrain from making such an overt statement, perhaps because, as their texts state, these two writers have found the writing process more personally reconstitutive. Thus, the revision, deconstruction and reconstruction of personal identity is re-enacted textually in the hope that it may lead to political reconstruction. This hope was realised. During the United States redress hearings held in the 1980s, Okubo's *Citizen 13660*, amongst others, was actually used as a testimony of the internment story, and Okubo herself was also asked to testify orally.[37] This serves to demonstrate how successful these Japanese American narratives were in offering alternative versions of the national story of internment, as well as rejecting dominant versions of national identity in favour of their own reformulated assertions of Americanness.

Viewed within a psychoanalytic framework, these texts also emerge as heavily invested in the Freudian idea of a talking cure.[38] Each expresses the desire for the storytelling act to be purgative as well as politically useful. In this sense, each text succeeds, although some more obviously or completely than others. Jeanne Wakatsuki Houston has spoken of the complete regeneration and release brought to her through the storytelling act.[39] Monica Sone, in contrast, desires that the process of narrating the internment experience will reconcile her problems of identity, but the ending, as discussed in this chapter, shows that this is clearly not the case. Distance from the trauma is often necessary in order for the story to emerge. Tal notes that 'Survival literature tends to appear at least a decade after the traumatic experience in question'.[40] Japanese American narratives vary in distance from the closure of the camps. Sone's *Nisei Daughter* appeared seven years later, whereas Houston's *Farewell to Manzanar* appeared in 1973, about thirty years after the camps were closed. This may explain the difference in the rejuvenative effects in writing. Sone clearly wants an early resolution of the problematics of identity she feels as a Japanese American, yet the swift publication of *Nisei Daughter* seems to have been premature. Without the accompanying healing effects of time, her story fails to be personally reconstitutive.

Miné Okubo, *Citizen 13660* (1946)

The very title of Miné Okubo's *Citizen 13660* announces the contradictions of citizenship and the internment experience which form the subject of her text. Although she was a US citizen, Okubo was interned at Tanforan Assembly Center, then Topaz Camp. Upon internment her family was assigned the number 13660. Thus the title of her autobiography places in ironic juxtaposition her two contradictory official identities. The text consists of a preface and then the autobiographical account written at the time of internment. The preface, written and appended to the text in 1983, speaks at a distance from internment of forty-one years. In this, she looks back at her experience with the benefit of hindsight and she re-evaluates her story within the wider history of the Second World War. She claims an academic historical interest as the impetus for her autobiographical narrative: 'to see what happens to people when reduced to one status and condition', thus assuming the stance of observer/witness of the period rather than victim (p. ix). The autobiographical narrative itself is quite unusual, in that it is comprised of pages split in half, with Okubo's own pictorial records above, and textual glosses and discussion below the illustrations. In the preface, though, Okubo tells us that the illustrations and text were never meant to appear together. The illustrations were originally intended as a picture of camp life for her friends on the outside, but Okubo later widened her projected viewership by planning an exhibition. The pictures have therefore always had a projected public viewership, and it is the consciousness of this that perhaps causes Okubo to place herself at the margins of her story, preferring to offer a more ostensibly objective record of the period. Okubo herself always appears in the pictures, but crucially as an observer, rather than participant. This may betray her desire to be an onlooker rather than victim of the experience, and can be seen as a means of managing her history. Depersonalising internment in this way also offers Okubo a politically effective location from which to speak. Able to claim the authority of witness, she remains sufficiently removed from the story of internment to avoid charges of overt bias. This move on Okubo's part can also thus be regarded as an attempt to obtain an 'objective', culturally legitimated (i.e. *detached*) subject position from which to speak.

It is the relationship between the illustrations and the text which makes *Citizen 13660* particularly interesting. The text mainly comprises a brief accompaniment elaborating or explicating the pictures, which span Okubo's late teenagerhood, through internment and culminating in the final picture which depicts Okubo leaving Tanforan. Sometimes the text accompanying the pictures is little more than a brief gloss on the pictures, at other times it is a more extensive exploration of an area of internment. The text becomes noticeably sparse at critical times in Okubo's story, when her identity is particularly threatened: such as at the moment of declaration of war; the move to the camp; the arrival at Topaz; the search for privacy. In addition, at points when her individual female identity is placed in jeopardy, the text also becomes sparse, for example, when female dress changes in the camp and all the women are forced to wear trousers, or when all the women are later forced to wear the same dresses due to clothing shortages. Even more revealing, however, are the instances of pictorial ellipsis which occur at several points in the text. These points also correspond to moments of threat to Okubo's identity, and serve to demonstrate the psychoactive effects of internment and its aftermath. It is as if Okubo cannot represent certain aspects of the internment story; as if her history becomes so unmanageable as to be unrepresentable. These points include the moment when the possibility of internment is raised, then announced, the move to Topaz, the arrival at Topaz, the description of the spartan accommodation, the distribution of the loyalty questionnaire, the move to Tule Lake 'disloyalty' centre and finally relocation. Viewed psychoanalytically, these omissions thus show Okubo's self-negation at certain moments. The channel of self-representation – her pictures – becomes blocked as a symptom of selfhood under stress. This blockage contradicts Okubo's attempt to place herself at a distance from her story: her inability to document certain parts of her story reveal her continuing psychological investment in that history (she significantly did not fill in the pictorial gaps later), and speaks counter to her claim that 'Time mellows the harsh and the grim' (p. ix).

Okubo's narrative is firmly located within the context of both personal and social reconstitution. Her impetus was to tell the story to non-witnesses – by implication, non-Japanese Americans. We may therefore assume that Okubo wrote and drew for at least a majority white audience. Her preface further establishes her text within this context by claiming that her work was intended for exhibition. Likewise, Okubo tells her reader that she both testified at the US reparation hearings held in 1982, and that *Citizen 13660* was used as evidence at those hearings:

> I testified at the hearing in New York City. As *Citizen 13660* had been widely reviewed and was considered an important reference book on the Japanese American evacuation and internment, I presented the commission with a copy of the book in addition to my oral testimony. In my

testimony I stressed the need for young people from grade school through college to be educated about the evacuation. (p. xi)

And later: 'I hope that things can be learned from this tragic episode, for I believe it could happen again' (p. xii). These statements from the preface frame the narrative, and are in keeping with Kalí Tal's observation of survivors' needs to tell their stories for reconstitutive purposes. Her preface was written during the redress proceedings and at a point when it had become clear that redress would be granted. Thus, *Citizen 13660*'s quest to maintain identity in the face of national and personal erasure is framed by the self-affirming redress proceedings forty years later.

Okubo's narrative comprehensively explores the contradictions of Japanese American citizenship in the light of internment. She constantly emphasises her identity as a citizen: 'I was an American citizen' she sadly asserts (p. ix), and notes that 'generations of Americans did not know that this had ever happened in the United States to other American citizens' (p. xi); as well as stressing the collapse of politically inscribed difference between citizen and alien that resulted from the government's internment of both citizens and aliens alike, and from the loyalty questionnaire. Okubo masks the personal effect that this had upon her when she discusses its effects in the third, rather than first person:

> It brought about a dilemma. Aliens (Issei) would be in a difficult position if they renounced Japanese citizenship and thereby made themselves stateless persons. Many of the Nisei also resented the question because of the assumption that their loyalty might be divided; it was confusing that their loyalty to the United States should be questioned at a moment when the army was asking them to volunteer. (p. 176)

The state's failure to observe national identity differences between citizen and alien is posited by Okubo as the cause of her and others' crisis of self-confidence:

> We had not believed at first that evacuation would affect the Nisei, American citizens of Japanese ancestry, but thought perhaps the Issei, Japanese-born mothers and fathers who were denied naturalization by American law, would be interned in case of war between Japan and the United States. It was a real blow when everyone, regardless of citizenship, was ordered to evacuate. (p. 17)

Mid-narrative, mid-internment, however, references to Okubo's citizenship disappear and she is instead defined only by a different, externally imposed identity – her relocation number, 13660.

The only point at which Okubo's identity truly emerges is at the very end, with her deceptively simple sentence: 'I was now *free*' (p. 208). In sharp contrast to the only occasional 'I' or 'we' throughout, this sentence betrays Okubo's distinct emergence from a period of self-erasure, illustrated textually through her limited ability to claim the use of the first-person pronoun. Although Okubo adopts a distanced stance from her own story, this narrative remains very much the tale of one *nisei*. The *issei* are rarely mentioned, and significantly, Okubo does not pass judgement on the internment of *issei* as enemy aliens. She is only concerned with the plight of the *nisei*, and the contradictory official identity they held at this time. In fact, none of the autobiographical narratives focus in any real detail upon the story of the *issei*. All the autobiographical writers are *nisei*, and thus are mainly concerned with their situation. This highlights the extraordinary generational split in national identity amongst Japanese Americans at this time. It is only Joy Kogawa, in her fictional renderings of internment in *Obasan* and *Itsuka*, who deals with the *issei* plight and response to internment, and even this is a third-person rendition, attempting to contrast *issei* compliance with their treatment with *nisei* protest at their contradictory status.

Monica Sone, *Nisei Daughter* (1953)

If the importance of omission is demonstrated by ellipsis in Okubo's text, then the awareness of her readership dominates Monica Sone's *Nisei Daughter*. Like Okubo, Sone opens with a preface appended long after the narrative itself was written. This preface, although not viewing internment from the vantage point of the post-redress condemnation of internment, does focus upon Sone's successful life after internment in the light of forthcoming anticipated redress, and thus from a point when she *seems* to have psychologically overcome the detrimental effects of that period. Sone adopts a more overtly political and emotional stance in her preface, which also functions to frame her story: 'The Nikkeis are telling the nation about 1942, a time when they became prisoners of their own government, without charges, without trials'.[41] Like Okubo, Sone stresses the fundamental contradiction to the promises of citizenship engendered by group-based incarceration: 'the Court carefully avoided ruling on the basic constitutional issue of curfew and mass incarceration of a particular group of citizens, selected solely on the basis of ancestry' (p. xvi). Sone's narrative seems to desire her reader to turn juror, and condemn the state's actions. She is also acutely conscious of a projected white readership, and throughout the narrative seeks to present an accommodating image of Japanese Americans. She is particularly concerned early in the text to present a harmonious picture of her dual identity as Japanese and American, and discusses aspects of both elements of her identity in relation to food and cultural practices, and in fact she actually stresses the dominance of her Americanness. For example, when she visits Japan with her family, she views it through the eyes of a foreigner, and expresses a desire to return to America: 'This America, where I was born, surrounded by people of different extractions, was still my home' (p. 108). As noted in chapter 1, although she retains the ethnic 'piquancy' of descriptions of the odd Japanese meal, or celebration, Sone emphasises that this does not interfere with her overriding identification as a 'Yankee'. Her story follows a fairly traditional autobiographical pattern, starting with early childhood, with considerable detail about her family life. The establishment of a relatively uncontradictory sense of a stable Japanese American identity is a means of throwing the events following the bombing of Pearl Harbor into question. Ironically, Sone's response to the news of the bombing unconsciously replicates assumptions about Japanese American identity made by the government which instigated internment in the first place. She feels a sense of contradictory identity for the first time, which mirrors the external conflict between Japan and the United States: 'I found myself shrinking inwardly from my Japanese blood, the blood of an enemy. I knew instinctively that the fact that I was an American by birthright was not going to help me escape the consequences of this unhappy war' (p. 146). Crucially, the conflict that Sone feels is not between Japanese and American loyalties, but between her declared 'instinctual' American identification and the knowledge that she will externally be identified as Japanese, which is of course exactly what happens. Sone, like Okubo, is really only concerned with the situation of the *nisei* citizens. She suggests that while *issei* may remain loyal to Japan, *nisei*'s primary allegiance is to the United States, which she highlights through discussing generational differences between *issei* and *nisei* within her own family:

> Henry and I used to criticise Japan's aggressions in China and Manchuria while Father and Mother condemned Great Britain and America's superior attitude towards Asiatics and their interference with Japan's economic growth. During these arguments, we had eyed each other like strangers, parents against children. (p. 148)

Sone shows that loyalty differences did exist between *issei* and *nisei*, alien and citizen, predating Pearl Harbor. Events on the world stage were figured within Sone's family. But, she asserts, her loyalty and her brother's were never in question. Against this backdrop, the elision of any distinction between *issei* aliens and *nisei* citizens is thrown into accentuated focus. Sone reports her investment in the protections and rights afforded her as an American citizen and her certainty that she would escape internment: 'We were quite sure that our rights as American citizens would not be violated, and we would not be marched out of our homes on the same basis as enemy aliens' (p. 158). Her realisation that she is branded with *issei* aliens produces in Sone a crisis on both national and personal levels:

> My citizenship wasn't real, after all. Then what was I? I was certainly not a citizen of Japan as my parents were. On second thought, even Father and Mother were more alien residents of the United States than Japanese nationals for they had little tie with their mother country ... Of one thing I was sure. The wire fence was real. I no longer had the right to walk out of it. It was because some people had little faith in the ideas and ideals of democracy. They said that after all these were but words and could not possibly insure loyalty. (pp. 177–8)

Sone suggests that the state's betrayal of members of Japanese American polity who possessed citizenship was also a betrayal of the very institution of citizenship itself, as its actions undermined the assumptions from which the state of citizenship itself proceeds: that citizenship is reciprocal, demanding loyalty in return for protection.

As Sone emerges from the internment experience, she starts to search for ways in which to mend her fractured sense of national and racial identity: 'Up till then America ... had meant ... a desperate struggle to be just myself. Now that I had shed my past, I hoped that I might come to know another aspect of America which would inject strength into my hyphenated Americanism instead of pulling it apart' (p. 216). Sone does seem to be able to partly mend her fractured identity. Yet she continues to experience racism on a regular basis, a fact which continues to highlight an externally imposed identity stressing her difference in the eyes of others from other members of the polity. Her final statement, 'The Japanese and American parts of me were now blended into one', asserts the reconciliation of her bifurcated identity, as well as conforming to a traditional *bildungsroman* ending (p. 238). Yet, as many critics have noted, this final resolutionary statement seems premature and unconvincing.[42] Sone's resolutionary ending seems to signal her *desire* for a reconciliation of her problems of identity, rather than a resolution itself. Sone is clearly addressing a white readership and her premature claims of the resolution of her hyphenated identity may signal an attempt to plead a harmonious existence of Japanese Americans in the United States to a white reader during a particularly charged moment in American race relations. Sone's learning process in *Nisei Daughter* is that choices of identity are not always available and unlimited. The earlier part of her narrative dealing with her pre-internment years depict her clarifying what is American and Japanese both on the inside and outside, and show Sone choosing identifications. Internment brings with it the shock of recognition that identity for racialised Americans may be externally imposed, for Sone as an enemy Japanese, however strange that identity may feel, and that American identity could remain out of reach. This process may be traced through a discernible loss in the narrator's confidence in herself. Early on, Sone's confidence in her ability to choose identifications shines through: 'I was a Yankee', she tells us proudly (p. 18). This contrasts sharply with her later professed need to revitalise and replenish her damaged identity. Like Okubo, Sone's dampened self-confidence nearly silences her: 'I was so overcome with self-consciousness I would not bring myself to speak' (p. 131). Likewise, the style of the text, as Elaine Kim has noted, shifts from exuberance to a subdued and even stilted style later on.[43] It seems that in the process of writing, Sone has relived the effects of internment upon her identity and this has translated into a noticeable shift in style through the narrative.

Yoshiko Uchida, *Desert Exile: The Uprooting of a Japanese–American Family* (1966)

Yoshiko Uchida's narrative, *Desert Exile: The Uprooting of a Japanese–American Family*, differs from both Okubo's *Citizen 13660* and Sone's *Nisei Daughter* in that there is no framing preface. Instead it is at the end of the autobiographical narrative that we find an epilogue, in which Uchida discusses internment experience at a distance and from a wider world viewpoint. This difference may be because *Desert Exile* appeared much later than the two autobiographical accounts discussed so far, and was written with the benefit of hindsight. Thus, there was no need for a lengthy preface bridging the temporal gap between internment experience and the later publication of writing about that experience. Like Okubo and Sone, Uchida devotes the early part of her story to establishing a relatively concordant picture of her and her family's life in the United States. Chapters 1 and 2 deal with Uchida's life in Berkeley, California and with the question of her Japanese American identity. Like Sone, Uchida sees no conflict within her hyphenated identity. Like

Sone too, she uses cultural activities like eating as a means of expressing this lack of conflict: 'While Keiko and I were still having our toast and steaming cups of cocoa on Sunday mornings, Mama would cook a large pot of rice to be eaten with the food she had prepared the night before' (p. 32). Like Sone as well, Uchida, while acknowledging the Japanese influence upon her life, also stresses the dominance of her Americanness: 'In spite of the complete blending of Japanese qualities and values into our lives, neither my sister nor I, as children, ever considered ourselves anything other than Americans. At school we saluted the American flag and learned to become good citizens' (p. 40). Pearl Harbor is introduced and dealt with in chapter 3 and as in those texts discussed so far, the careful establishment of a harmonious view of the Uchida family's life in the United States is all the more forcefully shattered by the onset of the moves towards internment. Like Sone, Uchida also emphasises the loyalty of her and other *nisei* to the state, thus by implication questioning the need for internment:

> We tried to go on living as normally as possible, behaving as other American citizens. Most nisei had never been to Japan. The United States of America was our only country and we were totally loyal to it. Wondering how we could make other Americans understand this, we bought defense bonds, signed up for civilian defense, and cooperated fully with every wartime regulation. (p. 53)

The rise in anti-Japanese sentiment, culminating in internment, is located by Uchida within a wider history of anti-Asian feeling, legislation and exclusions: 'At the time California already had a long history of anti-Asian activity, legitimised by such laws as those restricting immigration and land ownership' (p. 53). Uchida's discussion of internment and its meaning is very politically astute and engaged. She cites the history leading up to the events of 1941–45, quotes senators' views on the issue and names the amendments to the Constitution discussing citizenship and the rights which were flouted. Even more than Sone, she desires a readership which will judge the actions of the United States, and states the case against the government in a clear and detailed way. Like Okubo and Sone, Uchida also emphasises the loss of individual identity which stemmed from internment, telling us that 'from that day on we became Family Number 13453' (p. 59). The latter part of the autobiography, chapters 4 to 8, deal with internment itself, from evacuation through the move to Tanforan Assembly Center, the move to Topaz Camp and the life there. Uchida's tone describing these events is one of cutting, condemning sarcasm, in sharp contrast to Monica Sone's more conciliatory tone, as this example shows: 'I wondered how much the nation's security would have been threatened had the army permitted us to remain in our homes a few more days' (p. 70). Like Sone, Uchida also asserts that the state's treatment of Japanese Americans undermined the very institution of citizenship itself. She observes that Japanese Americans 'realized that the deprivation of the rights of one minority undermined the rights of the majority as well' (p. 85). The implication of this, of course, is that the reader should realise this too. In keeping with Uchida's style of close political commentary, the issue of the distribution of the loyalty questionnaires is covered in detail as well.

Kalí Tal's observation of the need for political reconstruction to frame the telling of traumatic stories characterises the impetus of Uchida's work, as she emphasises the responsibilities of memory: 'We must provide them with the cultural memory they lack', Uchida says of the younger generations of Japanese Americans (p. 147). But Uchida's narrative does not just aim for political reconstruction; it also deals with the personal effects of internment upon her individuality. Autobiographies usually document the *formative* moments in the life of the teller. *Desert Exile*, like *Nisei Daughter* and *Citizen 13660*, charts the *deformative* moments of the internment experience and its aftermath upon the individual. This is clearly signalled by Uchida's chosen title for her work, *Desert Exile*, which emphasises the family's relegation to the edges of the polity, and the de-formation of personal, social and familial structures in the subtitle: *The Uprooting of a Japanese–American Family*.

Significantly for Uchida, personal reconstruction does not come through telling, as she stresses in her epilogue: 'If my story has been long in coming, it is not because I did not want to remember our incarceration or to make this interior journey into my earlier self, but because it took so many years for these words to find a home' (p. 154). By 'home', Uchida means both a context for her telling in a post-redress, conciliatory climate, and also the textual container itself, the autobiographical form. This form allows Uchida to integrate her personal story with political comment for politically reconstructive purposes: 'I wrote it … for all Americans, with the hope that through knowledge of the past, they will never allow another group of people in America to be sent into a desert exile ever again' (p. 154). Personal reconstruction for Uchida also comes through her visit to Japan after the end of the war. Whereas Monica Sone's visit to her ancestral country had stirred within her a recognition of her Americanness, for Uchida the experience makes her turn to her Japaneseness as an alternative to an American identity she desired but was disallowed: 'My experience in Japan was as positive and restorative as the evacuation had been negative and depleting. I came home aware of a new dimension of myself as a Japanese American and with new respect and admiration for the culture which made my parents what they were. The circle was complete' (p. 152). Uchida's earlier assertion of her desire to be American, and her relatively successful attainment of an American identity contrasts strongly with her adoption of the Japanese side so wholeheartedly at the end of her story. The message is that if Japanese Americans remain outside of mainstream American society it is not because of their continuing affiliation with Japan, but because the United States has rejected them as Americans on a par with other American citizens.

As with *Citizen 13660*, the pictorial accompaniments to the text are often more revealing than the textual content itself. Sau-ling Wong's discussion of the process of 'undoing' in *Desert Exile* highlights this well. She demonstrates that the photographs Uchida chooses to illustrate her story tell a different tale than the text may suggest. They move from pre-immigration photographs, establishing origins, to pictures of Uchida's family and community, group pictures which establish order, community, stability and continuity, to anti-Japanese headlines which mark a shift from internal and subjective viewpoints to an exteriorised and objectified view of the community. These detached and depersonalised records of the internment experience, like those that we find in Okubo's pictures, chart the depersonalising and self-alienating effects of internment upon the individual. Then the pictures shift to represent disintegration through pictures of the camp in stages of dilapidation, as well as a distant view of Camp Topaz, again showing the distancing and depersonalising effects of internment. Post-internment, we see a return to two final family pictures. Wong reads these as an attempt to affirm regeneration and family togetherness as 'pathetically ineffective'.[44] So these twin photographs seem to be weak attempts at suggesting restoration. Uchida textually asserts the rediscovery of her Japanese identity as restorative, and through these pictures of her family symbolically reflects a return to an original pre-internment time of togetherness, but they fail to address the question of Uchida's continuing existence in the United States, a country which has robbed her of a politically legitimate national identity. Therefore, this personal reconstitution must be seen as only partial. The version of selfhood offered at the end of *Desert Exile*, as in *Nisei Daughter*, thus fails to fulfil its author's desired purpose of personal as well as political change.

Jeanne Wakatsuki Houston, *Farewell to Manzanar* (1973)

Most problematic in both its handling of the internment experience and its aftermath is Jeanne Wakatsuki Houston's *Farewell to Manzanar*. This text was actually written by Houston's husband, James Houston, after hours of taped conversations with his wife.[45] The mediated nature of the text, then, as Patricia A. Sakurai has noted, problematises assumptions we are able to make about the Japanese American female voice in the text, as well as its negotiation of self-identity.[46] Jeanne Wakatsuki Houston and James Houston have disclosed how James Houston turned what was often Jeanne's tearful recollections into a well-structured narrative. Unlike the other narratives, *Farewell to Manzanar* opens with the events at Pearl Harbor as a catalytic moment. This suggests that what went before this event does not matter in Houston's story. By page 34, the narrative sees Houston at the camp at Manzanar. Thus the internment story is not so much central to the wider story of development, but is embedded within it. The text has a curious relationship with its female subject. At times, it is acutely conscious of Houston's father's story rather then Houston's own tale. For example, the lengthy section in which Jeanne Houston is interrogated by the FBI is italicised. The debates that take place between Houston's father and her brother regarding the loyalty questionnaire are likewise given extensive textual space. Houston suggests that internment proved an emasculating experience for her father, and uses castration metaphors to describe this effect. Yet she fails to sufficiently explore the effects of internment upon herself, who, as a child internee, must have been highly impressionable, as well as extensively affected by the experience. This may be due to James Houston's mediating influence: possibly he was drawn to and interested in male versions of the story and therefore inflected the narrative accordingly. However, it also seems to be a part of the self-negation on the part of Jeanne that saturates this text. She repeatedly desires invisibility – 'part of me yearned to be invisible'[47] she notes – and she also discusses the erosion of individual identity which was the result of internment: 'You cannot deport 110,000 people unless you have stopped seeing individuals' (p. 137).

The entire narrative, despite James' influence, appears self-deprecating, as Elaine Kim observes: 'the narrator is plagued, both in camp and after release, by the idea that she deserves hatred'.[48] Later in the story we see Houston's rather pathetic attempts to assimilate as an American girl. At one point she enters a beauty contest, and decides that in order to win this most American of phenomena, she must capitalise upon her exotic, Asian identity and thus dresses up accordingly.

Of course, such a desperate plea to win approval in the eyes of others fails. Overall, the sense of Jeanne Wakatsuki Houston with which we are left is of a flailing selfhood and a desperate search for individuality. This is in spite of Houston's own assertion that the process of writing was enormously rejuvenative. This can be seen in the focus in the text upon the psychological effects of internment, as we are told: 'Much more than a remembered place it [Manzanar] had become a state of mind'.[49] Houston is not really concerned with the politically reconstructive function of her telling, although she does analyse the various political facets of the experience in some detail. The text instead represents Jeanne's confrontation with her own unmanageable history, and her subsequent reconciliation with her past. The title, *Farewell to Manzanar*, reflects this, suggesting as it does that the autobiographical process allows her to leave the story behind.

These autobiographical narratives reveal a crisis of the self on both a national and a personal, subjective level. The autobiographical form that each writer adopts as the medium of her story is only partly compatible with the purpose it is adopted to serve. Each uses a very traditional autobiographical form, which conforms to the style of the *bildungsroman*. This paradigm tracks the subject's life from genesis through the formative periods of childhood and early adulthood through to the successes of later life. Such a structure has no room for the sudden rupture of identity to be found in these Japanese American stories, nor to track the *de-formation* rather than the *formation* of the subject. It is this incompatibility which accounts for the tension detected earlier in these texts between the seamless, continuous narratives that these women want to produce, and the far more fractured, uncertain and discontinuous stories straining to be heard. The autobiographical form may be seen as delimiting these women's stories in terms of their identified goals of personal reconstruction. Yet in terms of political reconstruction, the autobiography proves highly effective. As witness/victim testimonies, these narratives assert the authority of personal experience in a way that renders them potent alternative narratives to the national story of internment. This is highlighted by the role that many of these texts played as documentation in the later redress hearings.

Joy Kogawa, *Obasan* (1981)

Joy Kogawa's novels about Japanese Canadian relocation, *Obasan* and *Itsuka*, while based upon the author's personal experience, assume a less delimiting genre in which to relate the experience of relocation.

The novelistic form of these two texts affords Kogawa a greater freedom to tell her story. In particular, the stories are freed from a restrictive framework of a *bildungsroman*-style structure, so, as Lisa Lowe has observed, they are able to refuse the premature reconciliation of Asian American particularity and identity that was evident at the end of both *Nisei Daughter* and *Desert Exile*.[50] Of the two novels, *Obasan* is the most interesting and relevant here. Whereas *Itsuka* picks up the story of the redress movement, *Obasan* deals with the relocation experience itself and its effects upon the individual, and uses a cyclical, rather than chronological and linear narrative structure. Although the time of the narrative present is the post-relocation life of protagonist Naomi Nakane, the continuing dominance of the past upon Naomi's present is signalled through the repeated returns to her history through her consciousness. Thus, the identity crisis engendered by the Canadian government's treatment of Japanese Canadians emerges as continuing beyond the particular moment of its production. The novel's structure allows the twin aims of personal and political reconstruction to be separated. Naomi Nakane, the central female character, and her elderly female relative, Obasan of the novel's title, together illustrate the debilitating effects of relocation upon individual identity. Both women are depicted as stultified by their histories, unable to free themselves from the memories of relocation. Through Naomi's consciousness and Obasan's reliance upon pictures and other records, the stasis of their current lives in the shadow of relocation is communicated. In contrast, Naomi's other older female relative, Aunt Emily, represents the desire for political reconstruction. Emily is described as a 'word warrior', and works ceaselessly for the redress movement.[51] Rather than becoming trapped or controlled by her past, Emily uses it, and the various documents of the time, such as her diary, to attain a recognition of the wrongdoing as well as to claim a Canadian identity. *Itsuka* develops this endeavour more thoroughly, culminating at the end of the text in the announcement that redress will proceed. Both texts, like the Japanese American internment narratives earlier, have an interesting extra-textual relationship with their subjects. Both document the struggle for redress and the struggle to assert an alternative version of the national story of relocation in opposition to official versions. This involves the use of personal narratives, like Aunt Emily's diary, charting relocation. Both *Obasan* and *Itsuka* were used in the redress hearings in Canada.[52] Therefore, both intra-textually and extra-textually, these two novels challenge national versions of the relocation story. It is also arguable that the adoption of a novel form, offering as it does in these cases a more complex formal structure than any of the earlier narratives, attains a wider critical and lay readership. Both texts have been phenomenally successful, even more so, arguably, than the most successful internment autobiography, *Citizen 13660*.[53] If the political aim of these texts is their intervention in national versions of their stories, and their assertion of alternative national identities, then the route to that outcome via fiction has proved more successful than via autobiography, due to the wider readerly cultural space that these novels have claimed.

Considered together, these texts document the ongoing negotiation of Japanese American female identity by subjects still fractured by the internment and relocation experiences. It is noticeable that cultural reactions and responses to this period are dominated by female texts. There are few equivalent texts of note by male authors, with the exceptions of John Okada's complex and haunting novel, *No-No Boy* (1957), and Toshio Mori's lesser-known collection of short stories, *Yokohama, California*.[54] Neither are autobiographies. Why, then, did this group of women alone put pen to paper in this way? It may be that Japanese American male cultural production dealing with this period was stifled by the widely discussed emasculating effects of internment upon the Japanese American male population. John Okada's novel, *No-No Boy*, documents this through the representation of the *nisei* soldier and central character, Kenji. Despite this, though, it is questionable whether these women writers suffered any less than their male counterparts in terms of the detrimental effects of internment and relocation upon their female identity. Camp life de-emphasised gender differences: all internees could work, and had equal access to the social life of the community, as well as the same lack of access to educational facilities. However we explain the lack of versions of the internment story by men, it remains the case that in recording the experience of internment and relocation, it is these Japanese American women who have spoken for their cultural group. This is also the case if we turn to consider Chinese American experience and national identity, as it is Maxine Hong Kingston who has spoken for her 'China men' forebears.[55]

Maxine Hong Kingston, *China Men* (1981)

As discussed in chapter 1, Chinese Americans contributed immeasurably to the economic development of the United States: from their earliest contribution to Western expansion through the construction of the railroad across the nation, their role in the development of the sugar cane industry to the later twentieth-century growth of Chinese American presence in service industries like laundry work.[56] It is this history of Chinese American economic fortunes, spanning the mid-nineteenth to the early twentieth centuries, that is the focus of Maxine Hong Kingston's novel/memoir/biography/history *China Men*. This critical period of Chinese American consolidation in the United States and the struggle for inclusion into the polity via citizenship is the subject of Kingston's text, which juxtaposes the national history of the Chinese exclusion acts and anti-Asian prejudices, with the international history of immigration, and, later, war in Asia, with the personal, local and subjective histories of the China men in Kingston's narrative. These histories recount the China men's struggles for citizenship and for a subsequent sense of national belonging and identity. *China Men* investigates American cultural exclusivity embedded as it is in concepts of 'the nation' and national identity, as it is manifested in political, legal and social structures. Jeff Spinner has written that 'the nation ... is an organic group of people possessing a unique culture'.[57] Kingston's project in *China Men* is to expose definitions of the nation as *inorganic* ideological constructions, and to reveal the racism implicit in such constructions. Definitions of the American nation exclude migrants like Hong Kingston's China men, because as new ethnically liminal presences in a white exclusionist environment, they are defined as non-members of the dominant group, by that group. In *China Men*, fiction, history, biography, cartography and law are all discussed as discourses producing ideas of national identity and nationhood. The text itself is at times fiction, at others times biography, memoir or history. Kingston's traversing of discursive boundaries is a strategy to reveal the ways in which the authority of such discourses is employed to legitimate and fix images of the nation as an organic in-group. Thus, *China Men* explores what it means to be an 'American', and demonstrates how concepts of 'American', national identity and the American 'nation' signify a particular cultural and geographical terrain, and thus also interrogates 'American' history as a grand – and self-aggrandising – narrative. So Kingston's text seeks to challenge ideas of nationhood and national identity through the discourses of citizenship, biography, history and fiction, in a way that attempts to claim both textual and actual territory for her ancestors.

Fiction, Jeff Spinner tells us, is a battleground of identity, along with other cultural media like state legislature and newspapers.[58] Different kinds of narration create the nation, which in turn, defines the individual either as part of that nation or as an outsider. To use Benedict Anderson's definition, the nation is an *imagined* political community, with *imagined* boundaries and collective traits, and the location of these imaginings are the cultural arenas of literature, history, legislature as well as other textual media. Anderson's argument, which has been elaborated upon by Homi Bhabha in his essay 'DissemiNation', links nationalism to various nation-making texts, thus attempting to make visible literature's function as a cultural producer as well as product of nationalist discourses and sentiments.[59] Implicit in this argument is the recognition that the nation is not fixed, but shifting, not organic but inorganic, and that it does not correspond to actual, but rather to conceptual spatial and territorial boundaries. As already stated, the boundaries of national membership – or more accurately non-membership – are inscribed in citizenship legislature, as well as public, economic and social structures and institutions. It is therefore these legal and institutional sites, as well as other cultural media like literary and historical texts, where fights over identity take place. *China Men* tells the story of the male Chinese immigrants' embattled quest for membership of the nation, to become Americans, citizens of the American state and to gain the accompanying entitlement to ownership of the land. The ascription of national membership within the pages of *China Men* means that the text itself, as a physical entity, claims its place as a nation-making text, revising and re-imagining the community of the American nation to take account of ethnic subjects and diaspora presences like the China men. Homi Bhabha writes that: 'counter narratives of the nation ... continually evoke and erase its totalising boundaries – both actual and conceptual – disturb those ideological manoeuvres through which 'imagined communities' are given essentialist identities'.[60] *China Men* contests and disrupts the ideological manoeuvres of the nation-state which define Kingston, as well as the China men, as outsiders of the imagined communities of the nation.

China Men makes use of inter-textual, intra-textual and extra-textual contestation. In this sense, it is also an example of what Linda Hutcheon calls 'historiographic metafiction'[61] in terms of its theoretical and discursive self-awareness and its project of rethinking and questioning the epistemological status of historical, geographical and theoretical discourses, as they are seen to participate in the production of ideologies of national identity. The problems identifying the discursive status of Kingston's work are well documented.[62] Yet it is important to recognise that the traversing of discursive categories by Kingston is quite deliberate. Variously described as 'history', 'fiction', 'memoir' or 'biography', *China Men* encapsulates the ongoing contest between different kinds of narratives in order to highlight how our attempts to delimit our cultural chronicles and stories produce epistemologically deceptive versions of our realities. Kingston herself has written: 'The mainstream culture doesn't know the history of Chinese-Americans, ... so all of a sudden, right in the middle of the stories, plunk – there is an eight-page section of pure history ... there are no characters in it. It really affects the shape of the book and it might look quite clumsy.'[63] Whether 'clumsy' or not, to have 'pure history' embedded in the middle of the stories produces a contestation or confrontation between two different discourses, which 'jars' the reader. The subjective, personal and fictionalised histories of the China men in the text serve to challenge and often to contradict the 'official' version of history to be found in 'pure history' ('The Laws') section.[64] Thus, official and non-official versions of history co-exist in such a way that the 'pure history' sections are exposed as far from 'pure', but are instead simply different ways of telling the same story, equally 'contaminated' by personal biases and viewpoints. The juxtaposition of ostensibly very different genres, history and fiction, one claiming more epistemological authority than the other, therefore uncovers the precarious status of the 'truth claim' of history and the inherent fictionality of historical discourse. In addition, the exposure of history as an ideologically constructed and value-loaded narrative highlights history's role in the production of 'nation' as a 'unisonant',[65] and legitimate entity.

History and fiction are not the only discursive sites of contestation, however. The authority of autobiography is treated with equal mistrust. Once again, the jostle between the traditionally conflicting and very separate discourses of autobiography and fiction is enacted in the text, with the fictional versions of the China men's stories again querying the authority of autobiographical 'truth'. Kingston continually emphasises how incomplete and often uncertain her knowledge of her grandfathers' stories is. She even questions her biographical subjects for information within the text: 'Did you cut your pigtail to show your support for the public? Or have you always been American?', she asks at one point (p. 18). Both autobiography and biography are narratives of genesis. Kingston's deployment of autobiographical discourse to tell the story of the China men's claim to the United States and to American nationality and citizenship has ironic resonances for the genealogies of origins that she is concerned with questioning.

Kingston has another purpose in throwing the discourses of history, fiction, autobiography and biography into contestation with each other. The strategy of mixing discourses prevents the reader from reading the text in just one way – as history *or* autobiography *or* fiction, and making corresponding assumptions about the referentiality of that discourse. She is counteracting the tendency to read all texts by 'ethnic' or 'minority' writers (whatever the *declared* discursive status of the text) as being in some way representative.[66] Cross-generic texts like *China Men* resist interpretation as an authoritative version of that ethnic group's story. For example, Kingston tells the story of several 'grandfathers' in her text. Grandfathers become almost generic;[67] there are simply too many to be blood relatives, and each grandfather represents part of the wider Chinese American immigrant story: of the search for gold; of working on the railroad, or on a sugarcane farm, or setting up a laundry. Yet the strategy of presenting these stories as the biographies of her grandfathers allows Kingston to offer them as textual warnings against the conflation of all ethnic or minority subjects as 'other' to a white readership.

The competition between fictional, historical and autobiographical discourses is further complicated by Kingston's use and abuse of myth in her text. *China Men* opens with a story about a man called Tang Ao, who went looking for the Gold Mountain (the United States), but instead found the Land of Women, where he underwent enforced feminisation through ear-piercing, epilation and footbinding. As Donald C. Goellnicht has pointed out, this myth has been adapted from the nineteenth-century Chinese novel *Flowers in the Mirror* by Li Ju-Chen.[68] Kingston has altered the myth to suit her own purposes (as she did in *The Woman Warrior*). She also highlights the precarious nature of myth-as-history by offering two conflicting dates for the mythic story – in AD 694–705 or in AD 441. As 'The Laws' form the structural centre of the text, so here this myth 'On Discovery' constitutes the beginning, signalling to the reader that myth should be accorded equal validity as a legitimate version of the past as history or autobiography or biography, discourses more commonly supposed to be grounded in 'fact'. Or, to read Kingston's purpose another way: she demonstrates the *il*legitimacy of all of these discourses as factual retrospectives. Thus, in *China Men* history, autobiography, biography and fiction are all placed on a discursive continuum.

The power of mythical fictions is emphasised in the Lo Bun Sun story, discussed later in this chapter. Intended as an auditory pun[69] on *Robinson Crusoe*, this story echoes Defoe's narrative, charting the protagonist's journey to a deserted island, his struggle for survival and eventual establishment of a colony on the island. The purpose of this myth is twofold. Again, the myth is accorded equal weight as more factual narratives in terms of its potency and endurance as an inherited cultural tale. The Lo Bun Sun story also interrogates and contests American myths of origins. It is a story of colonisation, but here is both inverted and subverted, because the subject position of coloniser is here inhabited by a Chinese, rather than a white, British man (Robinson Crusoe). Thus in the story that Kingston relates, the coloured man gets there first. This reflects back on American myths of origins where it is the white man who civilises and colonises, and with regard to Chinese American history, in the myth it is the Chinese rather than the white Americans who arrive first. The use of the Lo Bun Sun story therefore not only highlights the provisionality of narrative, but also becomes part of Kingston's wider project of re-colonisation, to '(re)claim America', as she puts it, for her male ancestors. In this manner, the revision by a 'minority' writer of a dominant cultural myth of origin serves to disrupt claims by that culture of cultural supremacy and to question such a genealogy of origin. So, Kingston's rewriting of both the Tang Ao Chinese myth and the Lo Bun Sun Western myth serve to literally authorise competing versions of history in her text, as well as the Chinese American claim to America.

China Men as frontier literary history

The way in which territory and territoriality meet textuality, as already discussed in this chapter, also represents an example of the kind of frontier literary history advocated by Annette Kolodny in her essay 'Letting Go Our Grand Obsessions'.[70] Kolodny's vision of frontier literary history points to the duality of meaning in the word 'authorise'. To write history, she suggests, is to both inscribe ownership and to colonise (as in 'inhabit'). Kolodny emphasises that frontiers – cultural as well as geographical – are created out of contestation of territory (again, cultural as well as geographical territory), or confrontation, so that cultural and geographical spaces are only defined in opposition to something: the presence of another culture, territory or interest group.[71] Thus, in Kolodny's model the frontier is as much human as geographical, and results from human/cultural contestations: 'there always stands at the heart of frontier literature … a physical terrain that, for at least one group of participants, is newly encountered and is undergoing change because of that encounter'.[72] The frontier, then, is an imagined boundary between nation and non-nation, so that a cultural group excluded from national membership would be forced, as is the case with the China men, to inhabit the border between nation and non-nation. I would suggest that China Men is one such frontier literary

history. The text is a historical, geographical as well as literary palimpsest, which reflects the continually evolving territory of the American
West. *China Men* charts the cultural frontier contests between the already resident white Americans and the newly arrived China men, and
the ways in which this contestation transmutes and transforms geographical and cultural frontiers. Kolodny suggests that it is human encounters with each other and with the physical environment that create
the frontier.[73] *China Men* tells the story of the grandfather China men's
interactions with their new physical environment, the mythologised
Gold Mountain. The China men working in the mines and on the railroad transform the physical environment: 'China men banded the nation North and South, East and West, with criss-crossing steel. They
were the binding and building ancestors of this place' (p. 145). Kingston
continually suggests that the Chinese American role in the metamor-
phosis of the United States accords the China men a right of ownership
of the land through her creation of atavistic narratives. As Jeff Spinner
makes clear, ancestry, and the evocation of ancestral connection, is one
way in which a sense of belonging is asserted.[74] Here, Kingston constantly evokes the language of ancestry in order to press her – and her
male forebears' – claims to American territory. Repeated references to
ancestorship include the chapter titles: 'Grandfather of the Sierra Ne-
vada Mountains'; 'The American Father', 'The Great-Grandfather of the
Sandalwood Mountains', all signifying ownership. This refers back to
the idea of colonisation of a country, mentioned earlier, where the inhabiting of a country signals ownership. In *China Men* this is suggested
through the chapter titles, but also more forcefully in particular through
the actions of the character Ah Goong. In a memorable scene, the grandfather of the railroad both urinates off a mountain face and mastur-
bates: '"I am fucking the world", he said. The world's vagina was big …
he fucked the world' (p. 132). Here, Ah Goong marks his territory in
the manner of a tom cat with his urine. In addition, his act of masturbation is both an attempt to master his environment in a rape-like act,
and to again mark his territory, so that the act of masturbation becomes
a kind of sexual graffiti. It is almost a literalisation of the interpenetra-
tion between a human and his environment that Kolodny described
earlier. In this example, Kingston links the language of procreation with
possession to intervene in dominant cultural narratives of origins in an
ironic parody of the creation myth. Furthermore, the sexual defilement
of the landscape in this manner has ironic resonances for notions of
national (read racial) purity in the context of the assumed link between nationality and territoriality. In her work on metaphors of

experience and history of the frontier, Kolodny charts the growth of frontier metaphors of 'psychosexual dramas of men intent on possessing a virgin continent';[75] and the ways in which this 'land – as woman symbolisation'[76] engendered an 'eroticised intimacy with the environment'.[77] As Kingston took up myths of colonisation like the *Robinson Crusoe*/Lo Bun Sun story and undermined them, here she engages with these metaphors and fantasies of sexual control over the land. By depicting her characters' re-enactment of the 'psychosexual drama', Kingston appropriates this metaphor for *her* pioneers' experience, while at the same time firmly locating the Asian American creation and experience of the frontier within a dominant psychohistory of the frontier.

Kingston's appropriation of dominant metaphors of the United States frontier is also gendered. Kolodny demonstrates how the metaphor and experience of the frontier has always been different for men and for women. While men, as already discussed in this chapter, reacted to the frontier in sexual terms, with images of sexual domination, women responded with Edenic metaphors and images of tending the land. Rather than producing the urge to dominate, encounters with the frontier for women produced the desire to domesticate, as Kolodny writes, to 'domesticate the strangeness of America'.[78] This metaphor is also used by Kingston in relation to the China men. At the very beginning of the text, Kingston indicates that she intends to present the China men's experience in America as not only an experience of estrangement, but also of emasculation, through her representation of the story 'On Discovery'.[79] The thesis that the immigrant experience is emasculating is continued when Kingston depicts the Asian American immigrants responding to the land in female terms by tending a garden:

> For recreation, because he was a farmer and as an antidote for the sameness of the cane, he planted a garden near the huts ... he ticked off in a chant the cuttings, seeds and bulbs he had brought across the ocean – pomelo, kumquat, which is "golden luck", tangerines, citron also known as five fingers and Buddha's hand, ginger, bitter melon and other kinds of melon. (p. 106)

For Bak Goong, the act of tending the land is a literal domestication: the transformation of the land into a more Asian landscape through the flora. Tending a garden thus is a strategy to combat the estrangement accompanying immigration. Kingston also shows how immigration has been emasculating by locating Bak Goong's reaction to the landscape within a female tradition of gardening the frontier. However, the China men's response to the frontier is also allied with the male desire for domination that Kolodny discusses. As Ah-Goong sought to have sex with the land, so Bak Goong and the other sugarcane workers worked the land in sexual terms:

> The land was ready to be sown. They bagged the slips in squares of cloth tied over their shoulders. Flinging the seed cane into ditches, Bak Goong wanted to sing like a farmer in an opera. When his bag was empty, he stepped into the furrow and turned the seed cane so the nodes were to the sides, nodes on either side of the stick like an animal's eyes. He filled the trenches and patted the pregnant earth. (p. 105)

Here again, like Ah-Goong's masturbation, Bak Goong spills seed, impregnates the land and thus becomes a kind of father of the American landscape. Through these metaphors of impregnation, Kingston both echoes a long dominant cultural tradition of responses to the frontier and also again asserts a paternity claim to the land on behalf of her China men forebears. Again, Kingston suggests that living in – and changing – the environment entitles ownership. Kolodny writes that the role the Asian American presence had in the American West was in transforming the agrarian landscape into an 'industrial frontier',[80] here illustrated in the stories of Ah Goong, Bak Goong and Bak Sook Goong, and is an example of the physical terrain and cultural landscape changing as a result of the cultural contact between Chinese and Americans. The physical terrain in one case is actually named after those who transformed it: Mokoli'i Island is called 'Chinaman's Hat'; language, in the form of nomenclature, is used as a way of inscribing the claim to territory. Kingston writes: 'It's a tribute to the pioneers to have a living island named after their workhat' (p. 91). Kingston seems to suggest that it is the transformation of the land that makes Chinese into Chinese Americans. It is significant that the 'railroad demons' set up a contest between different ethnic groups in building the railroad, which can be symbolically read as a contest for colonisation: 'Day shifts raced against night shifts, China Men against Welshmen, China Men against Irishmen, China Men against Injuns and black demons' (p. 138). In this quotation, 'Americans' are simply not present in the contest for ownership of the land; rather, new immigrant groups are seen engaged in competition for possession of the land, and, through that, for national belonging.

Kingston ultimately questions whether changing the land and inhabiting the land can lead to a claim to that land, though. Certainly, she suggests that within an 'American' frame of reference, this is not the case. Like Kolodny, Kingston recognises (although does not approve) that within an 'American' legal discursive system ownership must be circumscribed textually in the form of legal or historical documentation in order to be legitimate. Textual possession both facilitates and engenders physical possession.

In *China Men*, we also see Kingston interrogating the ways in which 'Americanness', as a sign of 'national' belonging, is engendered and inscribed on other battlefields of identity, such as language, cultural practices and occupations.[81] For instance, Ah Goong mistakenly believes that his part in the creation of the new frontier will make him American: 'Only Americans could have done it ... he was an American for having built the railroad', he decides (p. 144). Some of the other China men believe that American dress, names and pastimes constitute Americanness: they name themselves Ed, Woodrow, Roosevelt and Worldster, go to tea parties and 'looked all the same Americans' in suits (p. 65).

The need for 'Americanness' as a national identity to be inscribed officially as nationality and citizenship becomes clear to the China men, who are barred from citizenship because of their ethnicity. As 'The Laws' section tells us, 'national origin' upon which the qualification for citizenship is based, did not mean 'country of birth' until 1965, and Chinese Americans were barred from naturalising for many years too. In the China men who yearn to be fully fledged citizens, the confidence men who pose as 'citizenship judges' find easy prey: 'The demon said "I Citizenship Judge invite you to be US citizen. Only one bag gold." Ah Goong was thrilled. What an honor' (p. 141). The citizenship judges prey on the need for official recognition of Americanness, as one China man notes: 'he was already a part of this new country, but now he had it in writing' (p. 141). Of course, Kingston's intention here is ironic: the official circumscription of citizenship that Ah Goong has acquired is worthless. His misplaced faith in the authority of official texts is emphasised: 'If he got kidnapped, Ah Goong planned, he would whip out his Citizenship paper and show that he was an American' (p. 147). The precarious nature of 'official' 'legal' documentation is illustrated when the Hall of Records burned down: 'Citizenship papers burned, Residency certificates, passenger lists, Marriage certificates – every paper a China man wanted for citizenship and legality burned in that fire. An authentic citizen, then, had no more papers than an alien ... every Chinaman was reborn out of that fire a citizen' (p. 149). Significantly, the citizenship judges/confidence men take advantage of the China men at the point at which the labour on the railroad ceases because of a battle over wages, the moment when the China men feel most insecure in their new country. In addition, once the railroad is finished, the China men are driven out, so the legitimation through transforming the landscape by working on the railroad is lost, and it is at this point that Ah Goong considers returning to China.

For several of the China men, citizenship is defined through contestation. For example, Mad Sao 'proves' his Americanness by fighting in the Second World War for the United States. Similarly, Kingston tells us: 'Chinese Americans talk about how when they set foot in China, they realise their Americanness' (p. 287). The 'Vietnam Brother' who is given Q Clearance (high-level security clearance) by the US government becomes aware of his Americanness: 'the government was certifying that the family was really American, not precariously American but super-American' (p. 291). Here, the brother is forced to choose between contesting national allegiances, and he makes his initial choice, the United States, and receives Q clearance. Kingston ironically notes: 'maybe that Grandfather's Citizenship Judge was real and legal after all' (p. 291). However, the Vietnam brother finally rejects his American allegiance as he realises that he remains loyal to his Chinese identity too.[82] Another figure, Uncle Bun, comes to the same recognition, implied through his fear of the House Un-American Activities Committee. Here, 'citizenship' or 'subjecthood', meaning 'under the authority or law of a country' or 'in political and legal subjection to a country', whereby that country must reciprocate with obligations to the individual, collapses, becoming 'subject to', that is, conditional and provisional, and also 'in subjection to', suggesting subordination and domination. Ultimately, neither the Vietnam brother nor Uncle Bun can meet the demands that the dominant culture places upon them as citizens. By placing Chinese and American allegiances in contestation with each other, Kingston effectively exposes the ironies and pressures the qualifications for citizenship and subjecthood in a country slow to reciprocate with legitimating, if not welcoming, gestures, as illustrated in 'The Laws' section. Near the end of *China Men*, these conflicting national allegiances are represented symbolically in the Confucius Hall: 'Sun Yat Sen's and Chiang Kai Shek's pictures were on the stage next to the American and Chinese flags' (p. 261).

The ironies of citizenship are echoed in Kingston's father's experience at the Immigration station on Angel Island. The president of the Self Governing Organisation invites Kingston's father to join, which will entitle him to vote and protect his immigration interests. The ironies of statesmanship are exposed when the president tells Kingston's father that he 'won his office by having been on the island the longest' (p. 55), which echoes the Lo Bun Sun story and highlights the irony of the white man's colonisation. In addition, the association itself is seen in an ironic light, since none of the newly arrived men possess any of the benefits of democratic citizenship: as detainees they are neither free nor franchised, and the Self Governing Organisation does not seem to contribute to the advancement of citizenship for its members. The creation of a micro state on Angel Island betrays the China men's desire for American citizenship and their need for official 'belonging'. Significantly, the tale of the China man's experience on Angel Island, his long detention and repeated interrogation is the story of the 'legal' father. Once again, the ironies of legal processes are exposed when juxtaposed with the altogether more congenial narrative of the illegal immigrant father, who is made welcome: 'Chinatown seemed to be waiting to welcome him' (p. 54). Significantly, the heightened sensation of the American land beneath his feet serves to engender in him the feeling of belonging. *Terra incognita* becomes terra firma: 'He disciplined his legs to step confidently, as if they belonged where they walked. He felt the concrete through his shoes' (p. 54). Physical contact with the ground is again seen to constitute belonging. The later cries of the new immigrants to 'let me land' (p. 58) take on new significance, as physical contact with the terrain psychologically confirms territoriality. This is in opposition to geographical or cartographical documentation, which, as a means of inscribing territory, is, like historical and legal inscriptions, questioned by Kingston. Benedict Anderson asserts that maps are an instrument of power like legal or historical texts, because as self-protective and self-legitimating devices, they are used by the state to imagine its domain.[83] As a form of totalising classification, Kingston mistrusts maps, and in *China Men* cartographic inscriptions of the world and of reality are highlighted as subjective and also as unreliable:

> The villagers unfolded their maps of the known world, which differed: turtles and elephants supported the continents, which were islands on their backs; in other cartographies, the continents were mountains with China the middle mountain, Han Mountain or Tang Mountain or the Wah Republic, a Gold Mountain to its west on some maps and to the east on others. (p. 49)

What is 'known' is shown to be precarious and shifting, so that through such cartographic uncertainty Kingston again questions epistemological certainty, here of a cartographic text. Subjective cartographies do not coincide with supposedly more referential maps: Gold Mountain, the mythologised site of Chinese dreams of America cannot be fixed geographically here, as Kingston shows; the Gold Mountain yearned for by the China man 'coming to claim the Gold Mountain, his own country' (p. 54), may not be where expected. Kingston tells us that one

of the China men went to 'live in California, which *some say* is the real
Gold Mountain anyway' (p. 74, my emphasis). Thus, real and imagined cartographies co-exist alongside real and imagined sites, again
rendering problematic assumptions about the referentiality of cartographic texts. It is therefore worth noting that the trajectories created
and through them the territories claimed by Kingston for her China
men ancestors are the work of someone with 'no map sense' (p. 198).

The *Li Sao* epic elegy, retold by Kingston towards the end of *China
Men*, echoes the China men's stories. Ch'u Yuan, 'wronged and exiled'
(p. 251), was forced to leave his kingdom and wander for the rest of
his life in barbarian lands, where he finally died by drowning. Kingston
always intends her retelling of myths to comment upon the narrative,
and here she uses the *Li Sao* to emphasise how displacement leads to
state- and law-sanctioned dispossession. We are told: 'He had to leave
the Centre; he roamed in the outer world for the rest of his life, twenty
years' (p. 250). The story of Ch'u Yuan, like the China men's stories, is
the diaspora story of the 'ex-centric'. The 'ex-centric', in Hutcheon's
definition, is someone who finds him or herself at the margins, and 'ex-
centricity' is the state of being at the margin, the border or the edge.
The ex-centric is marginal in terms of race, gender, ethnicity, class, sexuality or social role, as defined in opposition to the centre. Once again,
definition takes place through contestation, here the challenge to the
centre from the border. Again, the process of definition, as in Kolodny's
model of frontier evolution, is an *oppositional* paradigm. Hutcheon writes
that 'the ex-centric relies on the centre for its definition',[84] as in Kolodny's
model the frontier was the result of the con*front*ation between two
interest groups. Kingston's China men are all 'ex-centrics'. In Hutcheon's
words, the 'ex-centric' is 'the off-center, ineluctably identified with the
center it desires but is denied'.[85] The constant yearning for citizenship
by the 'ex-centric' China men marks their desire for centricity.

The China men's 'ex-centricity' results from their diasporic move
from China as 'centric' citizens to America where they are in exile. Centricity is thus always defined by context. The China men become 'ex-
centric' in the context of American nationalism; they are non-members
and are therefore relegated to the cultural, legal and social margins.
China Men constitutes a potent challenge to ethnocentrism, though, as
the previously silent, displaced China men's history and validity is reas-
serted by Kingston. She writes of the China men: 'You say with the few
words and the silences: No stories. No past. No China' (p. 18). The
inscription of Chinese American history and thus the shattering of the
ex-centric's silence results in a contestation of (but not for) the centre

and its historical legitimising texts. The project of claiming the United States for her ex-centric ancestors involves Kingston in a re-ordering of culture by re-valuing personal and subjective histories in opposition to monolithic history. Thus, in *China Men*, the 'official' text of history inscribed in 'The Laws' section co-exists with the vernacular histories of the China men fathers and grandfathers.[86] The homogenising tendency of frontier literary history described by Kolodny as the 'grand narrative of discovery and progress' is revised in the (literal) face of heterogenising testimonies like those of the China men, with the accompanying attentiveness of the text to the subjectivity of the enunciating presence. However, this does not result in a move on the part of the ex-centric from the margin to the centre, although this desire is displayed by Kingston's father, who 'inked each piece of our own laundry with the word *Centre*' (p. 18), as Hutcheon writes: 'it does not invert the valuing of centers into that of peripheries and borders'.[87] Kingston recognises that her father cannot tell her 'how we landed in a country where we are eccentric people' (p. 18). Rather, the *presence* of the ex-centric, and the articulation of the ex-centric's perspective, story and history, contests the epistemological status and homogenising tendency of the dominant cultural and physical centre – here the United States – and Anglo American perspectives. Thus, dominant versions of history are seen to be erroneous, and the United States is located geographically both to the east and the west of China, depending on which text is consulted. The presence of the ex-centric's perspective engenders the recognition that historical, auto/biographical, cartographic as well as fictional representations are never value-neutral. The new significance of the ex-centric or marginal perspective accompanies a recognition of the value of heterogeneity, so that 'otherness' is seen in a positive light, while remaining defined in opposition to the centre, as Kingston recognises: 'our dog tags had *O* for religion and *O* for race because neither black nor white … some kids said *O* was for "Oriental", but I knew it was for "Other" because the Filipinos, the Gypsies, and the Hawaiian boy were *Os*' (pp. 269–70).

By re-interpreting the frontier as 'a specifiable first moment on that liminal borderland between distinct cultures', Kolodny suggests that a previously 'narrow Eurocentric design' is decentred. Thus, Kolodny's vision of a new literary frontier history coincides with the project of challenging centres and revaluing borders. Texts and peoples previously liminal due to their ethnicity, race or gender, become the focus of attention here, because, as Kolodny notes, the frontier is displaced always to the geographical edges. Thus, the edge – geographical, cultural and literary – destabilises the centre as the emphasis shifts. *China Men*, because of its cross-generic texture, forces a questioning of what constitutes not just a literary, but also an historical text. It thus demonstrates that it is not just the centre which does not hold, but neither do those boundaries between different genres and discourses, so that the official voice of history co-exists alongside the more marginal diasporic voices of the ex-centric China men.

China Men's metafictional self-consciousness betrays Kingston's postmodernist caution regarding the relationship between world and text, as well as between different kinds of textual inscription. Joy Kogawa's *Obasan* and *Itsuka* likewise reveal their author's suspicion of the mimetic capabilities of narrative as they highlight the multifarious and constructed nature of the past as it is available to us. The Japanese American internment narratives and *China Men* are grounded in very different assumptions about the conditions, nature and uses of writing. These autobiographical texts attempt to emphasise both the referentiality and veracity of their accounts. In so doing, these writers betray their subscription to an unproblematically liberal humanist correspondence between writing and experience. The Japanese American autobiographies' narrative assaults upon legitimated national versions of their stories and thus their identities are launched from a realist position. As argued in this chapter, Kogawa's and Kingston's renderings of the past through a predominantly fictional discourse allows a more vigorous assault to be launched upon other discourses, as they are seen to produce versions of national identity delimiting and controlling to culturally marginal subjects like the Japanese Americans and Kingston's China men.

Notes

1   A note on terminology is necessary at this point. By 'nation' I mean a group of people forming one society under one government, inhabiting the same territory, and regarding themselves as one group. This corresponds to the 'state', as that organised political community. 'National identity' is one's status in relation to that community, as an insider or as an outsider. 'Citizenship' is the formal route by which an individual becomes a member of the nation, with the accompanying rights and privileges extended to her under that agreement. Citizenship is also reciprocal, so the individual agrees to conform to certain rules in accepting that identity. A 'citizen' is a member of that nation state. I am indebted to both Will Kymlicka, *Multicultural Citizenship: A Liberal Theory of Minority Rights* (Oxford: Clarendon, 1995) and Jeff Spinner, *The Boundaries of Citizenship: Race, Ethnicity and Nationality in the Liberal State* (Baltimore, MD: Johns Hopkins University Press, 1994), for these definitions.

2   Lisa Lowe, *Immigrant Acts: On Asian American Cultural Politics* (Durham, NC: Duke University Press, 1996), p. 2.

3   Spinner, *The Boundaries of Citizenship*, p. 170.

4   Tracey Hill and William Hughes (eds), Contemporary *Writing and National Identity* (Bath: Sulis Press, 1995), p. 2.

5   Spinner, *The Boundaries of Citizenship*, p. 39.

6   *Ibid.*, p. 46.

7   *Ibid.*

8   See Lowe, *Immigrant Acts*, pp. 22–6; see also, Kymlicka, *Multicultural Citizenship*.

9   Kymlicka, *Multicultural Citizenship*, p. 175.

10 Iris Marion Young, *Justice and the Politics of Difference* (Princeton, NJ: Princeton University Press, 1995), p. 179.

11 Lowe, *Immigrant Acts*, p. ix. Whilst I wish to acknowledge the influence Lowe's piece has had on my own work, I also want to note our points of departure. Lowe's materialist critique leads to a reluctance to explore the anxieties attendant upon the negotiation of identity as it is in the realm of psychoanalysis; my analysis proceeds from the recognition that in these cultural forms and formations, 'psychoanalytic formulations ... hover as felt presences', as Priscilla Wald notes in *Constituting Americans: Cultural Anxiety and Narrative Form* (Durham, NC: Duke University Press, 1995), p. 3.

12 Lowe, *Immigrant Acts*, p. ix.

13 *Ibid.*, p. x.

14 *Ibid.*, p. 3

15 *Ibid.*, p. 6.

16 *Ibid.*

17 See Roger Daniels, Sandra C. Taylor and Harry H. L. Kitano (eds), *Japanese Americans: From Relocation to Redress* (Seattle, WA: University of Washington Press, 1991), for a comprehensive overview of the relocation and internment experience.

18 Ronald Takaki, *Strangers from a Different Shore: A History of Asian Americans* (New York: Penguin, 1990), p. 15; also chapter 10, 'The Watershed of World War II'.

19 Lowe's point, see Lowe, *Immigrant Acts*, p. ix.

20 Stan Yogi has read these texts as attempts to resolve Japanese American identity, an identity – or identities – in flux. See Stan Yogi, 'Japanese American Literature', in King-kok Cheung, *An Interethnic Companion to Asian American Literature* (New York: Cambridge University Press, 1997), pp. 134–7.

21 In this sense, these narratives share an affinity with the texts about Communist China which were the subject of chapter 4.

22 Kalí Tal, *Worlds of Hurt: Reading the Literature of Trauma* (New York: Cambridge University Press, 1996), p. 6.

23 A point reiterated in many of the Japanese American internment narratives.

24 See Elaine Kim, *Asian American Literature: An Introduction to the Writings and Their Social Context* (Philadelphia, PA: Temple University Press, 1982), p. 133.

25 Amy Iwasaki Mass, 'Psychological Effects of the Camps on Japanese Americans', in Daniels et al. (eds), *Japanese Americans: From Relocation to Redress*, pp. 159–62; p. 159.

26 Wald, *Constituting Americans*, p. 3.

27   Yoshiko Uchida, *Desert Exile: The Uprooting of a Japanese-American Family* (Seattle, WA: University of Washington Press, 1982), p. 153. All further page references are to this edition and are cited in parentheses.

28   Lowe's point, see Lowe, *Immigrant Acts*, p. 48.

29   However, historical and sociological work has been undertaken, collecting the oral testimonies of those *issei* who experienced internment and relocation.

30   Tal, *Worlds of Hurt*, p. 6. Critical work looking at the idea of a literature of trauma is starting to proliferate. For example, see also Tim Woods, 'Mending the Skin of Memory: Ethics and History in Contemporary Narratives', *Rethinking History*, 2:3, December (1998), pp. 339–48, and Leona Toker, 'Testimony as Art: Varlam Shalamov's "Condensed Milk"', in Dominic Rainsford and Tim Woods (eds), *Critical Ethics: Text, Theory and Responsibility* (London: Macmillan, 1998), pp. 241–56.

31   For a more extensive discussion of *Obasan*'s cyclical structure, see Helena Grice, 'Reading the Nonverbal: The Indices of Space, Time, Taciturnity and Tactility in Joy Kogawa's *Obasan*', *Melus*, 24:4, Winter (1999), 93–106.

32   *Bildungsroman* is a type of developmental narrative ending in success. It has been discussed as a very prominent form in Asian American literature, particularly manifested as autobiography. See King-Kok Cheung's discussion of the autobiographical in Asian American cultural production in her introduction to *An Interethnic Companion*; and Lisa Lowe's discussions in *Immigrant Acts*.

33   Benedict Anderson, *Imagined Communities: Reflections on the Origins and Spread of Nationalism* (London: Verso, 1994), p. 204.

34   Sau-ling Wong, *Reading Asian American Literature: From Necessity to Extravagance* (Princeton, NJ: Princeton University Press, 1993), pp. 120–30; p. 120.

35   Tal, *Worlds of Hurt*, p. 120.

36   *Ibid.*

37   Miné Okubo, *Citizen 13660* (Seattle, WA: Washington University Press, 1983), p. xi. All further page references are to this edition and are cited in parentheses.

38   See Tal, *Worlds of Hurt* for a discussion of this.

39   Quoted in Kim, *Asian American Literature*, p. 88.

40   Tal, *Worlds of Hurt*, p. 125.

41   Monica Sone, *Nisei Daughter* (Seattle, WA: University of Washington Press, 1979), p. xvi. All further page references are to this edition and are cited in parentheses.

42   See, for example, Kim, *Asian American Literature*, p. 80; Lowe, *Immigrant Acts*, pp. 48–9.

43   Kim, *Asian American Literature*, p. 80.

44   Wong, *Reading Asian American Literature*, p. 137.

45   Kim, *Asian American Literature*, p. 84.

46   Patricia A. Sakurai, 'The Politics of Possession: The Negotiation of Identity in *American in Disguise, Homebase* and *Farewell to Manzanar*', in Gary Y. Okihiro et al., *Privileging Positions: The Sites of Asian American Studies* (Pullman, WA: Washington State University Press, 1995), pp. 157–70; p. 165.

47   Jeanne Wakatsuki Houston and James D. Houston, *Farewell to Manzanar* (San Francisco, CA: Houghton Mifflin, 1973), p. 137. All further page references are to this edition, and are cited in parentheses.

48 Kim, *Asian American Literature*, p. 86.

49 Quoted in Kim, *Asian American Literature*, p. 88.

50 Lowe, *Immigrant Acts*, p. 48.

51 Joy Kogawa, *Obasan* (New York: Anchor Books, 1994). All further page references are to this edition, and are cited in parentheses.

52 A point made by Scott McFarlane, 'Covering *Obasan* and the Narrative of Internment', in Okhiro et al., *Privileging Positions*, pp. 401–11; p. 402.

53 See *Citizen 13660*, p. xi. For a discussion of the success of *Obasan* and *Itsuka*, see Wong, *Reading Asian American Literature*, pp. 16–17; see also McFarlane, 'Covering *Obasan*', pp. 401–2.

54 Of the two, Okada's novel is the better-known and the more widely discussed. See, for example, Jinqi Ling, 'Race, Power, and Cultural Politics in John Okada's *No-No Boy*', *American Literature*, 67:2, June (1995), pp. 359–81.

55 Kingston is often viewed as a spokesperson for Chinese Americans, both by Asian American and other critics, particularly in her position as probably the most prominent Asian American writer today.

56 Takaki notes that in 1867, 90 per cent of the Central Pacific Railroad workforce was comprised of Chinese Americans. And at the same time, Chinese labour was contributing significantly to the growth of the sugar cane industry in both Hawaii and on the mainland. By 1853, Chinese labourers constituted 9.2 per cent of the Hawaiian population as a result of this growth. The period after the completion of the railroad coincided with the decline of labour opportunities for Chinese in the sugar cane industry, mainly as a result of the new recruitment of cheaper and less organised ethnic labour groups. Chinese Americans were forced to search for new and different work opportunities. The early part of the twentieth century saw an economic slump, too, which partly engendered the rise in anti-Asian sentiment, also a factor in the Chinese banishment from white labour markets and the subsequent growth of a Chinese economic enclave. This period saw a move on the part of Chinese Americans into the service industries, especially the establishment of Chinese laundries. By 1920, 58 per cent of Chinese were engaged in service industries like laundry work.

57 Spinner, *The Boundaries of Citizenship*, p. 141.

58 See Spinner, *The Boundaries of Citizenship*, p. 168, for a more expansive discussion of the 'battlegrounds' of identity.

59 See Homi Bhabha (ed.), *Nation and Narration* (London: Routledge, 1990), pp. 1–6.

60 *Ibid.*, p. 300.

61 Linda Hutcheon, *A Poetics of Postmodernism: History, Theory, Fiction* (London: Routledge, 1988), pp. 5–6.

62 For discussions of the generic confusion surrounding Kingston's work, see LeiLani Nishime, 'Engendering Genre: Gender and Nationalism in *China Men* and *The Woman Warrior*', *Melus*, 20:1, Spring (1995), pp. 67–82; also Sauling Cynthia Wong, 'Autobiography as Guided Chinatown Tour? Maxine Hong Kingston's *The Woman Warrior* and the Chinese-American Autobiographical Controversy', in J. R. Payne (ed.), *Multicultural Autobiography*, (Knoxville, TN: University of Tennessee Press, 1992), pp. 248–79. For perhaps the most vitriolic discussion of Kingston's use of genre, see Frank Chin, 'This Is Not an Autobiography', *Genre*, 18:2 (1985), pp. 109–30.

63 Kingston quoted in Timothy Pfaff, 'Talk with Mrs. Kingston', *New York Times Book Review*, 15 June 1980, p. 26.

64 Maxine Hong Kingston, *China Men* (London: Picador, 1981), pp. 151–8. All further page references are to this edition and are cited in parentheses.

65 Bhabha's term, 'DissemiNation: time, narrative, and the margins of the modern nation', in Bhabha (ed.), *Nation and Narration*, pp. 291–322; p. 315.

66 See Wong, 'Autobiography as Guided Chinatown Tour' for a discussion of the demand for ethnic autobiography to be representative, especially pp. 258–9.

67 This is LeiLani Nishime's phrase. The same can be seen in the 'On Fathers' section in *China Men*, an introductory piece discussing the way that 'fathers' look and behave in the same way. In 'Alaska China Men', Kingston writes that 'perhaps any China Man was China Joe' (p. 160).

68 See Donald C. Goellnicht, 'Tang Ao in America: Male Subject Positions in *China Men*', in Shirley Goek-lin Lim and Amy Ling (eds), *Reading the Literatures of Asian America* (Philadelphia, PA: Temple University Press, 1992), pp. 191–212. Goellnicht is citing Amy Ling here, see p. 207.

69 Again, Nishime's term. See Nishime, 'Engendering Genre', p. 74.

70 Annette Kolodny, 'Letting Go Our Grand Obsessions: Notes Toward a New Literary History of the American Frontier', in Michael Moon and Cathy Davidson (eds), *Subjects and Citizens: Nation, Race And Gender From Oroonoko To Anita Hill*, (Durham, NC: Duke University Press, 1995), pp. 9–26.

71 She cites Howard Lamar and Leonard Thompson's definition of the frontier as 'a territory or zone of *inter*penetration between … previously distinct societies' (my italics).

72 *Ibid.*, p. 13.

73 *Ibid.*, p. 11.

74 Spinner, *The Boundaries of Citizenship*, p. 10.

75 Annette Kolodny, *The Lay of the Land: Metaphor as Experience and History in American Life and Letters* (Chapel Hill, NC: University of North Carolina Press, 1975), p. xiii.

76 *Ibid.*, p. ix.

77 Annette Kolodny, *The Land Before Her: Fantasy and Experience of the American Frontier, 1630–1860* (Chapel Hill, NC: University of North Carolina Press, 1984), p. 5.

78 *Ibid.*, p. 37; p. 237.

79 This is the story of enforced feminisation in the Land of Women; see Kingston, *China Men*, pp. 9–10.

80 Kolodny, 'Letting Go Our Grand Obsessions', p. 17.

81 See Spinner, *The Boundaries of Citizenship*, p. 10.

82 Another example of the way that the Second World War forced Asian Americans to choose between conflicting national allegiances can be found in John Okada, *No-No Boy* (Seattle, WA: University of Washington Press, 1979).

83 Anderson, *Imagined Communities*, p. 164.

84 Hutcheon, *A Poetics of Postmodernism*, p. 73.

85 *Ibid.*, p. 60.

86 Kingston indicates the official status of 'The Laws' section structurally too: the 'chronology' format she adopts signals a departure from her fictional text.

87 Hutcheon, *A Poetics of Postmodernism*, p. 69.

Homes and homecomings

Of course, places are both a location on earth and a state of mind
(Maxine Hong Kingston, email to the author, 15 April 2000)

A person's geography is both inward and outward
(Aimee Liu, *Face*)

I have been asked the 'home' question (when are you going home) peri-
odically for fifteen years now. Leaving aside the subtly racist implications
of the question (go home you don't belong), I am still not satisfied with my
response. What is home? The place I was born? Where I grew up? Where
my parents live? Where I live and work as an adult? Where I locate my
community – my people? Is home a geographical space, an historical space,
an emotional, sensory space?
(Chandra Talpade Mohanty, 'Defining Genealogies: Feminist Reflections
on being South Asian in North America')

Asian American women writers are extensively preoccupied with issues of space, place and the idea of 'home'. As Meena Alexander recently wrote in an email to the author, 'Places are so close to my nerves.
I sometimes think that's how my imagination works, by stitching through
these disparate places. What else is time, in so far as it makes the self
real to us, by which I mean palpable?'[1] This, the final chapter, explores
various Asian American women writers' use of the tropes of place, space
and home. In order to do this use is made of the recently emergent
critical discourse of space in literature, in which space is often used as
a metaphor for the dynamics of identity.[2] In the introduction to Monica
Sone's *Nisei Daughter*, S. Frank Miyamoto notes: 'I believe it is illuminating to regard *Nisei Daughter* as a statement of self-identity … The
identity question asks, "Who am I?", or more specifically, "What is my
place in the world?"'[3] The slippage from 'Who am I?' to 'What is my
place in the world?' is seen in many texts by Asian American women. In
her memoir, *Fault Lines*, for example, Meena Alexander asks: 'Who are
we? What selves can we construct to live by? How shall we mark out

space?'[4] However, space in these works does not just act as a metaphor for identity; it also, as Shirley Ardener notes, 'defines people and people define space'.[5] Thus, this discussion explores several Asian American women writers' searches, both in their fictions and autobiographies, for self through place. For example, in Chuang Hua's autobiographical novel, *Crossings*, a novel about the cultural crossings and wanderings that the central character Fourth Jane makes, she is repeatedly described in relation to the places and spaces that she has inhabited: 'She stood in the center of the square carpet of faded reds greens and blues and whites in which she discerned oases and deserts, scorpions and camels, departures, wanderings and homecomings woven inextricably.'[6] Many of the texts discussed here also have departures, wanderings and homecomings woven into their fabric as a dominant preoccupation in relation to the exploration of identity.

Places and spaces are charged sites, pregnant with our meanings and associations. As Edward Relph notes: 'There is for virtually everyone a deep association with and consciousness of the places where we were born and grew up, where we live now, or where we have had particularly moving experiences. This association seems to constitute a vital source of both individual and cultural identity and security'.[7] If places are ideologically charged sites, then the house, in Gaston Bachelard's words, is 'the most powerful psychospatial image'.[8] The 'house', in this sense, is interchangeable with the concept of 'home'. 'Home' is not just the dwelling place, but also carries nuances of belonging, nurturance and origins. 'Home', as Kathleen Kirby puts it, is 'a walled site of belonging'.[9] More than 'a three-dimensional structure', it is a 'densely signifying marker in ideology', demonstrated by the myriad of terms to describe the home: as dwelling, homestead, homeplace, habitation, domicile, abode, residence, amongst others.[10] 'Home' often carries a heavy ideological weight for the Asian American woman writer, who, in common with other ethnic or diasporic writers, may have undergone a separation from the ancestral homeland. In many texts, the idea of the homeland looms large in the search for identity, whether it is an actual remembered site, or a mythologised location.[11] Two key autobiographical texts, Lydia Minatoya's *Talking to High Monks in the Snow* (1992) and Kyoko Mori's *The Dream of Water* (1995), for instance, chart odysseys in search of identity which involve a journey back to Japan and China respectively, as the ancestral homeland. For other women writers, Asia remains an imagined homeplace, and these include Maxine Hong Kingston, the daughters in Amy Tan's novels,[12] Mona and Callie in Gish Jen's novels, and the character Nomi in Julie

Shigekuni's *A Bridge Between Us*.[13] For Meena Alexander, Sara Suleri and Shirley Geok-lin Lim, three writers whose memoir work is informed by a post-structuralist strain of postcolonial theory, 'home' can only ever be an imagined place.[14] And finally, for many earlier immigrants and their children, such as autobiography writers Monica Sone, Mary Paik Lee, Yoshiko Uchida, Jeanne Wakatsuki Houston and Jade Snow Wong, and fictionalists Joy Kogawa, Ronyoung Kim, as well as Tan's fictional mothers, the desire to make the United States their home is repeatedly repulsed by denials of citizenship, internment as enemy aliens and other racist exclusionary practices, even though the respective Asian country has long since been psychologically relinquished as the home-land.

Many of these women become wanderers in search of their iden-tity. Some, like the Korean American writer Theresa Hak Kyung Cha, and Ronyoung Kim's fictional characters, are in exile. Some, like Chuang Hua's protagonist Fourth Jane in *Crossings*, the character Ralph and his family in Gish Jen's *Typical American*, Amy Tan's *Joy Luck Club* mothers and Winnie Louie in *The Kitchen God's Wife*, many of Bharati Mukherjee's women characters (notably Dimple and Jasmine in *Wife*), Sara Suleri and Meena Alexander, are emigrés. The final group are the children, grandchildren and even the great grandchildren of immigrants who have never visited the ancestral homeland, despite its enduring psy-chological significance in their lives, and for whom the United States is home: Maxine Hong Kingston, Tan's *Joy Luck Club* daughters and Pearl Louie in *The Kitchen God's Wife*, Naomi in Joy Kogawa's novels, Kyoko Mori, Lydia Minatoya, Monica Sone, Yoshiko Uchida, Jeanne Wakatsuki Houston, Kadohata's protagonist in *The Floating World* and Jade Snow Wong. For these writers, the homeland is a mythologised location, in the manner described by Patricia Duncker: 'There is always a danger that the Homeland, the remembered, imagined or recon-structed country of origin ... can become an ideal dream, untouched by history, conflict, poverty or corruption'.[15]

Psychologies of exile and narratives of migration

In the discussion here of the wanderings that many of these women engage in, both geographically and textually, in their pursuit of self-definition, a distinction is made between what can be termed 'psycholo-gies of exile' and 'narratives of migration'. Home is where you belong, and 'psychology of exile' is used to indicate a state of unbelonging.[16] Many of the women here undergo different kinds of displacement:

geographical, social and familial, amongst others, and so the search for self is also the search for place and the desire for home. This state of unbelonging is paradigmatically expressed by female emigré Mai-mai Sze in her autobiography, *Echo of a Cry: A Story Which Began in China*:

> Fervently we have wanted to belong somewhere at the same time that we have often wanted to run away. We reached out for something, and when by chance grasped it, we often found that it wasn't what we wanted at all. There is one part of us that is always lost and searching. It is an echo of a cry that was a longing for warmth and safety. And through our adolescent fantasies, and however our adult reasoning may disguise it, the search continues.[17]

The gradual shift in many texts towards a narrative of migration is indicative of the Asian American woman's reconciliation of her particular displaced/migratory identity or her move towards the recovery of a state of belonging. This often involves a rethinking of the meanings of home and belonging, as John McLeod observes:

> Conventional ideas of 'home' and 'belonging' depend upon clearly defined, static notions of being 'in place', firmly rooted in a community or particular geographical location. But these models or 'narratives' of belonging no longer seem suited to a world where the experience and legacy of migration are altering the ways in which individuals think of their relation to place.[18]

Homes and houses: owning space

The sense of belonging is intimately bound up with the notion of ownership, of space and territory. The feeling of belonging is very specifically linked to a move towards home ownership in many narratives. As Marilyn Chandler makes clear in *Dwelling in the Text*, social and psychological stability is partly engendered through economic security and thus the goal of home ownership is a preoccupation in much ethnic fiction.[19] The desire to own and occupy space is likewise linked to the idea of the homeplace as a refuge: for the ethnic writer frequently a refuge from the destructive effects of racism. Using Gaston Bachelard's work on the phenomenology of space, in particular his notion of a spatial inside–outside dialectic, it can be suggested that several texts may usefully be read as inscribing the desire for a shelter from a hazardous racist environment. In particular, this desire is a feature of many Second World War internment narratives by Japanese Americans, for whom issues of home and homelessness became especially acute.

The house or home has other meanings in relation to Asian American women's writing, though. Houses often have their own identities created by the events that take place within their walls, and this chapter explores both the house of secrets and the house of ghosts. In addition, several writers employ architectural metaphors in order to describe both woman-to-woman and generational relationships within the household, so that in fact the house becomes spatially representative of its inhabitants. The house is also often the domain of a dominant family member: the patriarchal places of Chuang Hua's, Jade Snow Wong's and Fiona Cheong's texts come to mind, as do the ancestral halls of *The Woman Warrior* and Amy Tan's novels. Or the house may be the realm of maternalism: mothers loom large and even dominate in many houses. Likewise, the house often features as a domestic space where the Asian American daughter is confined, controlled or exploited. Much is made, too, of gendered zones within the house, with the kitchen being only the most prominent example. Gillian Rose has noted that feminism has often made use of a spatial politics,[20] and this chapter will explore this in relation to several Asian American women writers' reworking of Virginia Woolf's assertion of the need for a room of one's own.[21] The house may also be the textual container itself and I finally discuss the position of the ethnic woman writer in the house of fiction. Autobiography in particular has a large room here as a favoured way to create a textual home for the self.

In *Dwelling in the Text*, Marilyn Chandler explores the predominance of houses as a cultural preoccupation, as well as a nationally-sanctioned narrative in the United States: 'Our literature reiterates with remarkable consistency the centrality of the house in American cultural life and imagination'.[22] Chandler argues that, as a postcolonial country itself, the United States' cultural production has focused upon the necessity of carving out and claiming territory: 'In a country whose history has been focused for so long on the question of settlement and "development", the issue of how to stake out territory, clear it, cultivate it, and build on it has been of major economic, political and psychological consequence'.[23] Consequently, part of the process of American self-definition has always been the definition of its space. And dominant nation-making ideologies have apprized the goal of home ownership: 'The American dream still expresses itself in the hope of owning a freestanding single-family dwelling, which to many remains the most significant measure of ... cultural enfranchisement'.[24] For many ethnic writers in a state of unbelonging, as new immigrants or exiles, the objective of home ownership especially signifies the move towards belonging to, as well as owning, a corner in the world.

Gish Jen, *Typical American* (1992)

The desire for home ownership is particularly sharply defined in the novels of Gish Jen, a writer often concerned with ethnic peoples' attempts to belong. This is illustrated in the very title of her first work, *Typical American*, a novel which charts the Chang family's new immigrant efforts to become 'typical' Americans. David Leiwei Li describes *Typical American* as 'a new Asian American homesteading narrative', and observes that the novel's preoccupation is with 'belonging through materialist self-possession'.[25] Part of this preoccupation is with home ownership, which comes to be regarded by the Changs as one yardstick by which to measure the success of assimilation. Initially, the family's stay in the United States is temporary. The central male character, Ralph Chang, arrives on a Chinese government scholarship to study for a PhD in engineering. Circumstances conspire against him, however, and he soon finds himself stranded in the United States, without a living. During this period, he marries and he and his wife have two daughters. Eventually, he becomes involved in the restaurant business, and soon he becomes a successful businessman.

The desire for a home preoccupies Ralph during his first few months in America: 'He missed his home, missed having a place that was home. Home!'[26] The second section of the novel, entitled 'The House Holds', deals with Ralph's wife Helen's own desire for a *home*, rather than a *house*, and her attempt to achieve this. She moves from a decision to make herself 'at home': 'it was time to make herself as at home as she could' (p. 63), to wondering whether such a feat is possible in a strange country: 'could this place ever be a home?' (p. 66), to the decision to devote all of her energies to the endeavour: 'It was as if, once she'd resigned herself to her new world, something had taken her over – a desire to make it hers' (p. 76). Jen's concern is not solely the new ethnic's yearning to belong, but is also the ethnic woman's role as 'homemaker'. Traditionally a female role, in many ethnic texts, *Typical American* included, it is the women to whom the task falls of home-making, transforming the house from a three dimensional structure into a walled site of belonging. Jen ironises this process, as Helen, the character who most fervently yearns for a home, asks, '"A house! What is it? Four walls and a roof!"' (p. 154). For the Changs, house-hunting becomes almost a form of tourism, and at the stage that they move from being sight-seers to house-owners, they feel that they have 'arrived': 'When did they realize that a town like this was their destiny ... for some time they would dwell in a house like one of these, with a yard and garage?' (p. 135). And later: 'How lucky they were! How many people came to this country and bought a house just like that?' (p. 156). Helen rapidly turns home-maker, preoccupied with colour schemes and interior design. Through her efforts, the house gradually comes to affirm the position of the people within it: 'could a house give life to a family? A foolish idea. And yet, the house did seem to have filled itself, to have drawn out of the family roomfuls of activity' (p. 160). Because of this narrative emphasis upon women's roles as homemakers, Rachel Lee views the text as a particularly gendered fiction, especially in relation to the trope of home, as the following quotation attests:

> Domestic tranquillity, seemingly inherent in that product called 'home,' is forged by women's labor, specifically their accomodating to the rule of the patriarch. Moreover, Helen and Theresa's arduous efforts to make stable the home becomes a Sisyphean task: making Ralph 'at home' is already an impossibility by virtue of an national Home narrative that excludes 'Chinamen.' Asian American women thus labor against a double exclusion – they are those whose silences enable an Asian American 'home' already disabled by America's 'Home,' which is the exclusive terrain of whites.[27]

Typical American ends with the Changs comfortably ensconced in their home in America, well on the way to becoming 'typical' Americans. The sequel, *Mona in the Promised Land*, opens with the question, 'Where should they live next?'[28] In this novel, Jen ironises the ethnic success story. As the Changs become successful, they move to a desirable residential location in New York: 'Their house is still of the upstanding-citizen type. *Remember the Mayflower!* it seems to whisper, in dulcet tones'.[29] If the home is a walled site of belonging, then the mansion seems to underscore and authenticate the Changs' perception of themselves as Americans even further.

Although it was published in the relatively multi-ethnic 1990s, as Rachel Lee reminds us, *Typical American* is actually set in 'the Cold War era of suburbanization' of the 1950s.[30] Lee argues that this historical setting imbricates the novel in a whole series of xenophobic and nativist trends, such as shifting political relations with Asia and Russia, and alterations in US immigration law to favour professionals and economically privileged foreign nationals, so that in effect in relation to this context the idea of 'home' ultimately 'emerges as a conflicted trope in the novel'.[31] The attainment of 'home' in the novel is thus dependent upon the Changs' adherence to modes of Americanisation.

The internment and relocation experiences of Japanese North Americans during the Second World War threw issues of home and homelessness into particularly sharp relief. As discussed in chapter 6, many texts by Japanese Americans written about this time explore the ways that debarment from home ownership rendered them outsiders, and this often resulted in a psychology of exile. Most Japanese Americans were interned by the American government after the bombing of Pearl Harbor, shipped en masse to camps in deserts and other remote locations where they remained for the duration of the war. They were given next to no warning of this move and consequently had little time to sell or rent their houses. The army were ill-prepared for this evacuation, and the camps were ill-equipped and inhospitable. 'Home' sometimes became a former stable, unheated, draughty and sparsely furnished. Sanitation provision was communal and inadequate. Narratives about this period emphasise their authors' feelings of betrayal, displacement and uprootedness, as Yoshiko Uchida notes: 'I felt degraded, humiliated, and overwhelmed with a longing for home'.[32] All juxtapose their harsh camp surroundings with their (albeit often tenuous) sentiments of belonging they had felt in the homes that they had made in America. Jeanne Wakatsuki Houston writes: 'Remembering her warm apartment in East Los Angeles, the large three rooms above Nishio's Shoe Store, Yuki often wondered what bad karma she had earned to end up in such a place'.[33] Despite the inhospitable conditions, many Japanese Americans managed to make homes of their barracks. 'Home' is not just where one belongs, it is also the personalised and lived-in space of a family. Many camp quarters became microcosmic homes in this way: 'It had only been a crude community of stables and barracks but it had been home', and 'Our mothers had made homes in the bleak barrack rooms', one former internee recalls in *Desert Exile* (p. 103).

Joy Kogawa, *Obasan* (1981)

Although the internment autobiographies relate harsh tales of displacement and homelessness, it is Joy Kogawa's fictional rendering of the relocation experience in *Obasan* which most potently juxtaposes the feeling of *un*belonging alongside the desire for a home. As outlined in chapter 2, *Obasan* tells the story of Japanese Canadian internment and relocation through the chronologically jumbled and fractured narration of Japanese Canadian Naomi Nakane. Kogawa's chosen narrative style allows her to closely juxtapose Naomi's memories of the family home in Vancouver with the huts to which she and her family were relocated in Slocan, British Columbia and Lethbridge, Alberta. In particular, she remembers the family home: 'The house in which we live is in Marpole, a comfortable residential district of Vancouver. It is more splendid than any house I have lived in since. It does not bear remembering'.[34] For Naomi, as in the camp autobiographies, 'home' signifies a past that must be buried in order to cope with the present, a nostalgic pre-time that is lost: 'these are the bits of the house I remember. If I linger in the longing, I am drawn into a whirlpool' (p. 64). The house in Vancouver assumes an even more charged significance as it was Naomi's childhood home. In J. Gerald Kennedy's words, the childhood home especially becomes an 'almost magical site … associated with indelible, formative experiences'.[35] For Naomi, the childhood home bespeaks the maternal, as her memories of home are indelibly intertwined with her recollections of her mother, before she left the family for Japan. The construction of this association is complex, connecting Naomi's experience of the home with the nightly ritual of storytelling, predominantly enacted by her mother: 'My mother's voice is quiet and the telling is a chant. I snuggle into her arms, listening and watching the shadows of the peach tree outside my window' (p. 66). The Japanese folk story of Momotaro acts as the connective tissue, as it is always this story that the young Naomi requests as her bedtime story. Momotaro is a story of exile and homecoming. It is a simple tale: Momotaro is a young boy who is born of a peach, who is reared and nurtured by an old childless couple in their home. When he reaches adulthood, he travels and conquers bandits, returning in glory to his family. Momotaro's story does not just symbolise the move from exile to return, it also symbolises the crucial distinction between inside and outside of the home, as outlined in Gaston Bachelard's *The Poetics of Space*. Bachelard suggests that the house as an image contrasts with the outside world it is distinct from: 'between the house and the non-house it is easy to establish all sorts of contradictions'.[36] He asserts that 'outside and inside form a dialectic of division'.[37] Inside, there is shelter, nurturance and warmth, protection from a hostile environment. Naomi, hearing Momotaro, imagines her own house in this way: 'Inside the house in Vancouver there is confidence and laughter, music and mealtimes, games and storytelling. But outside, even in the backyard, there is an infinitely unpredictable, unknown and often dangerous world' (p. 69). Not only does inside provide nurturance and outside represent danger, Bachelard sees these different locations in terms of affirmed or negated subjectivity: 'when confronted with outside and inside, think in terms of being and non-being'.[38] As discussed in chapter 2 on mothers and daughters, Naomi's selfhood is bound up with her mother and here we can see this interconnectedness working spatially too. The dialectic of inside and outside is most vividly highlighted,

Bachelard suggests, when the homestead is contrasted with a snowy landscape: 'snow, especially, reduces the exterior world to nothing … it gives a single color to the entire universe'.[39] He continues:

> in the outside world, snow covers all tracks, blurs the road, muffles every sound, conceals all colors. As a result of this universal whiteness, we feel a form of cosmic negation in action. The dreamer of houses knows and senses this, and because of the diminished entity of the outside world, experiences all the qualities of intimacy with increased intensity.[40]

Naomi is a dreamer, and, during the Momotaro story, inhabits a quasi-dreamworld, in which she exhibits a heightened identification with Momotaro. In the Momotaro story, the dialectic of inside and outside is exaggerated in the way Bachelard suggests through a snowy landscape: 'the time comes when Momotaro must go and silence falls like feathers of snow all over the rice-paper hut' (p. 67). Naomi's empathy with Momotaro's story is carried beyond the terms of the tale into her later experiences of inside and outside dialectics. She carries this with her when she observes the house to which the family are first relocated in Slocan. But here, unlike Momotaro's and the Vancouver homes, the house does not provide protection from the surrounding environment. Rather, Naomi's description emphasises the house's inability to provide shelter and to be a distinct place from its surroundings:

> almost hidden from sight off the path, is a small grey hut with a broken porch camouflaged by shrubbery and trees. The color of the house is that of sand and earth. It seems more like a giant toadstool than a building. The mortar between the logs is crumbling and the porch roof dives down in the middle. … From the road, the house is invisible, and the path to it is overgrown with weeds. (p. 143)

The inside–outside dialectic is critical in imagining the home as a protective haven in hostile surroundings. For these people seeking refuge from racism, especially at a time of heightened anti-Japanese American sentiment, the hut in Slocan offers flimsy security, and crucially even fails to keep the outside out: even the weeds are invasive.

The inside–outside dialectic dissolves further in the family's next relocation to Lethbridge, Alberta: 'Our hut is at the edge of a field that stretches as far as I can see and is filled with an army of spartan plants fighting in the wind' (p. 230). Here we see the outside threatening to overcome the inside. Naomi emphasises the inadequacy of this house as shelter as well as its inability to become a home, when she describes it as: 'One room, one door, two windows', and 'uninsulated unbelievable thin-as-a-cotton-dress hovel' (p. 233). Naomi's desire for her home and this fear of inadequate housing begin to lead her to fear open spaces. As Naomi and her family's political situation in Canada becomes increasingly tenuous, so the family's physical space shrinks, until they inhabit this draughty hut. This is coupled with Naomi's growing fear of space and she registers her awareness of 'a strange empty landscape', which is almost devoid of shelter (p. 228). This feeling is carried with her, and she tells us in the preface, at a point chronologically at the end of the narration: 'I hate the staring into the night. The questions thinning into space. The sky swallowing the echoes'.

In addition to Momotaro, Naomi uses a European story of a homecoming to highlight her own displacement. This is the story of Goldilocks, and she tells it at the point in her narration when as a child she is being transferred from one site of relocation to another:

> In one of Stephen's books, there is a story of a child with long golden ringlets called Goldilocks who one day comes to a quaint house in the woods lived in by a family of bears. Clearly, we are that bear family in this strange house in the middle of the woods. ... In the morning, will I not find my way out of the forest and back to my room where the picture bird sings above my bed ... No matter how I wish it, we do not go home. (p. 149)

When Naomi's father returns to the family, Naomi again believes that his homecoming will lead to all their homecomings: 'I am Goldilocks, I am Momotaro. I am leaf in the wind restored to its branch, child of my father come home. The world is safe once more and Chicken Little is wrong. The sky is not falling down after all' (p. 202). Ultimately, though, her homecoming, together with that of her mother, does not take place: 'Trains do not carry us home. Ships do not return again', she laments (p. 225).

Bharati Mukherjee, *Wife* (1975)

Several other contemporary Asian American novels deal with the desire for the house to provide a haven from a hostile place. As Shirley Ardener notes: 'communities often regard the space closest to that occupied by the family as a relatively secure and predictable inner world in contrast to the potentially hostile and untrustworthy space outside'.[41] Bharati Mukherjee's novel *Wife*, is one such example. *Wife* tells the story of Dimple Dasgupta, the daughter of middle-class Indian parents, who marries Amit Basu, an engineer, and emigrates to the United States. Dimple has high expectations of her life in the United States, but her experiences are very different. She encounters a world of racism and prejudice, where Amit cannot obtain trained work and she herself is increasingly isolated, huddled inside her claustrophobic flat. Dimple sees her flat as her only refuge from New York: 'The air was never free of the sounds of sirens growing louder, or gradually fading. They were reminders of a dangerous world (even the hall was dangerous, she thought, let alone the playground and streets'.[42] The sense of both Dimple's social and cultural isolation, and gradual psychological deterioration as the novel progresses is acute, and, as Ketu Katrak observes, 'America hardly exists except as a backdrop, a physical location where she finds herself geographically'.[43]

Dimple eventually goes insane and kills her husband. This may be symptomatic of her inability to resolve a tension between inside–outside, similar to that experienced by Naomi in *Obasan*, as Sheng-mei Ma notes: 'Dimple's unresolved dilemma between her wish to remain a traditional Indian wife and the irresistible influences of the New York world … lead to her insanity'.[44] Ma has read *Wife* as representing an 'immigrant schizophrenic', or inability to reconcile two worlds, here both cultural *and* physical. In fact, this, Mukherjee's second novel, is typical of a phase in her long writing career when she herself felt something of an immigrant schizophrenic, or exile, too. Five years after Mukherjee published *Wife*, she moved to America from Canada, and has since felt far more comfortable with her 'between worlds' status, as she has documented at length in a well-known article in *The New York Times Book Review*, and this is reflected in her later novels.[45] In reviewing this shift in Mukherjee's own experience and writing, Polly Shulman has remarked that whereas *Wife* deals with 'the aloofness of expatriation', subsequent novels exhibit 'the exuberance of immigration'.[46]

Inside–outside may be interpreted in another way in relation to Asian American women's writing, and the ethnic woman's ownership of space. Many texts relate the experience of exclusion when debarred from living in certain areas. These texts are mainly early immigrant narratives of the pre–1960s period, and include Uchida's *Desert Exile*, Kim's *Clay Walls* and Lee's *Quiet Odyssey*, which relate to a time when blatant racism to these new immigrant groups was openly admissible, particularly through the unofficial enforcement of racist housing policies.[47] In Mary Paik Lee's *Quiet Odyssey*, for example, it is their house which reflects their position in society: 'We lived in a small one-room shack built in the 1880's. The passing of time had made the lumber shrink, so the wind blew through the cracks in the walls. There was no pretense of making it livable – just four walls, one window, and one door – nothing else'.[48] Here, as in *Obasan*, the house does not provide adequate shelter and thus lacks the potential to become a home. But it is not just the home per se which reflects its occupants' place in society, the location of the homestead likewise functions as an indicator of social, as well as economic, (dis)enfranchisement, as Lee observes: 'In those days, Orientals and others were not allowed to live in town with the white people' (p. 14). Mary Paik Lee relates her own experiences between 1905 and the Second World War where even though the family elect to place themselves in a subordinate position in relation to their white neighbours (as a strategy of self-preservation), this self-placement is nevertheless rewarded with ostracism: 'Although we found a house on the outskirts of town, the townspeople's attitude towards us was chilling' (p. 22). Gary Okihiro has written that Lee's narrative is characterised by a series of enforced displacements: colonisation, labour migration and racism, and this is a typical feature of narratives written by Asian American women at the time.[49] Other women encounter a spatial racism even more directly. Haesu, the main female character in Ronyoung Kim's novel *Clay Walls*, set in the 1930s, finds herself excluded from most forms of habitation. Barred from citizenship, she and her family are unable to buy a house, and local racist exclusions prohibit her from renting: 'He doesn't want "Orientals"', Haesu is repeatedly told.[50] Finally, Haesu is forced to sublet from a sympathetic white neighbour. Yoshiko Uchida recounts a similar experience at the same time, in *Desert Exile*: 'It seemed the realtors of the area had drawn an invisible line through the city and agreed among themselves not to rent or sell homes above that line to Asians' (p. 4). Debarment from home ownership in this manner engenders feelings of legal disentitlement and the desire for home ownership consequently assumes an even greater value. In both narratives Mary Paik Lee and Ronyoung Kim's character Haesu later communicate their awareness of the worth of their position when they finally buy houses: in *Quiet Odyssey*, 'The house had five rooms, a bathroom with a real bathtub and toilet, and a gas stove in the kitchen with a hot water tank on the back porch. We had a real house at last, with a big backyard and a fig tree. It was the first time we ever had everything just like the white people did. It really felt good' (p. 74).

Many ethnic subjects' search for home in the United States may stretch beyond the domain of the domicile, and 'home' may also signify the locale inhabited by ethnically similar groups of people. One notable example is the significance attached to Chinatowns as home. As K. Scott Wong has made clear, 'Chinatown' is both a residential and business space which is framed by outsiders.[51] It functions, therefore, as an 'inside' space in terms of inside–outside dialectics. It is also, as

Kay Anderson notes, 'a dominant community inferring identity'.[52] To live within it is to assume its identity, and also to take advantage of the protection it affords as a sympathetic, rather than racist, community in which to live. For instance, two contemporary novels, Aimee Liu's *Face* (1994) and Fae Myenne Ng's *Bone* (1993), are mainly set in the Chinatowns of New York and San Francisco respectively. For both main female characters in these works, Chinatown remains the charged site of childhood long after they leave, a place which they are by turns drawn towards and repelled from. Maibelle Chung notes in *Face*: 'I would not be able to live in Chinatown again. I understood that now. But I could not escape it either' (p. 325). Both novels chart women's identity crises which stem from events which took place in Chinatown during childhood. For Leila, in *Bone*, this is her sister's suicide and Chinatown remains for both Leila and her sister Nina the site of loss: 'When I suggested Chinatown, Nina said it was too depressing. ... At Chinatown places, you can only talk about the bare issues'.[53] And yet, despite this, Chinatown remains home: 'Salmon Alley's always been home'.[54] In *Face*, Maibelle Chung seeks to escape Chinatown as the site of a childhood rape, but finds herself constantly called back, as her friend Li tells her: 'this your home' (p. 230).

Exile, displacement, migration

Home represents the past. So the quest to recover or discover 'home' is also the search for identity, as Andrew Gurr suggests: 'The need for a sense of home as a base, a source of identity even more than a refuge, has grown powerfully in the last century or so. This sense of home is the goal of all voyages of self discovery'.[55] Thus, the search for and the pull of 'home' both resonate in several Asian American women's fictions of self-discovery, which deal at length with the roots/routes dynamic. Asian American women both within and without these texts become wanderers and engage in odysseys to Asia in search of their identity.[56] Lydia Minatoya's *Talking to High Monks in the Snow: An Asian American Odyssey* and Kyoko Mori's *The Dream of Water* are two prominent autobiographical examples, and Andrea Louie's *Moon Cakes* a fictional case. All three women – Minatoya, Mori and Louie's central character Maya Li – set out without knowing whether they will find their home. Minatoya: 'And so my road meanders. Taking detours, I pause here and there to sample the hospitality of strangers. Wondering, Is this where I belong? But always I return to my road, wanting to find home, before the darkness falls.'[57] Mori: 'I am taking a trip to Japan for the first time in thirteen years. "A trip" is how I think of it, not "going back" or "returning", which would imply that my destination is a home or a familiar place'.[58] And later: 'leaving the last city and boarding the train to Kobe, I wondered if my remaining three weeks might still offer some kind of homecoming ... I cannot decide how I feel, lost or at home'.[59] And finally, in Louie's *Moon Cakes*: 'I am not by nature a wanderer, but I feel I have become one'. 'So this is it. I know why I am here. I am looking for what it means to be Chinese ... I am looking for that pull of home'.[60] For all three, the respective Asian country is a partly mythologised homeland, as all have made the United States their home (although Mori spent early childhood in Japan). For Louie's character Maya Li and Minatoya, the Asian country, rather than the United States, initially seems to hold the key to identity, as their parents' orientation towards it as origin of their own identities has engendered their own psychological attachments.

For Mori, Japan has been an actual home and remains so for her parents. Yet her own problematic relationship with them has prohibited her return earlier. For Mori, as with Maya Li and Minatoya, the Asian country is a site associated with formative experiences and their return catalyses their discovery/recovery of a sense of their multiply-situated identity. All find a home of sorts in Asia: as Maya Li notes: 'I do not know when I began to love China, when I began to soak in her landscape like a luxurious, curative balm'.[61] And Mori, despite her trepidation at returning, realises that 'Kobe will always be ... a place to think of with nostalgia, from far away'.[62] The discovery of a home in each Asian country is tempered, however, by a recognition of equal rootedness in America, as Minatoya notes: 'in Asia I had found acceptance. But there were things that I wanted in America. Family. Work. To be a citizen once again. Trust and risk, I told myself. And when June came, I went home'.[63]

Chuang Hua, *Crossings* (1968)

Perhaps the most memorable itinerant in Asian American fiction by women is the character Fourth Jane in Chuang Hua's autobiographical novel about her search for identity, *Crossings*. In many ways, *Crossings* is *the* paradigmatic diasporic story. It tracks the central character Fourth Jane's life across different countries, the United States and France, as she struggles to find a stable sense of selfhood. The plot structure is sparse, with the only real developments in the text being Jane's affair with a married man and her mother's birthday party. Partly this is so that the plot does not detract from the sense of emptiness and space in the text, which strengthens our sense of Jane's homelessness. The narrative is framed by the crossings that Fourth Jane makes across seas, continents and cultural borders. Amy Ling describes Fourth Jane's cosmos as a 'shifting world',[64] and this is reflected textually through a spatially disjunctive and chronologically fragmented narrative style. As Amy Ling observes, there are 'seven ocean crossings and four major cultural transitions' and these passages chart Fourth Jane's search for self through place.[65] Fourth Jane's many displacements mark her self-imposed exile from both the United States and China as sources of selfhood. She describes her sense of needing to find home in both places:

> I couldn't live without America. It's a part of me by now. For years I used to think I was dying in America because I could not have China. ... When it had been possible to return to China while still living in America I loved America and China as two separate but equal realities of my existence. Before the outbreak of civil war in China I lived for the day when I could bring America with me to China. Selfishly I wanted both my worlds. (p. 122)

If 'place proves ... a nurturing medium, a source of both thought and identity',[66] then the dual ties to the United States and China engender in Fourth Jane a bifurcation of her identity. For Fourth Jane, a separation of the two realities of her existence is not possible, however, as they are inextricably connected: 'Moments I thought of giving up one for the other, I had such longings to make a rumble in the silence. But both parts equally strong canceled out choice' (p. 122). Fourth Jane's intensified awareness of her alienated self is tentatively alleviated, as it is for Mori, Maya Li and Minatoya earlier, through the recognition that 'home' resides as much within her as she resides within it: 'Quite unexpectedly one day it ended when I realized I had it in me and not being able to be there physically no longer mattered. Those wasted years when I denied America because I had lost China. In my mind I expelled myself from both' (p. 121). Fourth Jane's recognition of home as an imagined site is not, however, the culmination of her search for identity, as it is in the texts discussed so far. Textually, the fragmented and sequentially disordered narrative disallows any such solution. As Fourth Jane's lover tells her, she remains in exile even after moving to Paris: 'You are an exile in America as you are in exile here' (p. 121), because Fourth Jane has an exile mentality. Her narrative never changes from this dominant sense of a psychology of exile, and any homecoming is precluded as Fourth Jane remains stultified by her many displacements: 'On certain days moving from one room to another in her apartment was the only displacement she felt capable of undertaking' (p. 116).

Within Fourth Jane and other women like her, place and displacement have left an indelible mark upon her identity and she is a spatial hybrid. When her lover suggests she return to China, she replies: 'Too late now. Farm house, field, solitary tree, the distant mountains have fused, have become one with the American landscape. I can't separate any more. ... I belong to both, am both' (p. 125). *Crossings* does not, however, offer a synergistic vision of spatial hybridity and the problems and contradictions associated with place and displacement endure. It is partly the sense of the inevitability of the loss of home that blocks a synergistic reconciliation of Fourth Jane's different worlds, who describes it as a state of 'paralysis', 'I lived in no man's land, having also lost America since the loss of one entailed the loss of the other' (p. 122). Like Kyoko Mori, Fourth Jane's reconciliation of different places is complicated by the sense of loss associated with the home-as-past: 'How can I feel comforted by the past when loss is the most constant thing in it?'[67] Fourth Jane's crisis of the placeless self is never fully resolved and the sense of loss of place pervades the whole text. Michael Seidel has defined an exile as 'someone who inhabits one place and remembers or projects the reality of another'.[68] It is precisely this situation which produces in *Crossings* a sense of spatial palimpsest of Fourth Jane's many real and imagined locations.

Sara Suleri, *Meatless Days* (1989) and Meena Alexander, *Fault Lines: A Memoir* (1993)

For two very self-conscious South Asian writers of memoir, Sara Suleri and Meena Alexander, not only is the home-as-past inevitably lost, but place as home *only* exists in relation to the interpreting consciousness. Suleri and Alexander share with Fourth Jane this kind of exile psychology. Suleri constantly asserts that 'home' only exists within the imagination: 'When I teach topics in third world literature, much time is lost in trying to explain that the third world is locatable only as a discourse of convenience. Trying to find it is like pretending that history or home is real and not located precisely where you're sitting'.[69] Meena Alexander likewise locates 'home' within the imagination: 'the house of memory is fragile; made up in the mind's space'.[70] For both these writers, it is the existence of home only as a discourse, and not as an identifiable location, that engenders the loss associated with it: 'In my dreams, I am haunted by thoughts of a homeland I will never find', Alexander

tells us (p. 27). Suleri recounts the experience of her mental relin-
quishment of the 'home': 'One morning I awoke to find that ... my
mind had completely ejected the names of all the streets in Pakistan, as
though to assure that I could not return, or that if I did, it would be
returning to a loss'.[71]

Both Suleri and Alexander go further than many writers in their
interrogation of the particulars of the ethnic woman writer's search for
home. Alexander interestingly posits marriage as the catalyst of displacement: 'But for a woman, marriage makes a gash. It tears you from
your original home. Though you may return to give birth, once married
you are part and parcel of the husband's household' (p. 23). The first
severance from home that Alexander describes is irrevocable and can
never be recovered. Alexander's own perspective on her search for home
is focused upon the desire (which is always thwarted) to recover the
original home, which for Alexander is always the realm of the maternal. Although she admits that both maternal and paternal ancestral
homesteads define her: '*Nadu* is the Malayalan word for home, for homeland. Tiruvella, where my mother's home, Kuruchiethu House, stands,
Kozencheri, where appa's home, Kannadical House stands together
compose my nadu, the dark soil of self' (p. 23), it is predominantly
Tiruvella, the maternal homestead, which functions psychologically for
Alexander as the site of selfhood. She writes of her mother's home: 'the
rooms of the house are filled with darkness. I am in that house, some-
where in between my parents, hovering as a ghost might. I cannot
escape. This is the house of my blood, the whorl of flesh I am' (p. 30).
And at another point: 'I think of the Tiruvella house ... It is where I
trace my beginning' (p. 8). Like Fourth Jane, as Alexander resides imaginatively in these houses, so these houses imaginatively reside within
her: 'Those corridors wind through my blood' (p. 31). Thus, for
Alexander, home is associated with the mother. Suleri elaborates upon
this orientation: for her, home is also where the mother is. As her sister
tells her: 'A woman can't come home ... home is where your mother is,
one; it is where you are mother, two; and in between ... your spirit
must become a tiny, concentrated little thing, so that your body feels
like a spacious place in which to live'.[72] As discussed in the next section, the inevitability of the loss of home is tied up with the loss of the
maternal, as the ineluctable psychological severance from the maternal which is part of the bid for self-identity on the part of the daughter.[73] Thus the psychological orientation towards the mother mirrors
the psychological as well as physical orientation towards home as the
site of the maternal. *Fault Lines* is considerably more explicit than

Meatless Days in its confessed search for self, though. As Alexander tells us in the first few pages, she is both 'writing in search of a homeland' and writing about 'the difficulty of living in space' (p. 4). Alexander's search is for her identity through an imaginative exploration of space. As J. Gerald Kennedy notes, 'place enters importantly into the day-to-day construction of the self'.[74] Alexander envisages her textual construction of her identity as a stitching together of all the places where she has lived: 'Place names litter ... Allahabad, Tiruvella, Kozencheri, Pune, Dubai, London, New York, Minneapolis, Saint Paul, New Delhi, Trivandum. Sometimes I think I could lift these scraps of space and much as an indigent dressmaker, cut them into shape. Stitch my days into a patchwork garment fit to wear' (p. 30). And yet Alexander, like Fourth Jane, is both more and less than the sum of her spatial parts. 'Home' will never be a single place, and therefore will never exist outside of her desiring imagination: 'this Other who I am ... has no home. ... History is maquillage. No homeland here' (p. 193). Alexander sees the home-as-past as imaginative, and therefore the home – as history – cannot be externally located.

Alexander's experiences, like Suleri's, mean that as postcolonial women, the world and space cannot be taken for granted, and the memory of colonialism highlights the charged nature of space as territory to be colonised, owned, exploited. 'After all', Alexander writes, 'for such as we are the territories are not free. The world is not open. That endless space, the emptiness of the American sublime is worse than a lie' (p. 199). Exilic identity reflects this through the yearning to return and colonise space. Writers like Alexander, Suleri, and Bharati Mukherjee emphasise that the ownership of space cannot be taken for granted. Even for upper-class emigrés like Chuang Hua (*Crossings*) and Mai-mai Sze (*Echo of a Cry*), women who have actively chosen an exilic life,[75] rootlessness is a burden. It is only those women who choose to travel in search of the home of their identity, and find it, like Lydia Minatoya, Kyoko Mori and Maya Li, who are able to transmute their journeys into narratives of migration, in which they are able to emphasise the more positive side of diasporic identity, whereby one may have the best of both worlds.[76]

Domestic spaces and ghostly places

The house of ghosts is recurrent in ethnic fiction; we may think of Toni Morrison's *Beloved* or Ana Castillo's *So Far From God*, for example. Ghosts, both literal, and figurative, also inhabit many houses in Asian

American women's writing, where both the house of ghosts and the house of secrets feature. In this sense, houses assume the identities of the activities which have taken place within them. The house is represented as an especially charged space, haunted by the spectres of familial crimes, in Maxine Hong Kingston's *The Woman Warrior* and also in Fiona Cheong's *The Scent of the Gods*. Both of these texts relate the tale of fallen women and shameful pregnancies. Houses in Kingston's fiction always reflect their occupants. In *The Woman Warrior*, the house which forms the location of Kingston's aunt's shameful pregnancy reflects the weight of familial ancestry both inside: 'we stood together in the middle of our house, in the family hall with the pictures and the tables of the ancestors around us', and outside: 'At that time the house had only two wings. When the men came back, we would build two more to enclose our courtyard and a third one to begin a second courtyard'.[77] The villagers' discovery of and reaction to the no name aunt's unmarried pregnancy is charted in spatial terms. They break into the family home and search through the home for the aunt's room: 'the villagers pushed through both wings, even your grandparents' rooms, to find your aunt's, which was also mine until the men returned. From this room a new wing for one of the younger families would grow' (p. 12). Spatially, until this point the aunt's position within the house was amongst the family, so the villagers' invasion of the Hong homestead affects all of the family: they trample through *everyone's* rooms. The villagers destroy much of the internal structure of the house, literalising the image of the 'broken house', as Kingston notes: 'The villagers came to show my aunt and her lover-in-hiding a broken house' (p. 20). Both the no name aunt's self-inflicted and imposed punishments are also meted out in spatial ways. Once the secret is out, the aunt is relegated to an 'outcast' table: 'My aunt must have lived in the same house as my parents and eaten at an outcast table' (p. 15). The aunt's crime is described by Kingston spatially: 'my aunt crossed boundaries not delineated in space' (p. 15), describing social rules using spatial metaphors. The aunt's self-imposed punishment is therefore enacted through the observation of spatial rules, and as an outsider now, she must leave the house: 'She ran out into the fields, far enough from the house so that she could no longer hear their voices, and pressed herself against the earth, her land no more' (p. 20). In this extract, the aunt's dispossession is measured spatially – she no longer may claim the right to ancestral land. Then follows a proliferation of descriptions of the aunt, cast out, literally lost in space: 'She was one of the stars, a bright dot in blackness, without home, without a companion, in eternal cold and silence'; 'Flayed, unprotected against space, she felt pain return'; 'Black space opened' (p. 20). The aunt's position as outsider now she has been expelled from her place within the family, is completed by her own placement in a subordinate space: she drowns herself in the family well. Paradoxically, then, the house was rid of her and her secret, only for the memory of her, and the fear of her ghost, to remain on the doorstep.

In Fiona Cheong's novel *The Scent of the Gods*, the ancestral home is patriarchal, and the phrase 'in Great-Grandfather's house' is a recurrent refrain.[78] The story is of eleven year old Su Yen's struggle to locate the actual and imagined ghosts that haunt her family's house in 1960s Singapore. This house of secrets, like Kingston's, shrouds a shameful pregnancy resulting from rape, of Su Yen's Auntie Daisy, who remains behind closed doors, and is only ever fleetingly glimpsed by the young protagonist Su Yen, whose task it is, like it was for Kingston, to discover and reconstruct her story. In this novel, too, it is the seeping of the secret outside of the family home, that seems to start the destructive chain of events that finally rupture the family. The house of secrets is also common in Amy Tan's fiction. Many of the Joy Luck mothers, notably An-Mei Hsu, as well as Winnie Louie in *The Kitchen God's Wife*, describe childhood, as well as adult, houses with secrets, and often it transpires that a woman's shame is the secret. In fact, most of Tan's houses contain familial secrets, and warring family members, especially mothers and daughters, who must divulge their secrets in order for reconciliation to be achieved. This is the case in *The Kitchen God's Wife* and also, to a lesser extent, in *The Hundred Secret Senses*.

Ghosts also represent loss. For Kingston, this is not the loss of familial and ancestral dignity, but it is the loss of the maternal. As asserted in chapter 2 on mothers and daughters, for Kingston the maternal is represented not just by her biological mother, but also by other mother-figures, of whom the no name aunt is but one. This aunt's relegation from the house is also therefore for Kingston the loss of the maternal. In fact, the house is often the domain of the mother, so her loss is often measured spatially through her absence within the house. This is the case in Kogawa's novel *Obasan*, as well as for An-Mei Hsu in Amy Tan's *The Joy Luck Club*, where the mother is described as a 'ghost' because of her absence.[79] In *The Joy Luck Club*, Kingston's *The Woman Warrior* and Julie Shigekuni's novel *A Bridge Between Us*, a return home is the return to the mother, as it is her space. This is particularly the case in Shigekuni's novel, where the house becomes a space full of mothers and daughters, with the accompanying intergenerational conflicts, as explored in detail in chapter 2.

Julie Shigekuni, *A Bridge Between Us* (1995)

In Shigekuni's novel, the house functions as an architectural metaphor of the family within it, so that it becomes a spatial representation of its occupants. It is, predominantly, a house of women, and each level represents a generational stage of the family. Nomi, the youngest female of the family, writes:

> The house where I live with my mother, Grandma Rio and Granny Reiko looks like the Japanese word for gossip. I know this because Granny Reiko showed me how to draw it. First you make the three women: Granny Reiko who is my great-grandmother, and my mother, and below them Grandma Rio. You draw them sitting down, as close together as you can without making them touch. Then you put the roof over their heads, which Granny Reiko says belongs to her and keeps them inside.[80]

The story charts the lives of four generations of Japanese American women who all live together, united by familial ties but separated from each other by mother–daughter distances engendered by secrets. The title itself, *A Bridge Between Us*, deploys an architectural metaphor to indicate the obligation which forms a tie between all of the women. Nomi's comparison of the house with the Japanese character for gossip draws upon the traditional connecting tissue between women. Crucially, gossip is the spilling of secrets, but in this house, by and large, secrets are not shared and this blocks maternal–daughterly communication.[81]

The four women's different relationships with each other are also figured spatially. In the familial hierarchy, Granny Reiko is the great-grandmother, Grandma Rio is her daughter, Tomoe her daughter-in-law, and Nomi Tomoe's daughter. In the family house, Granny Reiko occupies the top floor, Tomoe and her daughters the middle floor, and Grandma Rio the bottom floor. This indicates both Grandma Rio's subordinate position within the household, and also the psychological distance between her and her mother: the rest of the household are located between them both, and thus separate them. Granny Reiko's position as dominant matriarch is likewise figured by her physical place at the top of the house.

Significantly, all of the women envisage the properties of the house in different ways, according to their position within it, as well as within the maternal–daughterly hierarchy. Granny Reiko's presence dominates, and she regards the house as a reflection of her own strength as well as her domain: 'This house has survived earthquake, fire, blood, my father's death, I want it to be the house where I too will die' (p. 20). Tomoe also sees the house as a strength, but a strength in itself, and this marks her desire for the home to be a refuge, as well as her subscription to domestic ideologies in which the woman is a homemaker. She recognises that although identical on the outside, each house has many problems within it: 'I steer the car past rows of houses, colorful boxes stacked up and down the hills, one after another, each one holding another family, each family with its own problems' (p. 67). So that although Tomoe desires her house to be a nurturing homestead, she is able to see through this ideology, that it is not just her own family with problems. Both Tomoe and Granny Reiko, for different reasons, have an interest in preserving the homestead. Grandma Rio and Nomi, by contrast, seek to escape it. Home for Rio has always been the site of maternal domination. She sees the house as repressive and this manifests itself in her dreams. She dreams of the outside with longing: 'I began visiting an old part of the country in my sleep, maybe it was Japan … I found myself wandering' (p. 137). Coupled with the desire to wander, Rio dreams of the emptiness of the house, the home-space as a void, both literally, and metaphorically, as it is not a nurturing space for Rio:

> when I was a child, I dreamed of falling off the earth. I saw myself walking up the hill toward home – that old, blue house where I still live. I'd walk to the top of the hill, climb the sixteen steps that led to the front door, and on the other side would be nothing. I'd fall through the air as if through water. I'd sink lower and deeper, unable to breathe. As a child, the dream came routinely as a nightmare. (pp. 50–1)

Rio's sense of the home as a void space changes as she grows older, and her inability to escape her mother's influence leads her to desire an escape from the house, which she increasingly finds to be a stifling environment. This is exacerbated by her husband's well-meaning attempts to make the house a safe place himself: 'Tadashi came home with storm windows, which he said he got to shut the draft out of the downstairs part of the house … I complained that there wasn't enough air' (pp. 136–7). For Rio, whose mother has always been a stifling influence, peril lies within rather than without the house, as Tadashi assumes. The same is true for her granddaughter Nomi, who feels not only the repressive influence of her mother, but also the weight of three generations of dominant mother-figures. Thus, Nomi, like Rio, seeks to escape the house-space. She leaves to escape the weight of maternal influence and notes that 'I knew I could never return home' (p. 205). She likens this weight to a house collapsing, again using an architectural description: 'My life is a burning house collapsing in on itself. There is too much weight' (p. 227). The novel ends with Nomi and Rio both escaping the weight of the collapsing house across a bridge of sorts and the final image is of the two escaping down a river on a raft, away from the house.

Domestic spaces often prove oppressive for Asian American daughters, because of the onus upon them, as women, to become skilled in house work. Maxine Hong Kingston, Aimee Liu's character Maibelle and Jade Snow Wong, for example, all feel the weight of maternal pressure to be good daughters with the accompanying home skills. Kingston, for one, rejects this: 'I refused to cook. When I had to wash dishes, I would crack one or two. "Bad girl," my mother yelled, and sometimes that made me gloat rather than cry' (p. 49). But domestic spaces within the house are not always associated with repressive maternal control. Frequently, domestic spaces become the sites of maternal–daughterly communication and reconciliation. Brave Orchid's laundry, for example, is the place that the young Kingston chooses as the location for her recitation of two hundred grievances that she has saved for her mother to hear. In Tan's novels, the kitchen is often the location for truthful or private exchange between mother and daughter. The decision to choose the domestic space of the homestead as the location of these tales of self-discovery is one way of subverting the notion of women 'as properly belonging to the domestic sphere'.[82] The domestic space becomes, in many accounts, the space that is rejected in favour of self-expression. In Tan's texts, Kingston's *The Woman Warrior*, Jade Snow Wong's *Fifth Chinese Daughter* and Aimee Liu's *Face*, the domicile is deserted by the Asian American daughter unwilling to assume the identity afforded her within that space. White feminists have argued that the house is 'the central site of the oppression of women'.[83] For ethnic women, too, the home is often the location of oppression, often rendered doubly so by the inhibitions placed upon her by the fear of a racist world beyond the homestead. This is notably the case for many of Bharati Mukherjee's characters, and even for Maxine Hong Kingston.

Ethnic women in the house of fiction: narrative homecomings

Feminism, as Gillian Rose has noted, has often made use of a spatial politics. The notions of the woman's need for a room of her own (Virginia Woolf), and of women in the house of fiction (Lorna Sage's use of a Jamesian image), are two prominent examples.[84] These images are pertinent to the analysis here as we consider the idea of the ethnic woman's room in the house of fiction. 'Home' may also be understood as both psyche and as the textual container itself.[85] In this sense, fictions of self-discovery by Asian American women are fictions of homecoming. All of the texts under consideration in this chapter, whether fictional or autobiographical in emphasis, chart their subjects' search for identity. The autobiography, though, in particular, functions as a home for one's history. Autobiography, as Lloyd S. Kramer has made clear, represents an attempt by the writer to make a fictional home for the textual self.[86] In this sense, the autobiography itself bears testimony to the woman writer's emerging sense of her own selfhood: as retrospective narratives, autobiographies chart the process (or may even *be* the process) whereby that textual self has come into being. As Yoshiko Uchida writes of her own work, *Desert Exile*: 'it took so many years for these words to find a home' (p. 154). The autobiography itself, is often a largely developmental narrative, even in the more experimental and chronologically fragmented accounts like those of Meena Alexander, Sara Suleri and Maxine Hong Kingston. For these writers, 'the blank page symbolises a location of self-birth'.[87] As 'home' is only ever an imagined place, so the self solely exists textually for many of these women, whose textual constructions of selfhood link identity with the psychological attachment to place. Lydia Minatoya's *Talking to High Monks in the Snow*, for example, is organised textually around the places where she has lived, each representing a development in her life.[88] Autobiography, though, must be placed alongside fiction on a generic continuum, and many other texts, whilst not overtly acknowledged as autobiography, nevertheless betray autobiographical emphases.[89] Chuang Hua's *Crossings*, Joy Kogawa's *Obasan* and Tan's *The Joy Luck Club* are three such examples. J. Gerald Kennedy has argued that: 'a writer's fixation with place may signal the *desire* of autobiography: the longing to reconstruct – albeit in fictive terms – the relation between the authorial self and a world of located experience'.[90] In these texts, the heightened significance of and attachment to place bears testimony to an autobiographical impulse: to investigate the role of space and place in the construction of identity.

Space has always been of particular interest to both women and feminist writers, as Margaret R. Higonnet has noted: 'the implications of a *space*, which intertwine physical, social and political territories, offer particularly rich material for feminist analysis today'.[91] Feminist literary theory since the 1970s has busied itself claiming space for woman writers in the house of fiction, from the early work of Elaine Showalter, Tillie Olsen and Mary Ellmann onwards. More recent excavations have been concerned to uncover the forgotten work of ethnic women. Most prominent is the work of African American women writers.

But in Asian American studies, too, disremembered women writers have been republished.[92] Alongside this has been an explosion of writing activity in the area of Asian American studies, particularly by Asian American women, so that it would not be an exaggeration to claim that Asian American women currently have a rather popular room in the house of fiction. In particular, the spectacular success stories of Maxine Hong Kingston, Amy Tan and Joy Kogawa come to mind.[93] Hot on their heels, however, come a whole crowd of new writers, many of whom have been discussed in these pages, and who are now enjoying the wider readership initially attracted by Kingston's, Tan's and Kogawa's work. These ethnic writers are the cross-over success stories.[94] This is the first step towards opening the canon, that most exclusive of spaces, and we are already witnessing the appearance of Asian American women writers on school and university curricula, both in the United States and, increasingly, in Britain.[95] More writers will certainly follow.

Many of the women discussed in this book are acutely aware of their place in the house of fiction. Several, for instance, have bemoaned their tokenist presence on curricula and within the pages of academic works.[96] Both within and without the text, Asian American women are concerned with defining their own space. As Higgonet asserts, 'the double displacement of subaltern women writers weighs not only on their physical depiction of place but on their general writing strategies. Space becomes a writerly problem'.[97] In *The Woman Warrior*, Kingston writes: 'we belong to the planet now' (p. 99). Part of a space-claiming project is the appropriation of both fictional and autobiographical forms as the mediums of self-expression. The success of the Asian American woman writer in carving out space has recently led to white readers clamouring at the door of ethnic fiction. One reviewer has written in relation to Tan's work: 'Tan is handing us [the white reader] a key with no price tag and letting us open the brass-bolted door'.[98]

That door may be ajar, but it is not yet entirely open. This study does not offer a comprehensive survey of Asian American women's writing, partly due to the cultural conditions of dissemination outlined in the introduction. Instead, it draws attention to distinctive elements within a range of Asian American women's writing, from early twentieth-century texts to works published as recently as 2001. These distinctive elements may be a preoccupation with issues of identity and identity formation, itinerancy, history, culture, or feminism; or generic experimentation, and as this book has, hopefully, demonstrated, often involve the writers concerned in a negotiation with current discourses of identity to be found in a wide range of cultural and epistemological locations, including psychoanalysis, literary theory and linguistics. The eminent critic of Native American literature, Arnold Krupat, has noted: 'Who are you, who are you? Identity questions are everywhere today'.[99] In an age when the United States has witnessed increasing racial tension, from legal battles like the Anita Hill vs. Clarence Hill rape trial of 1991, to the O. J. Simpson trial, or the racial riots in Los Angeles in the spring of 1992, the question 'What is an American?' has become increasingly critical.

In the foreword to the 1997 anthology *Making More Waves: New Writing by Asian American Women*, Jessica Hagedorn observes the 'growing audience of readers for writing by and about Asian American women'.[100] Acknowledging this fact, the editors of *Making More Waves* consciously sought to include pieces of writing which in terms of theme and plot moved beyond the better-known examples of writing by Asian American women, many of which 'moved characters along a linear continuum from Asian immigrant to American citizen to a happy ending suggesting the superiority of the latter over the former'.[101] Instead, they included pieces in which 'multiple identities emerge as irregularities and discontinuities'.[102] This is one way in which the current generation of Asian American women writers is answering the questions 'Who am I?' and 'What is an American?' Perhaps Renee Tajima-Peña best sums up this shift: 'When I was growing up, identity was always framed in terms of assimilation, "How do people become American?" Today the question is more aptly, "How has America become its people?"'[103]

Notes

1 Meena Alexander, email to the author, 16 March 2000.
2 The literature on space is vast, and growing. I have made use only of the examples most pertinent to my discussion.
3 S. Frank Miyamoto, Introduction, in Monica Sone, *Nisei Daughter* (Seattle, WA: University of Washington Press, 1979), p. vii.
4 Meena Alexander, *Fault Lines: A Memoir* (New York: The Feminist Press, 1993), p. 174. All further page references are to this edition, and are cited in parentheses.
5 Shirley Ardener (ed.), *Women and Space: Ground Rules and Social Maps* (Oxford: Berg, 1993), p. 3.
6 Chuang Hua, *Crossings* (Boston, MA: Northeastern University Press, 1986), p. 187. All further page references are to this edition, and are cited in parentheses.
7 Edward Relph, *Place and Placelessness* (London: Plon, 1976), p. 43.
8 Gaston Bachelard, *The Poetics of Space: The Classic Look At How We Experience Intimate Places* (Boston, MA: Beacon Press, 1989), p. 7.
9 Kathleen Kirby, *Indifferent Boundaries: Spatial Concepts of Human Subjectivity*

(New York: Guildford Press, 1996), p. 21.

10 *Ibid.*, p. 27.

11 Amy Ling discusses the longing for homeland, and the subsequent importance of 'home' in the fictions of Virginia Lee, Hazel Lin and Bette Bao Lord, in detail. I have been unable to trace these texts myself, but Ling's discussion does reflect my own view on later writers. Of particular relevance is Ling's emphasis on the *imagined* nature of home in these fictions, a point reiterated in my own argument. She writes: 'For some people whom time has distanced from their ancestral homeland, memory has become amber-tinted by nostalgia and the landscapes that they paint in this condition reflect more the imagination of the artists than the reality of the land being depicted'. See Amy Ling, *Between Worlds: Women Writers of Chinese Ancestry* (New York: Pergamon, 1990), pp. 97–103.

12 With the exception of Jing-mei Woo, who travels back to China at the end of the novel.

13 Nomi, too, goes to Japan, but lives as a virtual recluse there, and does not involve herself at all in her surroundings.

14 Shirley Geok-lin Lim's memoir, *Among the White Moon Faces: An Asian American Memoir of Homelands* (1996), extensively addresses issues of place and placelessness. This can be seen in some of the chapter titles: 'Geographies of Relocation', and 'Moving Home' for example.

15 Patricia Duncker, *Sisters and Strangers: An Introduction to Contemporary Feminist Fiction* (Oxford: Blackwell, 1992), p. 221.

16 This term owes much to Jamaican British novelist Joan Riley's novel of the same name, which deals with the state of unbelonging. See Joan Riley, *The Unbelonging* (London: Women's Press, 1985).

17 Mai-mai Sze, *Echo of a Cry: A Story Which Began In China* (New York: Harcourt Brace, 1945), p. 108.

18 John McLeod, *Beginning Postcolonialism* (Manchester: Manchester University Press, 2000), p. 214.

19 Marilyn R. Chandler, *Dwelling in the Text: Houses in American Fiction* (Berkeley, CA: University of California Press, 1991), p. 1.

20 See Gillian Rose, *Feminism and Geography: The Limits of Geographical Knowledge* (Cambridge: Polity, 1993), p. 26. Rose is referring to a remark made by Carole Pateman. See Carole Pateman, *The Disorder of Women: Democracy, Feminism and Political Theory* (Cambridge: Polity, 1989), p. 118.

21 See Virginia Woolf, *A Room of One's Own* (London: Grafton, 1977).

22 Chandler, *Dwelling in the Text*, p. 1.

23 *Ibid.*

24 *Ibid.*

25 David Leiwei Li, *Imagining the Nation: Asian American Literature and Cultural Consent* (Stanford: Stanford University Press, 1998), pp. 102–3. Li describes the 'house metaphor' as 'central' to Gish Jen's characterisation of the Chang family's Americanisation.

26 Gish Jen, *Typical American* (London: Plume, 1992), p. 33. All further page references are to this edition, and are cited in parentheses.

27 Rachel C. Lee, *The Americas of Asian American Literature: Gendered Fictions of Nation and Transnation* (Princeton: Princeton University Press, 1999), p. 50.

28 Gish Jen, *Mona in the Promised Land* (New York: Knopf, 1996), p. 3.

29 *Ibid.*, p. 4.

30 Lee, *The Americas of Asian American Literature*, p. 44.

31 *Ibid.*

32 Yoshiko Uchida, *Desert Exile: The Uprooting of a Japanese–American Family* (Seattle, WA: University of Washington Press, 1987), p. 71. All further page references are to this edition, and are cited in parentheses.

33 Jeanne Wakatsuki Houston, 'O Furo', in Sylvia Watanabe and Carol Bruchac (eds), *Into the Fire: Asian American Prose* (New York: Greenfield Review Press, 1996), p. 176.

34 Joy Kogawa, *Obasan* (New York: Anchor Books, 1994), p. 60. All further page references are to this edition, and are cited in parentheses.

35 J. Gerald Kennedy, *Imagining Paris: Exile, Writing and American Identity* (New Haven, CT: Yale University Press, 1993), p. 24.

36 Bachelard, *The Poetics of Space*, p. 40.

37 *Ibid.*, p. 211.

38 *Ibid.*, p. 212.

39 *Ibid.*, p. 40.

40 *Ibid.*, pp. 40–1.

41 Ardener (ed.), *Women and Space*, p. 10.

42 Bharati Mukherjee, *Wife* (New York: Fawcett Crest, 1975), p. 120.

43 Ketu Katrak, 'South Asian American Literature', in King-kok Cheung (ed.), *An Interethnic Companion to Asian American Literature* (New York: Cambridge University Press, 1997), pp. 192–218; p. 212.

44 Sheng-mei Ma, *Immigrant Subjectivities in Asian American and Asian Diaspora Literatures* (New York: SUNY Press, 1998), p. 56.

45 See Bharati Mukherjee, 'Immigrant Writing: Give Us Your Maximalists', *New York Times Book Review*, 28 August 1988, pp. 1, 28–9.

46 Polly Shulman, 'Home Truths: Bharati Mukherjee, World Citizen', *Voice Literary Supplement*, 66, June (1988), p. 9.

47 Although all published in the 1980s and 1990s, all these texts deal with a period spanning the Second World War and shortly afterwards.

48 Mary Paik Lee, *Quiet Odyssey: A Pioneer Korean–American Woman in America*, ed. Sucheng Chan (Seattle, WA: University of Washington Press, 1990), p. 15. All further page references are to this edition, and are cited in parentheses.

49 Gary Y. Okihiro, *Margins and Mainstreams: Asians in American History and Culture* (Seattle, WA: University of Washington Press, 1994), pp. 86–91.

50 Ronyoung Kim, *Clay Walls: A Novel* (Seattle, WA: University of Washington Press, 1994), p. 121.

51 K. Scott Wong, 'Chinatown: Conflicting Images, Contested Terrain', *Melus*, 20:1, Spring (1995), p. 14.

52 Kay Anderson, *Vancouver's Chinatown: Racial Discourse in Canada, 1875–1980* (Montreal, Quebec: McGill-Queen's University Press, 1991), p. 8.

53 Fae Myenne Ng, *Bone* (New York: Hyperion, 1993), p. 26.

54 *Ibid.*, p. 51.

55 Andrew Gurr, *Writers in Exile: The Identity of Home in Modern Literature* (Brighton: Harvester Press, 1981), p. 13.

56 Journeying is a trope which surfaces repeatedly in these texts. This can be seen in the many titles which indicate travels of some kind: Minatoya's *Talking to High Monks in the Snow: An Asian American Odyssey*; Kadohata's *The*

Floating World, Lee's *Quiet Odyssey*, Chuang's *Crossings*, all of which are discussed in this book. Also see Suyin's *Destination Chungking*, Uchida's *Journey to Topaz*, Kogawa's *Jericho Road*, and Kuo's *I've Come a Long Way* and *Westward to Chungking*, texts which lie beyond the boundaries of my own discussion, mainly because they are out of print.

57 Lydia Minatoya, *Talking to High Monks in the Snow: An Asian American Odyssey* (New York: Harper Collins, 1992), p. 66.

58 Kyoko Mori, *The Dream of Water* (New York: Ballantine, 1995), p. 9.

59 *Ibid.*, p. 48.

60 Andrea Louie, *Moon Cakes* (New York: Ballantine, 1995), p. 22; p. 267.

61 *Ibid.*, p. 324.

62 Kyoko Mori, *The Dream of Water: A Memoir* (New York: Ballantine, 1995), p. 274.

63 Minatoya, *Talking to High Monks in the Snow*, p. 265.

64 Amy Ling, Introduction, in Chuang Hua, *Crossings*, p. 2.

65 *Ibid.*, p. 3.

66 Kennedy, *Imagining Paris*, p. 24.

67 Mori, *The Dream of Water*, p. 186.

68 Michael Seidel, *Exile and the Narrative Imagination* (New Haven, CT: Yale University Press, 1986), p. ix.

69 Sara Suleri, *Meatless Days* (Chicago, IL: University of Chicago Press, 1989), p. 20. Suleri's argument here is in line with much postcolonial theory which utilises spatial metaphors to discuss the process of 'othering'. A notable example is Edward Said's *Orientalism*, which asserts that the 'orient' or 'east' is a cultural construction designed to place its inhabitants, cultures and institutions beyond the self-defined space of 'occidental' or 'western' culture.

70 Meena Alexander, *Fault Lines* (New York: The Feminist Press, 1993), p. 3.

71 Suleri, *Meatless Days,* p. 18.

72 *Ibid.*, p. 147.

73 See chapter 2 on mother–daughter discourses for a discussion of the loss of the maternal.

74 Kennedy, *Imagining Paris*, p. 14.

75 Or, at least, have elected to continue the exilic lifestyle imposed upon them as children by their parents.

76 I am thinking here of Amy Ling's suggestion in *Between Worlds* that the 'between worlds condition', characteristic of postcolonial writers, may carry positive charges too. See Ling, *Between Worlds*, pp. 177–9.

77 Maxine Hong Kingston, *The Woman Warrior* (London: Picador, 1977), p. 12. All further page references are to this edition, and are cited in parentheses. Ghost stories such as the one told by Kingston here, often work through a dialectic of inside and outside.

78 See Fiona Cheong, *The Scent of the Gods* (New York: Norton, 1991), p. 172, for example. Most haunted spaces, both literal and figurative, in Asian American writing by women are patriarchal places. These include Kingston's ancestral home, Cheong's house, the ancestral home in Chuang Hua's *Crossings*, and Winnie Louie's ancestral home in Amy Tan's *The Kitchen God's Wife*. Crucially, all these homes are haunted by the spectres of women who have fallen foul of patriarchal codes of conduct.

79 There is an obvious connection with Kingston's *The Woman Warrior* here.

80 Julie Shigekuni, *A Bridge Between Us* (New York: Anchor, 1995), p. 33. All further page references are to this edition, and are cited in parentheses.

81 This is a point first made in relation to Asian American writing by women by Julie Sze, 'Have You Heard?: Gossip, Silence and Community in *Bone*', *Critical Mass: A Journal of Asian American Cultural Criticism*, 2.1 (Winter, 1994), pp. 59–69.

82 Rose, *Feminism and Geography*, p. 35.

83 See Michelle Barrett, *Women's Oppression Today: Problems in Marxist Feminist Analysis* (London: Verso, 1980), p. 211.

84 See Lorna Sage, *Women in the House of Fiction: Post-War Women Novelists* (London: Macmillan, 1992).

85 A point made by Arnold Weinstein. See Arnold Weinstein, *Nobody's Home: Speech, Self and Place in American Fiction from Hawthorne to DeLillo* (New York: Oxford University Press, 1993), p. 5.

86 Lloyd S. Kramer, *Threshold of a New World: Intellectuals and the Exile Experience in Paris, 1830–1848* (Ithaca, NY: Cornell University Press, 1988), p. 28.

87 Margaret R. Higgonet and Joan Templeton (eds), *Reconfigured Spheres: Feminist Explorations of Literary Space* (Amherst: University of Massachusetts Press, 1994), p. 15.

88 She begins in America, travels through Asia, and the final section, entitled 'The Journey Home', marks her return to America.

89 See chapter 3 for discussion of the relationship between genre and identity.

90 Kennedy, *Imagining Paris*, p. 23.

91 Higgonet and Templeton (eds), *Reconfigured Spheres*, p. 1.

92 Republished Asian American women writers include Chuang Hua, Monica Sone, Diana Chang, Jade Snow Wong, Winnifred Eaton and Miné Okubo.

93 Sau-ling C. Wong pointed this out to me. See also, Sau-ling C. Wong, 'Sugar Sisterhood: Situating the Amy Tan Phenomenon', in David Palumbo-Liu (ed.), *The Ethnic Canon: Histories, Institutions and Interventions*, (Minneapolis, MN: University of Minnesota Press, 1995), pp. 174–210.

94 Such space-claiming has not been welcomed by all Asian Americanists. Frank Chin, the most vociferous of Asian American critics, has bewailed the success stories of Tan, Kingston and others as 'fakery' and 'racist love'. See Elaine Kim's discussion of Chin's objections in Kim, *Asian American Literature: An Introduction to the Writings and Their Social Context* (Philadelphia, PA: Temple University Press, 1982), pp. 178–9.

95 A point first made by Lisa Lowe. See 'Canon, Institutionalization, Identity', in Palumbo (ed.), *The Ethnic Canon*, p. 52.

96 Notably Maxine Hong Kingston. See Guy Amirthayagam (ed.), 'Cultural Misreadings by American Reviewers', in *Asian and Western Writers in Dialogue* (London: Macmillan, 1992), pp. 55–65.

97 Higgonet and Templeton (eds), *Reconfigured Spheres*, p. 12.

98 Elgy Gillespie, 'Amy, Angst, and the Second Novel', *San Francisco Review of Books*, Summer (1991), 33–4; p. 34.

99 Arnold Krupat, *The Turn to the Native: Studies in Criticism and Culture* (Lincoln: University of Nebraska Press, 1996), p. 88.

100 Jessica Hagedorn, 'Foreword', in Elaine Kim et al. (eds), *Making More Waves: New Writing by Asian American Women*, (Boston, MA: Beacon Press, 1997), p. x.

101 *Ibid.*, p. xi.
102 *Ibid.*, p. xiii.
103 Renée Tajima-Peña, 'Cinemaya', in Kim et al. (eds), *Making More Waves*, p. 108.

SELECT BIBLIOGRAPHY

Primary texts

Aihara, Kyoko, *Geisha* (London: Carlton Books, 2000)

Alexander, Meena, *Manhattan Music* (San Francisco, CA: Mercury House, 1987)

—— *Nampally Road* (San Francisco, CA: Mercury House, 1991)

—— *Fault Lines: A Memoir* (New York: The Feminist Press, 1993)

Asian Women United of California (eds), *Making Waves: An Anthology of Writings by and about Asian American Women* (Boston, MA: Beacon Press, 1991)

—— *Making More Waves: New Writing by Asian American Women* (Boston, MA: Beacon Press, 1997)

Badami, Anita Rau, *Tamarind Mem* (New York: South Asia Books, 1996)

Bruchac, Joseph (ed.), *Breaking Silence: An Anthology of Contemporary Asian American Poets* (New York: Greenfield Review Press, 1983)

Bulosan, Carlos, *America is in the Heart* (1943; Seattle, WA: University of Washington Press, 1994)

Cha, Theresa Hak Kyung, *Dictee* (1982; Berkeley, CA: Third Woman Press, 1995)

Chai, Arlene J., *The Last Time I Saw Mother* (New York: Fawcett Columbine, 1995)

Chang, Diana, *The Frontiers of Love* (1956; Seattle, WA: University of Washington Press, 1994)

Chang, Eileen, (Zhang Ai-ling), *The Rice Sprout Song* (1955; Berkeley, CA: University of California Press, 1998)

—— *The Rouge of the North* (1968; Berkeley, CA: University of California Press, 1998)

Chang, Jung, *Wild Swans: Three Daughters of China* (1991; London: Flamingo, 1993)

Chang, Pang-Mei, *Bound Feet and Western Dress* (London: Bantam, 1997)

Chao, Patricia, *Monkey King* (New York: HarperCollins, 1997)

Cheng, Nien, *Life and Death in Shanghai* (London: Flamingo, 1995)

Cheong, Fiona, *The Scent of the Gods* (New York: Norton, 1991)

Chin, Sara, *Below the Line* (San Francisco: City Lights, 1997)

Ching, C., A. Kim, and A. Khemeshewsky (eds), *Between the Lines: An Anthology by Pacific/Asian Lesbians of Santa Cruz* (Santa Cruz, CA: Dancing Bird Press, 1987)

Chow, Claire S., *Leaving Deep Water: Asian American Women at the Crossroads of Two Cultures* (New York: Plume, 1999)

Chu, Louis, *Eat a Bowl of Tea* (1961; Seattle, WA: University of Washington Press, 1979)

Chuang, Hua, *Crossings* (1968; Boston, MA: Northeastern University Press, 1985)

Dalby, Liza, *Geisha* (London: Vintage, 2000)

Divakaruni, Chitra Banerjee, *Arranged Marriage* (London: Black Swan, 1997)

—— *The Mistress of Spices* (London: Doubleday, 1997)

—— *Sister of My Heart* (London: Doubleday, 1999)

Downer, Lesley, *Geisha* (London: Headline, 2000)

Eaton, Edith Maude, aka Sui Sin Far, *Mrs. Spring Fragrance and Other Writings*, ed. Amy Ling and Annette White-Parks (Urbana, IL: University of Illinois Press, 1995)

Eng, Phoebe, *Warrior Lessons: An Asian American Woman's Journey Into Power* (New York: Pocket Books, 1999)

Far, Sui Sin (pseud. Edith Maude Eaton), 'Leaves from the Mental Portfolio of an Eurasian', in Edith Blicksilver (ed.), *The Ethnic American Woman: Problems, Protests, Lifestyles* (Dubuque, IA: Kendall/Hunt, 1978), pp. 187–9

Galang, M. Evelina, *Her Wild American Self* (Minneapolis, MN: Coffee House Press, 1996)

Gao, Anhua, *To The Edge of the Sky* (London and New York: Viking, 2000)

Golden, Arthur, *Memoirs of a Geisha* (1991; London: Vintage, 1998)

Hagedorn, Jessica, *Dogeaters* (New York: Pantheon, 1991)

—— (ed.), *Charlie Chan is Dead: An Anthology of Contemporary Asian American Fiction* (New York: Penguin, 1993)

—— *The Gangster of Love* (New York: Penguin, 1996)

Hahn, Kimiko, *Air Pocket* (New York: Hanging Loose Press, 1989)

Han, Suyin, *Destination Chungking* (1942; Harmondsworth: Penguin, 1960)

—— *A Many Splendoured Thing* (Boston, MA: Little, Brown, 1956)

—— *… And the Rain My Drink* (Harmondsworth: Penguin, 1961)

—— *The Crippled Tree: China, Biography, History, Autobiography* (London: Lowe and Brydore, 1965)

—— *The Enchantress* (New York: Bantam, 1985)

—— *Wind in My Sleeve: China, Autobiography, History* (London: Jonathan Cape, 1992)

—— *Winter Love* (London: Virago, 1994)

Hara, Marie, and Nora Okja Keller (eds), *Intersecting Circles: The Voices of Hapa Women in Poetry and Prose* (Honolulu, HI: Bamboo Ridge Press, 1999)

Harrison, Katherine, *The Binding Chair* (London: Fourth Estate, 2000)

Hong, Liu, *Startling Moon* (London: Headline, 2001)

Hong, Maria (ed.), *Growing Up Asian American* (New York: Avon, 1993)

Hongo, Garrett (ed.), *The Open Boat: Poems From Asian America* (New York: Anchor, 1993)

Houston, Jeanne Wakatsuki, and James D. Houston, *Farewell to Manzanar* (San Francisco, CA: Houghton Mifflin, 1973)

Jen, Gish, *Typical American* (London: Plume, 1992)

—— *Mona in the Promised Land* (New York: Knopf, 1996)

Jicai, Feng, *Voices From the Whirlwind: An Oral History of the Chinese Cultural Revolution* (New York: Pantheon, 1991)

Kadohata, Cynthia, *The Floating World* (New York: Viking, 1989)

—— *In The Heart of The Valley of Love* (New York: Viking, 1992)

Kang, Younghill, *The Grass Roof* (New York: Charles Scribner, 1931)

—— *East Goes West* (New York: Charles Scribner, 1937)

Keller, Nora Okja, *Comfort Woman: A Novel* (New York: Penguin, 1997)

Kim, Elaine H., and Janice Otani (eds), *With Silk Wings* (Oakland, CA: Asian Women United of California, 1983)

Kim, Elizabeth, *Ten Thousand Sorrows* (London: Transworld, 2000)

Kim, Patti, *A Cab Called Reliable* (New York: St. Martin's Press, 1997)

Kim, Ronyoung, *Clay Walls: A Novel* (Seattle, WA: University of Washington Press, 1994)

Kingston, Maxine Hong, *The Woman Warrior* (London: Picador, 1976)

—— *China Men* (London: Picador, 1981)

—— *Tripmaster Monkey: His Fake Book* (London: Picador, 1989)

—— *Hawai'i One Summer* (Honolulu, HI: University of Hawaii Press, 1998)

Kogawa, Joy, *Obasan* (1981; New York: Anchor Books, 1994)

—— *Itsuka* (New York: Anchor Books, 1994)

Kudaka, Geraldine, *Numerous Avalanches at the Point of Intersection* (New York: Greenfield Review Press, 1979)

—— (ed.), *On a Bed of Rice: An Asian American Erotic Feast* (New York: Anchor, 1995)

Lai, Him Mark, Genny Lim, and Judy Yung (eds), *Island* (Seattle, WA: University of Washington Press, 1995)

Lau, Evelyn, *You Are Not Who You Claim* (Victoria: Porcepic Books, 1990)

—— *Runaway: Diary of a Street Kid* (Victoria: Minerva, 1996)

—— *Other Women* (New York: Simon and Schuster, 1996)

Lee, Chang-Rae, *Native Speaker* (London: Granta, 1995)

Lee, Marie G., *Necessary Roughness* (New York: HarperCollins, 1996)

Lee, Mary Paik, *Quiet Odyssey: A Pioneer Korean Woman in America*, ed. S. Chan (Seattle, WA: University of Washington Press: 1990)

Lee, Sky, *Disappearing Moon Café* (Seattle, WA: Seal Press, 1990)

Lee, Virginia, 'The House that Tai Ming Built', in Kai-yu Hsu and Helen Palubinskas (eds), *Asian American Authors* (Boston, MA: Houghton Mifflin, 1972), 38–46

Lim, Genny, *Winter Place* (San Francisco, CA: Kearny Street Workshop, 1989)

Lim, Shirley Geok-lin, *Among the White Moon Faces: An Asian American Memoir of Homelands* (New York: The Feminist Press, 1996)

Lim, Shirley Goek-lin and Mayumi Tsutakawa (eds), *The Forbidden Stitch: An Asian American Women's Anthology* (Corvallis, OR: Calyx, 1989)

Liu, Aimee E., *Face* (London: Headline Review Press, 1994)

—— *Cloud Mountain* (New York: Warner, 1997)

Louie, Andrea, *Moon Cakes* (New York: Ballantine, 1995)

Mah, Adeline Yen, *Falling Leaves: The True Story of an Unwanted Chinese Daughter* (New York: Penguin, 1998)

McCunn, Ruthanne Lum, *Thousand Pieces of Gold: A Biographical Novel* (San Francisco, CA: Design Enterprises of San Francisco, 1981)

—— *Wooden Fish Songs* (New York: Plume, 1995)

Min, Anchee, *Red Azalea* (London: Victor Gollancz, 1993)

Minatoya, Lydia, *Talking to High Monks in the Snow: An Asian American Odyssey* (New York: HarperCollins, 1992)

Mirikitani, Janice, *Shedding Silence* (Berkeley: Celestial Arts, 1987)

—— *We, The Dangerous* (London: Virago, 1995)

—— Mori, Kyoko, *The Dream of Water: A Memoir* (New York: Ballantine, 1995)

Mori, Toshio, *Yokohama, California* (Seattle, WA: University of Washington Press, 1949)

Mu, Aiping, *Vermilion Gate* (London: Little, Brown, 2000)

Mukherjee, Bharati, *The Tiger's Daughter* (New York: Fawcett Crest, 1971)
——— *Wife* (New York: Fawcett Crest, 1975)
——— *Jasmine* (London: Virago, 1990)
——— *The Middleman and Other Stories* (London: Virago, 1990)
——— *The Holder of the World* (London: Virago, 1994)
Ng, Fae Myenne, 'A Red Sweater', *The American Voice*, 4 (1986) 47–58
——— *Bone* (New York: Hyperion, 1993)
Ng, Mei, *Eating Chinese Food Naked* (London: Hamish Hamilton, 1998)
Nieh, Hualing, *Mulberry and Peach* (Boston, MA: Beacon, 1988)
Okada, John, *No-No Boy* (1957; Seattle, WA: Washington University Press, 1980)
Okubo, Miné, *Citizen 13660* (1946; Seattle, WA: Washington University Press, 1983)
Pai, Margaret K., *The Dreams of Two Yi-Min* (Honolulu, HI: University of Hawaii Press, 1989)
Phou, Lee Yan, *When I Was a Boy in China* (Boston, MA: D. Lothrop, 1887)
Santos, Bienvenido N., *Scent of Apples: A Collection of Stories* (1955; Seattle, WA: University of Washington Press, 1979)
Sasaki, R. A., *The Loom and Other Stories* (St Paul, MN: Graywolf Press, 1991)
See, Lisa, *On Gold Mountain: The One Hundred Year Odyssey of a Chinese–American Family* (New York: St. Martin's Press, 1995)
Shigekuni, Julie, *A Bridge Between Us* (New York: Anchor, 1995)
Sone, Monica, *Nisei Daughter* (1953; Seattle, WA: University of Washington Press, 1979)
Song, Cathy, *Frameless Windows, Squares of Light* (New York: Norton, 1988)
Sugimoto, Etsu, *A Daughter of the Samurai* (New York: Doubleday, 1925)
Suleri, Sara, *Meatless Days* (Chicago, IL: University of Chicago Press, 1989)
Sze, Mai-mai, *Echo of a Cry: A Story Which Began In China* (New York: Harcourt Brace, 1945)
Tan, Amy, *The Joy Luck Club* (London: Minerva, 1989)
——— *The Kitchen God's Wife* (London: Flamingo, 1992)
——— *The Hundred Secret Senses* (London: Flamingo, 1996)
——— *The Bonesetter's Daughter* (London: Flamingo, 2001)
Tsukiyama, Gail, *Women of the Silk* (New York: St Martin's Press, 1991)
Tyau, Kathleen, *A Little Too Much is Enough* (London: The Women's Press, 1996)
Uchida, Yoshiko, *Desert Exile: The Uprooting of a Japanese–American Family* (1966; Seattle, WA: University of Washington Press, 1994)
Villanueva, Marianne, *Ginseng and Other Tales From Manila* (Corvallis, OR: Calyx, 1991)
Watanabe, Sylvia, *Talking to the Dead* (New York: Doubleday, 1992)
Watanabe, S. and Carol Bruchac (eds), *Home To Stay: Asian American Women's Fiction* (New York: Greenfield Review Press, 1990)
——— *Into the Fire: Asian American Prose* (New York: Greenfield Review Press, 1996)
Watanna, Onoto, *Me, a Book of Remembrance* (1915; Jackson, MN: University of Mississippi Press, 1997)
——— *His Royal Nibs* (New York: W. J. Watt, 1925)
White-Parks, Annette, *Sui Sin Far/Edith Maude Eaton: A Literary Biography*

(Urbana, IL: University of Illinois Press, 1995)
Wong, Jade Snow, *Fifth Chinese Daughter* (1945; Seattle, WA: University of Washington Press, 1989)
Wong, Jan, *Red China Blues* (London: Bantam, 1997)
Wong, Shawn Hsu, *Homebase* (New York: Reed Books, 1979)
—— *Asian American Literature: A Brief Introduction and Anthology* (New York: HarperCollins, 1996)
Xu, Meihong, *Daughter of China: The True Story of Forbidden Love in Modern China* (London: Headline, 1999)
Yamada, Mitsuye, *Camp Notes and Other Poems* (New York: Kitchen Table, 1982)
—— *Desert Run: Poems and Stories* (New York: Kitchen Table, 1988)
Yamamoto, Hisaye, *Seventeen Syllables and Other Stories* (New York: Kitchen Table: Women of Color Press, 1988)
—— *"Seventeen Syllables"*, ed. King-kok Cheung (New Brunswick, NJ: Rutgers University Press, 1994)
Yamanaka, Lois-Ann, *Blu's Hanging* (New York: Bard, 1997)
Yamashita, Karen Tei, *Through the Arc of the Rainforest* (Minneapolis: Coffee House Press, 1990)
—— *Tropic of Orange* (Minneapolis: Coffee House Press, 1997)
Yamauchi, Wakako, *Songs My Mother Taught Me: Stories, Plays, and Memoir* (New York: The Feminist Press, 1994)
Ye, Ting-xing, *A Leaf in the Bitter Wind* (London: Bantam, 2000)
Ying, Hong, *Daughter of the River* (London: Bloomsbury, 1998)

Secondary texts

Abel, Elizabeth, 'Black Writing, White Reading: Race and the Politics of Feminist Interpretation', in Henry Louis Gates, Jr., and Kwame Anthony Appiah (eds), *Identities* (Chicago, IL: University of Chicago Press, 1995), 242–70
Aguilar-San Juan, Karin (ed.), *The State of Asian America: Activism and Resistance in the 1990s* (Boston, MA: South End Press, 1994)
Alexander, Meena, *The Shock of Arrival: Reflections on Postcolonial Experience* (Boston, MA: South End Press, 1996)
Amirthayagam, Guy (ed.), *Asian and Western Writers in Dialogue* (London: Macmillan, 1982)
Anderson, Benedict, *Imagined Communities: Reflections on the Origin and Spread of Nationalism* (London: Verso, 1994)
Anderson, Kay, *Vancouver's Chinatown: Racial Discourse in Canada, 1875–1980* (Montreal, Quebec: McGill-Queen's University Press, 1991)
Anderson, Linda, *Women and Autobiography in the Twentieth Century: Remembered Futures* (Hemel Hampstead: Harvester Wheatsheaf, 1997)
Andrews, Geoff, *Citizenship* (London: Lawrence and Wishart, 1991)
Anzaldúa, Gloria, *Borderlands/La Frontera: The New Mestiza* (San Francisco, CA: Aunt Lute, 1987)
—— *Making Face, Making Soul/Haciendo Caras: Creative and Critical Perspectives by Women of Color* (San Francisco, CA: Aunt Lute, 1990)
Ardener, Shirley, *Women and Space: Ground Rules and Social Maps* (Oxford:

Berg, 1993)

Armitt, Lucie, *Theorising the Fantastic* (London: Edward Arnold, 1996)

Bachelard, Gaston, *The Poetics of Space: The Classic Look At How We Experience Intimate Places* (Boston, MA: Beacon Press, 1989)

Baker, Houston A., Jr. (ed.), *Three American Literatures: Essays in Chicano, Native American, and Asian American Literature for Teachers of American Literature* (New York: MLA, 1982)

—— and Patricia Redmond (eds), *Afro-American Literary Study in the 1990s* (Chicago, IL: University of Chicago Press, 1990)

Barrett, Michele, *Women's Oppression Today: Problems in Marxist Feminist Analysis* (London: Verso, 1980)

Benstock, Shari, *The Private Self* (Chapel Hill, NC: University of North Carolina Press, 1988)

—— *Textualising the Feminine: On the Limits of Genre* (Norman, OK: University of Oklahoma Press, 1991)

Bentley, Nancy, 'White Slaves: The Mulatto Hero in Antebellum Fiction', in Michael Moon and Cathy Davidson (eds), *Subjects and Citizens: Nation, Race, and Gender from Oroonoko to Anita Hill*, (Durham, NC: Duke University Press, 1995), 195–216

Bergland, Betty Ann, 'Representing Ethnicity in Autobiography: Narratives of Opposition', *The Yearbook of English Studies*, 24 (1994), 67–93

Bhabha, Homi K. (ed.), *Nation and Narration* (London: Routledge, 1990)

—— *The Location of Culture* (London: Routledge, 1994)

Bim Yim, Sun, *Korean Women in America* (Seoul, Korea: Ehwa University, 1978)

Birch, Eva Lenox, *Black American Women's Writing: A Quilt of Many Colours* (Hemel Hampstead: Harvester Wheatsheaf, 1994)

Bloom, Harold (ed.), *Asian American Women Writers* (Philadelphia, PA: Chelsea House, 1997)

Boelhower, William, 'The Immigrant Novel as Genre', *Melus*, 8:1, Spring (1981), 3–13

—— *Through a Glass Darkly: Ethnic Semiosis in American Literature* (New York: Oxford University Press, 1984)

—— 'Ethnographic Politics: The Uses of Memory in Ethnic Fiction', in Amritjit Singh et al. (eds), *Memory and Cultural Politics: New Approaches to American Ethnic Literatures* (Boston, MA: Northeastern University Press, 1996), 19–40

Brah, Avtar, *Cartographies of Diaspora: Contesting Identities* (London and New York: Routledge, 1996)

Brodzki, Bella, and Celeste Schenck (eds), *Life/Lines: Theorizing Women's Autobiography* (Ithaca, NY: Cornell University Press, 1988)

Brooks, Ann, *Postfeminisms: Feminism, Cultural Theory and Cultural Forms* (London and New York: Routledge, 1997)

Brown, Linda Keller, and Kay Mussell, *Ethnic and Regional Foodways in the United States: The Performance of Group Identity* (Knoxville, TN: University of Tennessee Press, 1984)

Bruss, Elizabeth W., *Autobiographical Acts: The Changing Situation of a Literary Genre* (Baltimore, MD: Johns Hopkins University Press, 1976)

Butler, Judith, *Gender Trouble: Feminism and the Subversion of Identity* (New York: Routledge, 1990)

Cameron, Deborah, *Verbal Hygiene* (London: Routledge, 1995)

Carr, Helen (ed.), *From My Guy to Sci-Fi: Genre and Women's Writing in the Postmodern World* (London: Pandora, 1989)

Carrera-Levillain, Pilar and Jose-Miguel Fernandez-Dols, 'Neutral Faces in Context: Their Emotional Meaning and their Function', *Journal of Nonverbal Behaviour*, 18:4, Winter (1994), 281–301

Cashmore, Ellis (ed.), *A Dictionary of Ethnic and Racial Theory* (New York: Routledge, 1996)

Castillo, Ana, *So Far From God* (New York: Plume, 1994)

Chan, Jeffery Paul, 'Letters: The Mysterious West', *New York Review of Books*, 28 April 1977, 41

—— et al., 'An Introduction to Chinese-American and Japanese-American Literatures', in Houston A. Baker, Jr. (ed.), *Three American Literatures: Essays in Chicano, Native American, and Asian American Literature for Teachers of American Literature*, (New York: MLA, 1982), 197–228

Chandler, Marilyn R., *Dwelling in the Text: Houses in American Fiction* (Berkeley: University of California Press, 1991)

Chang, Grace, 'The Global Trade in Filipina Workers', in Sonia Shah (ed.), *Dragon Ladies: Asian American Feminists Breathe Fire* (Boston, MA: South End Press, 1997), 132–51

Cheung, King-kok, '"Don't Tell": Imposed Silences in *The Color Purple* and *The Woman Warrior*', *PMLA*, 103, March (1988), 162–74

—— 'The Woman Warrior versus The Chinaman Pacific: Must a Chinese American Critic Choose Between Feminism and Heroism?', in Marianne Hirsch and Evelyn Fox Keller (eds), *Conflicts in Feminism*, (New York: Routledge, 1990), 234–51

—— *Articulate Silences: Hisaye Yamamoto, Maxine Hong Kingston, Joy Kogawa* (Ithaca, NY: Cornell University Press, 1993)

—— 'Of Men and Men: Reconstructing Chinese American Masculinity', in Sandra Kumamoto Stanley (ed.), *Other Sisterhoods: Literary Theory and U.S. Women of Color* (Urbana, IL: University of Illinois Press, 1998), 173–99

—— (ed.), *An Interethnic Companion to Asian American Literature* (New York: Cambridge University Press, 1997)

Chin, Frank, 'This Is Not An Autobiography', *Genre*, 18:2 (1985), 109–30

—— et al., *Aiiieeeee! An Anthology of Asian-American Writers* (Washington DC, WA: Howard University Press, 1983)

Chodorow, Nancy, *The Reproduction of Mothering: Psychoanalysis and the Sociology of Gender* (Berkeley, CA: University of California Press, 1978)

—— *Femininities, Masculinities, Sexualities: Freud and Beyond* (Lexington, KY: University of Kentucky Press, 1994)

Chow, Esther Ngan-ling, 'The Feminist Movement: Where are all the Asian American Women?' in Elaine Kim et al. (eds), *Making Waves: An Anthology of Writing by and about Asian American Women* (Boston, MA: Beacon Press, 1989), 362–77

—— , Doris Wilkinson and Maxine Baca Zinn (eds), *Race, Class, and Gender:*

Common Bonds, Different Voices (Thousand Oaks, CA: Sage, 1996)

Chu, Patricia, *Assimilating Asians: Gendered Strategies of Authorship in Asian America* (Durham, NC: Duke University Press, 2000)

Chua, Chen Lok, 'Two Chinese Versions of the American Dream: The Golden Mountain in Lin Yutang and Maxine Hong Kingston', *Melus*, 8:4, Winter (1981), 61–70

—— Cisneros, Sandra, *The House on Mango Street* (New York: Vintage, 1984)

Clark, VéVe A., et al. (eds), *Revising the Word and the World: Essays in Feminist Literary Criticism* (Chicago, IL: University of Chicago Press, 1993)

Coward, Rosalind, *Female Desire: Women's Sexuality Today* (London: Paladin, 1984)

Cranny-Francis, Anne, *Feminist Fiction* (Cambridge: Polity Press, 1990)

Culler, Jonathan, 'Towards a Theory of Non-Genre Literature', in Raymond Federman (ed.), *Surfiction* (Chicago, IL: Swallow Press, 1981)

Daniels, Roger, Sandra C. Taylor and Harry L. Kitano (eds), *Japanese Americans: From Relocation to Redress* (Seattle, WA: University of Washington Press, 1991)

Davé, Shilpa, 'The Doors to Home and History: Post-colonial Identities in Meena Alexander and Bharati Mukherjee', *Amerasia*, 19:3 (1993), 103–13

Davidson, Cathy N. and E. M. Broner (eds), *The Lost Tradition: Mothers and Daughters in Literature* (New York: Frederick Ungar, 1980)

Davies, Carole Boyce, *Black Women, Writing and Identity: Migrations of the Subject* (London: Routledge, 1994)

De Lauretis, Teresa, *Alice Doesn't: Feminism, Semiotics, Cinema* (London: Macmillan, 1984)

—— *Technologies of Gender: Essays on Theory, Film, and Fiction* (London: Macmillan, 1987)

Dearborn, Mary V., *Pocahontas's Daughters: Gender and Ethnicity in American Culture* (New York: Oxford University Press, 1986)

Derrida, Jacques, 'The Law of Genre', *Glyph 7* (Baltimore, MD: Johns Hopkins University Press, 1980)

—— *Acts of Literature*, ed. Derek Attridge (London: Routledge, 1992)

Dick, Leslie, 'Feminism, Writing, Postmodernism', in Helen Carr (ed.), *From My Guy to Sci-Fi: Genre and Women's Writing in the Postmodern World*, (London: Pandora, 1989), 204–14

Duncker, Patricia, *Sisters and Strangers: An Introduction to Contemporary Feminist Fiction* (Oxford: Blackwell, 1992)

DuPlessis, Rachel Blau, *Writing Beyond the Ending: Narrative Strategies of Twentieth-Century Women Writers* (Bloomington, IN: Indiana University Press, 1985)

Eakin, Paul (ed.), *American Autobiography: Retrospect and Prospect* (Madison, WI: University of Wisconsin Press, 1991)

Featherston, Elena (ed.), *Skin Deep: Women Writing on Color, Culture and Identity* (Freedom, CA.: The Crossing Press, 1994)

Felski, Rita, *Beyond Feminist Aesthetics: Feminist Literature and Social Change* (Cambridge, MA: Harvard University Press, 1989)

Ferraro, Thomas J., *Ethnic Passages: Literary Immigrants in Twentieth Century*

America (Chicago, IL: University of Chicago Press, 1993)

Fisher, Dexter (ed.), *The Third Woman: Minority Women Writers of the United States* (Dallas, TX: Houghton Mifflin, 1980)

Fischer, Michael M. J., 'Ethnicity and the Postmodern Arts of Memory', in James Clifford and George E. Marcus (eds), *Writing Culture: The Poetics and Politics of Ethnography*, (Berkeley, CA: University of California Press, 1986), 194–233

Fong, Katheryn, 'Woman's Review of "Woman Warrior"', *San Francisco Journal*, 25 January 1978, 6

Frankenberg, Ruth, *White Women, Race Matters: The Social Construction of Whiteness* (Minneapolis: University of Minnesota Press, 1993)

Franklin, Cynthia G., *Writing Women's Communities: The Politics and Poetics of Contemporary Multi-Genre Anthologies* (Madison, WI: University of Wisconsin Press, 1997)

Fugita, Stephen S., and David O'Brien, *Japanese American Ethnicity: The Persistence of Community* (Seattle, WA: University of Washington Press, 1991)

Fuss, Diana, 'Fashion and the Homospectatorial Look', in Henry Louis Gates, Jr. and Kwame Anthony Appiah (eds), *Identities*, (Chicago, IL: University of Chicago Press, 1995), 90–114

Gardiner, Judith Kegan, 'On Female Identity and Writing by Women', *Critical Inquiry* 8:2, Winter (1981), 347–61

Gates, Henry Louis, Jr. (ed.), *'Race,' Writing, and Difference* (Chicago, IL: University of Chicago Press, 1985)

—— *Loose Canons: Notes on the Culture Wars* (Oxford: Oxford University Press, 1992)

—— and Kwame Anthony Appiah (eds), *Identities* (Chicago, IL: University of Chicago Press, 1995)

—— Gee, Emma (ed.), *Asian Women* (Berkeley, CA: University of California Press, 1971)

Ghymn, Esther Mikyung, *Images of Asian American Women by Asian American Women Writers* (New York: Peter Lang, 1995)

—— (ed.), *Asian American Studies: Identity, Images, and Issues Past and Present* (New York: Peter Lang, 2000)

Gillespie, Elgy, 'Amy, Angst, and the Second Novel', *San Francisco Review of Books*, Summer (1991), 33–4

Gilmore, Leigh, *Autobiographics: A Feminist Theory of Self-Representation* (Ithaca, NY: Cornell University Press, 1994)

Gilroy, Paul, 'Diaspora and the Detours of Identity', in Kathryn Woodward (ed.), *Identity and Difference* (Milton Keynes: Open University Press, 1997), 299–343

Goellnicht, Donald C., 'Tang Ao in America: Male Subject Positions in *China Men*', in Amy Ling and Shirley Geok-lin Lim (eds), *Reading the Literatures of Asian America* (Philadelphia, PA: Temple University Press, 1992), 191–212

—— 'Blurring Boundaries: Asian American Literature as Theory', in King-kok Cheung (ed.), *An Interethnic Companion to Asian American Literature* (New York: Cambridge University Press, 1996), 338–65

Gossett, Thomas F., *Race: The History of an Idea in America* (Dallas, TX: Southern Methodist University Press, 1975)

Grice, Helena, 'Asian American Writing in a European Context: Problems and Paradigms', *Hitting Critical Mass*, 4:1, Autumn (1996), 11–26

—— 'Reading the Nonverbal: The Indices of Space, Time, Taciturnity and Tactility in Joy Kogawa's *Obasan*', *Melus*, 24:4, Winter (1999), 93–106

—— 'Asian American Women's Prose Narratives: Genre and Identity', in Esther Mikyung Ghymn (ed.), *Asian American Studies: Identity, Images, and Issues Past and Present* (New York: Peter Lang, 2000), 179–204

—— 'Placing the Korean American Subject: Theresa Hak Kyung Cha's *Dictee*', in Pauline Polkey and Alison Donnell (eds), *Representing Lives* (London: Macmillan, 2000), 43–52

—— 'Face-ing/De-Face-ing Racism: Physiognomy and Racism in Eur/Amerasian Women's Texts', in Josephine Lee, Yuko Matsukawa and Imogene Lim (eds), *Re/Collecting Early Asian America: Readings in Cultural History*, (Philadelphia, PA: Temple University Press, 2002)

—— 'Trauma and Memory: Patricia Chao's *Monkey King*, Aimee Liu's *Face* and Joy Kogawa's *Obasan*', in Rocío G. Davis and Sami Ludwig (ed.), *Asian American Ceremonies: Ritual, Rupture, Departure* (Madison, WI: University of Wisconsin Press, forthcoming)

—— (ed.), 'Asian American Literary Feminisms', special issue of *Hitting Critical Mass: A Journal of Asian American Cultural Criticism*, 6:2, Spring (2000)

Gurr, Andrew, *Writers in Exile: The Identity of Home in Modern Literature* (Sussex: The Harvester Press, 1981)

Gutman, Huck, *As Others Read Us: International Perspectives on American Literature* (Amherst, MA: University of Massachusetts Press, 1991)

Hagedorn, Jessica, 'Travels in the Combat Zone', in Lyn Lifshin (ed.), *Lips Unsealed: Confidences from Contemporary Women Writers* (Santa Barbara, CA: Capra Press, 1990), 119–22

Hamalian, Leo, 'A *Melus* Interview: Diana Chang', *Melus*, 20:4, Winter (1995), 29–43

Harris, Virginia, 'Prison of Color', in Elena Featherston (ed.), *Skin Deep: Women Writing on Color, Culture and Identity*, (Freedom, CA: The Crossing Press, 1994), 9–16

Heung, Marina, 'Mother Text/Daughter Text: Matrilineage in Amy Tan's *The Joy Luck Club*', *Feminist Studies*, 19:3, Autumn (1993), 597–616

Higgonet, Margaret R., and Joan Templeton (eds), *Reconfigured Spheres: Feminist Explorations of Literary Space* (Amherst, MA: University of Massachusetts Press, 1994)

Hill, Tracey, and William Hughes (eds), *Contemporary Writing and National Identity* (Bath: Sulis Press, 1995)

Hirsch, Marianne, 'Mothers and Daughters: A Review Essay', *Signs*, 7:1, Autumn (1981), 200–22

—— *The Mother/Daughter Plot: Narrative, Psychoanalysis, Feminism* (Bloomington, IN: Indiana University Press, 1989)

Holton, Robert, *Jarring Witnesses: Modern Fiction and the Representations of History* (Hemel Hampstead: Harvester Wheatsheaf, 1994)

Hongo, Garrett, 'Asian American Literature: Questions of Identity', *Amerasia*, 20:3 (1994), 1–8

—— (ed.), *Under Western Eyes: Personal Essays from Asian America* (New York: Anchor, 1995)

Hsia, C.T., *A History of Modern Chinese Fiction* (1961; Bloomington, IN: Indiana University Press, 1999)

Humm, Maggie, *The Dictionary of Feminist Theory* (Hemel Hempstead: Harvester Wheatsheaf, 1989)

Hune, Shirley, et al. (eds), *Asian Americans: Comparative and Global Perspectives* (Pullman, WA: Washington State University Press, 1991)

—— 'Rethinking Race: Paradigms and Policy Formation', *Amerasia*, 21:1 & 2 (1995), 29–40

Hunt, Linda, '"I Could Not Figure Out What Was My Village": Gender vs. Ethnicity in Maxine Hong Kingston's *The Woman Warrior*', *Melus*, 12:3, Autumn (1985), 5–12

Hutcheon, Linda, *A Poetics of Postmodernism: History, Theory, Fiction* (London: Routledge, 1988)

Jameson, Frederic, 'Postmodern Consumer Society', in Hal Foster (ed.), *Postmodern Culture* (London: Pluto, 1985), 111–25

Jelinek, Estelle C. (ed.), *Women's Autobiography: Essays in Criticism* (Bloomington, IN: Indiana University Press, 1980)

Kafka, Phillipa, *(Un)Doing the Missionary Position: Gender Asymmetry in Contemporary Asian American Women's Writing* (Westport, CT: Greenwood Press, 1997)

Kauffman, Linda S., *American Feminist Thought at Century's End: A Reader* (Cambridge, MA: Blackwell, 1993)

Kennedy, J. Gerald, *Imagining Paris: Exile, Writing and American Identity* (New Haven, CT: Yale University Press, 1993)

Ketrak, Ketu H., 'South Asian American Literature', in King-kok Cheung (ed.), *An Interethnic Companion to Asian American Literature* (New York: Cambridge, 1996), 192–218

Kim, Elaine H., 'Visions and Fierce Dreams: A Commentary on the Works of Maxine Hong Kingston', *Amerasia*, 8:2 (1981), 145–61

—— *Asian American Literature: An Introduction to the Writings and their Social Context* (Philadelphia, PA: Temple University Press, 1982)

—— 'Beyond Railroads and Internment: Comments on the Past, Present, and Future of Asian American Studies', in Gary Okihiro et al. (eds), *Privileging Positions: The Sites of Asian American Studies* (Pullman, WA: Washington State University Press, 1995), 11–19

—— and Norma Alarcón (eds), *Writing Self, Writing Nation: Essays on Theresa Hak Kyung Cha's DICTEE* (Berkeley, CA: Third Woman Press, 1994)

—— and Chungmoo Choi (eds), *Dangerous Women: Gender and Korean Nationalism* (New York: Routledge, 1998)

—— et al. (eds), *Making Waves: An Anthology of Writing by and about Asian American Women* (Boston, MA: Beacon Press, 1991)

King, Katie, *Theory in its Feminist Travels: Conversations in U.S. Women's Movements* (Bloomington, IN: Indiana University Press, 1994)

Kingston, Maxine Hong, 'Cultural Misreadings by American Reviewers', in Guy Amirthayagam (ed.), *Asian and Western Writers in Dialogue* (London: Macmillan, 1982) 55–65

—— 'San Francisco's Chinatown: A View from the Other Side of Arnold Genthe's Camera', *American Heritage*, December (1978) 35–47

—— '"How Are You?" "I am Fine, Thankyou. And You?"', in Leonard Michaels and Christopher Ricks (eds), *The State of the Language* (Berkeley, CA: University of California Press, 1980), 152–7

—— 'Personal Statement', in Shirley Geok-lin Lim (ed.), *Approaches to Teaching Maxine Hong Kingston's 'The Woman Warrior'* (New York: MLA, 1991), 23–5

Kirby, Kathleen, *Indifferent Boundaries: Spatial Concepts of Human Subjectivity* (New York: Guildford Press, 1996)

Kolodny, Annette, *The Lay of the Land: Metaphor as Experience and History in American Life and Letters* (Chapel Hill, NC: University of North Carolina Press, 1975)

—— *The Land Before Her: Fantasy and Experience of the American Frontier, 1630–1860* (Chapel Hill, NC: University of North Carolina Press, 1984)

—— 'Letting Go Our Grand Obsessions: Notes Toward a New Literary History of the American Frontier', in Michael Moon and Cathy Davidson (eds), *Subjects and Citizens: Nation, Race, and Gender from Oroonoko to Anita Hill* (Durham, NC: Duke University Press, 1995), 9–26

Kothari, Geeta, 'Where Are You From?', in Garrett Hongo (ed.), *Under Western Eyes: Personal Essays from Asian America* (New York: Anchor, 1995), 151–74

Kramer, Lloyd S., *Threshold of a New World: Intellectuals and the Exile Experience in Paris, 1830–1848* (Ithaca, NY: Cornell University Press, 1988)

Krupat, Arnold, *The Turn to the Native: Studies in Criticism and Culture* (Lincoln, NE: University of Nebraska Press, 1996)

Kymlicka, Will, *Multicultural Citizenship: A Liberal Theory of Minority Rights* (Oxford: Clarendon, 1995)

Le Espiritu, Yen, *Asian American Panethnicity: Bridging Institutions and Identities* (Philadelphia, PA: Temple University Press, 1992)

—— *Asian American Women and Men: Labor, Laws, and Love* (Thousand Oaks, CA: Sage, 1997)

Lee, A. Robert, 'Eat a Bowl of Tea: Asian America in the Novels of Gish Jen, Cynthia Kadohata, Kim Ronyoung, Jessica Hagedorn, and Tran Van Dinh', *The Yearbook of English Studies*, 24 (1994), 263–80

Lee, Josephine, *Performing Asian America: Race and Ethnicity on the Contemporary Stage* (Philadelphia, PA: Temple University Press, 1997)

Lee, Rachel C., *The Americas of Asian American Literature: Gendered Fictions of Nation and Transnation* (Princeton, NJ: Princeton University Press, 1999)

Lejeune, Philippe, *Le Pacte Autobiographique* (Paris: Seuil, 1975)

Leong, Russell C., 'Lived Theory (*notes on the run*)', *Amerasia*, 21:1 & 2 (1995), v–x

—— (ed.), *Asian American Sexualities: Dimensions of the Gay and Lesbian Experience* (New York: Routledge, 1996)

Li, David Leiwei, 'The Naming of a Chinese-American "I": Cross-Cultural Sign/
ifications in *The Woman Warrior*', *Criticism*, 30:4, Autumn (1988), 497–
515

—— *Imagining the Nation: Asian American Literature and Cultural Consent*
(Stanford, CA: Stanford University Press, 1998)

Lidoff, Joan, 'Autobiography in a Different Voice: *The Woman Warrior* and the
Question of Genre', in Shirley Geok-lin Lim (ed.), *Approaches to Teaching
Maxine Hong Kingston's 'The Woman Warrior'* (New York: MLA, 1991), pp.
112–21

Lim, Shirley Geok-lin, 'Japanese American Women's Life Stories: Maternality in
Monica Sone's *Nisei Daughter* and Joy Kogawa's *Obasan*', *Feminist Studies*,
16:2, Summer (1990), 289–312

—— 'Hegemony and "Anglo-American Feminism"': Living in the Funny House',
Tulsa Studies in Women's Literature, 12:2, Autumn (1993), 279–87

—— 'Feminist and Ethnic Literary Theories in Asian American Literature', *Feminist Studies*, 19:3, Autumn (1993), 571–95

—— (ed.), *Approaches to Teaching Maxine Hong Kingston's 'The Woman Warrior'* (New York: MLA, 1991)

—— and Amy Ling (eds), *Reading the Literatures of Asian America* (Philadelphia, PA: Temple University Press, 1992)

—— and Mayumi Tsutakawa (eds), *The Forbidden Stitch: An Asian American
Women's Anthology* (Corvallis, OR: Calyx Books, 1989)

—— Lim-Hing, Sharon (ed.), *The Very Inside: An Anthology of Writing by Asian
and Pacific Islander Lesbian and Bisexual Women* (Toronto: Sister Vision,
1994)

Ling, Amy, 'A Rumble in the Silence: Chuang Hua's *Crossings*', *Melus*, 9:3, Winter (1982), 29–37

—— *Between Worlds: Women Writers of Chinese Ancestry* (New York and London: Pergamon, 1990)

—— '"Emerging Canons" of Asian American Literature and Art', in Shirley Hune
et al. (eds), *Asian Americans: Comparative and Global Perspectives* (Pullman, WA: Washington State University Press, 1991), 191–8

—— 'I'm Here: An Asian American Women's Response', in Diane Price Herndyl
and Robyn Warhol (eds), *Feminisms: An Anthology of Literary Theory and
Criticism* (New Brunswick: Rutgers University Press, 1991), 738–745

Ling, Jinqi, *Narrating Nationalisms: Ideology and Form in Asian American Literature* (New York: Oxford University Press, 1993)

—— 'Race, Power, and Cultural Politics in John Okada's *No-No Boy*', *American
Literature*, 67:2, June (1995), 359–81

Ling, Susie Hsiuhan, 'The Mountain Movers: Asian American Women's Movement in Los Angeles', *Amerasia*, 15:1, 51–67

Lionnet, Françoise, *Autobiographical Voices: Race, Gender, Self-Portraiture* (Ithaca,
NY: Cornell University Press, 1989)

—— *Postcolonial Representations: Women, Literature, Identity* (Ithaca, NY: Cornell
University Press, 1995)

Lorde, Audre, *Zami: A New Spelling of My Name* (London: Pandora, 1982)

Lowe, Lisa, 'Heterogeneity, Hybridity, Multiplicity: Marking Asian American

Differences', *Diaspora*, Spring (1981), 24–44

—— 'Unfaithful to the Original: the Subject of *Dictee*', in Elaine Kim and Norma Alarcón (eds), *Writing Self, Writing Nation: Essays on Theresa Hak Kyung Cha's DICTEE* (Berkeley, CA: Third Woman Press, 1994), 35–69

—— 'Canon, Institutionalization, Identity', in David Palumbo-Liu (ed.), *The Ethnic Canon: Histories, Institutions, and Interventions* (Minneapolis, MN: University of Minnesota Press, 1995), 48–68

—— *Immigrant Acts: On Asian American Cultural Politics* (Durham, NC: Duke University Press, 1996)

Lury, Celia, *Consumer Culture* (Cambridge: Polity, 1996)

McFarlane, Scott, 'Covering *Obasan* and the Narrative of Internment', in Gary Okihiro et al. (eds), *Privileging Positions: The Sites of Asian American Studies* (Pullman, WA: Washington State University Press, 1995), 400–11

Madsen, Deborah L., '(Dis)figuration: The Body as Icon in the Writings of Maxine Hong Kingston', *The Yearbook of English Studies*, 24 (1994), 237–50

Maglin, Nan Bauer, '"Don't Never Forget the Bridge That You Crossed Over On": The Literature of Matrilineage', in Cathy Davidson and E. M. Broner (eds), *The Lost Tradition: Mothers and Daughters in Literature* (New York: Frederick Ungar, 1980), 257–67

Marcus, Jane, 'Storming the Toolshed', *Signs*, 7:3, Spring (1982), 622–41

Mariani, Philomena (ed.), *Critical Fictions: The Politics of Imaginative Writing* (Seattle, WA: Bay Press, 1991)

Mass, Amy Iwasaki, 'Psychological Effects of the Camps on Japanese Americans', in Roger Daniels et al. (eds), *Japanese Americans: From Relocation to Redress* (Seattle, WA: University of Washington Press, 1991), 159–62

Massardier-Kenney, Françoise, '*Indiana*: a Textual Analysis of Facial Description', *International Fiction Review*, 15:2, Summer (1988), 117–23

Matsui, J., 'Asian Americans', *Pacific Citizen*, 6 September 1968, 6

Matsukawa, Yuko, '*Melus* Interview: Gish Jen', *Melus*, 18:4, Winter (1993), 111–20

Mazumbar, Sucheta, 'General Introduction: A Woman-Centred Perspective on Asian American History', in Asian Women United of California (eds), *Making Waves: An Anthology of Writings by and about Asian-American Women* (Boston, MA: Beacon Press, 1991), 1–22

—— 'Asian American Studies and Asian Studies: Rethinking Roots', in Shirley Hune et al. (eds), *Asian Americans: Comparative and Global Perspectives* (Pullman, WA: Washington State University Press, 1991), 29–48

Meese, Elizabeth A., *Crossing the Double-Cross: The Practice of Feminist Criticism* (Chapel Hill, NC: The University of North Carolina Press, 1986)

Mehta, Gita, *Karma Cola: Marketing the Mystic East* (New York: Vintage, 1979)

Michaels, Leonard, and Christopher Ricks (eds), *The State of the Language* (Berkeley, CA: University of California Press, 1980)

Miller, Lucien, and Hui-chuan Chang, 'Fiction and Autobiography: Spatial Form in *The Golden Cangue* and *The Woman Warrior*', *Tamkang Review*, 15 (1984–85), 75–96

Mills, Sara et al., *Feminist Readings, Feminists Reading* (Hemel Hempstead: Harvester Wheatsheaf, 1989)

Mirza, Heidi Safia, *Black British Feminism: A Reader* (London and New York: Routledge, 1997)

Miyamoto, S. Frank, Introduction, *Nisei Daughter* (Seattle, WA: University of Washington Press, 1979)

Mohanty, Chandra Talpade, 'Defining Genealogies: Feminist Reflections on Being South Asian in North America', in Elaine Kim et al. (eds), *Making More Waves: New Writing by Asian American Women* (Boston, MA: Beacon Press, 1997), 119–27

Moi, Toril, *Sexual/Textual Politics: Feminist Literary Theory* (London: Routledge, 1993)

Moon, Michael, and Cathy N. Davidson (eds), *Subjects and Citizens: Nation, Race, and Gender From Oroonoko to Anita Hill* (Durham, NC: Duke University Press, 1995)

Moraga, Cherríe, and Gloria Anzaldúa (eds), *This Bridge Called My Back: Writings by Radical Women of Color* (New York: Kitchen Table: Women of Color Press, 1981)

Morante, Linda, 'From Silence to Song: The Triumph of Maxine Hong Kingston', *Frontiers*, 9:2 (1987), 78–82

Morgan, Janice, and Colette T. Hall (eds), *Gender and Genre in Literature: Redefining Autobiography in Twentieth-Century Women's Fiction* (New York: Garland, 1991)

Morrison, Toni, 'Rootedness: The Ancestor as Foundation', in Mari Evans (ed.), *Black Women Writers: A Critical Evaluation* (New York: Anchor/Doubleday, 1984), 339–45

—— *Beloved* (London: Picador, 1987)

—— *The Bluest Eye* (London: Picador, 1990)

Mulvey, Laura, 'Visual Pleasure and Narrative Cinema', *Screen*, 16:3, Autumn (1975), 6–18

Munt, Sally R., *Murder by the Book? Feminism and the Crime Novel* (London: Routledge, 1994)

Nishime, LeiLani, 'Engendering Genre: Gender and Nationalism in *China Men* and *The Woman Warrior*', *Melus*, 20:1, Spring (1995), 67–82

Nomura, Gail, 'Issei Working Women in Hawaii', in Elaine Kim et al. (eds), *Making Waves: An Anthology of Writing by and about Asian American Women* (Boston, MA: Beacon Press, 1989), 135–48

Okihiro, Gary Y., *Margins and Mainstreams: Asians in American History and Culture* (Seattle, WA: University of Washington Press, 1994)

—— 'Theory, Class, and Place', in *Privileging Positions: The Sites of Asian American Studies* (Pullman: Washington State University Press, 1995), 1–9

—— et al. (eds), *Privileging Positions: The Sites of Asian American Studies* (Pullman: Washington State University Press, 1995)

Olney, James, *Metaphors of Self: The Meaning of Autobiography* (Princeton, NJ: Princeton University Press, 1972)

—— (ed.), *Autobiography: Essays Theoretical and Critical* (Princeton, NJ: Princeton University Press, 1980)

Omi, Michael, and Howard Winant, *Racial Formation in the US: From the 1960's to 1980's* (New York: Routledge, 1986)

Ono, Kent A., 'Re/signing "Asian American": Rhetorical Problematics of Na-
    tion', *Amerasia*, 21:1 & 2 (1995), 67–78
Osajima, Keith, 'Postmodern Possibilities: Theoretical and Political Directions
    for Asian American Studies', *Amerasia*, 21:1 & 2 (1995), 79–87
Ostriker, Alice, 'The Thieves of Language: Women Poets and Revisionist
    Mythmaking', in Elaine Showalter (ed.), *The New Feminist Criticism* (Lon-
    don: Virago, 1982), 314–38
Palumbo-Liu, David, 'Theory and the Subject of Asian American Studies',
    Amerasia, 21:1 & 2 (1995), 55–65
—— *Asian/American: Historical Crossings of a Racial Frontier* (Stanford, CA:
    Stanford University Press, 1999)
—— 'Model Minority Discourse and the Course of Healing', in Abdul
    JanMohamed (ed.), *Minority Discourse: Ideological Containment and Uto-
    pian/Heterotopian Potentials* (New York: Oxford University Press, forth-
    coming)
—— (ed.), *The Ethnic Canon: Histories, Institutions and Interventions* (Minne-
    apolis: University of Minnesota Press, 1995)
Payne, James R. (ed.), *Multicultural Autobiography: American Lives* (Knoxville:
    University of Tennessee Press, 1992)
Pearlman, Mickey, *Mother Puzzles: Daughters and Mothers in Contemporary
    American Literature* (Westport, CT: Greenwood, 1989)
—— and Katherine Usher Henderson, 'Amy Tan', in *Inter/View: Talks with
    America's Writing Women* (Lexington, KY: Kentucky University Press, 1990),
    15–22
Perloff, Marjorie (ed.), *Postmodern Genres* (Norman, OK and London: Univer-
    sity of Oklahoma Press, 1989)
Perry, Donna, 'Maxine Hong Kingston', in *Backtalk: Women Writers Speak Out:
    Interviews* (New Brunswick, NJ: Rutgers University Press, 1993), 172–93
Pfaff, Timothy, 'Talk with Mrs. Kingston', *New York Times Book Review*, 15 June
    1980, 26
Phillipson Laing, H., and A. R. Lee, *Interpersonal Perception* (London: Tavistock
    Publications, 1966)
Rainwater, Catherine and William J. Scheick (eds), *Contemporary American
    Women Writers: Narrative Strategies* (Lexington, KY: The University Press
    of Kentucky, 1985)
Rau, Samantha Ramu, 'The Need to Belong', *The New York Times Book Review*,
    23 September 1956, 26
Ray, Sangeeta, 'Memory, Identity, Patriarchy: Projecting a Past in the Memoirs
    of Sara Suleri and Michael Ondaatje', *mfs*, 39:1, Spring (1993), 37–58
Rayson, Ann, 'Beneath the Mask: Autobiographies of Japanese-American
    Women', *Melus*, 14:1, Spring (1987), 43–57
Reed, Ishmael et al., 'Is Ethnicity Obsolete?', in Werner Sollors (ed.), *The Inven-
    tion of Ethnicity* (New York: Oxford University Press, 1992), 226–35
Relph, Edward, *Place and Placelessness* (London: Plon, 1976)
Rich, Adrienne, *Of Woman Born: Motherhood as Experience and as Institution*
    (London: Virago, 1977)
Riley, Joan, *The Unbelonging* (London: Women's Press, 1985)

Young, Iris Marion, *Justice and the Politics of Difference* (Princeton, NJ: Princeton University Press, 1995)

Yu, Connie Young, 'The World of our Grandmothers', in Elaine Kim et al. (eds), *Making Waves: An Anthology of Writing by and about Asian American Women* (Boston, MA: Beacon Press, 1989), 33–42.

Yung, Judy, *Chinese Women of America: A Pictorial History* (Seattle, WA: University of Washington Press, 1986)

—— *Unbound Feet: A Social History of Chinese Women in San Francisco* (Berkeley, CA: University of California Press, 1995)

—— *Unbound Voices: A Documentary History of Chinese Women in San Francisco* (Berkeley, CA: University of California Press, 1999)

Zia, Helen, *Asian American Dreams: The Emergence of an American People* (New York: Farrar, Straus and Giroux, 2000)

INDEX